MICROSOFT® VISUAL BASIC® .NET

LANGUAGE REFERENCE

Microsoft® .net

PUBLISHED BY
Microsoft Press
A Division of Microsoft Corporation
One Microsoft Way
Redmond, Washington 98052-6399

Library of Congress Cataloging-in-Publication Data
Microsoft Visual Basic .NET : Language Reference / Microsoft Corporation.
p. cm.
Includes index.
ISBN 0-7356-1552-7
1. Microsoft Visual BASIC. 2. BASIC (Computer program language) I. Microsoft Corporation.

QA76.73.B3 M5595 2002
005.26'8-dc21 2001056814

Printed and bound in the United States of America.

1 2 3 4 5 6 7 8 9 QWT 7 6 5 4 3 2

Distributed in Canada by Penguin Books Canada Limited.

A CIP catalogue record for this book is available from the British Library.

Microsoft Press books are available through booksellers and distributors worldwide. For further information about international editions, contact your local Microsoft Corporation office or contact Microsoft Press International directly at fax (425) 936-7329. Visit our Web site at www.microsoft.com/mspress. Send comments to *mspinput@microsoft.com*.

Acquisitions Editor: Juliana Aldous
Project Editor: Denise Bankaitis

Body Part No. X08-64076

Contents

APPENDIX E Visual Basic Compiler Options *(continued)*

Before You Begin

Typographic and Code Conventions

Visual Basic® documentation uses the following typographic and code conventions.

Typographic Conventions

Convention	Description
Sub, **If**, **ChDir**, **Print**, **True**, **Debug**	Words in bold with initial letter capitalized indicate language-specific keywords.
Setup	Words you are instructed to type appear in bold.
object, *varname*, *arglist*	Italic letters indicate placeholders for information you supply.
[*expressionlist*]	In syntax, items inside brackets are optional.
{ **Public** | **Private** }	In syntax, braces and a vertical bar indicate a mandatory choice between two or more items. You must choose one, and only one, of the items.
[**Protected** | **Friend**]	In syntax, a vertical bar separates alternative options. Within brackets, the alternatives are not exclusive. Within braces, the alternatives are exclusive.
[{ **ByRef** | **ByVal** }]	In syntax, brackets surrounding items within braces indicate that no more than one item may be included, and the items may also be omitted entirely.
$membname_1$, $membname_2$, $membname_3$	Subscripts differentiate multiple instances of the same placeholder.
$membname_1$ ... $membname_n$	In syntax, ellipses indicate an indefinite number of items of the kind immediately preceding the ellipses. In code, ellipses signify code omitted for the sake of clarity.
ESC, ENTER	Words in capital letters indicate key names and key sequences.
ALT+F1, CTRL+R	A plus sign (+) between key names indicates a combination of keys. For example, ALT+F1 means hold down the ALT key while pressing the F1 key.

Code Conventions

Sample code	Description
`MyString = "Hello, world!"`	This font is used for code, variables, and error message text.
`' This is a comment.`	An apostrophe (') introduces code comments.

`MyVar = "This is an " _`
`& "example" _`
`& " of how to continue code."`
	A space followed by an underscore (_) at the end of line continues a line of code.

Introduction to Visual Basic .NET

Language Changes in Visual Basic

While earlier versions of Visual Basic are targeted for Microsoft® Windows® client applications, Visual Basic .NET is intended for creating XML Web service applications as well. For this purpose, Visual Basic .NET generates managed code for the common language runtime. This entails changes to the language itself.

The changes in Visual Basic .NET are intended to:

- Simplify the language and make it more consistent.
- Add new features requested by users.
- Make code easy to read and maintain.
- Help programmers avoid introducing coding errors.
- Make applications more robust and easier to debug.

The following topics describe language changes from previous versions in Visual Basic .NET.

Programming Element Support Changes Summary

Visual Basic .NET changes the manner in which it supports various programming elements, mostly for interoperability with the common language runtime. Many Visual Basic 6.0 elements are renamed, reclassified, or combined with other programming elements for Visual Basic .NET. Several elements are no longer supported, because the common language runtime includes functionality that makes them unnecessary.

The following table lists changed programming elements and their replacements.

Visual Basic 6.0 programming element	Visual Basic .NET equivalent	Namespace, class, or run-time library location
Abs function	Abs Method	System Namespace, Math Class
AscB function	Asc Function	Visual Basic Run-Time Library Members, Strings module

(continued)

(continued)

Visual Basic 6.0 programming element	Visual Basic .NET equivalent	Namespace, class, or run-time library location
As Any keyword phrase	Not supported in Visual Basic .NET; see "Declaration Syntax Changes in Visual Basic"	Does not apply
Atn function	Atan Method	System Namespace, Math Class
Calendar property	CurrentCulture Property	System.Globalization Namespace, CultureInfo Class
ChDir statement	ChDir Function	Visual Basic Run-Time Library Members, FileSystem module
ChDrive statement	ChDrive Function	Visual Basic Run-Time Library Members, FileSystem module
Chr$, **ChrB**, functions	Chr Function	Visual Basic Run-Time Library Members, Strings module
Close statement	FileClose Function	Visual Basic Run-Time Library Members, FileSystem module
Cos function	Cos Method	System Namespace, Math Class
Currency data type	Decimal Data Type; see "Data Type Changes in Visual Basic"	Visual Basic Run-Time Library Members, VariantType Enumeration
CVDate function	DateValue Function	Visual Basic Run-Time Library Members, DateAndTime module
CVError function	Error Statement	Does not apply
Date function, **Date** statement	Now Property, Today Property	Visual Basic Run-Time Library Members, DateAndTime module
Date$ function	DateString Property	Visual Basic Run-Time Library Members, DateAndTime module
Debug.Assert method	Assert, Fail methods	System.Diagnostics Namespace, Debug Class
Debug.Print method	Write, WriteIf, WriteLine, and WriteLineIf methods	System.Diagnostics Namespace, Debug Class
Deftype statements	Not supported in Visual Basic .NET; see "Data Type Changes in Visual Basic"	Does not apply

Visual Basic 6.0 programming element	Visual Basic .NET equivalent	Namespace, class, or run-time library location
DeleteSetting statement	DeleteSetting Function	Visual Basic Run-Time Library Members, Interaction module
DoEvents function	DoEvents Method	System.Windows.Forms Namespace, Application Class
Empty keyword	Nothing	Does not apply
Eqv operator	= Operator; see "Boolean Operator Changes in Visual Basic"	Does not apply
Exp function	Exp Method	System Namespace, Math Class
FileCopy statement	FileCopy Function	Visual Basic Run-Time Library Members, FileSystem module
Get statement	FileGet Function	Visual Basic Run-Time Library Members, FileSystem module
GoSub statement	Not supported in Visual Basic .NET; use the Return Statement; see "Control Statement Changes in Visual Basic"	Does not apply
Initialize event	Not supported in Visual Basic .NET; use **Sub New**; see "Class and Interface Changes in Visual Basic"	Does not apply
Imp operator	Not supported in Visual Basic .NET; see "Not" and "Or" operators, and "Boolean Operator Changes in Visual Basic"	Does not apply
Input #, **Input$** statements, **Input$**, **InputB**, **InputB$** functions	Input Function	Visual Basic Run-Time Library Members, FileSystem module
Instancing property	Not supported in Visual Basic .NET; see "Class and Interface Changes in Visual Basic"	Does not apply
InStrB function	InStr Function	Visual Basic Run-Time Library Members, Strings module
IsEmpty function	IsNothing Function	Visual Basic Run-Time Library Members, Information module

(continued)

(continued)

Visual Basic 6.0 programming element	Visual Basic .NET equivalent	Namespace, class, or run-time library location
IsMissing function	Not supported in Visual Basic .NET; see "Procedure Declaration Changes in Visual Basic"	Does not apply
IsNull function	IsDbNull Function	Visual Basic Run-Time Library Members, Information module
IsObject function	IsReference Function	Visual Basic Run-Time Library Members, Information module
Kill statement	Kill Function	Visual Basic Run-Time Library Members, FileSystem module
LCase$ function	LCase Function	Visual Basic Run-Time Library Members, Strings module
Left$, **LeftB**, **LeftB$** functions	Left Function	Visual Basic Run-Time Library Members, Strings module
LenB function	Len Function	Visual Basic Run-Time Library Members, Strings module
Let, **Set** assignment statements	Not supported in Visual Basic .NET; the new **Set** statement is unrelated to the older one; see "Default Property Changes in Visual Basic"	Does not apply
Line Input # statement	LineInput Function	Visual Basic Run-Time Library Members, FileSystem module
Lock statement	Lock, Unlock Functions	Visual Basic Run-Time Library Members, FileSystem module
Log function	Log Method	System Namespace, Math Class
LSet, **RSet** statements	LSet Function, PadRight, PadLeft; see "Data Type Changes in Visual Basic"	Visual Basic Run-Time Library Members, Strings module and System Namespace, String Class
LTrim$ function	LTrim Function	Visual Basic Run-Time Library Members, Strings module
MidB function	Mid Function	Visual Basic Run-Time Library Members, Strings module
MidB statement	Mid Statement	Visual Basic Run-Time Library Members, Strings module

Visual Basic 6.0 programming element	Visual Basic .NET equivalent	Namespace, class, or run-time library location
MkDir statement	MkDir Function	Visual Basic Run-Time Library Members, FileSystem module
Name statement	Rename Function	Visual Basic Run-Time Library Members, FileSystem module
Now function	Now Property	Visual Basic Run-Time Library Members, DateAndTime module
Null keyword	Nothing	Does not apply
Oct$ function	Oct Function	Visual Basic Run-Time Library Members, Conversion module
On ... GoSub construction	Not supported in Visual Basic .NET; use Select Case Statement; see "Control Statement Changes in Visual Basic"	Does not apply
On ... GoTo construction	Not supported in Visual Basic .NET; use Select Case Statement; see "Control Statement Changes in Visual Basic"	Does not apply
Open statement	FileOpen Function	Visual Basic Run-Time Library Members, FileSystem module
Option Base statement	Not supported in Visual Basic .NET; see "Array Bound Changes in Visual Basic"	Does not apply
Option Private Module statement	Not supported in Visual Basic .NET; use Module Statement; see "Class and Interface Changes in Visual Basic"	Does not apply
Print # statement	Print, PrintLine Functions	Visual Basic Run-Time Library Members, FileSystem module
Property Get, **Property Let**, **Property Set** statements	Not supported in Visual Basic .NET; see "Property Changes in Visual Basic"	Does not apply
Put statement	FilePut Function	Visual Basic Run-Time Library Members, FileSystem module

(continued)

(continued)

Visual Basic 6.0 programming element	Visual Basic .NET equivalent	Namespace, class, or run-time library location
Reset statement	Reset Function	Visual Basic Run-Time Library Members, FileSystem module
Right$, **RightB** functions	Right Function	Visual Basic Run-Time Library Members, Strings module
RmDir statement	RmDir Function	Visual Basic Run-Time Library Members, FileSystem module
Round function	Round Method	System Namespace, Math Class
RSet, **LSet** statements	RSet Function; see "Data Type Changes in Visual Basic"	Visual Basic Run-Time Library Members, Strings module
RTrim$ function	RTrim Function	Visual Basic Run-Time Library Members, Strings module
SaveSetting statement	SaveSetting Function	Visual Basic Run-Time Library Members, Interaction module
Scale method	Not supported in Visual Basic .NET	Does not apply
Set, **Let** assignmenr statements	Not supported in Visual Basic .NET; the new **Set** statement is unrelated to the older one; see "Default Property Changes in Visual Basic"	Does not apply
SetAttr statement	SetAttr Function	Visual Basic Run-Time Library Members, FileSystem module
Sgn function	Sign Function	System Namespace, Math Class
Sin function	Sin Method	System Namespace, Math Class
Sqr function	Sqrt Function	System Namespace, Math Class
String function	String Constructor; see "String ($) Function Changes in Visual Basic"	System Namespace, String Class
String ($) functions	Not supported in Visual Basic .NET; see "String ($) Function Changes in Visual Basic"	Does not apply
Terminate event	Not supported in Visual Basic .NET; use **Sub Dispose** and **Sub Finalize**; see "Class and Interface Changes in Visual Basic"	Does not apply

Visual Basic 6.0 programming element	Visual Basic .NET equivalent	Namespace, class, or run-time library location
Time function, **Time** statement	TimeOfDay Property; see "DateTime Structure," "Date Data Type"	Visual Basic Run-Time Library Members, DateAndTime module
Time$ function	TimeString Property	Visual Basic Run-Time Library Members, DateAndTime module
Timer function	Timer Property	Visual Basic Run-Time Library Members, DateAndTime module
Trim$ function	LTrim, RTrim, and Trim Functions	Visual Basic Run-Time Library Members, Strings module
Type statement	Not supported in Visual Basic .NET; use Structure Statement; see "Structure Declaration Changes in Visual Basic"	Does not apply
UCase$ function	UCase Function	Visual Basic Run-Time Library Members, Strings module
Unlock statement	Lock, Unlock Functions	Visual Basic Run-Time Library Members, FileSystem module
Variant data type	Object Data Type; see "Universal Data Type Changes in Visual Basic"	Does not apply
Wend keyword	While...End While Statements and End Statement; see "Control Statement Changes in Visual Basic"	Does not apply
Width # statement	FileWidth Function	Visual Basic Run-Time Library Members, FileSystem module
Write # statement	Write, WriteLine Functions	Visual Basic Run-Time Library Members, FileSystem module

See Also

Language Changes in Visual Basic

Array Changes

The following topics describe changes to arrays between Visual Basic 6.0 and Visual Basic .NET:

- **Array Bound Changes in Visual Basic** Discusses changes to array bounds and default bounds.
- **Array Size Declaration Changes in Visual Basic** Describes changes to the specification of array sizes.
- **ReDim Statement Changes in Visual Basic** Discusses changes to declarations that include the **ReDim** statement.

Array Bound Changes in Visual Basic

Visual Basic .NET updates the declaration of array bounds to provide interoperability with arrays in other programming languages.

Visual Basic 6.0

In Visual Basic 6.0, the default lower bound of every dimension of an array is 0. You can change this to 1 with the **Option Base** statement. You can also override the default lower bound in individual array declarations.

If you leave the default at 0, the number of elements in the array is equal to the upper bound plus one. The following declaration reserves 21 elements for the array `Weight`:

```
Dim Weight(20) As Single
```

Visual Basic .NET

In Visual Basic .NET, the lower bound of every array dimension is 0, and you cannot declare it to be otherwise. The **Option Base** statement is not supported.

The number you specify for each dimension in the declaration is the upper bound, and the initial element count is equal to the upper bound plus one. The declaration in the preceding example reserves 21 elements for `Weight`, with subscripts 0 through 20.

See Also

Declaration Syntax Changes in Visual Basic, Array Size Declaration Changes in Visual Basic, Dim Statement, UBound Function, Programming Element Support Changes Summary

Array Size Declaration Changes in Visual Basic

Visual Basic .NET updates array size declaration for interoperability with the common language runtime.

Visual Basic 6.0

In Visual Basic 6.0, you can specify the size of an array in its declaration, as in the following example:

```
Dim Month(0 To 11) As Integer
```

This causes the array to have a fixed size, which you cannot change with the **ReDim** statement.

Visual Basic .NET

In Visual Basic .NET, an array cannot have a fixed size. The preceding example can be rewritten as either of the following declarations:

```
Dim Month(11) As Integer   ' Reserves 12 elements -- (0) through (11).
Dim Month() As Integer = New Integer(11) {}
```

These declarations are equivalent. Each specifies an initial size, which you can change during execution with the **ReDim** statement. To initialize the elements, you can use the following syntax:

```
Dim Month() As Integer = {1, 2, 3, 4, 5, 6, 7, 8, 9, 10, 11, 12}
```

Number of Dimensions

Although an array's size can change in Visual Basic .NET, the number of dimensions must be fixed. The following example declares a three-dimensional array:

```
Dim Point( , , ) As Double
```

The **ReDim** statement can set or change the size of each dimension, but the array always remains three-dimensional.

See Also

Dim Statement, New, ReDim Statement, Programming Element Support Changes Summary

ReDim Statement Changes in Visual Basic

Visual Basic .NET updates declaration with the **ReDim** statement for simplification and improved readability.

Visual Basic 6.0

In Visual Basic 6.0, you can use the **ReDim** statement to serve as the initial declaration of a dynamic array. The array does not have to be declared anywhere else.

Visual Basic 6.0 also allows you to change the rank of an array with **ReDim**, as in the following example:

```
Dim X(10) As Single
ReDim X(10, 10)
```

Visual Basic .NET

In Visual Basic .NET, you cannot use **ReDim** as a declaration. You must declare an array just like any other variable, using **Dim** or an equivalent statement, before it can appear in a **ReDim** statement.

You cannot change the rank of an array in Visual Basic .NET. The code in the preceding example causes an error.

See Also

ReDim Statement, Dim Statement, Programming Element Support Changes Summary

Control Flow Changes

The following topics describe changes to control flow between Visual Basic 6.0 and Visual Basic .NET:

- **Control Statement Changes in Visual Basic** Covers changes to statements controlling execution flow.
- **Exception Handling Changes in Visual Basic** Discusses new support for structured exception handling, and continued support for unstructured exception handling.

Control Statement Changes in Visual Basic

Visual Basic .NET updates several statements controlling the flow of execution.

Visual Basic 6.0

In Visual Basic 6.0, the **GoSub** statement calls a sub-procedure within a procedure. The **On ... GoSub** and **On ... GoTo** constructions, also known as computed **GoSub** and computed **GoTo**, provide compatibility with early versions of BASIC.

The **While ... Wend** construction loops through code while a specified condition is true.

Visual Basic .NET

In Visual Basic .NET, you can call procedures with the **Call** statement, and the **GoSub** statement is not supported. You can perform multiple branching with **Select...Case** statements, and the **On ... GoSub** and **On ... GoTo** constructions are not supported. However, Visual Basic .NET still supports the **On Error** statement.

Visual Basic .NET retains the **While ... Wend** construction, but replaces the **Wend** keyword with the **End** statement. The **Wend** keyword is not supported.

See Also

Procedure Calling Sequence Changes in Visual Basic, Call Statement, Function Statement, Sub Statement, Return Statement, Select...Case Statements, On Error Statement, End Statement, Programming Element Support Changes Summary

Exception Handling Changes in Visual Basic

Visual Basic .NET adds support for structured exception handling, and continues support for unstructured exception handling.

Visual Basic 6.0

In Visual Basic 6.0, you use unstructured exception handling to deal with errors in your code. Placing the **On Error** statement at the beginning of a block of code handles any errors that occur within that block. Unstructured exception handling also employs the **Error** and **Resume** statements.

Visual Basic .NET

In Visual Basic .NET, structured exception handling code detects and responds to errors during execution by combining a control structure with exceptions, protected blocks of code, and filters. Structured exception handling is done through a **Try** statement, which is made up of three kinds of blocks: **Try**, **Catch**, and **Finally**. A **Try** block is a statement block that contains the statement to be executed. A **Catch** block is a statement block that handles an exception. A **Finally** block contains statements to be run when the **Try** statement is exited, regardless of whether an exception has occurred. The **Throw** statement, used in conjunction with a **Catch** block, raises an exception that is represented by an instance of a type derived from the **System.Exception** class.

See Also

Try...Catch...Finally Statements, Throw Statement, On Error Statement, Error Statement, Resume Statement, Programming Element Support Changes Summary

Data Type Changes

The following topics describe changes to data types between Visual Basic 6.0 and Visual Basic .NET:

- **Data Type Changes in Visual Basic** Describes data type declaration, usage, and conversion.
- **Integer Data Type Changes in Visual Basic** Covers integer data type updates.
- **Universal Data Type Changes in Visual Basic** Covers universal data type updates.

Data Type Changes in Visual Basic

Visual Basic .NET updates data types for interoperability with other programming languages and the common language runtime. The changes affect data type declaration, usage, and conversion.

Visual Basic 6.0

In Visual Basic 6.0, you use the **Deftype** statements—**DefBool**, **DefByte**, **DefCur**, **DefDate**, **DefDbl**, **DefDec**, **DefInt**, **DefLng**, **DefObj**, **DefSng**, **DefStr**, and **DefVar**—to set a variable's default type.

You use the **Currency** data type for calculations involving money and for fixed-point calculations.

A **Date** is stored in a **Double** format using eight bytes.

If two **Variant** variables containing integers are multiplied, an overflow condition causes the data type of the result to be changed to **Double**.

You can use the **LSet** and **RSet** statements to copy a variable of one user-defined type to another variable of a different user-defined type.

Visual Basic .NET

The **Deftype** statements are not supported in Visual Basic .NET. Nor is the **Currency** data type. Instead, use the new **Decimal** data type, which can handle more digits on both sides of the decimal point, for all money variables and calculations. **Decimal** is also directly supported by the common language runtime.

In Visual Basic .NET, the **Date** data type uses the common language runtime **DateTime** data type, which is an eight-byte integer value. Because of these different representations, there is no implicit conversion between the **Date** and **Double** data types. To convert between **Double** and the Visual Basic 6.0 representation of **Date**, use the **ToOADate** and **FromOADate** methods of the **DateTime** structure in the **System** namespace.

If multiplication of two **Object** variables containing integers results in an overflow, the result is changed to the 64-bit **Long** data type.

You cannot use **LSet** and **RSet** to assign one data type to another. Doing so entails a type-unsafe operation, particularly with structures, which could result in unverifiable code.

See Also

Decimal Data Type, Date Data Type, Val Function, Type Conversion Functions, Data Type Summary, Double Data Type, Long Data Type, Programming Element Support Changes Summary

Integer Data Type Changes in Visual Basic

Visual Basic .NET updates the integer data types for interoperability with other programming languages and with the common language runtime.

The following table shows correspondences between integer types in Visual Basic 6.0 and Visual Basic .NET.

Integer Size	Visual Basic 6.0 type and type character	Visual Basic .NET type and type character	Common language runtime type
8 bits, signed	(none)	(none)	**System.SByte**
16 bits, signed	**Integer** (%)	**Short** (none)	**System.Int16**
32 bits, signed	**Long** (&)	**Integer** (%)	**System.Int32**
64 bits, signed	(none)	**Long** (&)	**System.Int64**

On 32-bit systems, 32-bit integer operations are faster than either 16-bit or 64-bit integer operations. This means that in Visual Basic .NET, **Integer** is the most efficient and fundamental numeric type. You can improve performance in your applications by changing your **Long** declarations to **Integer** when you migrate to Visual Basic .NET.

Note If you are interfacing with components created on platforms other than Visual Basic .NET, you must take care that your data types correspond to those of the other components. For example, if you use a **Declare** statement to refer to an external procedure created in Visual Basic 6.0, and the procedure defines an **Integer** argument (two bytes in Visual Basic 6.0), you must identify that argument as **Short** in the **Declare** statement, because that is the two-byte integer type in Visual Basic .NET.

See Also

Data Type Summary, Integer Data Type, Short Data Type, Long Data Type, Programming Element Support Changes Summary, Declare Statement

Universal Data Type Changes in Visual Basic

Visual Basic .NET updates the universal data type for interoperability with the common language runtime.

Visual Basic 6.0

In Visual Basic 6.0, **Variant** serves as the universal data type. This means that you can store data of any type in a variable of type **Variant**.

Visual Basic .NET

In Visual Basic .NET, **Object** is the universal data type. A variable of type **Object** can hold data of any type. The **Variant** type is not supported, and all its functionality is supplied by **Object**.

Variant is still a reserved word in Visual Basic .NET, even though it has no syntactical use. This helps avoid confusion with its former meanings.

The **VarType** function returns a member of the **VariantType** enumeration that provides the data type classification of an object variable. You can also use classes in the **System** namespace to obtain numeric data type information for an **Object** instance, as shown in the following code:

```
Dim SomeObj As Object
' ... ... ... ...  SomeObj is assigned some value during processing.
' ... ... ... ...  Now we want to find out the data type of SomeObj.
Dim Dtype As Integer       ' To hold numeric data type result.
Dtype = Type.GetTypeCode(SomeObj)
```

See Also

Object Data Type, VarType Function, VariantType Enumeration, Programming Element Support Changes Summary

Declaration Changes

The following topics describe changes to declarations between Visual Basic 6.0 and Visual Basic .NET:

- **Declaration Syntax Changes in Visual Basic** Describes multiple variable declaration and return type declaration.
- **String Length Declaration Changes in Visual Basic** Discusses the specification of string length.
- **Structure Declaration Changes in Visual Basic** Discusses structures, also known as user-defined types (UDTs).
- **Variable Scope Changes in Visual Basic** Discusses the scope of variables inside a block.

Declaration Syntax Changes in Visual Basic

Visual Basic .NET introduces several changes related to the declaration of programming elements.

Multiple Variable Declaration

Visual Basic .NET revises simultaneous declaration of several variables for simplification.

Visual Basic 6.0

In Visual Basic 6.0, you can declare variables of different types in the same statement, but you must specify the data type of each variable or it defaults to **Variant**. The following example shows multiple declarations and their resulting data types:

```
Dim I, J As Integer              ' I is Variant, J is Integer.
Dim L As Integer, M As Integer   ' L is Integer, M is Integer.
Dim N As Integer, X As Double    ' N is Integer, X is Double.
```

Visual Basic .NET

In Visual Basic .NET, you can declare multiple variables of the same data type without having to repeat the type keyword. The declarations equivalent to those in the preceding example are as follows:

```
Dim I                              ' I is Object.
Dim J As Integer                   ' J is Integer.
' -- OR --
Dim I As Object, J As Integer      ' I is Object, J is Integer.
Dim L, M As Integer                ' L is Integer, M is Integer.
Dim N As Integer, X As Double      ' N is Integer, X is Double.
```

External Procedure Declaration

Visual Basic 6.0

In Visual Basic 6.0, when you declare a reference to an external procedure with the **Declare** statement, you can specify **As Any** for the data type of any of the arguments and the return type. The **As Any** keywords disable type checking and allow any data type to be passed in or returned.

Visual Basic .NET

Visual Basic .NET does not support the **Any** keyword. In a **Declare** statement, you must specifically declare the data type of every argument and the return if **Option Strict** is **On**. This improves type safety. You can overload your procedure declaration to accommodate various argument data types. You cannot overload only on return types, but you can use the argument type overloads to vary the return type, or you can turn **Option Strict Off**.

Line Label Declaration

Visual Basic 6.0

In Visual Basic 6.0, a line number can directly precede a statement on the same line, without any separating character.

Visual Basic .NET

Visual Basic .NET requires that every line label be followed by a colon (**:**). A statement can optionally follow the colon on the same line, or the line label and colon can stand alone on the line.

See Also

Universal Data Type Changes in Visual Basic, Declare Statement, Option Strict Statement, Programming Element Support Changes Summary

String Length Declaration Changes in Visual Basic

Visual Basic .NET updates string length declaration for interoperability with the common language runtime.

Visual Basic 6.0

In Visual Basic 6.0, you can specify the length of a string in its declaration. This causes the string to have a fixed length, as in the following example:

```
Dim Name As String * 30
```

Visual Basic .NET

In Visual Basic .NET, you cannot declare a string to have a fixed length unless you use the VBFixedStringAttribute Class attribute in the declaration. The code in the preceding example causes an error.

You declare a string without a length. When your code assigns a value to the string, the length of the value determines the length of the string, as in the following example:

```
Dim Name As String
' ...
Name = "Name is now 30 characters long" ' Length can be changed later.
```

See Also

String Data Type, Dim Statement, Programming Element Support Changes Summary

Structure Declaration Changes in Visual Basic

Visual Basic considers structures and user-defined types (UDTs) to be the same type of programming element. Visual Basic .NET updates structure declaration for unification and improved readability.

Visual Basic 6.0

In Visual Basic 6.0, you declare a structure using the **Type ... End Type** construction. The structure and its members all default to public access. Explicit access declaration is optional. The following example shows a valid structure declaration:

```
Type Employee
   EmpNumber As Integer      ' Defaults to Public access.
   EmpOfficePhone As String
   EmpHomePhone As String    ' Cannot be declared Private inside Type.
End Type
```

Visual Basic .NET

In Visual Basic .NET, the **Type** statement is not supported. You must declare structures using the **Structure** statement as part of a **Structure ... End Structure** construction. Every member of a structure must have an access modifier, which can be **Public**, **Friend**, or **Private**. You can also use the **Dim** statement, which defaults to public access. The structure in the preceding example can be declared as follows:

```
Structure Employee
   Public EmpNumber As Integer      ' Must declare access, even if Public.
   Dim EmpOfficePhone As String     ' Still defaults to Public access.
   Private EmpHomePhone As String   ' Can be made Private inside Structure.
End Structure
```

Visual Basic .NET unifies the syntax for structures and classes. Structures support most of the features of classes, including methods.

See Also

Structure Statement, Dim Statement, Public, Private, Programming Element Support Changes Summary

Variable Scope Changes in Visual Basic

Visual Basic .NET updates local variable scope to support block scope and improve structured programming.

Visual Basic 6.0

In Visual Basic 6.0, any variable declared inside a procedure has procedure scope, so it can be accessed anywhere else within the same procedure. If the variable is declared inside a block—that is, a set of statements terminated by an **End**, **Loop**, or **Next** statement—the variable is still accessible outside the block. The following example illustrates procedure scope:

```
For I = 1 To 10
   Dim N As Long ' N has procedure scope although it was declared within a block.
   N = N + Incr(I)
Next
W = Base ^ N    ' N is still visible outside the block it is declared in.
```

Visual Basic .NET

In Visual Basic .NET, a variable declared inside a block has block scope, and it is not accessible outside the block. The preceding example can be rewritten as follows:

```
Dim N As Long   ' N is declared outside the block and has procedure scope.
For I = 1 To 10
   N = N + Incr(I)
Next
W = Base ^ N   ' N is visible outside the block but I is not.
```

However, a variable's lifetime is still that of the entire procedure. This is true whether the variable has block scope or procedure scope. If you declare a variable inside a block, and if you enter that block several times during the lifetime of the procedure, you should initialize the variable to avoid unexpected values.

See Also

Programming Element Support Changes Summary

Function Changes

The following topics describe changes to functions between Visual Basic 6.0 and Visual Basic .NET:

- **Format Function Changes in Visual Basic** Discusses date/time, numeric, and string format changes to the **Format** function.
- **Date and Time Changes in Visual Basic** Discusses changes to the **Date**, **Date$**, **Time**, and **Time$** functions.
- **String ($) Function Changes in Visual Basic** Discusses functions that include the **String** ($) suffix.

Format Function Changes in Visual Basic

The Visual Basic .NET **Format** function now follows the common language runtime specification for formatting data.

The following sections detail the changes Visual Basic .NET makes to the date/time, numeric, and string formats.

Date/Time Format

Visual Basic 6.0

In Visual Basic 6.0, to display a short or long date, you use either the "ddddd" or "dddddd" format specifier. The **DayOfWeek** ("w") and **WeekOfYear** ("ww") specifiers display the day considered to be the first day of the week, and the week considered to be the first week of the year. The lowercase "m" character displays the month as a number without a leading zero. The **Quarter** specifier ("q") displays the quarter of the year as a number from 1–4.

To display a minute as a number with or without leading zeros, you use either the "Nn" or the "N" format specifier. The characters "Hh" display the hour as a number with leading zeros, and "ttttt" displays the time as a complete time. To display either an uppercase or lowercase "A" or "P" with any hour before or after noon, you use either "AM/PM", "am/pm", "A/P", "a/p", or "AMPM."

Visual Basic .NET

In Visual Basic .NET, "ddddd" and "dddddd" behave the same as "dddd", displaying the full name of the day. They do not display the short date and long date. **DayOfWeek** ("w") and **WeekOfYear** ("ww") are not supported; instead, use the **DatePart** function as follows:

```
Format(Datepart(DateInterval.Weekday, Now))
Format(Datepart(DateInterval.WeekOfYear, Now))
```

"M" and "m" apply to different things, so both are now case sensitive. Use uppercase "M" only for the month in the date portion of a date/time format, and lowercase "m" only for the minutes in the time portion.

The **Quarter** format specifier is not supported; instead, use the **DatePart** function as follows:

```
Format(DatePart(DateInterval.Quarter, Now))
```

To display the minute as a number with or without leading zeros, use "m" or "mm". The "ttttt" format is no longer supported. "H" and "h" apply to different things, so both are now case sensitive. Use uppercase "H" only for a 24-hour clock, and lowercase "h" only for a 12-hour clock. The AM/PM formats are replaced with "t" and "tt."

Numeric Format

Visual Basic 6.0

In Visual Basic 6.0, the **Format** function converts strings to numbers for you.

Negative numbers with an empty negative format string display an empty string.

Trailing decimal points are displayed.

Visual Basic 6.0 supports four format sections—positive, negative, zero, and null.

The exponent for formatting scientific notation supports the "#" placeholder.

The **Short Date/Time** specifier ("c"), displays a date and time in the ddddd ttttt format.

Visual Basic .NET

In Visual Basic .NET, the **Format** function does not convert strings to numbers for you. Thus, the first of the following two lines of code is invalid in Visual Basic .NET, while the second is valid:

```
Format("1.234", "#.#")    ' Displays "#.#".
Format(CSng("1.234"),"#.#")    ' Displays "1.234".
```

Negative numbers with an empty negative format string display a minus sign, as in the following example:

```
Format(-1, ";")    ' Displays "-".
```

Trailing decimal points are not displayed, as in the following examples:

```
Format(123, "###.")    ' Displays "123"
Format(123, "###.#")    ' Displays "123"
```

Visual Basic .NET supports three format sections—positive, negative, and zero. If a non-zero value rounds to zero according to the first or second format section, the resulting zero is formatted according to the third section.

The exponent for formatting scientific notation does not support the "#" placeholder; use the "0" (zero) placeholder instead. Thus, the first of the following two lines of code is invalid in Visual Basic .NET, while the second is valid:

```
Format(123, "#e+#")    ' Displays "12e+3".
Format(123, "#e+0")    ' Displays "1e+2".
```

The short date/time specifier ("c") is now reserved for **Currency** formatting; for date formatting, use the **General Date/Time** ("g") format.

String Format

Visual Basic 6.0

In Visual Basic 6.0, you create expressions for user-defined format strings with the @, &, <, >, and ! specifiers.

Visual Basic .NET

Visual Basic .NET eliminates support for user-defined format strings, so the @, &, <, >, and ! format specifiers have no meaning and are no longer supported.

See Also

Date and Time Changes in Visual Basic, Format Function, DatePart Function, Programming Element Support Changes Summary

Date and Time Changes in Visual Basic

Visual Basic .NET updates the **Date**, **Date$**, **Time**, and **Time$** functions, and replaces the **Now** and **Timer** functions with properties.

Visual Basic 6.0

In Visual Basic 6.0, the **Date** and **Time** functions return the system date and time in the four-byte **Date** format. Similarly, the **Date** and **Time** statements use the Visual Basic 6.0 format to set the system date and time.

The **Date$** and **Time$** functions return the system date and time in **String** format.

The **Now** and **Timer** functions specify the current date and time and the number of seconds elapsed since midnight.

Visual Basic .NET

Visual Basic .NET replaces **Date** and **Time** with the **Today** and **TimeOfDay** properties, which use the eight-byte common language runtime (CLR) **DateTime** structure. This corresponds with the **Date** data type in Visual Basic .NET. You can use **Today** and **TimeOfDay** to both set and fetch the system date and time.

Visual Basic .NET replaces the **Date$** and **Time$** functions with the **DateString** and **TimeString** properties. You can use **DateString** and **TimeString** to both set and fetch the system date and time.

The **Now** and **Timer** functions are replaced by read-only properties of the same names. Their calling sequences remain unchanged.

See Also

Format Function Changes in Visual Basic, Format Function, Today Property, TimeOfDay Property, Date Data Type, DateString Property, TimeString Property, Now Property, Timer Property, Programming Element Support Changes Summary

String ($) Function Changes in Visual Basic

Visual Basic .NET eliminates the need for some functions to have both a **String** version and a **Variant** version.

Visual Basic 6.0

In Visual Basic 6.0, some functions have two versions, one that returns a **String** value and one that returns a **Variant** value. These function pairs are differentiated by a dollar sign ($) suffix for the **String** version; for example, **Chr** and **Chr$**.

Visual Basic .NET

Visual Basic .NET replaces each function pair with a single function. The **Variant** versions are discontinued, and you can call the **String** versions either with or without the $ suffix.

Although only **Trim** is defined, Visual Basic .NET accepts **Trim$** because the $ works as an identifier type character for the **String** data type.

See Also

Format Function Changes in Visual Basic, Date and Time Changes in Visual Basic, Programming Element Support Changes Summary, LTrim, RTrim, and Trim Functions

Object and Component Changes

The following topics describe changes to objects and components between Visual Basic 6.0 and Visual Basic .NET:

- **Object Creation Changes in Visual Basic** Covers implicit object creation.
- **Binary Compatibility Changes in Visual Basic** Discusses updates to the mechanism for preserving compatibility with older versions of a component.
- **Class and Interface Changes in Visual Basic** Discusses declaration and usage of classes and interfaces.

Object Creation Changes in Visual Basic

Visual Basic .NET revises object creation for improved readability and to support constructors with arguments.

Visual Basic 6.0

In Visual Basic 6.0, an object variable declared with the keywords **As New** is initialized to **Nothing**, meaning that no object has yet been created. Every time the variable is encountered during execution, it is evaluated before the code executes. If the variable contains **Nothing**, an object of the appropriate class is created prior to execution of the code that uses it.

Visual Basic .NET

In Visual Basic .NET, there is no implicit object creation. If an object variable contains **Nothing** when it is encountered, it is left unchanged and no instance is automatically created.

You can create an object with the same statement that declares the object variable. Each of the following two lines of code creates an object from a class, `EmpObj`, that is already defined in the application. The two lines are treated as equivalent, with the first being taken as shorthand for the second:

```
Dim Emp As New EmpObj           ' Shorthand for next line.
Dim Emp As EmpObj = New EmpObj  ' EmpObj created; Emp points to EmpObj.
```

In both cases, an instance of the `EmpObj` class is created as soon as the **Dim** statement is executed, and `Emp` is initialized to a reference to the new object.

Parameterized Constructors

Some classes have constructors that take arguments. If you are creating an object from such a class, you can include its arguments in the declaration. The following example shows two equivalent declarations that pass arguments to the object's constructor, with the first being taken as shorthand for the second:

```
Dim Q As New Quark(12, 0.0035)          ' Shorthand for next line.
Dim Q As Quark = New Quark(12, 0.0035)  ' Parameterized constructor.
```

See Also

Dim Statement, New, Nothing, Programming Element Support Changes Summary

Binary Compatibility Changes in Visual Basic

Visual Basic .NET updates the mechanism for preserving compatibility with older versions of a component.

Visual Basic 6.0

In Visual Basic 6.0, the Binary Compatibility option allows you to automatically retain class and interface identifiers from a previous version of a component when you compile a new version. The new version contains both the old identifiers and the new identifiers, and client applications can continue using the old interface to your component without having to be updated.

Visual Basic .NET

In Visual Basic .NET, binary compatibility is accomplished using attributes. This gives you direct control over the information placed in your compiled component, such as class and interface identifiers, virtual table offsets, and any appropriate COM attributes. Because you can explicitly select attributes for preservation, the Binary Compatibility option is not supported.

See Also

ComClassAttribute Class, Programming Element Support Changes Summary

Class and Interface Changes in Visual Basic

Visual Basic .NET introduces a number of changes that affect the declaration and usage of classes and interfaces.

Implements Statement

Visual Basic 6.0

In Visual Basic 6.0, a class definition implicitly includes a default interface, which defines the public members of the class. This interface can be referenced by another class. In particular, a class can specify another class name in an **Implements** statement.

Visual Basic .NET

In Visual Basic .NET, classes can have methods, and you can define interfaces explicitly. The properties and methods of a class belong exclusively to the class itself. The **Implements** statement can specify only an interface, not another class.

Late Binding

Visual Basic 6.0

In Visual Basic 6.0, you can assign an interface reference to a variable of the **Object** data type, enabling late-bound access to the interface's methods and properties. This behavior is limited to in-process calls on the same thread. The following example shows skeleton code for late binding to an interface:

```
Dim Int As Interface1
Dim Cls As New Class1    ' Class1 implements Interface1.
Dim Obj As Object
' ...
Set Int = Cls            ' Gets a reference to the Interface1 interface.
Set Obj = Int            ' Assigns the Interface1 reference to Obj.
Obj.Property1 = Value    ' Late-bound call to Interface1.
```

Visual Basic .NET

Visual Basic .NET allows late binding only to public members of a class, and not to interface members. To accomplish the binding of the preceding example, you must set `Obj` directly to `Cls` to be able to reference `Property1`. The late binding code can be rewritten as follows:

```
Obj = Cls                ' Assigns the Class1 reference to Obj.
Obj.Property1 = Value    ' Late-bound call to Class1.
```

Global Classes

Visual Basic 6.0

When you create a new class in Visual Basic 6.0, the allowable values of the **Instancing** property include **GlobalSingleUse** and **GlobalMultiUse**. These indicate that other components can invoke the properties and methods of the new class as if they were global functions. An instance of the class is implicitly created the first time one of its members is called. This functionality enables a server to expose properties and methods that can be accessed without qualification.

Visual Basic .NET

Visual Basic .NET provides the same functionality by allowing you to expose standard module members from a server. You can add properties and methods of a shared class to the **System** namespace using the **Imports** statement. Visual Basic .NET does not support the **Instancing** property. You can achieve the effect of **GlobalMultiUse** with **Public** class access and the appropriate constructor access.

Option Private Module Statement

Visual Basic 6.0

In Visual Basic 6.0, the **Option Private Module** statement indicates that the entire module is private, and its components are not accessible outside its project.

Visual Basic .NET

Visual Basic .NET does not support the **Option Private Module** statement. This specification is handled by access modifiers in the **Module** statement.

Default Members

Visual Basic 6.0

In Visual Basic 6.0, you can specify that any particular method or data member is the default member of a class.

Visual Basic .NET

In Visual Basic .NET, a default member of a class can only be a property that takes one or more arguments. This enables interoperability with other programming languages.

Initialization and Termination

Visual Basic 6.0

In Visual Basic 6.0, class modules use the **Initialize** and **Terminate** events to perform any necessary actions at the time of creation and destruction. The **Initialize** event is raised when the object is first encountered following a **New** statement, and **Terminate** is raised as soon as the last reference to the object is released. However, you can also call these event methods directly at any time during execution.

Visual Basic .NET

Visual Basic .NET uses the constructor/destructor model, and does not support **Class_Initialize** and **Class_Terminate**. A class uses the **Sub** statement to declare its constructor. This enables support of inheritance, which requires parameterized constructors. It also protects the constructor and destructor from being called except at creation and termination.

Indeterminate Lifetime

Object lifetime is determined by the creation and termination of the object instance. The program determines the creation time of the objects it declares, but termination involves a more complex mechanism.

Visual Basic 6.0

In Visual Basic 6.0, every object instance maintains a reference count. When the last reference to an instance is released and the count goes to zero, the object is terminated immediately.

Visual Basic .NET

In Visual Basic .NET, a destructor is not necessarily called as soon as the last reference is released. This is because the common language runtime maintains a reference tree instead of individual reference counts. The garbage collector traces the reference tree in the background. If it finds an object or group of objects that have no reference from any currently executing code, it calls the destructors of all such objects. It is impossible to predict either the order of this destruction or the time it takes the garbage collector to trace the reference tree. Therefore, the lifetime of an object is indeterminate.

See Also

Implements Statement, Imports Statement, Object Data Type, Class Statement, Module Statement, Sub Statement, New, Programming Element Support Changes Summary

Procedure Changes

The following topics describe changes to procedures between Visual Basic 6.0 and Visual Basic .NET:

- **Parameter Passing Mechanism Changes in Visual Basic** Describes passing arguments to procedures.
- **Procedure Calling Sequence Changes in Visual Basic** Discusses procedure calls and returns.
- **Procedure Declaration Changes in Visual Basic** Describes optional procedure arguments and static local variables.

Parameter Passing Mechanism Changes in Visual Basic

Visual Basic .NET introduces several changes affecting the mechanism of passing arguments to procedures.

Default Passing Mechanism

Visual Basic 6.0

In Visual Basic 6.0, if you do not specify **ByVal** or **ByRef** for a procedure argument, the passing mechanism defaults to **ByRef**. This allows the variable passed into the procedure to be modified in the calling program.

Exposing a variable to modification can lead to a pitfall. In the following example, the passing mechanism defaults to **ByRef**, the value of `ElapsedSeconds` gets altered by **MinutesPastHour**, and `ElapsedSeconds` is displayed incorrectly by **MsgBox**:

```
Function MinutesPastHour(Seconds As Integer) As Integer
   Dim Hours As Integer = Seconds \ 3600
   Seconds = Seconds Mod 3600
   MinutesPastHour = Seconds \ 60
End Function
' ...
ElapsedSeconds = CInt(Timer( ))  ' Integer seconds since midnight.
ExtraMinutes = MinutesPastHour(ElapsedSeconds)
MsgBox "Total seconds: " & ElapsedSeconds & _
       "; minutes past hour: " & ExtraMinutes
```

Passing an argument **ByRef** allows a procedure to change it in the calling program, which can lead to unexpected behavior. And if that procedure calls another procedure and passes the same argument **ByRef**, the chances of unintentionally changing the original variable are increased.

Visual Basic .NET

When you declare a procedure in Visual Basic .NET, the passing mechanism defaults to **ByVal** for every argument. This protects arguments against modification. The declaration in the preceding example can be rewritten as follows:

```
Function MinutesPastHour(ByVal Seconds As Integer) As Integer
```

Passing `Seconds` by value prevents the procedure from accessing the variable in the calling program, and helps avoid the pitfall just described.

Although **ByVal** is the default mechanism, specifying it explicitly for every argument removes uncertainty and makes your code easier to read.

ByRef Property Arguments

Visual Basic 6.0

In Visual Basic 6.0, a property passed to a procedure as a **ByRef** argument is copied into the procedure but not copied out. This means that any modification to such a property argument is not reflected back to the original property in the calling program, even though it was passed **ByRef**.

Visual Basic .NET

In Visual Basic .NET, a property argument passed **ByRef** is copied both into and out of the procedure. The following example demonstrates how a property can be changed by a procedure:

```
Sub Reduce(ByRef Height As Single)
' ... ... ... ... ... ... ...   ' Code to modify Height argument.
End Sub
' ...
Dim Sq As Square = New Square   ' Square has property Side of type Single.
Reduce(Sq.Side)                 ' Side is changed when Reduce returns.
```

When a procedure modifies a property argument, the value of the original property is not changed immediately in the calling program. Instead, it is copied out when the procedure returns.

ParamArray Arguments

Visual Basic 6.0

In Visual Basic 6.0, a procedure can specify the **ParamArray** keyword on the last of its arguments to accept an array of **Variant** arguments. You cannot declare the passing mechanism of these arguments. They are always passed **ByRef**.

Visual Basic .NET

In Visual Basic .NET, **ParamArray** arguments are always passed **ByVal**. The arguments in the array must all be of the data type of the **ParamArray** argument.

See Also

Procedure Declaration Changes in Visual Basic, Procedure Calling Sequence Changes in Visual Basic, Function Statement, Sub Statement, ByVal, ByRef, ParamArray, Programming Element Support Changes Summary

Procedure Calling Sequence Changes in Visual Basic

Visual Basic .NET introduces several changes affecting procedure calling sequences. These changes improve syntax consistency.

Parentheses in Procedure Calls

Visual Basic 6.0

In Visual Basic 6.0, parentheses are required around the argument list in **Function** calls. In **Sub** calls, they are required if you use the **Call** statement and forbidden if you do not. The following example shows valid calling statements:

```
Y = Sqrt(X)
Call DisplayCell(2, 14, Value)
DisplayCell 2, 14, Value  ' Variation on previous statement.
```

Visual Basic .NET

In Visual Basic .NET, parentheses are always required around a non-empty argument list in any procedure call. In **Sub** calls, the **Call** statement is optional. The preceding example can be rewritten as follows:

```
Y = Sqrt(X)
DisplayCell(2, 14, Value)
```

If you are calling a procedure without supplying any arguments, you can include empty parentheses or leave them out altogether.

Return Statement

Visual Basic 6.0

In Visual Basic 6.0, you use the **Return** statement only to branch back to the code following a **GoSub** statement. Both statements must be in the same procedure.

Visual Basic .NET

In Visual Basic .NET, the **GoSub** statement is not supported, and you can use the **Return** statement to return control to the calling program from a **Function** or **Sub** procedure.

See Also

Declaration Syntax Changes in Visual Basic, Procedure Declaration Changes in Visual Basic, Parameter Passing Mechanism Changes in Visual Basic, Control Statement Changes in Visual Basic, Return Statement, Call Statement, Programming Element Support Changes Summary

Procedure Declaration Changes in Visual Basic

Visual Basic .NET introduces several changes related to the declaration of procedures.

Optional Arguments

Visual Basic 6.0

In Visual Basic 6.0, you can declare a procedure argument as **Optional** without specifying a default value. If an optional argument is of the **Variant** type, the procedure code can use the **IsMissing** function to determine whether the argument is present.

Visual Basic .NET

In Visual Basic .NET, every optional argument must declare a default value, which is passed to the procedure if the calling program does not supply that argument. The **IsMissing** function is not needed to detect a missing argument, and it is not supported. The following example shows an optional argument declaration:

```
Sub Calculate(Optional ByVal Switch As Boolean = False)
```

Static Local Variables

Visual Basic 6.0

In Visual Basic 6.0, you can declare a procedure with the **Static** modifier. This causes every local variable within the procedure to be static and to retain its value between calls.

Visual Basic .NET

In Visual Basic .NET, the **Static** keyword is not supported in a **Function** or **Sub** statement. You must individually declare each local variable you want to be **Static**.

See Also

Procedure Calling Sequence Changes in Visual Basic, Parameter Passing Mechanism Changes in Visual Basic, Optional, Static, Programming Element Support Changes Summary

Property Changes

The following topics describe changes to properties between Visual Basic 6.0 and Visual Basic .NET:

- **Default Property Changes in Visual Basic** Covers changes to default property support.
- **Property Changes in Visual Basic** Covers changes to property procedures and arguments.

Default Property Changes in Visual Basic

Visual Basic .NET updates default property support for simplification and improved readability.

Visual Basic 6.0

In Visual Basic 6.0, default properties are supported on objects. On a **Label** control, for example, **Caption** is the default property, and the two assignments in the following example are equivalent:

```
Dim L As Label
L = "Important"
L.Caption = "Important"
```

While default properties enable a certain amount of shorthand in writing Visual Basic code, they have several drawbacks:

- They can make code more difficult to read. In the preceding example, if you are not familiar with the **Label** control, you cannot tell from the first assignment whether the string `"Important"` is being stored directly in the variable `L` or in a default property.
- Given an object that you plan to use in your code, it is not always easy to discover whether it has a default property, and if so, which property that is.
- Default properties make the **Set** statement necessary in the Visual Basic language. The following example shows how **Set** is needed to indicate that an object reference, rather than a default property, is to be assigned:

  ```
  Dim L1 As Label, L2 As Label
  L1 = "Saving"   ' Assign a value to L1's Caption property.
  L2 = L1         ' Replace L2's Caption property with L1's.
  Set L2 = L1     ' Replace L2 with an object reference to L1.
  ```

Visual Basic .NET

In Visual Basic .NET, default properties are not supported unless they take arguments. Because of this syntax change, the **Let** and **Set** statements are not needed to specify what is to be assigned, and they are not used in assignment statements. The **Text** property replaces the **Caption** property on the **Label** control, and the preceding example can be rewritten as follows:

```
Dim L1, L2 As Label    ' Both become type Label in Visual Basic .NET.
L1.Text = "Saving"     ' Assign Text property.
L2.Text = L1.Text      ' Copy Text property.
L2 = L1                ' Copy object reference.
```

Let is still a reserved word in Visual Basic .NET, even though it has no syntactical use. This helps avoid confusion with its former meanings. Visual Basic .NET uses the **Set** statement for property procedures that set the value of a property.

Parameterized Properties

Default properties that take arguments are not ambiguous, and they are supported in Visual Basic .NET. Default properties appear most commonly on collection classes. In the **System.Windows.Forms** namespace, for example, the **Form** class supports the following hierarchy:

Form object

- **Controls** property (returns a **ControlCollection** object for this form)
  - **ControlCollection** object (default property is **Item**)
    - **Item** property (returns a **Control** object for one item in the collection)
      - **Control** object

The **Form.Controls** property returns a **ControlCollection** object, and the **ControlCollection.Item** property returns a **Control** object. The following example shows both valid and invalid use of default properties in Visual Basic .NET:

```
Dim F As Form   ' Assume F has been created and initialized.
' ...
F.Controls.Item(0).Text = "Stop"   ' Valid -- no default properties used.
F.Controls(0).Text = "Stop"   ' Valid -- Item is parameterized.
' ...
F(0).Text = "Stop"   ' INVALID -- Form does not have a default property.
F.Controls(0) = "Stop"   ' INVALID -- No default property on Control.
```

Default Property Declaration

In Visual Basic .NET, you specify a property as the default property by beginning its declaration with the **Default** keyword. If you overload the property name, you must specify **Default** in every overload declaration. You cannot declare a default property to be **Shared** or **Private**.

See Also

Property Changes in Visual Basic, Set Statement, Default, Programming Element Support Changes Summary

Property Changes in Visual Basic

Visual Basic .NET updates the declaration of property procedures and arguments for simplification and interoperability with other programming languages.

Visual Basic 6.0

In Visual Basic 6.0, you use the **Property Get**, **Property Let**, and **Property Set** statements to get and set property values.

Passing a variable the **ByRef** property argument allows a procedure to change that variable in the calling code.

Visual Basic .NET

Visual Basic .NET introduces a unified property declaration syntax that includes the procedures for getting and setting the property's value. This guarantees consistency of property attributes such as access level and overloading. The following example shows the declaration of a property that does not take arguments:

```
Private MonthNum As Integer = 1  ' Internal storage for property value.
Property Month( ) As Integer
   Get
      Return MonthNum
   End Get
   Set(ByVal Value As Integer)
      If Value < 1 Or Value > 12 Then
         ' Error processing for invalid value.
      Else
         MonthNum = Value
      End If
   End Set
End Property   ' Month
```

You can use any name you want for the argument to **Set**. If you do not supply an argument, `Value` is automatically generated.

This syntax change makes the **Property Get** and **Property Set** statements unnecessary, and they are not supported. Because Visual Basic .NET does not allow default properties without arguments, **Property Let** and **Property Set** are not needed to distinguish whether an object reference or a default property is to be assigned. Therefore, the **Property Let** statement also is not supported.

Visual Basic .NET does not support **ByRef** property arguments. If a property procedure has a **ByRef** argument and changes the variable underlying that argument, the property can behave in an unexpected manner. Therefore, all declarations of parameterized properties must specify **ByVal** for the arguments.

See Also

Default Property Changes in Visual Basic, ByVal, Programming Element Support Changes Summary

Miscellaneous Changes

The following topics describe changes to operators and file handling between Visual Basic 6.0 and Visual Basic .NET:

- **Boolean Operator Changes in Visual Basic** Describes Boolean operators and logical expressions.
- **File Handling Changes in Visual Basic** Discusses expansion of file handling capabilities, and compatibility with previous versions of Visual Basic file I/O functions.

Boolean Operator Changes in Visual Basic

Visual Basic .NET removes two Boolean operators and adds two others to improve performance.

Visual Basic 6.0

In Visual Basic 6.0, Boolean operators—**And**, **Or**, **Not**, and **Xor**—always evaluate all the expressions in their operands.

You use the **Eqv** and **Imp** operators to perform logical equivalences and implications on two expressions.

Visual Basic .NET

In Visual Basic .NET, the **And**, **Or**, **Not**, and **Xor** operators still evaluate all expressions contributing to their operands. Visual Basic .NET also introduces two new operators, **AndAlso** and **OrElse**, that can reduce execution time by *short-circuiting* logical evaluations. If the first operand of an **AndAlso** operator evaluates to **False**, the second operand is not evaluated. Similarly, if the first operand of an **OrElse** operator evaluates to **True**, the second operand is not evaluated.

> **Note** You should be careful using short-circuiting operators. If the second operand contains a procedure call, you cannot rely on that procedure being called every time the operator executes.

The **Eqv** and **Imp** operators are not supported. Use the equals (=) comparison operator in place of **Eqv** for both logical and bitwise evaluations. You can replace the logical **Imp** operator with an expression using the **Not** and **Or** operators, as shown in the following example:

```
Result = A Imp B           ' True unless A is True and B is False.
Result = (Not A) Or B      ' Same as A Imp B.
```

You can replace a bitwise **Imp** in the same manner, using **Not** and **Or** on numeric operands.

See Also

And Operator, AndAlso Operator, Or Operator, OrElse Operator, Not Operator, Xor Operator, Programming Element Support Changes Summary

File Handling Changes in Visual Basic

Visual Basic .NET expands file handling capabilities while providing compatibility with previous versions of Visual Basic file I/O functions.

Visual Basic 6.0

In Visual Basic 6.0, file handling is accomplished using various file I/O functions such as **Open**, **Input**, **Output**, and **Append**. The File System Object provides an object-oriented method of working with files.

Visual Basic .NET

In Visual Basic .NET, file handling is accomplished through the **System.IO** namespace, which duplicates and expands upon the File System Object. In addition, the **System.IO.File** namespace includes functions that provide compatibility with the older Visual Basic file I/O functions.

The **FileStream** class provides access to standard input and output files and error devices.

The following table lists file-related enumerations available in Visual Basic .NET.

Enumeration	Purpose
FileAccess Enumeration	Defines constants for read, write, or read/write access to a file.
FileMode Enumeration	Specifies how the operating system opens a file.
FileShare Enumeration	Provides constants for controlling the level of access other FileStream members have to the same file.
FileAttributes Enumeration	Provides access to stored attributes, such as whether a file is a directory, is encrypted, hidden, or read-only, or is a system file or a temporary file.

See Also

FileAttribute Enumeration; Programming Element Support Changes Summary

Overview of Visual Basic Concepts

Classes

ComClassAttribute Class

VBFixedArrayAttribute Class

VBFixedStringAttribute Class

Constants

Print and Display Constants

Constructors

ComClassAttribute Constructor

VBFixedArrayAttribute Constructor

VBFixedStringAttribute Constructor

Data types

Boolean Data Type

Byte Data Type

Char Data Type

Date Data Type

Decimal Data Type

Double Data Type

Integer Data Type

Long Data Type

Object Data Type

Short Data Type

Single Data Type

String Data Type

User-Defined Data Type

Directives

#Const Directive

#ExternalSource Directive

#If...Then...#Else Directives

#Region Directive

Enumerations

AppWinStyle Enumeration

CallType Enumeration

CompareMethod Enumeration

DateFormat Enumeration

DateInterval Enumeration

DueDate Enumeration

FileAttribute Enumeration

FirstDayOfWeek Enumeration

FirstWeekOfYear Enumeration

MsgBoxResult Enumeration

MsgBoxStyle Enumeration

OpenAccess Enumeration

OpenMode Enumeration

OpenShare Enumeration

Tristate Enumeration

VariantType Enumeration

VbStrConv Enumeration

Fields

VBFixedArrayAttribute.FirstBound Field

VBFixedArrayAttribute.SecondBound Field

VBFixedStringAttribute.SizeConst Field

Functions

AppActivate Function

Asc, AscW Functions

Beep Function

CallByName Function

ChDir Function

ChDrive Function

Choose Function

Chr, ChrW Functions

Command Function

CreateObject Function

CType Function

CType Function

CurDir Function

DateAdd Function

DateDiff Function

DatePart Function

DateSerial Function

DateValue Function

Day Function

DDB Function

DeleteSetting Function

Derived Math Functions

Different Formats for Different Numeric Values (Format Function)

Dir Function

Environ Function

EOF Function

ErrorToString Function

FileAttr Function

FileClose Function

FileCopy Function

FileDateTime Function

FileGet Function

FileGetObject Function

FileLen Function

FileOpen Function

FilePut Function

FilePutObject Function

FileWidth Function

Filter Function

Format Function

FormatCurrency Function

FormatDateTime Function

FormatNumber Function

FormatPercent Function

FreeFile Function

FV Function

GetAllSettings Function

GetAttr Function

GetChar Function

GetException Function

GetObject Function

GetSetting Function

Hex Function

Hour Function

IIf Function

Input Function

InputBox Function

InputString Function

InStr Function

InStrRev Function

Int, Fix Functions

IPmt Function

IRR Function

IsArray Function

IsDate Function

IsDBNull Function

IsError Function

IsNothing Function

IsNumeric Function

IsReference Function

Join Function

Kill Function

LBound Function

LCase Function

Left Function

Len Function

LineInput Function

Loc Function

Lock, Unlock Functions

LOF Function

LSet Function

LTrim, RTrim, and Trim Functions

Math Functions

Mid Function

Minute Function

MIRR Function

MkDir Function

Month Function

MonthName Function

MsgBox Function

NPer Function

NPV Function

Oct Function

Partition Function

Pmt Function

PPmt Function

Predefined Date/Time Formats (Format Function)

Predefined Numeric Formats (Format Function)

Print, PrintLine Functions

PV Function

QBColor Function

Rate Function

Rename Function

Replace Function

Reset Function

RGB Function

Right Function

RmDir Function

Rnd Function

RSet Function

SaveSetting Function

Second Function

Seek Function

SetAttr Function

Shell Function

SLN Function

Space Function

SPC Function

Split Function

Str Function

StrComp Function

StrConv Function

StrDup Function

StrReverse Function

Switch Function

SYD Function

SystemTypeName Function

TAB Function

TimeSerial Function

TimeValue Function

Type Conversion Functions

TypeName Function

UBound Function

UCase Function

User-Defined Date/Time Formats (Format Function)

User-Defined Numeric Formats (Format Function)

Val Function

Val Function

VarType Function

VbTypeName Function

Weekday Function

WeekdayName Function

Write, WriteLine Functions

Year Function

Keywords

Alias

Ansi

As

Assembly

Auto

ByRef

ByVal

Case

Default

DirectCast

Each

Else

ElseIf

End

Error

Explicit

FALSE

For

Friend

Handles

Implements

In

Is

Lib

Loop

Me

Module

MustInherit

MustOverride

MyBase

MyClass

New

Next

Nothing

NotInheritable

NotOverridable

Off

On

Option

Optional

Overloads

Overridable

Overrides

ParamArray

Preserve

Private

Protected

Public

ReadOnly

Resume

Shadows

Shared

Static

Step

Then

To

TRUE

TypeOf

Unicode

Until

When

While

WithEvents

WriteOnly

Methods

Add Method

Clear Method

GetEnumerator Method

Raise Method

Remove Method

Objects

Collection Object

Err Object

Operators

- Operator
& Operator
&= Operator
* Operator
*= Operator
/ Operator
/= Operator
\ Operator
\= Operator
^ Operator
^= Operator
+ Operator
+= Operator
= Operator
-= Operator
AddressOf Operator
And Operator
AndAlso Operator
Comparison Operators
GetType Operator
Is Operator
Like Operator
Mod Operator
Not Operator
Or Operator
OrElse Operator
Xor Operator

Properties

ComClassAttribute.ClassID Property
ComClassAttribute.EventID Property
ComClassAttribute.InterfaceID Property
ComClassAttribute.InterfaceShadows Property
Count Property
DateString Property
Description Property
Erl Property
HelpContext Property
HelpFile Property
Item Property
LastDLLError Property
Now Property
Number Property
ScriptEngine Property
ScriptEngineBuildVersion Property
ScriptEngineMajorVersion Property
ScriptEngineMinorVersion Property
Source Property
TimeOfDay Property
Timer Property
TimeString Property
Today Property

Statements

- AddHandler Statement
- Call Statement
- Class Statement
- Const Statement
- Declare Statement
- Delegate Statement
- Dim Statement
- Do...Loop Statements
- End Statement
- Enum Statement
- Erase Statement
- Error Statement
- Event Statement
- Exit Statement
- For Each...Next Statements
- For...Next Statements
- Function Statement
- Get Statement
- GoTo Statement
- If...Then...Else Statements
- Implements Statement
- Imports Statement
- Inherits Statement
- Interface Statement
- Mid Statement
- Module Statement
- Namespace Statement
- On Error Statement
- Option Compare Statement
- Option Explicit Statement
- Option Strict Statement
- Property Statement
- RaiseEvent Statement
- Randomize Statement
- ReDim Statement
- REM Statement
- RemoveHandler Statement
- Resume Statement
- Return Statement
- Select...Case Statements
- Set Statement
- Stop Statement
- Structure Statement
- Sub Statement
- SyncLock Statement
- Throw Statement
- Try...Catch...Finally Statements
- While...End While Statements
- With...End With Statements

Visual Basic Language Keywords

The following is a listing of the Visual Basic .NET language keywords. All language keywords are reserved.

#Const
#ExternalSource
#If...Then...#Else
#Region
&
&=
*
*=
+
+=
-
-=
/
/=
=
\
\=
^
^=
AddHandler
AddressOf
Alias
And
AndAlso
Ansi
As
Assembly
Auto
Boolean
ByRef
Byte
ByVal
Call
Case
Catch
CBool
CByte
CChar
CDate
CDec
CDbl
Char
CInt
Class
CLng
CObj
Const
CShort
CSng
CStr
CType
Date
Decimal
Declare
Default
Delegate
Dim
DirectCast
Do
Double
Each
Else
ElseIf
End
Enum
Erase
Error
Event
Exit
False
Finally
For
Friend
Function
Get
GetType
GoTo
Handles
If
Implements
Imports
In
Inherits
Integer
Interface
Is
Let
Lib
Like
Long
Loop
Me
Mod
Module
MustInherit
MustOverride
MyBase
MyClass
Namespace
New
Next
Not
Nothing
NotInheritable

NotOverridable	Property	Shadows	To
Object	Protected	Shared	True
On	Public	Short	Try
Option	RaiseEvent	Single	TypeOf
Optional	ReadOnly	Static	Unicode
Or	ReDim	Step	Until
OrElse	#Region	Stop	**Variant**
Overloads	REM	String	When
Overridable	RemoveHandler	Structure	While
Overrides	Resume	Sub	With
ParamArray	Return	SyncLock	WithEvents
Preserve	Select	Then	WriteOnly
Private	Set	Throw	Xor

Note **Variant** and **Let** are retained as keywords, although they are no longer used in Visual Basic .NET.

A–Z Reference

#Const Directive

Defines conditional compiler constants for Visual Basic.

```
#Const constname = expression
```

Parts

constname
: Required. **String**. Name of the constant being defined.

expression
: Required. Literal, other conditional compiler constant, or any combination that includes any or all arithmetic or logical operators except **Is**.

Remarks

Conditional compiler constants are always private to the file in which they appear. You cannot create public compiler constants using the **#Const** directive; you can create them only in the user interface.

You can use only conditional compiler constants and literals in *expression*. Using a standard constant defined with **#Const** causes an error. Conversely, you can use constants defined with the **#Const** keyword only for conditional compilation. Constants also can be undefined, in which case they have a value of **Nothing**.

Example

This example uses the **#Const** directive.

```
#Const MyCountry = "USA"
#Const Version = "8.0.0012"
#Const CustomerNumber = 36
```

See Also

#If...Then...#Else Directives, Const Statement

#ExternalSource Directive

Indicates a mapping between source lines and text external to the source, such as an .aspx file.

```
# ExternalSource( StringLiteral , IntLiteral )
   [ LogicalLine+ ]
# End ExternalSource
```

Parts

StringLiteral
The path to the external source.

IntLiteral
The line number of the first line of the external source.

Logical Line
The line where the error occurs in the external source.

 # End ExternalSource
Terminates the **#ExternalSource** block.

Remarks

A source file may include external source directives that indicate a mapping between source lines and text external to the source, so if errors are encountered during compilation, they are identified as coming from the external source. External source directives have no effect on compilation and may not be nested. They are intended for internal use by the application only.

#If...Then...#Else Directives

Conditionally compiles selected blocks of Visual Basic code.

```
#If expression Then
   statements
[ #ElseIf expression Then
   [ statements ]
...
#ElseIf expression Then
   [ statements ] ]
[ #Else
   [ statements ] ]
#End If
```

Parts

expression

Required for **If** and **ElseIf** statements, optional elsewhere. Any expression, consisting exclusively of one or more conditional compiler constants, literals, and operators, that evaluates to **True** or **False**. Three conditional compilation constants are provided: **Config**, **Debug**, and **Trace**. **Debug** and **Trace** are **Boolean** datatypes and can be set in the Project Properties dialogue. When **Debug** is defined, Debug class methods generate output to the **Output** window. When it is not defined, Debug class methods are not compiled and no Debug output is generated. Similarly, when **Trace** is defined, Trace class methods generate output to the **Output** window. When it is not defined, Trace class methods are not compiled and no Trace output is generated. **Config** is a string datatype, which corresponds to the current setting in the Configuration Manager.

statements

Required for **If** statement block, optional elsewhere. Visual Basic program lines or compiler directives that are compiled if the associated expression evaluates to **True**.

#End If

Terminates the #**If** statement block.

Remarks

On the surface, the behavior of the **#If...Then...#Else** directives appears the same as that of the **If...Then...Else** statements. However, the **#If...Then...#Else** directives evaluate what is compiled by the compiler, whereas the **If...Then...Else** statements evaluate conditions at run time.

Conditional compilation is typically used to compile the same program for different platforms. It is also used to prevent debugging code from appearing in an executable file. Code excluded during conditional compilation is completely omitted from the final executable file, so it has no effect on size or performance.

Regardless of the outcome of any evaluation, all expressions are evaluated using **Option Compare Text**. The **Option Compare** statement does not affect expressions in **#If** and **#ElseIf** statements.

> **Note** No single-line form of the **#If**, **#Else**, **#ElseIf**, and **#End If** directives exists; that is, no other code can appear on the same line as any of the directives.

Example

This example uses the **#If...Then...#Else** construct to determine whether to compile certain statements.

```
#Const CustomerNumber = 36
#If CustomerNumber = 35 Then
    ' Insert code to be compiled for customer # 35.
#ElseIf CustomerNumber = 36 Then
    ' Insert code to be compiled for customer # 36.
#Else
    ' Insert code to be compiled for all other customers.
#End If
```

See Also

#Const Directive

#Region Directive

Collapses and hides sections of code in Visual Basic .NET files.

```
#Region "identifier_string"
#End Region
```

Parts

identifier_string
: Required. String that acts as the title of a region when it is collapsed. Regions are collapsed by default.

#End Region
: Terminates the **#Region** block.

Remarks

The **#Region** directive lets you specify a block of code that you can expand or collapse when using the outlining feature of the Visual Studio® Code Editor. **#Region** statements support block semantics (such as **#If...#End If**), meaning that the start and end must be in the same code block.

Example

This example uses the **#Region** directive.

```
#Region "MathFunctions"
' Insert code for the Math functions here.
#End Region
```

& Operator

Generates a string concatenation of two expressions.

```
result = expression1 & expression2
```

Parts

result
: Required. Any **String** or **Object** variable.

expression1
: Required. Any expression.

expression2
: Required. Any expression.

Remarks

If the data type of *expression1* or *expression2* is not **String**, it is converted to **String**. The data type of *result* is **String**. If one or both expressions are stated as Nothing or have a value of **DBNull.value**, they are treated as a string with a value of " ".

Example

This example uses the **&** operator to force string concatenation. The result is a string value representing the concatenation of the two string operands.

```
Dim myStr As String
myStr = "Hello" & " World"    ' Returns "Hello World".
```

The following example uses the & operator to force string concatentaion on the result of a database lookup. The result is the string value from the database or an empty string in the case of a null value.

```
Dim rs As Recordset = Cmd.Execute("Select * from …")
Dim myStr As String
myStr=rs("au_id") & ""
```

See Also

&= Operator, Concatenation Operators, Operator Precedence in Visual Basic, Operators Listed by Functionality

&= Operator

Concatenates a **String** expression to a **String** variable and assigns the result to the variable.

```
variable &= expression
```

Parts

variable
: Required. Any **String** variable.

expression
: Required. Any **String** expression.

Example

The following example uses the **&=** operator to concatenate two **String** variables and assign the result to the first variable.

```
Dim var1 As String = "Hello "
Dim var2 As String = "World!"
var1 &= var2    ' The value of var1 is now "Hello World!"
```

See Also

& Operator, *= Operator, += Operator, -= Operator, /= Operator, = Operator, \= Operator, ^= Operator

* Operator

Multiplies two numbers.

```
number1 * number2
```

Parts

number1
Required. Any numeric expression.

number2
Required. Any numeric expression.

Result

The result is the product of *number1* and *number2*.

Supported Types

Byte, **Short**, **Integer**, **Long**, **Single**, **Double**, **Decimal**

Remarks

The data type of the result is the same as that of the data type with the greatest range. The order of range, from least to greatest range, is Byte, Short, Integer, Long, Single, Double, and Decimal.

If an expression is stated as Nothing, or is Empty, it is treated as zero.

Example

This example uses the * operator to multiply two numbers. The result is the product of the two operands.

```
Dim myValue As Double
myValue = 2 * 2   ' Returns 4.
myValue = 459.35 * 334.90   ' Returns 153836.315.
```

See Also

*= Operator, Arithmetic Operators, Operator Precedence in Visual Basic, Operators Listed by Functionality

*= Operator

Multiplies the value of a variable by the value of an expression and assigns the result to the variable.

```
variable *= expression
```

Parts

variable
Required. Any numeric variable.

expression
Required. Any numeric expression.

Example

The following example uses the *= operator to multiply one **Integer** variable by a second and assign the result to the first variable.

```
Dim var1 As Integer = 10
Dim var2 As Integer = 3
var1 *= var2   ' The value of var1 is now 30.
```

See Also

&= Operator, * Operator, += Operator, -= Operator, /= Operator, = Operator, \= Operator, ^= Operator

+ Operator

Adds two numbers. Also used to concatenate two strings.

```
expression1 + expression2
```

Parts

expression1
Required. Any numeric expression or string.

expression2
Required. Any numeric expression or string.

Result

The value of the result will be the sum of *expression1* and *expression2* if *expression1* and *expression2* are numeric or the result of the concatenation of *expression1* and *expression2* if *expression1* and *expression2* are strings.

Supported Types

Byte, **Short**, **Integer**, **Long**, **Single**, **Double**, **Decimal**, **String**

Remarks

When you use the **+** operator, you may not be able to determine whether addition or string concatenation will occur. Use the **&** operator for concatenation to eliminate ambiguity and provide self-documenting code.

If neither expression is an **Object**, the following rules apply:

If	Then
Both expressions are the same numeric data types (**Byte**, **Short**, **Integer**, **Long**, **Single**, **Double**, or **Decimal**)	Add.
Both expressions are strings	Concatenate.
One expression is a numeric data type and the other is a string	If **Option Strict** is **On**, a compile error is generated; if **Option Strict** is **Off**, implicitly convert **String** to **Double** and add. If **String** cannot be converted to a numeric value, an **InvalidCastException** is thrown.
One expression is a numeric data type, and the other is **Nothing**	If **Option Strict** is **On** a compile error is generated; if **Option Strict** is **Off**, add, with **Nothing** valued at zero.
One expression is a string, and the other is **Nothing**	If **Option Strict** is **On** a compile error is generated; if **Option Strict** is **Off**, concatenation, with **Nothing** = " ".

If one expression is an **Object** expression, the following rules apply.

If	Then
One expression is a numeric **Object** expression and the other is a numeric value type	If **Option Strict** is **On**, a compiler error is generated; if **Option Strict** is **Off,** add.
One expression is a numeric **Object** expression and the other is a **String** type	If **Option Strict** is **On**, a compiler error is generated; if **Option Strict** is **Off**, implicitly convert **String** to **Double** and add. If **String** cannot be converted to a numeric value, an **InvalidCastException** is thrown.
One expression is a string **Object** expression and the other is a **String** type	If **Option Strict** is **On**, a compiler error is generated; if **Option Strict** is **Off**, implicitly convert **Object** to **String,** and then concatenate.
One expression is a string **Object** expression and the other is a numeric value type	If **Option Strict** is **On**, a compiler error is generated; if **Option Strict** is **Off**, implicitly convert **Object** to **Double** and add. If **Object** cannot be converted to a numeric value, an **InvalidCastException** is thrown.

If both expressions are **Object** expressions, the following rules apply (**Option Strict Off** only):

If	Then
Both **Object** expressions are numeric	Add.
Both **Object** expressions are strings	Concatenate.
One **Object** expression is numeric and the other is a string	Implicitly cast the numeric **Object** to **Double** and add. If **Object** cannot be converted to a numeric value, an **InvalidCastException** is thrown.

If one or both expressions are stated as Nothing or have a value of **DBNull**, they are treated as a string with a value of " ".

Example

This example uses the **+** operator to add numbers. You can also use the **+** operator to concatenate strings. However, to eliminate ambiguity, you should use the **&** operator instead. If the components of an expression created with the **+** operator are numeric, the arithmetic result is assigned. If the components are exclusively strings, the strings are concatenated. The expression cannot contain components of mixed types. The arithmetic result returns the sum of the two operands. The concatenation result returns a string representing the concatenation of the two operands.

```
Dim myNumber As Integer
Dim var1 As String
Dim var2 As Integer
myNumber = 2 + 2   ' Returns 4.
myNumber = 4257.04 + 98112   ' Returns 102369.04.

Option Strict On
' Initialize mixed variables.
var1 = "34"
var2 = 6
myNumber = var1 + var2   ' Generates a compile-time error.

Option Strict Off
Var1 = "34"
Var2 = 6
myNumber = var1 + var2
' Returns 40 (addition) after the string in var1 is
' converted to a numeric value. Use of Option Strict Off
' for these operations is not recommended.
```

See Also

& Operator, Concatenation Operators, Arithmetic Operators, Operators Listed by Functionality, Operator Precedence in Visual Basic

+= Operator

Adds the value of an expression to the value of a variable and assigns the result to the variable. Also concatenates a **String** expression to a **String** variable and assigns the result to the variable.

```
variable += expression
```

Parts

variable
Required. Any numeric or **String** variable.

expression
Required. Any numeric or **String** expression.

Remarks

This statement will implicitly perform widening but not narrowing conversions if the compilation environment is enforcing strict semantics. If permissive semantics are allowed, the operator will implicitly perform a variety of string and numeric conversions. These conversions are identical to the conversions described for the + operator. For details on how these conversions are performed, see "+ Operator." For more information on strict and permissive semantics, see "Option Strict Statement."

Example

These examples use the **+=** operator to combine the value of one variable with another. In the first example, **+=** is used with numeric variables to add one value to another. In the second example, **+=** is used with **String** variables to concatenate one value with another. In both cases, the result is assigned to the first variable.

```
Dim var1 As Integer = 10
Dim var2 As Integer = 3
var1 += var2    ' The value of var1 is now 13.

' This example uses string variables.
Dim var1 As String = "10"
Dim var2 As String = "3"
var1 += var2    ' The value of var1 is now "103".
```

See Also

+ Operator, Arithmetic Operators, Concatenation Operators, Operator Precedence in Visual Basic, Operators Listed by Functionality

- Operator

Yields the difference between two numbers or indicates the negative value of a numeric expression.

Syntax 1

```
expression1 - expression2
```

Syntax 2

```
-number
```

Parts

number

Required. Any numeric expression.

number1

Required. Any numeric expression.

number2

Required. Any numeric expression.

Result

The result will be the difference between *number1* and *number2*.

Supported Types

Byte, **Short**, **Integer**, **Long**, **Single**, **Double**, **Decimal**

Remarks

In Syntax 1, the **-** operator is the arithmetic subtraction operator for the difference between two numbers. In Syntax 2, the **-** operator is the unary negation operator for the negative value of an expression. The data type of the result is the same as that of the data type with the greatest range. The order of range, from least to greatest range, is Byte, Short, Integer, Long, Single, Double, and Decimal.

If an expression is stated as Nothing, it is treated as zero.

Example

This example uses the **-** operator to calculate and return the difference between two numbers.

```
Dim myResult As Double
myResult = 4 - 2   ' Returns 2.
myResult = 459.35 - 334.90   ' Returns 124.45.
```

See Also

-= Operator, Arithmetic Operators, Operator Precedence in Visual Basic, Operators Listed by Functionality

-= Operator

Subtracts the value of an expression from the value of a variable and assigns the result to the variable.

```
variable -= expression
```

Parts

variable

Required. Any numeric variable.

expression

Required. Any numeric expression.

Example

The following example uses the **-=** operator to subtract one **Integer** variable from another and assign the result to the latter variable.

```
Dim var1 As Integer = 10
Dim var2 As Integer = 3
var1 -= var2   ' The value of var1 is now 7.
```

See Also

&= Operator, *= Operator, += Operator, - Operator, /= Operator, = Operator, \= Operator, ^= Operator

/ Operator

Divides two numbers and returns a floating-point result.

```
number1 / number2
```

Parts

result

Required. Any numeric variable.

number1

Required. Any numeric expression.

number2

Required. Any numeric expression.

Result

The result is the quotient of *number1* divided by *number2*.

Supported Types

Byte, **Short**, **Integer**, **Long**, **Single**, **Double**, **Decimal**

Remarks

The data type of *result* is usually **Double**. The following are exceptions to this rule:

If	Then *result* is
One expression is **Single** and the other is any data type except **Double**	**Single**.
Both expressions are **Decimal** data types	**Decimal**. If a **Decimal** expression is divided by 0, a **DividebyZero** exception is raised. This exception only occurs with a **Decimal** expression.

If an expression is stated as Nothing, or is Empty, it is treated as zero.

Example

This example uses the / operator to perform floating-point division. The result is the quotient of the two operands.

```
Dim MyValue As Double
MyValue = 10 / 4   ' Returns 2.5.
MyValue = 10 / 3   ' Returns 3.333333.
```

See Also

\= Operator, \ Operator, Arithmetic Operators, Operator Precedence in Visual Basic, Operators Listed by Functionality

/= Operator

Divides the value of a variable by the value of an expression and assigns the result to the variable.

```
variable /= expression
```

Parts

variable
Required. Any numeric variable.

expression
Required. Any numeric expression.

Remarks

This statement assigns a **Double** to the variable on the left hand side. If **Option Strict** is **On**, *variable* must be a **Double**. If **Option Strict** is **Off**, an implicit conversion will be made and the resultant value assigned to *variable*, with a possible error at run time. For more information, see "Option Strict Statement."

Example

The following example uses the **/=** operator to divide one **Integer** variable by a second and assign the quotient to the first variable.

```
Dim var1 As Integer = 12
Dim var2 As Integer = 3
var1 /= var2    ' The value of var1 is now 4.
```

See Also

&= Operator, *= Operator, += Operator, -= Operator, / Operator, = Operator, \= Operator, ^= Operator

= Operator

Used to assign a value to a variable or property.

```
variable = value
```

Parts

variable
Any variable or any writable property.

value
Any literal, constant, or expression.

Remarks

The name on the left side of the equal sign can be a simple scalar variable, a property, or an element of an array. Properties on the left side of the equal sign can only be those properties that are writable at run time. When used, the value on the right side of the equation is assigned to the variable on the left side of the equation.

Example

This example demonstrates use of the assignment operator. The value on the right side of the expression is assigned to the variable on the left side of the expression.

```
Dim myInt as Integer
Dim myString as String
Dim myButton as System.Windows.Forms.Button
Dim myObject as Object
myInt = 42
myString = "This is an example of a string literal"
myButton = New System.Windows.Forms.Button()
myObject = myInt
myObject = myString
myObject = myButton
```

See Also

&= Operator, *= Operator, += Operator, -= Operator, /= Operator, \= Operator, ^= Operator

\ Operator

Divides two numbers and returns an integer result.

```
number1 \ number2
```

Parts

number1
Required. Any numeric expression of an integral type.

number2
Required. Any numeric expression of an integral type.

Supported Types

Byte, **Short**, **Integer**, or **Long**

Result

The result is the integer quotient of *number1* and *number2*, dropping the remainder.

Remarks

Before division is performed, any floating-point numeric expressions are coerced to **Byte**, **Short**, **Integer**, or **Long** expressions if **Option Strict** is **Off**. If **Option Strict** is **On**, a compiler error results.

The data type of the result is **Byte**, **Short**, **Integer**, or **Long**. Any fractional portion is truncated.

If any expression is stated as Nothing, or Empty, it is treated as zero. Attempting to perform integer division by zero causes a **DivideByZeroExeception** to be thrown.

Example

This example uses the \ operator to perform integer division. The result is an integer representing the integer quotient of the two operands.

```
Dim myValue As Integer
myValue = 11 \ 4   ' Returns 2.
myValue = 9 \ 3   ' Returns 3.
myValue = 100 \ 3   ' Returns 33.
MyValue = 67 \ -3   ' Returns -22.
```

See Also

\= Operator, / Operator, Arithmetic Operators, Operator Precedence in Visual Basic, Operators Listed by Functionality

\= Operator

Divides the value of a variable by the value of an expression and assigns the integer result to the variable.

```
variable \= expression
```

Parts

variable
Required. Any numeric variable.

expression
Required. Any numeric expression.

Remarks

For further information on integer division, see "\ Operator."

Example

The following example uses the **\=** operator to divide one **Integer** variable by a second and assign the integer result to the first variable.

```
Dim var1 As Integer = 10
Dim var2 As Integer = 3
var1 \= var2    ' The value of var1 is now 3.
```

See Also

&= Operator, *= Operator, += Operator, -= Operator, /= Operator, = Operator, \ Operator, ^= Operator

^ Operator

Raises a number to the power of another number.

```
Number ^ exponent
```

Parts

number
Required. Any numeric expression.

exponent
Required. Any numeric expression.

Result

The result value will be *number* raised to the *exponent* power.

Supported Types

Double. All operands of a different type will be converted to **Double**.

Remarks

Number can be negative only if *exponent* is an integer value. When more than one exponentiation is performed in a single expression, the ^ operator is evaluated as it is encountered from left to right.

Usually, the data type of *result* is **Double**.

Example

This example uses the ^ operator to raise a number to the power of an exponent. The result is the first operand raised to the power of the second.

```
Dim myValue As Double
myValue = 2 ^ 2    ' Returns 4.
myValue = 3 ^ 3 ^ 3    ' Returns 19683.
myValue = (-5) ^ 3    ' Returns -125.
myValue = (-5) ^ 4    ' Returns 625.
```

See Also

^= Operator, Arithmetic Operators, Operator Precedence in Visual Basic, Operators Listed by Functionality

^= Operator

Raises the value of a variable to the power of an expression and assigns the result back to the variable.

```
variable ^= expression
```

Parts

variable
    Required. Any numeric variable.

expression
    Required. Any numeric expression.

Example

The following example uses the ^= operator to raise the value of one **Integer** variable to the power of a second variable and assign the result to the first variable.

```
Dim var1 As Integer = 10
Dim var2 As Integer = 3
var1 ^= var2    ' The value of var1 is now 1000.
```

See Also

&= Operator, *= Operator, += Operator, -= Operator, /= Operator, = Operator, \= Operator, ^ Operator

Add Method

Adds a member to a **Collection** object.

```
Public Sub Add( _
   ByVal Item As Object, _
   Optional ByVal Key As String, _
   Optional ByVal { Before | After } As Object = Nothing _
)
```

Parameters

Item
  Required. An object of any type that specifies the member to add to the collection.

Key
  Optional. A unique **String** expression that specifies a key string that can be used instead of a positional index to access a member of the collection.

Before
  Optional. An expression that specifies a relative position in the collection. The member to be added is placed in the collection before the member identified by the *Before* argument. If *Before* is a numeric expression, it must be a number from 1 to the value of the collection's **Count** property. If *Before* is a **String** expression, it must correspond to the key string specified when the member being referred to was added to the collection. You cannot specify both *Before* and *After*.

After
  Optional. An expression that specifies a relative position in the collection. The member to be added is placed in the collection after the member identified by the *After* argument. If *After* is a numeric expression, it must be a number from 1 to the value of the collection's **Count** property. If *After* is a **String** expression, it must correspond to the key string specified when the member referred to was added to the collection. You cannot specify both *Before* and *After*.

Exceptions/Error Codes

Exception type	Error number	Condition
ArgumentException	5	Both *Before* and *After* are specified, or argument does not refer to an existing member of the collection.
ArgumentException	5	The specified *Key* already exists.

Remarks

The *Before* or *After* argument must refer to an existing member of the collection; otherwise, an error occurs.

An error also occurs if a specified *Key* value matches the key for an existing member of the collection.

Example

This example uses the **Add** method to add `Child` objects—instances of a class called `Child` containing a **Public** property `Name`—to a collection called `Family`. To see how this works, create a **Form** with two **Buttons** and set their **Text** properties to Add and List. Add the **Child** class definition and the **Family** declaration to the form code. Modify the **Click** events for the **Add** and **List** buttons as shown. The **Add** button allows you to add children. The **List** button will display the names of all the children.

```
Public Class Child
   Public Name As String
   Sub New(ByVal newName As String)
      Name = newName
   End Sub
End Class

Private family As New Collection() ' Create a Collection object.

Private Sub Add_Click(ByVal sender As System.Object, _
ByVal e As System.EventArgs) Handles Button1.Click
   Dim newName As String
   newName = InputBox("Name of new family member: ")
   If newName <> "" Then
      family.Add(New Child(newName), newName)
   End If
End Sub

Private Sub List_Click(ByVal sender As System.Object, _
ByVal e As System.EventArgs) Handles Button2.Click
   Dim aChild As Child
   For Each aChild In family
      MsgBox(aChild.Name)
   Next
End Sub
```

See Also

Item Property, Remove Method, ArgumentException

Applies To

Collection Object

AddHandler Statement

Associates an event with an event handler.

```
AddHandler event, AddressOf eventhandler
```

Parts

event

The name of the event to handle.

eventhandler

The name of a procedure that will handle the event.

Remarks

The **AddHandler** and **RemoveHandler** statements allow you to start and stop event handling at any time during program execution.

Example

```
Sub TestEvents()
   Dim Obj As New Class1()
   ' Associate an event handler with an event.
   AddHandler Obj.Ev_Event, AddressOf EventHandler
   Obj.CauseSomeEvent()    ' Ask the object to raise an event.
End Sub

Sub EventHandler()
   ' This procedure handles events raised by the object Obj.
   MsgBox("EventHandler caught event.")    ' Handle the event.
End Sub

Public Class Class1
   Public Event Ev_Event()    ' Declare an event.
   Sub CauseSomeEvent()
      RaiseEvent Ev_Event()    ' Raise an event.
   End Sub
End Class
```

See Also

RemoveHandler Statement, Handles

AddressOf Operator

Creates a procedure delegate instance that references the specific procedure.

```
AddressOf procedurename
```

The required *procedurename* specifies the procedure that will be referenced by the newly created procedure delegate.

Remarks

The **AddressOf** operator creates a function delegate that points to the function specified by *procedurename*. When the specified procedure is an instance method then the function delegate refers to both the instance and the method so that when the function delegate is invoked the specified method of the specified instance is called.

The AddressOf operator can be used as the operand of a delegate constructor or it can be used in a context in which the type of the delegate can be determined by the compiler.

Example

This example uses the **AddressOf** operator to designate a delegate to handle the **Click** event of a button.

```
Public Sub ButtonClickHandler(ByVal sender As Object, e As _
   System.EventArgs)
' Implementation code omitted.
End Sub

Public Sub New()
   AddHandler Button1.Click, AddressOf ButtonClickHandler
   ' Additional code omitted.
End Sub
```

The following example uses the **AddressOf** operator to designate the startup function for a thread.

```
Public Sub CountSheep()
   Dim i As Integer = 1 ' Sheep don't count from 0.
   Do While (True) ' Endless loop.
      Console.WriteLine("Sheep " & i & " Baah")
      i = i + 1
      Thread.Sleep(1000) 'Wait 1 second.
   Loop
End Sub

Sub UseThread()
   Dim t As New System.Threading.Thread(AddressOf CountSheep)
   t.Start()
End Sub
```

See Also

Declare Statement, Function Statement, Sub Statement

Alias

The **Alias** keyword indicates that an external procedure has another name in its DLL.

The **Alias** keyword is used in this context:

Declare Statement

See Also

Visual Basic Language Keywords

And Operator

Performs a logical conjunction on two **Boolean** expressions, or bitwise conjunction on two numeric expressions.

```
result = expression1 And expression2
```

Parts

result
Required. Any **Boolean** or numeric expression. The result for **Boolean** comparison is the **Boolean** result of comparison of the two expressions. The result for numeric comparison is a numeric value resulting from the bitwise conjunction of two numeric expressions

expression1
Required. Any **Boolean** or numeric expression.

expression2
Required. Any **Boolean** or numeric expression.

Remarks

For **Boolean** comparison, if both *expression1* and *expression2* evaluate to **True**, *result* is **True**. If *expression1* evaluates to **True** and *expression2* evaluates to **False**, *result* is **False**. If *expression1* evaluates to **False**, and *expression2* evaluates to True, the *result* is **False.** The following table illustrates how *result* is determined:

If *expression1* is	And *expression2* is	Value of *result* is
True	**True**	**True**
True	**False**	**False**
False	**True**	**False**
False	**False**	**False**

When applied to numeric values, the **And** operator performs a bitwise comparison of identically positioned bits in two numeric expressions and sets the corresponding bit in *result* according to the following table:

If bit in expression1 is	And bit in expression2 is	The result is
0	0	0
0	1	0
1	0	0
1	1	1

Note Since the logical/bitwise operators have a lower precedence than other arithmetic and relational operators, any bitwise operations should be enclosed in parentheses to insure accurate execution.

If the operands consist of one **Boolean** expression and one numeric expression, the result **Boolean** expression will be converted to a numeric value (–1 for True, and 0 for False) and the bitwise operation will result.

Example

This example uses the **And** operator to perform a logical conjunction on two expressions. The result is a **Boolean** value that represents whether the entire conjoined expression is true.

```
Dim A As Integer = 10
Dim B As Integer = 8
Dim C As Integer = 6
Dim myCheck As Boolean
myCheck = A > B And B > C   ' Returns True.
myCheck = B > A And B > C   ' Returns False.
```

This example uses the **And** operator to perform logical conjunction of the individual bits of two numeric expressions. The bit in the result pattern is set if the corresponding bits in the operands are both set.

```
Dim A As Integer = 10
Dim B As Integer = 8
Dim C As Integer = 6
Dim myCheck As Integer
myCheck = (A And B)   ' Returns 8.
myCheck = (A And C)   ' Returns 2.
myCheck = (B And C)   ' Returns 0.
```

See Also

Logical/Bitwise Operators, Operator Precedence in Visual Basic, Operators Listed by Functionality, AndAlso Operator, Logical Operators

AndAlso Operator

Performs short-circuiting logical conjunction on two expressions.

```
result = expression1 AndAlso expression2
```

Parts

result

Required. Any **Boolean** expression. The result is the **Boolean** result of comparison of the two expressions.

expression1

Required. Any **Boolean** expression.

expression2

Required. Any **Boolean** expression.

Remarks

If both *expression1* and *expression2* evaluate to **True**, *result* is **True**. If *expression1* evaluates to True and *expression2* evaluates to **False**, *result* is **False**. If *expression1* evaluates to **False**, *expression2* is not evaluated, and *result* is **False** (the operator is said to have short-circuited the expression). The following table illustrates how *result* is determined:

If ***expression1*** is	And ***expression2*** is	Value of ***result*** is
True	**True**	**True**
True	**False**	**False**
False	(not evaluated)	**False**

Example

This example uses the **AndAlso** operator to perform a logical conjunction on two expressions. The result is a **Boolean** value that represents whether the entire conjoined expression is true. If the first expression is **False**, the second is not evaluated.

```
Dim A As Integer = 10
Dim B As Integer = 8
Dim C As Integer = 6
Dim myCheck As Boolean
myCheck = A > B AndAlso B > C    ' True.
myCheck = B > A AndAlso B > C    ' False. Second expression not evaluated.
myCheck = A > B AndAlso C > B    ' False. Second expression evaluated.
```

```
' This example demonstrates using the AndAlso operator to search through
' array values. If i is greater than the upper bound of the array, it does
' attempt to find a corresponding value in the array.

Dim i As Integer = 0
While i <= UBound(arr) AndAlso arr(i) <> SearchValue
   i += 1
End While
```

See Also

Logical/Bitwise Operators, Operator Precedence in Visual Basic, Operators Listed by Functionality, Logical Operators

Ansi

The **Ansi** keyword indicates that strings are converted to American National Standards Institute (ANSI) values regardless of the name of the method being declared.

The **Ansi** keyword is used in this context:

Declare Statement

See Also

Visual Basic Language Keywords

AppActivate Function

Activates an application window.

```
Public Overloads Sub AppActivate( _
   ByVal { Title As String | ProcessID As Integer } _
)
```

Parameters

Title
String expression specifying the title in the title bar of the application window you want to activate. You can use the task ID returned by the **Shell** function.

ProcessID
Integer specifying the Win32® Process ID number assigned to this process.

Exceptions/Errors

Exception type	Error number	Condition
ArgumentException	5	*ProcessID* is not found.

Remarks

The **AppActivate** function changes the focus to the named application or window, but does not affect whether it is maximized or minimized. Focus moves from the activated application window when the user takes some action to change the focus or close the window. Use the **Shell** function to start an application and set the window style.

You can use **AppActivate** only with processes that own windows. Most console applications do not own windows, which means that they do not appear in the list of processes that **AppActivate** searches. When running from a console application, the system creates a separate process to run the application and returns the output to the console process. Consequently, when the current Process ID is requested, you get the created process's Process ID rather than the console application's Process ID.

At run time the **AppActivate** function activates any running application whose title matches *Title* or whose Process ID matches *ProcessID*. If there is no exact match, it activates any application whose title string begins with *Title*. If there is more than one application named by *Title*, the **AppActivate** function activates one at random.

Example

This example illustrates various uses of the **AppActivate** function to activate an application window. The **Shell** procedures assume the applications are in the paths specified.

```
Dim notepadID As Integer
' Activate a running notepad process.
AppActivate("Untitled - Notepad")
' AppActivate can also use the return value of the Shell function.
' Shell runs a new instance of notepad.
notepadID = Shell("C:\WINNT\NOTEPAD.EXE", AppWinStyle.MinimizedNoFocus)
' Activate the new instance of notepad.
AppActivate(notepadID)
```

See Also

Shell Function

AppWinStyle Enumeration

When you issue **Shell** commands, you can use the following enumeration members in your code in place of the actual values.

AppWinStyle Enumeration Members

The *Style* argument takes the following **AppWinStyle** enumeration members:

Member	Constant	Description
Hide	**vbHide**	Window is hidden and focus is passed to the hidden window.
NormalFocus	**vbNormalFocus**	Window has focus and is restored to its original size and position.
MinimizedFocus	**vbMinimizedFocus**	Window is displayed as an icon with focus.
MaximizedFocus	**vbMaximizedFocus**	Window is maximized with focus.
NormalNoFocus	**vbNormalNoFocus**	Window is restored to its most recent size and position. The currently active window remains active.
MinimizedNoFocus	**vbMinimizedNoFocus**	Window is displayed as an icon. The currently active window remains active.

See Also

Shell Function

As

The **As** keyword introduces an **As** clause, which identifies a data type.

The **As** keyword is used in these contexts:

- Const Statement
- Declare Statement
- Delegate Statement
- Dim Statement
- Enum Statement
- Event Statement
- Function Statement
- Property Statement
- Sub Statement
- Try...Catch...Finally Statements

See Also

Visual Basic Language Keywords

Asc, AscW Functions

Returns an **Integer** value representing the character code corresponding to a character.

```
Public Overloads Function Asc(ByVal String As Char) As Integer
Public Overloads Function AscW(ByVal String As Char) As Integer
```

-or-

```
Public Overloads Function Asc(ByVal String As String) As Integer
Public Overloads Function AscW(ByVal String As String) As Integer
```

Parameter

String

Required. Any valid **Char** or **String** expression. If *String* is a **String** expression, only the first character of the string is used for input. If *String* is **Nothing** or contains no characters, an **ArgumentException** error occurs.

Exceptions/Errors

Exception type	Error number	Condition
ArgumentException	5	*String* is not specified or is zero length.

Remarks

Asc returns the *code point*, or character code, for the input character. This can be 0 through 255 for single-byte character set (SBCS) values and –32768 through 32767 for double-byte character set (DBCS) values. The returned value depends on the code page for the current thread, which is contained in the **ANSICodePage** property of the **TextInfo** class. **TextInfo.ANSICodePage** can be obtained by specifying **System.Globalization.CultureInfo.CurrentCulture.TextInfo.ANSICodePage**.

AscW returns the Unicode code point for the input character. This can be 0 through 65535. The returned value is independent of the culture and code page settings for the current thread.

Example

This example uses the **Asc** function to return **Integer** character codes corresponding to the first letter in each string.

```
Dim MyInt As Integer
MyInt = Asc("A")    ' MyInt is set to 65.
MyInt = Asc("a")    ' MyInt is set to 97.
MyInt = Asc("Apple")    ' MyInt is set to 65.
```

See Also

Chr, ChrW Functions; Conversion Functions; Type Conversion Functions

Assembly

The **Assembly** keyword indicates that an attribute block at the beginning of a source file applies to the entire assembly and not only to the current module.

Auto

The **Auto** keyword indicates that strings are converted according to common language runtime rules based on the name of the method being declared.

The **Auto** keyword is used in this context:

Declare Statement

See Also

Visual Basic Language Keywords

Beep Function

Sounds a tone through the computer's speaker.

```
Public Sub Beep()
```

Remarks

The pitch and duration of the beep depend on your hardware and system software, and therefore vary among computers.

Example

This example uses the **Beep** function to sound a long, uninterrupted tone through the computer's speaker.

```
Dim I As Integer
For I = 1 To 100   ' Loop 100 times.
   Beep   ' Sound a tone.
Next I
```

See Also

Visual Basic Run-Time Library Members

Boolean Data Type

Boolean variables are stored as 16-bit (2-byte) numbers, but they can only be **True** or **False**. Use the keywords **True** and **False** to assign one of the two states to **Boolean** variables.

When numeric data types are converted to **Boolean** values, 0 becomes **False** and all other values become **True**. When **Boolean** values are converted to numeric types, **False** becomes 0 and **True** becomes –1.

> **Note** You should never write code that relies on equivalent numeric values for **True** and **False**. Whenever possible, you should restrict usage of **Boolean** variables to the logical values for which they are designed. If it is necessary to mix **Boolean** and numeric values, be sure to use the appropriate conversion keywords.

The equivalent .NET data type is **System.Boolean**.

See Also

Data Type Summary, Integer Data Type, Type Conversion Functions, Conversion Summary

ByRef

The **ByRef** keyword indicates that an argument is passed in such a way that the called procedure can change the value of a variable underlying the argument in the calling code.

The **ByRef** keyword is used in these contexts:

Declare Statement

Function Statement

Sub Statement

See Also

Visual Basic Language Keywords

Byte Data Type

Byte variables are stored as unsigned 8-bit (1-byte) numbers ranging in value from 0 through 255.

The **Byte** data type is used for containing binary data.

> **Note** The **Byte** data type can be converted to the **Short**, **Integer**, **Long**, **Single**, **Double**, or **Decimal** data type without encountering a **System.OverflowException** error.

The equivalent .NET data type is **System.Byte**.

See Also

Data Type Summary, Integer Data Type, Short Data Type, Type Conversion Functions, Conversion Summary

ByVal

The **ByVal** keyword indicates that an argument is passed in such a way that the called procedure or property cannot change the value of a variable underlying the argument in the calling code.

The **ByVal** keyword is used in these contexts:

Declare Statement

Function Statement

Property Statement

Sub Statement

See Also

Visual Basic Language Keywords

Call Statement

Transfers control to a **Sub** procedure, **Function** procedure, or dynamic-link library (DLL) procedure.

```
[ Call ] ProcedureName[(ArgumentList)]
```

Parts

ProcedureName
: Required. Name of the procedure to call.

ArgumentList
: Optional. List of variables or expressions representing arguments that are passed to the procedure when it is called. Multiple arguments are separated by commas. If you include *ArgumentList*, you must enclose it in parentheses.

Remarks

You are not required to use the **Call** keyword when calling a procedure; however, if you use the **Call** statement to call any intrinsic, DLL, or user-defined function, the function's return value is discarded.

Example

This example illustrates how the **Call** statement is used to transfer control to a **Sub** procedure, an intrinsic function, and a dynamic-link library (DLL) procedure.

```
' Call a Sub procedure.
Call PrintToDebugWindow("Hello World")
' The above statement passes control to the following Sub procedure.
Sub PrintToDebugWindow(ByVal AnyString As String)
   Debug.WriteLine(AnyString)   ' Print to the Output window.
End Sub

' Call an intrinsic function. The return value is discarded.
Call Shell("C:\Windows\calc.exe", AppWinStyle.NormalFocus)

' Call a Microsoft Windows DLL procedure. The Declare statement must be
' Private in a class, not in a module.
Private Declare Sub MessageBeep Lib "User" (ByVal N As Integer)
Sub CallMyDll()
   Call MessageBeep(0)   ' Call Windows DLL procedure.
   MessageBeep(0)   ' Call again without Call keyword.
End Sub
```

See Also

Declare Statement, Function Statement, Sub Statement

CallByName Function

Executes a method on an object, or sets or returns a property on an object.

```
Public Function CallByName( _
   ByVal Object As System.Object, _
   ByVal ProcName As String, _
   ByVal UseCallType As CallType, _
   ByVal ParamArrayArgs() As Object _
) As Object
```

Parameters

Object
: Required. **Object**. A pointer to the object exposing the property or method.

ProcName
: Required. **String**. A string expression containing the name of the property or method on the object.

UseCallType
: Required. An enumeration member of type **Microsoft.VisualBasic.CallType** representing the type of procedure being called. The value of **CallType** can be **Method**, **Get**, or **Set**.

ParamArrayArgs()
Optional. **ParamArray**. A parameter array containing the arguments to be passed to the property or method being called.

Exceptions/Errors

Exception type	Error number	Condition
ArgumentException	5	Invalid *UseCallType* value; must be **Method**, **Get**, or **Set**.

Remarks

The **CallByName** function is used to get or set a property, or to invoke a method, at run time, using a string to specify the name of the property or method.

Example

In the following example, the first line uses **CallByName** to set the **Text** property of a text box, the second line retrieves the value of the **Text** property, and the third line invokes the **Move** method to move the text box.

```
Imports Microsoft.VisualBasic.CallType
' Imports statements must be at the top of a module.
...
Sub TestCallByName1()
'  Set a property.
   CallByName(TextBox1, "Text", CallType.Set, "New Text")
'  Retrieve the value of a property.
   MsgBox(CallByName(TextBox1, "Text", CallType.Get))
'  Call a method.
   CallByName(TextBox1, "Hide", CallType.Method)
End Sub
```

The next example uses the **CallByName** function to invoke the **Add** and **Item** methods of a collection object.

```
Public Sub TestCallByName2()
   Dim col As New Collection()
'  Store the string "Item One" in a collection by
'  calling the Add method.
   CallByName(col, "Add", CallType.Method, "Item One")
'  Retrieve the first entry from the collection using the
'  Item property and display it using MsgBox().
   MsgBox(CallByName(col, "Item", CallType.Get, 1))
End Sub
```

See Also

CallType Enumeration, Parameter Arrays

CallType Enumeration

When you call the **CallByName** function, you can use the following **CallType** enumeration members in your code in place of the actual values:

CallType Enumeration Members

The *UseCallType* argument takes the following **CallType** values:

Member	Constant	Description
Method	**vbMethod**	A method is being invoked.
Get	**vbGet**	A property value is being retrieved.
Set	**vbSet**	A property value is being determined.

See Also

CallByName Function

Case

The **Case** keyword introduces a value or set of values against which the value of an expression is to be tested.

The **Case** keyword is used in this context:

Select...Case Statements

See Also

Visual Basic Language Keywords

Char Data Type

Char variables are stored as unsigned 16-bit (2-byte) numbers ranging in value from 0 through 65535. Each number represents a single Unicode character. Direct conversions between the **Char** data type and the numeric types are not possible, but you can use the **AscW** and **ChrW** functions for this purpose.

Appending the literal type character **C** to a single-character string literal forces it to the **Char** data type. This is required if the type checking switch (**Option Strict**) is on, as the following example shows:

```
Option Strict On
' ...
Dim CharVar As Char
CharVar = "Z"     ' Cannot convert String to Char with Option Strict On.
CharVar = "Z"C    ' Successfully assigns single character to CharVar.
```

The equivalent .NET data type is **System.Char**.

See Also

Data Type Summary; Integer Data Type; Type Conversion Functions; Conversion Summary; Asc, AscW Functions; Chr, ChrW Functions

ChDir Function

Changes the current directory or folder.

```
Public Sub ChDir(ByVal Path As String)
```

Parameter

Path

Required. A **String** expression that identifies which directory or folder becomes the new default directory or folder. *Path* may include the drive. If no drive is specified, **ChDir** changes the default directory or folder on the current drive.

Exceptions/Errors

Exception type	Error number	Condition
ArgumentException	52	*Path* is empty.
FileNotFoundException	76	Invalid drive is specified, or drive is unavailable.

Remarks

The **ChDir** function changes the default directory, but not the default drive. For example, if the default drive is C, the following statement changes the default directory on drive D, but C remains the default drive:

```
ChDir "D:\TMP"
```

Making relative directory changes is accomplished using "..", as follows:

```
ChDir ".." ' Moves up one directory.
```

Example

This example uses the **ChDir** function to change the current directory or folder.

```
' Change current directory or folder to "MYDIR".
ChDir("MYDIR")

' Assume "C:" is the current drive. The following statement changes
' the default directory on drive "D:". "C:" remains the current drive.
ChDir("D:\WINDOWS\SYSTEM")
```

See Also

ChDrive Function, CurDir Function, Dir Function, MkDir Function, RmDir Function

ChDrive Function

Changes the current drive.

```
Public Overloads Sub ChDrive(ByVal Drive As { Char | String })
```

Parameter

Drive

Required. String expression that specifies an existing drive. If you supply a zero-length string (" "), the current drive doesn't change. If the *Drive* argument is a multiple-character string, **ChDrive** uses only the first letter.

Exceptions/Errors

Exception type	Error number	Condition
IOException	68	Invalid drive is specified, or drive is unavailable.

Example

This example uses the **ChDrive** function to change the current drive.

```
ChDrive("D")    ' Make "D" the current drive.
```

See Also

ChDir Function, CurDir Function, MkDir Function, RmDir Function

Choose Function

Selects and returns a value from a list of arguments.

```
Public Function Choose( _
   ByVal Index As Double, _
   ByVal ParamArray Choice() As Object _
) As Object
```

Parameters

Index

Required. **Double**. Numeric expression that results in a value between 1 and the number of elements passed in the *Choice* argument.

Choice()

Required. **Object** parameter array. You can supply either a single variable or an expression that evaluates to the **Object** data type, to a list of **Object** variables or expressions separated by commas, or to a single-dimensional array of **Object** elements.

Exceptions/Errors

Exception type	Error number	Condition
ArgumentException	5	Rank of *Choice()* <> 1.

Remarks

The **Choose** function returns a member of the list passed in *Choice()*, based on the value of *Index*. The first member of the list is selected when *Index* is 1. The last member of the list is selected when *Index* is **UBound**(*Choice()*). If *Index* is outside these limits, **Choose** returns **Nothing**.

If *Index* is not a whole number, it is rounded to the nearest whole number before being evaluated.

You can use **Choose** to look up a value in a list of possibilities.

> **Note** The expressions in the argument list can include function calls. As part of preparing the argument list for the call to **Choose**, the Visual Basic compiler calls every function in every expression. This means that you cannot rely on a particular function not being called if a different expression is selected by *Index*.

Example

This example uses the **Choose** function to display a name in response to an index passed into the procedure in the `Ind` parameter.

```
Function GetChoice(Ind As Integer) As String
   GetChoice = CStr(Choose(Ind, "Speedy", "United", "Federal"))
End Function
```

See Also

IIf Function, Select...Case Statements, Switch Function

Chr, ChrW Functions

Returns the character associated with the specified character code.

```
Public Function Chr(ByVal CharCode As Integer) As Char
Public Function ChrW(ByVal CharCode As Integer) As Char
```

Parameter

CharCode

Required. An **Integer** expression representing the *code point*, or character code, for the character. If *CharCode* is outside the range –32768 through 65535, an **ArgumentException** error occurs.

Exceptions/Errors

Exception type	Error number	Condition
ArgumentException	5	*CharCode* < –32768 or > 65535.

Remarks

The asymmetric range accepted for *CharCode* compensates for the storage differences between the **Short** and **Integer** data types. For example, &H8E01 is –29183 as a **Short** but +36353 as an **Integer**. This also facilitates compatibility with Visual Basic 6.0.

Chr uses the **Encoding** class in the **System.Text** namespace to determine if the current thread is using a single-byte character set (SBCS) or a double-byte character set (DBCS). It then takes *CharCode* as a code point in the appropriate set. The range can be 0 through 255 for SBCS characters and –32768 through 65535 for DBCS characters. The returned character depends on the code page for the current thread, which is contained in the **ANSICodePage** property of the **TextInfo** class. **TextInfo.ANSICodePage** can be obtained by specifying **System.Globalization.CultureInfo.CurrentCulture.TextInfo.ANSICodePage**.

ChrW takes *CharCode* as a Unicode code point. The range is independent of the culture and code page settings for the current thread. Values from –32768 through –1 are treated the same as values in the range +32768 through +65535.

Numbers from 0 through 31 are the same as standard, nonprintable ASCII codes. For example, `Chr(10)` returns a linefeed character.

Example

This example uses the **Chr** function to return the character associated with the specified character code.

```
Dim MyChar As Char
MyChar = Chr(65)    ' Returns "A".
MyChar = Chr(97)    ' Returns "a".
MyChar = Chr(62)    ' Returns ">".
MyChar = Chr(37)    ' Returns "%".
```

See Also

Asc, AscW Functions; Str Function; Conversion Functions; Type Conversion Functions

Class Statement

Declares the name of a class, as well as a definition of the variables, properties, events, and methods that comprise the class.

```
[ <attrlist> ] [ Public | Private | Protected | Friend |
Protected Friend ] [ Shadows ] [ MustInherit | NotInheritable ] _
Class name
   [ Inherits classname ]
   [ Implements interfacenames ]
   [ statements ]
End Class
```

Parts

attrlist
: Optional. List of attributes that apply to this class. Multiple attributes are separated by commas.

Public
: Optional. Entities declared with the **Public** modifier have public access. There are no restrictions on the use of public entities.

Private
: Optional. Entities declared with the **Private** modifier have private access. A private entity is accessible only within its declaration context, including any nested entities.

Protected
: Optional. Entities declared with the **Protected** keyword have protected access. They are accessible only from within their own class or from a derived class. Protected access can be specified only on members of classes. It is not a superset of friend access.

Friend
: Optional. Entities declared with the **Friend** modifier have friend access. An entity with friend access is accessible only within the program that contains the entity declaration. Classes that do not specify an access modifier are declared as **Friend** by default.

Protected Friend
: Optional. Entities declared with the **Protected Friend** modifiers have the union of protected and friend accessibility.

Shadows
: Optional. Indicates that this class shadows an identically named programming element in a base class. You can shadow any kind of declared element with any other kind. A shadowed element is unavailable in the derived class that shadows it

MustInherit
: Optional. Indicates that non-shared members of the **Class** can only be accessed via derived classes. Instances of must-inherit classes cannot be created.

NotInheritable
Optional. Indicates that the **Class** is a class from which no further inheritance is allowed.

name
Required. Name of the **Class**; follows standard variable naming conventions.

Inherits
Optional. Indicates that this class inherits the members of another class. A class can inherit from only one other class.

classname
The name of base class that this class inherits.

Implements
Optional. Indicates that this class implements the members of an interface. If you use the **Implements** statement, it must immediately follow any **Inherits** statements after the **Class** statement, and you must implement every member defined by every interface you specify.

interfacenames
Required if the **Implements** statement is used. The names of the interfaces implemented by this class.

statements
Optional. Statements which comprise the variables, properties, events, methods and nested types of the class.

End Class
Terminates the **Class** block.

Each attribute in the *attrlist* part has the following syntax and parts:

```
attrname [({ attrargs | attrinit })]
```

attrlist Parts

attrname
Required. Name of the attribute. Must be a valid Visual Basic identifier.

attrargs
Optional. List of positional arguments for this attribute. Multiple arguments are separated by commas.

attrinit
Optional. List of field or property initializers for this attribute. Multiple initializers are separated by commas.

Remarks

Classes that do not specify an access modifier are declared as **Friend** by default. Within a **Class** block, members are declared as either **Public**, **Private**, **Protected**, **Friend**, or **Protected Friend** using the appropriate declaration statements. Anything declared as **Private** is visible only within the **Class** block. Anything declared as **Public** is visible within the **Class** block, as well as by code outside the **Class** block. Anything not explicitly declared is **Public** by default, except for fields and constants, which default to **Private**. **Public** variables, sometimes called Fields, serve as properties of the class, as do properties explicitly declared using **Property** declarations. Default properties and methods for the class are specified in their declarations using the **Default** keyword. See the individual declaration statement topics for information on how this keyword is used.

Binding of unqualified names in nested classes will search the members of the class itself, then the members of its containing class, and so on out to the outermost containing class. Private members of outer classes can be referenced but an error will be given for references to instance members of containing classes.

Nested classes cannot inherit from their containing class.

Example

This example uses the **Class** Statement to define a class, in which variables, properties, methods and events can be created.

```
Public Class ThisClass
   ' [variable, property, method and event declarations]
End Class
```

See Also

Inherits Statement, Implements Statement, Interface Statement, Property Statement

Clear Method

Clears all property settings of the **Err** object.

```
object.Clear
```

Parameter

object
Always the **Err** object.

Remarks

Use **Clear** to explicitly clear the **Err** object after an error has been handled, such as when you use deferred error handling with **On Error Resume Next**. The **Clear** method is called automatically whenever any of the following statements executes:

- Any type of **Resume** statement
- **Exit Sub**, **Exit Function**, or **Exit Property**
- Any **On Error** statement
- Any **Try...Catch...Finally** statement

> **Note** The **On Error Resume Next** construct may be preferable to **On Error GoTo** when handling errors generated during access to other objects. Checking **Err** after each interaction with an object removes ambiguity about which object was accessed by the code: you can be sure which object placed the error code in **Err.Number**, as well as which object originally generated the error (the object specified in **Err.Source**).

Example

This example uses the **Err** object's **Clear** method to reset the numeric properties of the **Err** object to zero and its string properties to zero-length strings. Without the call to **Clear**, the second call to **MsgBox** would display the same error message.

```
Sub ClearErr()
   ' Produce overflow error
   On Error Resume Next
   Dim zero As Integer = 0
   Dim result As Integer = 8 / zero
   MsgBox(Err.Description)
   Err.Clear()
   MsgBox(Err.Description)
End Sub
```

See Also

Description Property, Err Object, HelpContext Property, HelpFile Property, LastDLLError Property, Number Property, On Error Statement, Raise Method, Source Property

Applies To

Err Object

Collection Object

A **Collection** object is an ordered set of items that can be referred to as a unit.

Remarks

The **Collection** object provides a convenient way to refer to a related group of items as a single object. The items, or members, in a collection need only be related by the fact that they exist in the collection. Members of a collection do not have to share the same data type.

You can create a collection the same way you create other objects. For example:

```
Dim X As New Collection
```

Once you have created a collection, you can add members with the **Add** method and remove them with the **Remove** method. You can return specific members from the collection with the **Item** method, and iterate through the entire collection with the **For Each...Next** statement.

Note Although the **Collection** object in version 6 and in .NET have identical functionality, they cannot interoperate in a COM environment.

Example

This example creates a **Collection** object (`MyClasses`), and then creates a dialog box in which users can add objects to the collection. To see how this works, choose the **Class** command from the **Project** menu and declare a public variable called `InstanceName` at module level of `Class1` (type `Public InstanceName`) to hold the names of each instance. Leave the default name as `Class1`. Copy and paste the following code into the General section of another module, and then start it with the statement `ClassNamer` in another procedure. (This example only works with host applications that support classes.)

```
Public Class Class1
   Public InstanceName As String
End Class

Sub ClassNamer()
   Dim MyClasses As New Collection()   ' Create a Collection object.
   Dim number As Integer   ' Counter for individualizing keys.
   Dim Msg As String   ' Variable to hold prompt string.
   Dim name As String
   Dim oneInst As Class1
   Dim nameList As String = ""
   Do
      Dim inst As New Class1()   ' Create a new instance of Class1.
      number += 1   ' Increment Num, then get a name.
      Msg = "Please enter a name for this object." & ControlChars.CrLf _
         & "Press Cancel to see names in collection."
      name = InputBox(Msg, "Name the Collection Items")
      Inst.InstanceName = name   ' Put name in object instance.
```

(continued)

(continued)

```
      ' If user entered name, add it to the collection.
      If inst.InstanceName <> "" Then
         ' Add the named object to the collection.
         MyClasses.Add (inst, number.ToString())
      End If
   Loop Until name = ""

   For Each oneInst In MyClasses    ' Create list of names.
      nameList &= oneInst.InstanceName & ControlChars.CrLf
   Next

   ' Display the list of names in a message box.
   MsgBox (nameList, , "Instance Names In MyClasses Collection")

   Dim count As Integer
   For count = 1 To MyClasses.Count
      ' Remove name from the collection.
      MyClasses.Remove(1)
      ' Since collections are reindexed automatically, remove
      ' the first member on each iteration
   Next
End Sub
```

See Also

For Each...Next Statements

ComClassAttribute Class

The **ComClassAttribute** attribute instructs the compiler to add meta-data that allows a class to be exposed as a COM object.

```
<System.AttributeUsage(System.AttributeTargets.Class, _
   Inherited := False, AllowMultiple := False)> _
Public NotInheritable Class ComClassAttribute
   Inherits System.Attribute
```

Remarks

Use **ComClassAttribute** to simplify the process of creating COM components from Visual Basic .NET. COM objects are considerably different from .NET assemblies, and without the **ComClassAttribute**, you need to follow a number of steps to generate a COM object from Visual Basic .NET. For classes marked with **ComClassAttribute**, the compiler performs many of these steps automatically.

Example

To run this example, create a new **Class Library** application and add the following code to a class module.

```
<ComClass(ComClass1.ClassId, ComClass1.InterfaceId, ComClass1.EventsId)> _
Public Class ComClass1
   ' Use the Region directive to define a section named COM Guids.
#Region "COM GUIDs"
   ' These  GUIDs provide the COM identity for this class
   ' and its COM interfaces. You can generate
   ' these guids using guidgen.exe
    Public Const ClassId As String = "7666AC25-855F-4534-BC55-27BF09D49D46"
    Public Const InterfaceId As String = "54388137-8A76-491e-AA3A-853E23AC1217"
    Public Const EventsId As String = "EA329A13-16A0-478d-B41F-47583A761FF2"
#End Region

   Public Sub New()
      MyBase.New()
   End Sub

   Function AddNumbers(ByVal X As Integer, ByVal Y As Integer)
      AddNumbers = X + Y
   End Function
End Class
```

See Also

VBFixedArrayAttribute Class, VBFixedStringAttribute Class, ComClassAttribute Class Members

ComClassAttribute Constructor

Initializes a new instance of the **ComClassAttribute** class.

```
Public Sub New()
```

-or-

```
Public Sub New( _
   ByVal _ClassID As String _
)
```

-or-

```
Public Sub New( _
   ByVal _ClassID As String, _
   ByVal _InterfaceID As String _
)
```

-or-

```
Public Sub New( _
   ByVal _ClassID As String, _
   ByVal _InterfaceID As String, _
   ByVal _EventID As String _
)
```

Parameters

_ClassID
Initializes the value of the **ClassID** property that is used to uniquely identify a class.

_InterfaceID
Initializes the value of the **InterfaceID** property that is used to uniquely identify an interface.

_EventID
Initializes the value of the **EventID** property that is used to uniquely identify an event.

Remarks

The constructor for the **ComClassAttribute** class allows you to set the **ClassID**, **InterfaceID**, or **EventID** properties when applying the **ComClassAttribute** to a class.

See Also

ComClassAttribute Class

ComClassAttribute.ClassID Property

Gets a class ID used to uniquely identify a class.

```
Public ReadOnly Property ClassID As String
```

Property Value

Read only. A string that can be used by the compiler to uniquely identify the class when a COM object is created.

Remarks

The constructor sets this property when the **ComClassAttribute** is applied to a class.

See Also

ComClassAttribute Class

ComClassAttribute.EventID Property

Gets an event ID used to uniquely identify an event.

```
Public ReadOnly Property EventID As String
```

Property Value

Read only. A string that can be used by the compiler to uniquely identify an event for the class when a COM object is created.

Remarks

The constructor sets this property when the **ComClassAttribute** is applied to a class.

See Also

ComClassAttribute Class

ComClassAttribute.InterfaceID Property

Gets an interface ID used to uniquely identify an interface.

```
Public ReadOnly Property InterfaceID As String
```

Property Value

Read only. A string that can be used by the compiler to uniquely identify an interface for the class when a COM object is created.

Remarks

The constructor sets this property when the **ComClassAttribute** is applied to a class.

See Also

ComClassAttribute Class

ComClassAttribute.InterfaceShadows Property

Indicates that the COM interface name shadows another member of the class or base class.

```
Public Property InterfaceShadows As Boolean
```

Property Value

A **Boolean** value that indicates that the COM interface name shadows another member of the class or base class.

Remarks

Shadowing is when a member uses the same name as another member.

See Also

Shadowing, ComClassAttribute Class

Command Function

Returns the argument portion of the command line used to launch Visual Basic or an executable program developed with Visual Basic.

```
Public Function Command() As String
```

Remarks

For applications developed with Visual Basic and compiled to an .exe file, the **Command** function returns any arguments that appear after the name of the application on the command line, as in this example:

```
MyApp cmdlineargs
```

Example

This example uses the **Command** function to get the command-line arguments in a function that returns them in an object containing an array.

```
Function GetCommandLineArgs() As String()
   ' Declare variables.
   Dim separators As String = " "
   Dim commands As String = Microsoft.VisualBasic.Command()
   Dim args() As String = commands.Split(separators.ToCharArray)
   Return args
End Function
```

See Also

Visual Basic Run-Time Library Members

CompareMethod Enumeration

When you call comparison functions, you can use the **CompareMethod** enumeration in your code in place of the actual values.

CompareMethod Enumeration Members

The *Compare* argument takes the following **ComapreMethod** enumeration members:

Member	Constant	Description
Binary	**vbBinaryCompare**	Performs a binary comparison.
Text	**vbTextCompare**	Performs a textual comparison.

See Also

Filter Function, InStr Function, InStrRev Function, Replace Function, Split Function, StrComp Function

Const Statement

Used at module, class, structure, procedure, or block level to declare constants for use in place of literal values.

```
[ <attrlist> ] [{ Public | Protected | Friend | Protected Friend |
Private }] [ Shadows ] Const name [ As type ] = initexpr
```

Parts

attrlist
: Optional. List of attributes that apply to the constants declared in this statement. Multiple attributes are separated by commas.

Public
: Optional. Constants declared with the **Public** keyword have public access. There are no restrictions on the accessibility of public constants.

Protected
: Optional. Constants declared with the **Protected** keyword have protected access. They are accessible only from within their own class or from a derived class. Protected access can be specified only on members of classes. It is not a superset of friend access.

Friend
: Optional. Constants declared with the **Friend** keyword have friend access. They are accessible from within the program that contains their declaration and from anywhere else in the same assembly.

Protected Friend

Optional. Constants declared with the **Protected Friend** keywords have the union of protected and friend access. They can be used by code in the same assembly, as well as by code in derived classes. Protected friend access can be specified only on members of classes.

Private

Optional. Constants declared with the **Private** keyword have private access. They are accessible only from within their declaration context, including from members of any nested types such as procedures.

Shadows

Optional. Indicates that this constant shadows an identically named programming element, or set of overloaded elements, in a base class. You can shadow any kind of declared element with any other kind. A shadowed element is unavailable in the derived class that shadows it.

name

Required. Name of the constant. Must be a valid Visual Basic identifier. You can declare as many constants as you like in the same declaration statement, specifying the *name* and *initexpr* parts for each one. Multiple constants are separated by commas.

type

Optional unless **Option Strict** is **On**. Data type of the constant. Can be **Boolean**, **Byte**, **Char**, **Date**, **Decimal**, **Double**, **Integer**, **Long**, **Object**, **Short**, **Single**, **String**, or the name of an enumeration. You must use a separate **As** clause for each constant being defined.

You cannot use variables or functions in *initexpr*. However, you can use the conversion keywords such as **CInt** and **CDate**, and you can use the **AscW** and **ChrW** methods of the **Strings** class in the **Microsoft.VisualBasic** namespace.

If you do not specify *type*, the constant takes the data type of *initexpr*. If you do specify *type*, the data type of *initexpr* must be convertible to *type*.

If *type* is **Object**, *initexpr* must be **Nothing**.

initexpr

Required. Expression that is evaluated and assigned to the constant when it is created. Can consist of a literal; another constant that is already defined; a member of an enumeration; or any combination of literals, constants, and enumeration members. You can use arithmetic and logical operators to combine such elements.

Each attribute in the *attrlist* part has the following syntax and parts:

```
attrname [({ attrargs | attrinit })]
```

attrlist Parts

attrname

Required. Name of the attribute. Must be a valid Visual Basic identifier.

attrargs

Optional. List of positional arguments for this attribute. Multiple arguments are separated by commas.

attrinit

Optional. List of field or property initializers for this attribute. Multiple initializers are separated by commas.

Remarks

Constants declared in a **Sub**, **Function**, or **Property** procedure are local to that procedure. A constant declared outside a procedure is defined throughout the class, module, or structure in which it is declared.

You can use a constant anywhere you can use an expression.

Example

This example uses the **Const** statement to declare constants for use in place of literal values.

```
' Constants are shared by default.
Const MyVar As Integer = 459
' Declare Public constant.
Public Const MyString As String = "HELP"
' Declare Private Integer constant.
Private Const MyInt As Integer = 5
```

See Also

Enum Statement, #Const Directive, Dim Statement, ReDim Statement

Count Property

Returns an integer containing the number of objects in a collection. Read-only.

```
Overridable Public ReadOnly Property Count() As Integer
```

Example

This example uses the **Collection** object's **Count** property to specify how many iterations are required to remove all the elements of the collection called `Classes1`. When collections are numerically indexed, the base is 1 by default. Since collections are reindexed automatically when a removal is made, the following code removes the first member on each iteration.

```
Dim Num As Long
Dim Classes1 As New Collection()
For Num = 1 To Classes1.Count   ' Remove name from the collection.
   Classes1.Remove(1)   ' Default collection numeric indexes.
Next
```

See Also

Add Method, Item Property, Remove Method

Applies To

Collection Object

CreateObject Function

Creates and returns a reference to a COM object. **CreateObject** cannot be used to create instances of classes in Visual Basic unless those classes are explicitly exposed as COM components.

```
Public Shared Function CreateObject( _
   ByVal ProgId As String, _
   Optional ByVal ServerName As String = "" _
) As Object
```

Parameters

ProgId
Required. **String**. The program ID of the object to create.

ServerName
Optional. **String**. The name of the network server where the object will be created. If *ServerName* is an empty string (" "), the local machine is used.

Exceptions/Errors

Exception type	Error number	Condition
Exception	429	*ProgId* not found or not supplied.
Exception	462	Server is unavailable.
FileNotFoundException	53	No object of the specified type exists.

Remarks

To create an instance of a COM component, assign the object returned by **CreateObject** to an object variable:

```
xlApp = CreateObject("Excel.Application")
```

The type of object variable you use to store the returned object can affect your applications performance. Declaring an object variable with the **As Object** clause creates a variable that can contain a reference to any type of object. However, access to the object through that variable is late bound; that is, the binding occurs when your program is run. There are a lot of reasons why you should avoid late binding, including slower application performance. To create an object variable that results in early binding, that is, binding when the program is compiled, add a reference to the type library for your object from the **COM** tab of the **Add Reference** dialog box on the **Project** menu and declare the object variable of the specific type of your object. For example, you can declare and create the following Microsoft Excel references:

```
Dim xlApp As Excel.Application
Dim xlBook As Excel.Workbook
Dim xlSheet As Excel.WorkSheet
xlApp = CreateObject("Excel.Application")
```

The reference through an early-bound variable can give better performance, but can only contain a reference to the class specified in the declaration.

Another issue is that COM objects use unmanaged code—code without the benefit of the common language runtime. There is a fair degree of complexity involved in mixing the managed code of Visual Basic .NET with unmanaged code from COM. When you add a reference to a COM object, a search is made for a predefined interoperability assembly for that library; if one is found then it is used. If none is found you have the option of creating a local interoperability assembly that contains local interoperability classes for each class in the COM library.

You can create an object on a remote networked computer by passing the name of the computer to the *ServerName* argument of **CreateObject**. That name is the same as the Machine Name portion of a share name: for a share named "\\MyServer\Public," *ServerName* is "MyServer."

> **Note** Refer to COM documentation (see Microsoft Developer Network) for additional information on making an application visible on a remote networked computer. You may have to add a registry key for your application.

The following code returns the version number of an instance of Excel running on a remote computer named `MyServer`:

```
Dim xlApp As Object
' Replace string "\\MyServer" with name of the remote computer.
   xlApp = CreateObject("Excel.Application", "\\MyServer")
   MsgBox(xlApp.Version)
```

If the remote server name is incorrect, or if it is unavailable, a run-time error occurs.

> **Note** Use **CreateObject** when there is no current instance of the object. If an instance of the object is already running, a new instance is started, and an object of the specified type is created. To use the current instance, or to start the application and have it load a file, use the **GetObject** function. If an object has registered itself as a single-instance object, only one instance of the object is created, no matter how many times **CreateObject** is executed.

Example

This example uses the **CreateObject** function to set a reference (`xlApp`) to Microsoft Excel. It uses the reference to access the **Visible** property of Microsoft Excel, and then uses the Microsoft Excel **Quit** method to close it. Finally, the reference itself is released.

```
Sub TestExcel()
   Dim xlApp As Excel.Application
   Dim xlBook As Excel.Workbook
   Dim xlSheet As Excel.Worksheet
   xlApp = CType(CreateObject("Excel.Application"), Excel.Application)
   xlBook = CType(xlApp.Workbooks.Add, Excel.Workbook)
   xlSheet = CType(xlBook.Worksheets(1), Excel.Worksheet)
```

(continued)

(continued)

```
    ' Place some text in the second row of the sheet.
    xlSheet.Activate()
    xlSheet.Cells(2, 2) = "This is column B row 2"
    ' Show the sheet.
    xlSheet.Application.Visible = True
    ' Save the sheet to C:\test.xls directory.
    xlSheet.SaveAs("C:\Test.xls")
    ' Optionally, you can call xlApp.Quit to close the work sheet.
End Sub
```

See Also

GetObject Function, Declare Statement

CType Function

Returns the result of explicitly converting an expression to a specified data type, object, structure, class, or interface.

```
CType(expression, typename)
```

Parts

expression
: Any valid expression. If the value of *expression* is outside the range allowed by *typename*, an error occurs.

typename
: Any expression that is legal within an **As** clause in a **Dim** statement, that is, the name of any data type, object, structure, class, or interface.

Remarks

CType is compiled inline, meaning the conversion code is part of the code that evaluates the expression. Execution is faster because there is no call to a procedure to accomplish the conversion.

Example

This example uses the **CType** function to convert an expression to the specified data type.

```
Dim MyNumber As Long
Dim MyNewType As Single
MyNumber = 1000
MyNewType = CType(MyNumber,Single)    ' MyNewType is set to 1000.0.
```

See Also

Type Conversion Functions

CurDir Function

Returns a string representing the current path.

```
Public Overloads Function CurDir([ ByVal Drive As Char ]) As String
```

Parameter

Drive

Optional. **String** expression that specifies an existing drive. If no drive is specified, or if *Drive* is a zero-length string (" "), **CurDir** returns the path for the current drive.

Exceptions/Errors

Exception type	Error number	Condition
IOException	68	*Drive* is not found.
ArgumentException	68	Invalid *Drive* is specified.

Example

This example uses the **CurDir** function to return the current path.

```
' Assume current path on C drive is "C:\WINDOWS\SYSTEM".
' Assume current path on D drive is "D:\EXCEL".
' Assume C is the current drive.
Dim MyPath As String
MyPath = CurDir()   ' Returns "C:\WINDOWS\SYSTEM".
MyPath = CurDir("C")   ' Returns "C:\WINDOWS\SYSTEM".
MyPath = CurDir("D")   ' Returns "D:\EXCEL".
```

See Also

ChDir Function, ChDrive Function, MkDir Function, RmDir Function

Date Data Type

Date variables are stored as IEEE 64-bit (8-byte) integers that represent dates ranging from January 1 of the year 1 through December 31 of the year 9999, and times from 0:00:00 (midnight) through 11:59:59 PM.

Date values must be enclosed within number signs (#) and be in the format m/d/yyyy, for example `#5/31/1993#`. If you convert a **Date** value to the **String** type, the date is rendered according to the short date format recognized by your computer, and the time is rendered according to the time format (either 12-hour or 24-hour) in effect on your computer.

The equivalent .NET data type is **System.DateTime**.

See Also

Data Type Summary, Double Data Type, Type Conversion Functions, Conversion Summary

DateAdd Function

Returns a **Date** value containing a date and time value to which a specified time interval has been added.

```
Public Overloads Function DateAdd( _
   ByVal Interval As DateInterval, _
   ByVal Number As Double, _
   ByVal DateValue As DateTime _
) As DateTime
```

-or-

```
Public Overloads Function DateAdd( _
   ByVal Interval As String, _
   ByVal Number As Double, _
   ByVal DateValue As Object _
) As DateTime
```

Parameters

Interval

Required. **DateInterval** enumeration value or **String** expression representing the time interval you want to add.

Number

Required. **Double**. Floating-point expression representing the number of intervals you want to add. *Number* can be positive (to get date/time values in the future) or negative (to get date/time values in the past). It can contain a fractional part when *Interval* specifies hours, minutes, or seconds. For other values of *Interval*, any fractional part of *Number* is ignored.

DateValue

Required. **Date**. An expression representing the date and time to which the interval is to be added. *DateValue* itself is not changed in the calling program.

Settings

The *Interval* argument can have one of the following settings.

Enumeration value	String	Unit of time interval to add
DateInterval.Day	d	Day; truncated to integral value
DateInterval.DayOfYear	y	Day; truncated to integral value
DateInterval.Hour	h	Hour; rounded to nearest millisecond
DateInterval.Minute	n	Minute; rounded to nearest millisecond
DateInterval.Month	m	Month; truncated to integral value

Enumeration value	String	Unit of time interval to add
DateInterval.Quarter	q	Quarter; truncated to integral value
DateInterval.Second	s	Second; rounded to nearest millisecond
DateInterval.Weekday	w	Day; truncated to integral value
DateInterval.WeekOfYear	ww	Week; truncated to integral value
DateInterval.Year	yyyy	Year; truncated to integral value

Exceptions/Errors

Exception type	Error number	Condition
InvalidCastException	13	*DateValue* is not coercible to **Date.**
ArgumentException	5	*Interval* is invalid.
ArgumentOutOfRangeException	9	Calculated date is before 00:00:00 on January 1 of the year 1, or later than 23:59:59 on December 31, 9999.

Remarks

You can use the **DateAdd** function to add or subtract a specified time interval from a date. For example, you can calculate a date 30 days from today or a time 45 minutes before now.

To add days to *DateValue*, you can use **DateInterval.Day**, **DateInterval.DayOfYear**, or **DateInterval.Weekday**. These are treated as equivalent because **DayOfYear** and **Weekday** are not meaningful time intervals.

The **DateAdd** function never returns an invalid date. If necessary, the day part of the resulting date is adjusted downward to the last day of the resulting month in the resulting year. The following example adds one month to January 31:

```
Dim NextMonth As Date = DateAdd(DateInterval.Month, 1, #1/31/1995#)
```

In this example, **DateAdd** returns `#2/28/1995#`, not `#2/31/1995#`. If *DateValue* is `#1/31/1996#`, it returns `#2/29/1996#` because 1996 is a leap year.

If any argument has an invalid value, an **ArgumentException** error occurs. If the calculated date is earlier than 00:00:00 on January 1 of the year 1, or later than 23:59:59 on December 31, 9999, an **ArgumentOutOfRangeException** error occurs. If the *DateValue* argument has a value that cannot be coerced to a valid **Date** value, an **InvalidCastException** error occurs.

Note **DateAdd** uses the current calendar setting from the **CurrentCulture** property of the **CultureInfo** class in the **System.Globalization** namespace. The default **CurrentCulture** values are determined by **Control Panel** settings.

Since every **Date** value is supported by a **DateTime** structure, its methods give you additional options in adding time intervals. For example, you can add a fractional number of days, rounded to the nearest millisecond, to a **Date** variable as follows:

```
Dim NextTime As Date = Now          ' Current date and time.
NextTime = NextTime.AddDays(3.4)    ' Increment by 3 2/5 days.
```

Example

This example takes a date and, using the **DateAdd** function, displays a corresponding date a specified number of months in the future.

```
Dim Msg, Number, StartDate As String   'Declare variables.
Dim Months As Double
Dim SecondDate As Date
Dim IntervalType As DateInterval
IntervalType = DateInterval.Month    ' Specifies months as interval.
StartDate = InputBox("Enter a date")
SecondDate = CDate(StartDate)
Number = InputBox("Enter number of months to add")
Months = Val(Number)
Msg = "New date: " & DateAdd(IntervalType, Months, SecondDate)
MsgBox (Msg)
```

See Also

DateDiff Function, DatePart Function, Day Function, Format Function, Now Property, Weekday Function, Year Function, Date Data Type

DateDiff Function

Returns a **Long** value specifying the number of time intervals between two **Date** values.

```
Public Overloads Function DateDiff( _
   ByVal Interval As DateInterval, _
   ByVal Date1 As DateTime, _
   ByVal Date2 As DateTime, _
   Optional ByVal DayOfWeek As FirstDayOfWeek = FirstDayOfWeek.Sunday, _
   Optional ByVal  WeekOfYear As FirstWeekOfYear = FirstWeekOfYear.Jan1 _
) As Long
```

-or-

```
Public Overloads Function DateDiff( _
   ByVal Interval As String, _
   ByVal Date1 As Object, _
   ByVal Date2 As Object, _
   Optional ByVal DayOfWeek As FirstDayOfWeek = FirstDayOfWeek.Sunday, _
   Optional ByVal WeekOfYear As FirstWeekOfYear = FirstWeekOfYear.Jan1 _
) As Long
```

Parameters

Interval

Required. **DateInterval** enumeration value or **String** expression representing the time interval you want to use as the unit of difference between *Date1* and *Date2*.

Date1, Date2

Required. **Date**. The two date/time values you want to use in the calculation. The value of *Date1* is subtracted from the value of *Date2* to produce the difference. Neither value is changed in the calling program.

DayOfWeek

Optional. A value chosen from the **FirstDayOfWeek** enumeration that specifies the first day of the week. If not specified, **FirstDayOfWeek.Sunday** is used.

WeekOfYear

Optional. A value chosen from the **FirstWeekOfYear** enumeration that specifies the first week of the year. If not specified, **FirstWeekOfYear.Jan1** is used.

Settings

The *Interval* argument can have one of the following settings.

Enumeration value	String	Unit of time difference
DateInterval.Day	d	Day
DateInterval.DayOfYear	y	Day
DateInterval.Hour	h	Hour
DateInterval.Minute	n	Minute
DateInterval.Month	m	Month
DateInterval.Quarter	q	Quarter
DateInterval.Second	s	Second
DateInterval.Weekday	w	Week
DateInterval.WeekOfYear	ww	Calendar week
DateInterval.Year	yyyy	Year

The *DayOfWeek* argument can have one of the following settings.

Enumeration value	Value	Description
FirstDayOfWeek.System	0	First day of week specified in system settings
FirstDayOfWeek.Sunday	1	Sunday (default)
FirstDayOfWeek.Monday	2	Monday (complies with ISO standard 8601, section 3.17)
FirstDayOfWeek.Tuesday	3	Tuesday
FirstDayOfWeek.Wednesday	4	Wednesday
FirstDayOfWeek.Thursday	5	Thursday
FirstDayOfWeek.Friday	6	Friday
FirstDayOfWeek.Saturday	7	Saturday

The *WeekOfYear* argument can have one of the following settings.

Enumeration value	Value	Description
FirstWeekOfYear.System	0	First week of year specified in system settings
FirstWeekOfYear.Jan1	1	Week in which January 1 occurs (default)
FirstWeekOfYear.FirstFourDays	2	Week that has at least four days in the new year (complies with ISO standard 8601, section 3.17)
FirstWeekOfYear.FirstFullWeek	3	First full week in the new year

Exceptions/Errors

Exception type	Error number	Condition
ArgumentException	5	Invalid *Interval.*
ArgumentException	5	*Date* or *DayofWeek* are out of range.
InvalidCastException	13	*Date1* or *Date2* are invalid types.

Remarks

You can use the **DateDiff** function to determine how many specified time intervals exist between two date/time values. For example, you might use **DateDiff** to calculate the number of days between two dates, or the number of weeks between today and the end of the year.

If *Interval* is set to **DateInterval.DayOfYear**, it is treated the same as **DateInterval.Day**, because **DayOfYear** is not a meaningful unit for a time interval.

If *Interval* is set to **DateInterval.WeekOfYear**, the return value represents the number of weeks between the first day of the week containing *Date1* and the first day of the week containing *Date2*. The following example shows how this produces different results from **DateInterval.Weekday**.

```
Dim DatTim1 As Date = #1/4/2001#    ' This is a Thursday.
Dim DatTim2 As Date = #1/9/2001#    ' This is the next Tuesday.
' Assume Sunday is specified as first day of the week.
Dim WD As Long = DateDiff(DateInterval.Weekday, DatTim1, DatTim2)
Dim WY As Long = DateDiff(DateInterval.WeekOfYear, DatTim1, DatTim2)
```

In the preceding example, **DateDiff** returns **0** to `WD` because the difference between the two dates is less than seven days, but it returns **1** to `WY` because there is a seven-day difference between the first days of the respective calendar weeks.

If *Interval* is set to **DateInterval.Year**, the return value is calculated purely from the year parts of *Date1* and *Date2*.

Because *Date1* and *Date2* are of the **Date** data type, they hold date and time values accurate to 100-nanosecond ticks on the system timer. However, **DateDiff** always returns the number of time intervals as a **Long** value.

If *Date1* represents a later date and time than *Date2*, **DateDiff** returns a negative number.

If any argument has an invalid value, an **ArgumentException** error occurs. If either the *Date1* or *Date2* argument has a value that cannot be coerced to a valid **Date** value, an **InvalidCastException** error occurs.

Note When comparing December 31 to January 1 of the following year, **DateDiff** returns 1 for **DateInterval.Year**, **DateInterval.Quarter**, or **DateInterval.Month**, even though only one day has elapsed.

Since every **Date** value is supported by a **DateTime** structure, its methods give you additional options in finding time intervals. For example, you can use the **Subtract** method in either of its overloaded forms. One of these subtracts a **TimeSpan** from a **Date** variable to return another **Date** value; the other subtracts a **Date** value to return a **TimeSpan**. You can time a process to find out how many milliseconds it takes, as follows:

```
Dim StartTime As Date = Now    ' Starting date/time.
' Run the process that is to be timed.
Dim RunLength As System.TimeSpan = Now.Subtract(StartTime)
Dim Millisecs As Integer = RunLength.Milliseconds
```

Example

This example uses the **DateDiff** function to display the number of days between a given date and today.

```
Dim FirstDate, Msg As String    ' Declare variables.
Dim SecondDate As Date
FirstDate = InputBox("Enter a date")
SecondDate = CDate(FirstDate)
Msg = "Days from today: " & DateDiff(DateInterval.Day, Now, SecondDate)
MsgBox (Msg)
```

See Also

DateAdd Function, DatePart Function, Day Function, Format Function, Now Property, Weekday Function, Year Function, Date Data Type

DateFormat Enumeration

When you call the **DateValue** function, you can use the following enumeration members in your code in place of the actual values.

Member	Constant	Description
GeneralDate	**vbGeneralDate**	For real numbers, displays a date and time. If the number has no fractional part, displays only a date. If the number has no integer part, displays time only. Date and time display is determined by your computer's regional settings.
LongDate	**vbLongDate**	Displays a date using the long-date format specified in your computer's regional settings.
ShortDate	**vbShortDate**	Displays a date using the short-date format specified in your computer's regional settings.
LongTime	**vbLongTime**	Displays a time using the long-time format specified in your computer's regional settings.
ShortTime	**vbShortTime**	Displays a time using the short-time format specified in your computer's regional settings.

Note You can access your computer's regional settings by double-clicking the Regional Options icon, found in Control Panel.

See Also

DateValue Function

DateInterval Enumeration

When you call date-related functions, you can use enumeration members in your code in place of the actual values.

The **DateInterval** enumeration defines constants used with date-related functions to identify how date intervals are determined and formatted. The following table lists the **DateInterval** enumeration members.

Member	Description
DateInterval.Day	Day of month (1 through 31).
DateInterval.DayOfYear	Day of year (1 through 366).
DateInterval.Hour	Hour (1 through 24).
DateInterval.Minute	Minute (1 through 60).
DateInterval.Month	Month (1 through 12).
DateInterval.Quarter	Quarter of year (1 through 4).
DateInterval.Second	Second (1 through 60).
DateInterval.Weekday	Day of week (1 through 7).
DateInterval.WeekOfYear	Week of year (1 through 53).
DateInterval.Year	Year.

See Also

DateFormat Enumeration, DueDate Enumeration, DatePart Function, DateAdd Function, DateDiff Function

DatePart Function

Returns an **Integer** value containing the specified component of a given **Date** value.

```
Public Overloads Function DatePart( _
   ByVal Interval As DateInterval, _
   ByVal DateValue As DateTime, _
   Optional ByVal FirstDayOfWeekValue As FirstDayOfWeek = VbSunday, _
   Optional ByVal FirstWeekOfYearValue As FirstWeekOfYear = VbFirstJan1 _
) As Integer
```

-or-

```
Public Overloads Function DatePart( _
    ByVal Interval As String, _
   ByVal DateValue As Object, _
   Optional ByVal DayOfWeek As FirstDayOfWeek = FirstDayOfWeek.Sunday, _
   Optional ByVal WeekOfYear As FirstWeekOfYear = FirstWeekOfYear.Jan1 _
) As Integer
```

Parameters

Interval

Required. **DateInterval** enumeration value or **String** expression representing the part of the date/time value you want to return.

DateValue
Required. **Date** value that you want to evaluate.

FirstDayOfWeekValue
Optional. A value chosen from the **FirstDayOfWeek** enumeration that specifies the first day of the week. If not specified, **FirstDayOfWeek.Sunday** is used.

FirstWeekOfYearValue
Optional. A value chosen from the **FirstWeekOfYear** enumeration that specifies the first week of the year. If not specified, **FirstWeekOfYear.Jan1** is used.

Settings

The *Interval* argument can have one of the following settings.

Enumeration value	String	Part of date/time value to return
DateInterval.Day	d	Day of month (1 through 31)
DateInterval.DayOfYear	y	Day of year (1 through 366)
DateInterval.Hour	h	Hour
DateInterval.Minute	n	Minute
DateInterval.Month	m	Month
DateInterval.Quarter	q	Quarter
DateInterval.Second	s	Second
DateInterval.Weekday	w	Day of week (1 through 7)
DateInterval.WeekOfYear	ww	Week of year (1 through 53)
DateInterval.Year	yyyy	Year

The *FirstDayOfWeekValue* argument can have one of the following settings.

Enumeration value	Value	Description
FirstDayOfWeek.System	0	First day of week specified in system settings
FirstDayOfWeek.Sunday	1	Sunday (default)
FirstDayOfWeek.Monday	2	Monday (complies with ISO standard 8601, section 3.17)
FirstDayOfWeek.Tuesday	3	Tuesday
FirstDayOfWeek.Wednesday	4	Wednesday
FirstDayOfWeek.Thursday	5	Thursday
FirstDayOfWeek.Friday	6	Friday
FirstDayOfWeek.Saturday	7	Saturday

The *FirstWeekOfYearValue* argument can have one of the following settings.

Enumeration value	Value	Description
FirstWeekOfYear.System	0	First week of year specified in system settings
FirstWeekOfYear.Jan1	1	Week in which January 1 occurs (default)
FirstWeekOfYear.FirstFourDays	2	Week that has at least four days in the new year (complies with ISO standard 8601, section 3.17)
FirstWeekOfYear.FirstFullWeek	3	First full week in new year

Exceptions/Errors

Exception type	Error number	Condition
ArgumentException	5	*Interval* is invalid.
InvalidCastException	13	*DateValue* is not coercible to **Date**.

Remarks

You can use the **DatePart** function to evaluate a date/time value and return a specific component. For example, you might use **DatePart** to calculate the day of the week or the current hour.

If you choose **DateInterval.Weekday** for the *Interval* argument, the returned value is consistent with the values of the **FirstDayOfWeek** enumeration. If you choose **DateInterval.WeekOfYear**, **DatePart** uses the **Calendar** and **CultureInfo** classes of the **System.Globalization** namespace to determine your current settings.

The *FirstDayOfWeekValue* argument affects calculations that use the **DateInterval.Weekday** and **DateInterval.WeekOfYear** *Interval* settings. The *FirstWeekOfYearValue* argument affects calculations that specify **DateInterval.WeekOfYear** for *Interval*.

If any argument has an invalid value, an **ArgumentException** error occurs. If the *DateValue* argument has a value that cannot be coerced to a valid **Date** value, an **InvalidCastException** error occurs.

Since every **Date** value is supported by a **DateTime** structure, its methods give you additional options in retrieving date/time parts. For example, you can obtain the entire date value of a **Date** variable, with the time value set to midnight, as follows:

```
Dim CurrDatTim As Date = Now   ' Current date and time.
Dim LastMidnight As Date = CurrDatTim.Date   ' At midnight.
```

Example

This example takes a date and, using the **DatePart** function, displays the quarter of the year in which it occurs.

```
Dim FirstDate, Msg As String   'Declare variables.
Dim SecondDate As Date
FirstDate = InputBox("Enter a date:")
SecondDate = CDate(FirstDate)
Msg = "Quarter: " & DatePart(DateInterval.Quarter, SecondDate)
MsgBox (Msg)
```

See Also

DateAdd Function, DateDiff Function, Day Function, Format Function, Now Property, Weekday Function, Year Function, Date Data Type

DateSerial Function

Returns a **Date** value representing a specified year, month, and day, with the time information set to midnight (00:00:00).

```
Public Function DateSerial( _
   ByVal [Year] As Integer, _
   ByVal [Month] As Integer, _
   ByVal [Day] As Integer _
) As DateTime
```

Parameters

Year

Required. **Integer** expression from 1 through 9999. However, values below this range are also accepted. If *Year* is 0 through 99, it is interpreted as being between 1930 and 2029, as explained in the Remarks section below. If *Year* is less than 1, it is subtracted from the current year.

Month

Required. **Integer** expression from 1 through 12. However, values outside this range are also accepted. The value of *Month* is offset by 1 and applied to January of the calculated year. In other words, (*Month* –1) is added to January. The year is recalculated if necessary. The following results illustrate this effect:

- If *Month* is 1, the result is January of the calculated year.
- If *Month* is 0, the result is December of the previous year.
- If *Month* is –1, the result is November of the previous year.
- If *Month* is 13, the result is January of the following year.

Day

Required. **Integer** expression from 1 through 31. However, values outside this range are also accepted. The value of *Day* is offset by 1 and applied to the first day of the calculated month. In other words, (*Day* –1) is added to the first of the month. The month and year are recalculated if necessary. The following results illustrate this effect:

- If *Day* is 1, the result is the first day of the calculated month.
- If *Day* is 0, the result is the last day of the previous month.
- If *Day* is –1, the result is the penultimate day of the previous month.
- If *Day* is past the end of the current month, the result is the appropriate day of the following month. For example, if *Month* is 4 and *Day* is 31, the result is May 1.

Remarks

Under Windows 98 or Windows 2000, two-digit years for the *Year* argument are interpreted based on user-defined machine settings. The default settings are that values from 0 through 29 are interpreted as the years 2000–2029, and values from 30 through 99 are interpreted as the years 1930–1999. For all other *Year* arguments, use a four-digit year; for example, 1924.

Earlier versions of Windows interpret two-digit years based on the defaults described previously. To be sure the function returns the proper value, use a four-digit *Year*.

The following example demonstrates negative, zero, and positive argument values. Here, the **DateSerial** function returns a **Date** representing the day before the first day of March in the year 10 years before the current year; in other words, the last day of February ten years ago.

```
Dim EndFeb As Date = DateSerial(-10, 3, 0)
```

If either *Month* or *Day* exceeds its normal range, it is applied to the next larger unit as appropriate. For example, if you specify 32 days, it is evaluated as one month and from one to four days, depending on the value of *Month*. If *Year* is greater than 9999, or if any argument is outside the range –2,147,483,648 through 2,147,483,647, an **ArgumentException** error occurs. If the date specified by the three arguments is earlier than 00:00:00 on January 1 of the year 1, or later than 23:59:59 on December 31, 9999, an **ArgumentOutOfRangeException** error occurs.

The **Date** data type includes time components. **DateSerial** sets all of these to 0, so the returned value represents the beginning of the calculated day.

Since every **Date** value is supported by a **DateTime** structure, its methods give you additional options in assembling a **Date** value. For example, you can use one of the overloaded **DateTime** constructors to populate a **Date** variable using the desired combination of components. The following example sets `NewDateTime` to May 6, 1978 at one tenth of a second before 8:30 in the morning:

```
Dim NewDateTime As Date = New Date(1978, 5, 6, 8, 29, 59, 900)
```

Example

This example uses the **DateSerial** function to return the date for the specified year, month, and day.

```
Dim MyDate As Date
' MyDate contains the date for February 12, 1969.
MyDate = DateSerial(1969, 2, 12)   ' Return a date.
```

See Also

DateValue Function, Day Function, Month Function, Now Property, TimeSerial Function, TimeValue Function, Weekday Function, Year Function, Date Data Type

DateString Property

Returns or sets a **String** value representing the current date according to your system.

```
Public Property DateString As String
```

Exceptions/Errors

Exception type	Error number	Condition
InvalidCastException	5	Invalid cast.

Remarks

DateString always returns the system date as "MM-dd-yyyy", which uses the abbreviated month name. The accepted formats for setting the date are "M-d-yyyy", "M-d-y", "M/d/yyyy", and "M/d/y".

If you attempt to set **DateString** with an invalid value, an **InvalidCastException** occurs.

To get or set the current system time as a **String**, use the **TimeString** property.

To access the current system date as a **Date**, use the **Today** property.

Example

This example uses the **DateString** property to display the current system date.

```
MsgBox("The current date is " & DateString)
```

See Also

Now Property, TimeString Property, Today Property

DateValue Function

Returns a **Date** value containing the date information represented by a string, with the time information set to midnight (00:00:00).

```
Public Function DateValue(ByVal StringDate As String) As DateTime
```

Parameter

StringDate

Required. **String** expression representing a date/time value from 00:00:00 on January 1 of the year 1 through 23:59:59 on December 31, 9999.

Exceptions/Errors

Exception type	Error number	Condition
InvalidCastException	13	*StringDate* includes invalid time information.

Remarks

If *StringDate* includes only numbers from 1 through 12 separated by valid date separators, **DateValue** recognizes the order for month, day, and year according to the Short Date format specified for your system. **DateValue** uses the current calendar setting from the **CurrentCulture** property of the **CultureInfo** class in the **System.Globalization** namespace. The default **CurrentCulture** values are determined by **Control Panel** settings. You can override the Short Date format by setting the **ShortDatePattern** property of the **DateTimeFormatInfo** class in the **System.Globalization** namespace.

DateValue recognizes month names in long, abbreviated, and numeric form. For example, in addition to recognizing 12/30/1991 and 12/30/91, **DateValue** also recognizes December 30, 1991 and Dec 30, 1991.

If the year part of *StringDate* is omitted, **DateValue** uses the current year from your computer's system date.

If the *StringDate* argument includes time information, **DateValue** does not include it in the returned value. However, if *StringDate* includes invalid time information, such as "89:98", an **InvalidCastException** error occurs.

Example

This example uses the **DateValue** function to convert a string to a date. You can also use date literals to directly assign a date to an **Object** or **Date** variable, for example, `MyDate = #2/12/69#`.

```
Dim MyDate As Date
MyDate = DateValue("February 12, 1969")   ' Returns a date.
```

See Also

DateSerial Function, Day Function, Month Function, Now Property, TimeSerial Function, TimeValue Function, Weekday Function, Year Function, Date Data Type, System.Globalization Namespace

Day Function

Returns an **Integer** value from 1 through 31 representing the day of the month.

```
Public Function Day(ByVal DateValue As DateTime) As Integer
```

Parameter

DateValue
Required. **Date** value from which you want to extract the day.

If you use the **Day** function, you might have to qualify it with the **Microsoft.VisualBasic** namespace, because the **System.Windows.Forms** namespace defines **Day** as an enumeration. The following example shows how qualifying **Day** resolves this ambiguity:

```
Dim ThisDay As Integer = Microsoft.VisualBasic.Day(Now)
```

You can also obtain the day of the month by calling **DatePart** and specifying **DateInterval.Day** for the *Interval* argument.

Example

This example uses the **Day** function to obtain the day of the month from a specified date. In the development environment, the date literal is displayed in standard short format (such as "02/12/1969") using the locale settings of your code.

```
Dim MyDate As Date
Dim MyDay As Integer
MyDate = #2/12/1969#   ' Assign a date using standard short format.
MyDay = Microsoft.VisualBasic.Day(MyDate)   ' MyDay contains 12.
```

Day is qualified to distinguish it from the **System.Windows.Forms.Day** enumeration.

See Also

Hour Function, Minute Function, Month Function, Now Property, Second Function, Weekday Function, Year Function, DatePart Function

DDB Function

Returns a **Double** specifying the depreciation of an asset for a specific time period using the double-declining balance method or some other method you specify.

```
Function DDB( _
    ByVal Cost As Double, _
    ByVal Salvage As Double, _
    ByVal Life As Double, _
    ByVal Period As Double, _
    Optional ByVal Factor As Double = 2.0 _
) As Double
```

Parameters

Cost

Required. **Double** specifying initial cost of the asset.

Salvage

Required. **Double** specifying value of the asset at the end of its useful life.

Life

Required. **Double** specifying length of useful life of the asset.

Period

Required. **Double** specifying period for which asset depreciation is calculated.

Factor

Optional. **Double** specifying rate at which the balance declines. If omitted, 2 (double-declining method) is assumed.

Exceptions/Errors

Exception type	Error number	Condition
ArgumentException	5	Argument value < 0 or *Period* > *Life*.

Remarks

The double-declining balance method computes depreciation at an accelerated rate. Depreciation is highest in the first period and decreases in successive periods.

The *Life* and *Period* arguments must be expressed in the same units. For example, if *Life* is given in months, *Period* must also be given in months. All arguments must be positive numbers.

The **DDB** function uses the following formula to calculate depreciation for a given period:

```
Depreciation / Period = ((Cost - Salvage) * Factor) / Life
```

Example

This example uses the **DDB** function to return the depreciation of an asset for a specified period given the initial cost (`InitCost`), the salvage value at the end of the asset's useful life (`SalvageVal`), the total life of the asset in years (`LifeTime`), and the period in years for which the depreciation is calculated (`Depr`).

```
Sub testDDB()
   Dim InitCost, SalvageVal, MonthLife, DepYear As Double
   Dim Fmt As String
   Dim LifeTime, Depr As Double
   Const YRMOS As Integer = 12    ' Number of months in a year.
   Fmt = "###,##0.00"
   InitCost = CDbl(InputBox("What's the initial cost of the asset?"))
   SalvageVal = CDbl(InputBox("Enter the asset's value at end of its life.")
   MonthLife = CDbl(InputBox("What's the asset's useful life in months?")
   Do While MonthLife < YRMOS    ' Ensure period is >= 1 year.
      MsgBox("Asset life must be a year or more.")
      MonthLife = CDbl(InputBox("What's the asset's useful life in months?")
   Loop
   LifeTime = MonthLife / YRMOS    ' Convert months to years.
   If LifeTime <> Int(MonthLife / YRMOS) Then
      LifeTime = Int(LifeTime + 1)    ' Round up to nearest year.
   End If
   DepYear = CInt(InputBox("Enter year for depreciation calculation."))
   Do While DepYear < 1 Or DepYear > LifeTime
      MsgBox("You must enter at least 1 but not more than " & LifeTime)
      DepYear = CDbl(InputBox("Enter year for depreciation calculation.")
   Loop
   Depr = DDB(InitCost, SalvageVal, LifeTime, DepYear)
   MsgBox("The depreciation for year " & DepYear & " is " & _
   Format(Depr, Fmt) & ".")
End Sub
```

See Also

FV Function, IPmt Function, IRR Function, MIRR Function, NPer Function, NPV Function, Pmt Function, PPmt Function, PV Function, Rate Function, SLN Function, SYD Function

Decimal Data Type

Decimal variables are stored as signed 128-bit (16-byte) integers scaled by a variable power of 10. The scaling factor specifies the number of digits to the right of the decimal point; it ranges from 0 through 28. With a scale of 0 (no decimal places), the largest possible value is +/–79,228,162,514,264,337,593,543,950,335. With 28 decimal places, the largest value is +/–7.9228162514264337593543950335, and the smallest nonzero value is +/–0.0000000000000000000000000001 (+/–1E–28).

Appending the literal type character **D** to a literal forces it to the **Decimal** data type. Appending the identifier type character @ to any identifier forces it to **Decimal**. You might need to use the **D** type character to assign a large value to a **Decimal** variable or constant, as the following example shows:

```
Dim BigDec1 As Decimal = 9223372036854775807    ' No overflow.
Dim BigDec2 As Decimal = 9223372036854775808    ' Overflow.
Dim BigDec3 As Decimal = 9223372036854775808D   ' No overflow.
```

This is because without a literal type character the literal is taken as **Long**, and the value to be assigned to `BigDec2` is too large for the **Long** type.

The equivalent .NET data type is **System.Decimal**.

See Also

Data Type Summary, Type Conversion Functions, Conversion Summary

Declare Statement

Used at module level to declare references to external procedures in a dynamic-link library (DLL).

```
[ <attrlist> ] [ Public | Private | Protected | Friend | Protected Friend ] [
Shadows ] _
Declare [ Ansi | Unicode | Auto ] [ Sub ] name Lib "libname" _
[ Alias "aliasname" ] [([ arglist ])]
```

-or-

```
[ <attrlist> ] [ Public | Private | Protected | Friend | Protected Friend ] [
Shadows ] _
Declare [ Ansi | Unicode | Auto ] [ Function ] name Lib "libname" _
[ Alias "aliasname" ] [([ arglist ])] [ As type ]
```

Parts

attrlist

Optional. List of attributes that apply to this procedure. Multiple attributes are separated by commas.

Public

Optional. Entities declared with the **Public** modifier have public access. There are no restrictions on the use of public entities.

Private

Optional. Entities declared with the **Private** modifier have private access. A private entity is accessible only within its declaration context, including any nested entities.

Protected

Optional. Entities declared with the **Protected** keyword have protected access. They are accessible only from within their own class or from a derived class. Protected access can be specified only on members of classes. It is not a superset of friend access.

Friend

Optional. Entities declared with the **Friend** modifier have friend access. An entity with friend access is accessible only within the program that contains the entity declaration.

Protected Friend

Optional. Entities declared with the **Protected Friend** modifiers have the union of protected and friend accessibility.

Shadows

Optional. Indicates that this procedure shadows an identically named programming element in a base class. You can shadow any kind of declared element with any other kind. A shadowed element is unavailable in the derived class that shadows it

Ansi

Optional. Converts all strings to ANSI values. If no modifier is specified, **Ansi** is the default.

Unicode

Optional. Converts all strings to Unicode values.

Auto

Optional. Converts the strings according to common language runtime rules based on the name of the method (or the alias name, if specified).

Sub

Optional (either **Sub** or **Function** must appear). Indicates that the procedure does not return a value.

Function

Optional (either **Sub** or **Function** must appear). Indicates that the procedure returns a value that can be used in an expression.

name

Required. Any valid procedure name. Note that DLL entry points are case sensitive.

Lib

Required. Indicates that a DLL or code resource contains the procedure being declared. The **Lib** clause is required for all declarations.

libname

Required. Name of the DLL or code resource that contains the declared procedure.

Alias

Optional. Indicates that the procedure being called has another name in the DLL. This is useful when the external procedure name is the same as a keyword. You can also use **Alias** when a DLL procedure has the same name as a public variable, constant, or any other procedure in the same scope. **Alias** is also useful if any characters in the DLL procedure name are not allowed by the DLL naming convention.

aliasname

Optional. Name of the procedure in the DLL or code resource. If the first character is not a number sign (#), *aliasname* is the name of the procedure's entry point in the DLL. If (#) is the first character, all characters that follow must indicate the ordinal number of the procedure's entry point.

arglist

Optional. List of variables representing arguments that are passed to the procedure when it is called.

type

Optional. Data type of the value returned by a Function procedure; may be **Byte**, **Boolean**, **Char**, **Short**, **Integer**, **Long**, **Single**, **Double**, **Decimal**, **String** (variable length only), **Object**, or structure. Arrays of any type cannot be returned, but an object containing an array can.

> **Note** Functions declared with the **Declare** statement cannot return dates.

Each attribute in the *attrlist* part has the following syntax and parts:

```
attrname [({ attrargs | attrinit })]
```

attrlist Parts

attrname

Required. Name of the attribute. Must be a valid Visual Basic identifier.

attrargs

Optional. List of positional arguments for this attribute. Multiple arguments are separated by commas.

attrinit

Optional. List of field or property initializers for this attribute. Multiple initializers are separated by commas.

The *arglist* argument has the following syntax and parts:

```
[ <attrlist> ] [ Optional ] [ ByVal | ByRef ] [ ParamArray ] varname[( )]
[ As type ]
```

arglist Parts

attrlist

Optional. List of attributes that apply to this argument. Multiple attributes are separated by commas.

Optional

Optional. Indicates that an argument is not required. If used, all subsequent arguments in *arglist* must also be optional and declared using the **Optional** keyword. **Optional** can't be used for any argument if **ParamArray** is used.

ByVal
: Optional. Indicates that the argument is passed by value. **ByVal** is the default in Visual Basic.

ByRef
: Optional. Indicates that the argument is passed by reference.

ParamArray
: Optional. Used only as the last argument in *arglist* to indicate that the final argument is an **Optional** array of **Object** elements. The **ParamArray** keyword allows you to provide an arbitrary number of arguments. The **ParamArray** keyword can't be used with **ByVal**, **ByRef**, or **Optional**.

varname
: Required. Name of the variable representing the argument being passed to the procedure; follows standard variable naming conventions.

( )
: Required for array variables. Indicates that *varname* is an array.

type
: Optional. Data type of the argument passed to the procedure; may be **Byte**, **Boolean**, **Char**, **Short**, **Integer**, **Long**, **Single**, **Double**, **Decimal**, **String** (variable length only), **Object**, a user-defined type, or an object type.

Remarks

For **Function** procedures, the data type of the procedure determines the data type it returns. You can use an **As** clause following *arglist* to specify the return type of the function. Within *arglist*, you can use an **As** clause to specify the data type of any of the arguments passed to the procedure.

> **Note** If the external procedure was created on a platform other than Visual Basic .NET, you must take care that the data types correspond. For example, if you declare a reference to a Visual Basic 6.0 procedure with an **Integer** argument (two bytes in Visual Basic 6.0), you must identify that argument as **Short** in the **Declare** statement, because that is the two-byte integer type in Visual Basic .NET.

Example

The following example declares a function that returns the current user name.

```
Declare Function GetUserName Lib "advapi32.dll" Alias _
"GetUserNameA" (ByVal lpBuffer As String, ByRef nSize As Integer) As Integer
Function GetUser()
   Dim RetVal As Integer
   Dim UserName As String
   Dim Buffer As String
   Buffer = New String(CChar(" "), 25)
   RetVal = GetUserName(Buffer, 25)
   UserName = Strings.Left(Buffer, InStr(Buffer, Chr(0)) - 1)
   MsgBox(UserName)
End Function
```

The **DllImport** attribute provides an alternative way of using functions in unmanaged code. The following example declares an imported function without using a **Declare** statement.

```
' Add an Imports statement at the top of the class or module
' where the DllImport attribute will be used.
Imports System.Runtime.InteropServices
'...
<DllImport("KERNEL32.DLL", EntryPoint:="MoveFileW", SetLastError:=True, _
CharSet:=CharSet.Unicode, ExactSpelling:=True, _
CallingConvention:=CallingConvention.StdCall)> _
Public Shared Function _
MoveFile(ByVal src As String, ByVal dst As String) As Boolean
    ' This function copies a file from the path src to the path dst.
    ' Leave function empty - DLLImport attribute forces calls
    ' to MoveFile to be forwarded to MoveFileW in KERNEL32.DLL.
End Function
```

See Also

AddressOf Operator, Call Statement, Function Statement, LastDLLError Property, Sub Statement

Default

The **Default** keyword identifies a property as the default property of its class.

The **Default** keyword is used in this context:

Property Statement

See Also

Visual Basic Language Keywords

Delegate Statement

Used to declare a delegate. Delegates are a reference type that refers to a **Shared** method of a type or to an instance method of an object. Any procedure with matching parameters types and return type may be used to create an instance of this delegate class. The procedure can then later be invoked via the delegate instance.

```
[ <attrlist> ] [ Public | Private | Protected | Friend | Protected Friend ] _
[ Shadows ] Delegate [ Sub ] name [([ arglist ])]
```

-or-

```
[ <attrlist> ] [ Public | Private | Protected | Friend | Protected Friend ] _
[ Shadows ] Delegate [ Function ] name [([ arglist ])] As type
```

Parts

attrlist

Optional. List of attributes that apply to this delegate. Multiple attributes are separated by commas.

Public

Optional. Entities declared with the **Public** modifier have public access. There are no restrictions on the use of public entities.

Private

Optional. Entities declared with the **Private** modifier have private access. A private entity is accessible only within its declaration context, including any nested entities.

Protected

Optional. Entities declared with the **Protected** keyword have protected access. They are accessible only from within their own class or from a derived class. Protected access can be specified only on members of classes. It is not a superset of friend access.

Friend

Optional. Entities declared with the **Friend** modifier have friend access. An entity with friend access is accessible only within the program that contains the entity declaration.

Protected Friend

Optional. Entities declared with the **Protected Friend** modifiers have the union of protected and friend accessibility.

Shadows

Optional. Indicates that this delegate shadows an identically named programming element in a base class. You can shadow any kind of declared element with any other kind. A shadowed element is unavailable in the derived class that shadows it

Sub

Optional, but either **Sub** or **Function** must appear. Declares this procedure as a delegate subroutine that does not return a value.

Function

Optional, but either **Sub** or **Function** must appear. Declares this procedure as a delegate function that returns a value.

name

Required. Name of the delegate type; follows standard variable naming conventions.

arglist

Optional. List of variables representing arguments that are passed to the procedure when it is called.

type

Optional. Data type of the return value.

Each attribute in the *attrlist* part has the following syntax and parts:

```
attrname [({ attrargs | attrinit })]
```

attrlist Parts

attrname

Required. Name of the attribute. Must be a valid Visual Basic identifier.

attrargs

Optional. List of positional arguments for this attribute. Multiple arguments are separated by commas.

attrinit

Optional. List of field or property initializers for this attribute. Multiple initializers are separated by commas.

Each argument in the *arglist* part has the following syntax and parts:

```
[ <attrlist> ] [ ByVal | ByRef ] varname[( )] [ As type ]
```

arglist Parts

attrlist

Optional. List of attributes that apply to this argument. Multiple attributes are separated by commas.

ByVal

Optional. Indicates that the argument is passed by value. **ByVal** is the default in Visual Basic.

ByRef

Optional. Indicates that the argument is passed by reference.

varname

Required. Name of the variable representing the argument being passed to the procedure; follows standard variable naming conventions.

( )

Required for array variables. Indicates that *varname* is an array.

type

Optional. Data type of the argument passed to the procedure; may be **Byte**, **Boolean**, **Char**, **Short**, **Integer**, **Long**, **Single**, **Double**, **Decimal**, **Date**, **String** (variable length only), **Object**, a user-defined type, or an object type.

Remarks

The **Delegate** statement defines the parameter types and return type of a delegate class. Any procedure with matching parameters types and return type may be used to create an instance of this delegate class. The procedure can then later be invoked via the delegate instance, by calling the delegate's **Invoke** method.

Each delegate class defines a constructor that is passed the specification of an object method. The only thing that can be legally specified as an argument to such a delegate constructor is an expression of the form:

```
AddressOf [<expression>.]<methodname>
```

The compile-time type of the *expression* must be the name of a class or an interface that contains a method of the specified name whose signature matches the signature of the delegate class. The *methodname* can be either a shared method or an instance method. The *methodname* is not optional even if you create a delegate for the default method of the class.

Example

This example uses the **Delegate** statement to declare a delegate for comparing two integers and returning a Boolean. The `SelectionSort` method takes an instance of a delegate of this type and uses it to sort an integer array.

```
Public Class SortClass
   Delegate Function Compare(ByVal x As Integer, _
                              ByVal y As Integer) As Boolean

   Function CompareValues(ByVal X As Integer, _
                           ByVal Y As Integer) As Boolean
      If X > Y Then
         CompareValues = True
      Else
         CompareValues = False
      End If
   End Function

   Sub SelectionSort(ByVal IsGreaterThan As Compare, _
                     ByVal IntArray() As Integer)
      Dim MaxVal As Integer
      Dim MaxIndex As Integer
      Dim i, j As Integer

      ' Step through the elements in the array starting with the
      ' last element in the array.
      For i = UBound(IntArray) To 1 Step -1
         MaxVal = IntArray(i)
         MaxIndex = i
         For j = 1 To i
            ' Use the delegate to compare values.
            If IsGreaterThan.Invoke(IntArray(j), MaxVal) Then
               MaxVal = IntArray(j)
               MaxIndex = j
            End If
         Next j
```

```
         ' Use the delegate to compare values.
         If IsGreaterThan.Invoke(i, MaxIndex) Then
            IntArray(MaxIndex) = IntArray(i)
            IntArray(i) = MaxVal
         End If
      Next i
   End Sub
End Class

Class Class1
   Sub SortArray()
      Dim Sort As New SortClass()
      Dim arr1() As Integer = {1, 5, 3, 2, 7, 22, 5, 54, 12}
      Sort.SelectionSort(AddressOf Sort.CompareValues, arr1)
      MsgBox("Array sorted.")
   End Sub
End Class

' Add a button to your main form and insert the following code
' into the Click event handlr.
   Private Sub Button1_Click(ByVal sender As System.Object, _
                             ByVal e As System.EventArgs) _
                             Handles Button1.Click
      Dim c As New Class1()
      c.SortArray()
   End Sub
```

DeleteSetting Function

Deletes a section or key setting from an application's entry in the Windows registry.

```
Public Sub DeleteSetting( _
   ByVal AppName As String, _
   Optional ByVal Section As String = Nothing, _
   Optional ByVal Key As String = Nothing _
)
```

Parameters

AppName

Required. **String** expression containing the name of the application or project to which the section or key setting applies.

Section

Required. **String** expression containing the name of the section from which the key setting is being deleted. If only *AppName* and *Section* are provided, the specified section is deleted along with all related key settings.

Key

Optional. **String** expression containing the name of the key setting being deleted.

Exceptions/Errors

Exception type	Error number	Condition
ArgumentException	5	*Section, AppName,* or *Key* setting does not exist.
ArgumentException	5	User is not logged in.

Remarks

If all arguments are provided, the specified setting is deleted. A run-time error occurs if you attempt to use **DeleteSetting** on a nonexistent section or key setting.

DeleteSetting requires that a user be logged on since it operates under the HKEY_LOCAL_USER registry key, which is not active until a user logs on interactively.

Registry settings that are to be accessed from a non-interactive process (such as mtx.exe) should be stored under either the HKEY_LOCAL_MACHINE\Software\ or the HKEY_USER\DEFAULT\Software registry keys.

Example

The following example first uses the **SaveSetting** procedure to make entries in the Windows registry for the `MyApp` application, and then uses the **DeleteSetting** statement to remove them. Because no *Key* argument is specified, the whole `Startup` section is deleted, including the section name and all of its keys.

```
' Place some settings in the registry.
SaveSetting("MyApp", "Startup", "Top", "75")
SaveSetting("MyApp","Startup", "Left", "50")
' Remove section and all its settings from registry.
DeleteSetting ("MyApp", "Startup")
' Remove MyApp from the registry.
DeleteSetting ("MyApp")
```

See Also

GetAllSettings Function, GetSetting Function, SaveSetting Function

Derived Math Functions

The following is a list of non-intrinsic math functions that can be derived from the intrinsic math functions:

Function	Derived equivalents
Secant (Sec(x))	1 / **Cos**(x)
Cosecant (Csc(x))	1 / **Sin**(x)
Cotangent (Ctan(x))	1 / **Tan**(x)
Inverse sine (Asin(x))	**Atan**(x / **Sqrt**(-x * x + 1))
Inverse cosine (Acos(x))	**Atan**(-x / **Sqrt**(-x * x + 1)) + 2 * **Atan**(1)
Inverse secant (Asec(x))	2 * **Atan**(1) - **Atan**(**Sign**(x) / **Sqrt**(x * x - 1))
Inverse cosecant (Acsc(x))	**Atan**(**Sign**(x) / **Sqrt**(x * x - 1))
Inverse cotangent (Acot(x))	2 * **Atan**(1) - **Atan**(x)
Hyperbolic sine (Sinh(x))	(**Exp**(x) - **Exp**(-x)) / 2
Hyperbolic cosine (Cosh(x))	(**Exp**(x) + **Exp**(-x)) / 2
Hyperbolic tangent (Tanh(x))	(**Exp**(x) - **Exp**(-x)) / (**Exp**(x) + **Exp**(-x))
Hyperbolic secant (Sech(x))	2 / (**Exp**(x) + **Exp**(-x))
Hyperbolic cosecant (Csch(x))	2 / (**Exp**(x) - **Exp**(-x))
Hyperbolic cotangent (Coth(x))	(**Exp**(x) + **Exp**(-x)) / (**Exp**(x) - **Exp**(-x))
Inverse hyperbolic sine (Asinh(x))	**Log**(x + **Sqrt**(x * x + 1))
Inverse hyperbolic cosine (Acosh(x))	**Log**(x + **Sqrt**(x * x - 1))
Inverse hyperbolic tangent (Atanh(x))	**Log**((1 + x) / (1 - x)) / 2
Inverse hyperbolic secant (AsecH(x))	**Log**((**Sqrt**(-x * x + 1) + 1) / x)
Inverse hyperbolic cosecant (Acsch(x))	**Log**((**Sign**(x) * **Sqrt**(x * x + 1) + 1) / x)
Inverse hyperbolic cotangent (Acoth(x))	**Log**((x + 1) / (x - 1)) / 2

See Also

Math Functions

Description Property

Returns or sets a **String** expression containing a descriptive string associated with an error. Read/write.

For the **Err** object, returns or sets a descriptive string associated with an error.

```
Public Property Description() As String
```

Remarks

The **Description** property setting consists of a short description of the error. Use this property to alert the user to an error that you can't or don't want to handle. When generating a user-defined error, assign a short description of your error to the **Description** property. If the **Description** property isn't filled in, and the value of the Number property corresponds to a Visual Basic run-time error, then the string returned by the ErrorToString function is set in the **Description** property when the error is generated.

Example

This example assigns a user-defined message to the **Description** property of the **Err** object.

```
On Error Resume Next
Err.Raise(60000)
Err.Description = "Your Widget needs a new Frob!"
MsgBox(Err.Description)
```

See Also

ErrorToString Function, HelpContext Property, HelpFile Property, LastDLLError Property, Number Property, Source Property

Applies To

Err Object

Different Formats for Different Numeric Values (Format Function)

A user-defined format expression for numbers can have from one to three sections separated by semicolons. If the style argument of the **Format** function contains one of the Predefined Numeric Formats, only one section is allowed.

If you use	This is the result
One section only	The format expression applies to all values.
Two sections	The first section applies to positive values and zeros; the second applies to negative values.
Three sections	The first section applies to positive values, the second applies to negative values, and the third applies to zeros.

The following example has two sections: the first defines the format for positive values and zeros; the second section defines the format for negative values. Since the *Style* argument of the **Format** function takes a string, it is enclosed by quotation marks.

```
"$#,##0;($#,##0)"
```

If you include semicolons with nothing between them, the missing section is printed using the format of the positive value. For example, the following format displays positive and negative values using the format in the first section and displays `Zero` if the value is zero.

```
"$#,##0;;\Z\e\r\o"
```

See Also

Format Function

Dim Statement

Used at module, class, structure, procedure, or block level to declare and allocate storage space for variables.

```
[ <attrlist> ] [{ Public | Protected | Friend | Protected Friend |
Private | Static }] [ Shared ] [ Shadows ] [ ReadOnly ]
Dim [ WithEvents ] name[ (boundlist) ] [ As [ New ] type ] [ = initexpr ]
```

Parts

attrlist

Optional. List of attributes that apply to the variables declared in this statement. Multiple attributes are separated by commas.

Public

Optional. Variables declared with the **Public** keyword have public access. There are no restrictions on the accessibility of public variables.

You can use **Public** only at module, namespace, or file level. This means you can declare public variables in a source file or inside a module, class, or structure, but not inside a procedure. If you specify **Public**, you can optionally omit the **Dim** keyword.

Protected

Optional. Variables declared with the **Protected** keyword have protected access. They are accessible only from within their own class or from a derived class. Protected access is not a superset of friend access.

You can use **Protected** only at class level. This means you can declare protected variables inside a class but not inside a procedure, and not at module, namespace, or file level. You can use **Protected** only to declare members of the class. If you specify **Protected**, you can optionally omit the **Dim** keyword.

Friend

Optional. Variables declared with the **Friend** keyword have friend access. They are accessible from within the program that contains their declaration and from anywhere else in the same assembly.

You can use **Friend** only at module, namespace, or file level. This means you can declare friend variables in a source file or inside a module, class, or structure, but not inside a procedure. If you specify **Friend**, you can optionally omit the **Dim** keyword.

Protected Friend

Optional. Variables declared with the **Protected Friend** keywords have the union of protected and friend access. They can be used by code anywhere in the same assembly, by code in their own class, and by code in any derived classes.

You can use **Protected Friend** only at class level. This means you can declare protected friend variables inside a class but not inside a procedure, and not at module, namespace, or file level. You can use **Protected Friend** only to declare members of the class. If you specify **Protected Friend**, you can optionally omit the **Dim** keyword.

Private

Optional. Variables declared with the **Private** keyword have private access. They are accessible only from within their declaration context, including from members of any nested types such as procedures.

You can use **Private** only at module level. This means you can declare private variables inside a module, class, or structure, but not at namespace or file level and not inside a procedure. If you specify **Private**, you can optionally omit the **Dim** keyword.

Static

Optional. Variables declared with the **Static** keyword remain in existence and retain their latest values after termination of the procedure in which they are declared.

You can use **Static** only at procedure level. This means you can declare static variables inside a procedure or a block within a procedure, but not at class or module level. If you specify **Static**, you can optionally omit the **Dim** keyword.

You cannot specify **Static** together with either **Shared** or **Shadows** in the same variable declaration.

Shared

Optional. Indicates that this variable is shared. This means it is not associated with a specific instance of a class or structure. You can access a shared variable by qualifying it either with the class or structure name, or with the variable name of a specific instance of the class or structure.

You can use **Shared** only at module, namespace, or file level. This means you can declare shared variables in a source file or inside a module, class, or structure, but not inside a procedure. If you specify **Shared**, you can optionally omit the **Dim** keyword.

You cannot specify both **Static** and **Shared** in the same variable declaration.

Shadows

Optional. Indicates that this variable shadows an identically named programming element, or set of overloaded elements, in a base class. You can shadow any kind of declared element with any other kind. A shadowed element is unavailable in the derived class that shadows it.

You can use **Shadows** only at module, namespace, or file level. This means you can declare shadowing variables in a source file or inside a module, class, or structure, but not inside a procedure. If you specify **Shadows**, you can optionally omit the **Dim** keyword.

You cannot specify both **Static** and **Shadows** in the same variable declaration.

ReadOnly

Optional. Variables declared with the **ReadOnly** keyword can only be read and not written. This can be useful for creating constant members of reference types, such as an object variable with preset data members.

You can use **ReadOnly** only at module, namespace, or file level. This means you can declare read-only variables in a source file or inside a module, class, or structure, but not inside a procedure. If you specify **ReadOnly**, you can optionally omit the **Dim** keyword.

WithEvents

Optional. Keyword that specifies that *name* is an object variable that refers to an instance of a class that can raise events. You can declare as many individual variables as you like using **WithEvents**, but you cannot declare arrays this way.

If you use the **WithEvents** keyword, you cannot declare *name* as **Object**. You must declare it as the specific class that can raise the events.

name

Required. Name of the variable. Must be a valid Visual Basic identifier. You can declare as many variables as you like in the same declaration statement, specifying the *name* part for each one and supplying the *boundlist* part for arrays. Multiple variables are separated by commas.

You can declare several variables to be of the same data type. You can also specify different types for different variables or groups of variables. Each variable takes the data type specified in the first **As** clause encountered after its *name* part.

boundlist

Optional. List of non-negative integers representing the upper bounds of the dimensions of an array variable. Multiple upper bounds are separated by commas. An array can have up to 60 dimensions.

Each value in *boundlist* specifies the upper bound of a dimension, not the length. The lower bound is always zero, so the subscript for each dimension can vary from zero through the upper-bound value.

It is possible to use –1 to declare the upper bound of an array dimension. This signifies that the array is empty but not **Nothing**, a distinction required by certain common language runtime functions. However, Visual Basic code cannot successfully access such an array. If you attempt to do so, an **IndexOutOfRangeException** error occurs during execution.

New

Optional. Keyword that enables immediate creation of an object. If you use **New** when declaring the object variable, a new instance of the object is created when the **Dim** statement is executed.

type

Optional unless **Option Strict** is **On**. Data type of the variable. Can be **Boolean**, **Byte**, **Char**, **Date**, **Decimal**, **Double**, **Integer**, **Long**, **Object**, **Short**, **Single**, or **String**; or the name of an enumeration, structure, class, or interface. You can use a separate **As** clause for each variable being defined, or you can define several variables to be of the same type by using a common **As** clause.

If you do not specify *type*, the variable takes the data type of *initexpr*. If you do specify *type*, the data type of *initexpr* must be convertible to *type*. If neither *type* nor *initexpr* is present, the data type defaults to **Object**.

initexpr

Optional. Expression that is evaluated and assigned to the variable when it is created. If you declare more than one variable with the same **As** clause, you cannot supply *initexpr* for that group of variables.

Each attribute in the *attrlist* part has the following syntax and parts:

```
attrname [({ attrargs | attrinit })]
```

attrlist Parts

attrname

Required. Name of the attribute. Must be a valid Visual Basic identifier.

attrargs

Optional. List of positional arguments for this attribute. Multiple arguments are separated by commas.

attrinit

Optional. List of field or property initializers for this attribute. Multiple initializers are separated by commas.

Remarks

Variables declared with **Dim** are available to all code within the region containing the **Dim** statement. If they are declared in a module, class, or structure, but outside any procedure, they can be accessed from anywhere within that module, class, or structure. If they are declared inside a procedure or a block, they are accessible only from within that procedure or block. To specify their accessibility in more detail, include the **Public**, **Protected**, **Friend**, **Protected Friend**, **Private**, or **Static** keywords.

The **Dim** statement can declare the data type of a variable and initialize its contents. The declaration statements in the following example declare an **Integer** variable, a **Boolean** variable, and an object variable. These are initialized, respectively, to 10, **True**, and a newly created instance of the **Label** class.

```
Dim Quantity As Integer = 10
Private FirstTry As Boolean = True
Protected MyLabel As New Label
```

If you do not specify an initialization value for a variable, Visual Basic initializes it to the default value for its data type. The default initialization values are as follows:

- 0 for all numeric types (including **Byte**).
- Binary 0 for **Char.**
- **Nothing** for all reference types (including **Object**, **String**, and all arrays).
- **False** for **Boolean.**
- 12:00 AM of January 1 of the year 1 for **Date.**

Each element of a structure or array is initialized as if it were a separate variable.

You can initialize the values of an array by surrounding the initialization values with braces ({}). The following example creates an array with four elements:

```
Friend A() As Integer = {0, 1, 2, 3}
```

For multidimensional arrays, each separate dimension is surrounded with braces. The elements are specified in row-major order. The following example illustrates this:

```
' Initialize each array element to its row index + its column index.
Public A( , ) As Integer = {{0+0, 0+1, 0+2}, {1+0 ,1+1, 1+2}}
```

> **Note** You should put all your declaration statements at the beginning of the code region in which they appear, for example a module or a procedure. If a declaration statement initializes the value of a variable, it should be executed before any other statement makes reference to the variable.

A public variable can be either early bound or late bound. Protected, friend, and private variables cannot be late bound. This means you cannot access members on a late-bound object variable unless it is declared **Public**. If you attempt to do this, the compiler does not generate an error, but a **MissingMemberException** error occurs at run time.

A static variable has a longer lifetime than that of the procedure in which it is declared. The boundaries of the variable's lifetime depend on where the procedure is declared and whether or not it is **Shared**.

- If the procedure is declared in a module, its static variables are initialized the first time the procedure is called, and they continue to exist until your program terminates execution.
- If the procedure is declared as **Shared** within a class or structure, its static variables are initialized the first time the procedure is called either on a specific instance or on the class or structure itself. They remain in existence until the program terminates.
- If the procedure is declared within a class or structure and is not **Shared**, its static variables are associated with each individual instance of the class or structure. They are initialized the first time the procedure is called in that instance, and they continue to exist until that instance is released.

Example

This example uses the **Dim** statement to declare variables and arrays. The lower bound for array subscripts is always 0, and the upper bound is the value that appears in the **Dim** statement.

```
' Declarations do not have to initialize their variables.
' AnyValue and MyValue are initialized by default to Nothing.
Dim AnyValue, MyValue As Object
' Number is initialized by default to 0.
Dim Number As Integer
' Multiple declarations can be of the same data type or different types.
Dim FirstNumber, SecondNumber, ThirdNumber As Integer
Dim MyDate As Date, MyValue As Single, MySwitch As Boolean
' DayArray is an array of 51 Objects indexed from 0 through 50.
Dim DayArray(50) As Object
' Matrix2 is a two-dimensional array of type Integer.
Dim Matrix2(3, 4) As Integer
' Matrix3 is a three-dimensional array of type Double.
Dim Matrix3(5, 9, 5) As Double
' BirthDay is an array of 11 dates indexed from 0 through 10.
Dim BirthDay(10) As Date
' MyArray is an array of objects. The length of the array is assigned
' when another statement assigns an array object to MyArray.
Dim MyArray() As Object
```

See Also

Const Statement, ReDim Statement

Dir Function

Returns a string representing the name of a file, directory, or folder that matches a specified pattern or file attribute, or the volume label of a drive.

```
Public Overloads Function Dir() As String
```

-or-

```
Public Overloads Function Dir( _
   Optional ByVal PathName As String, _
   Optional ByVal Attributes As FileAttribute = FileAttribute.Normal _
) As String
```

Parameters

PathName
: Optional. **String** expression that specifies a file name, directory or folder name, or drive volume label. A zero-length string (" ") is returned if *PathName* is not found.

Attributes
: Optional. Enumeration or numeric expression whose value specifies file attributes. If omitted, returns files that match *PathName,* but have no attributes.

Settings

The *Attributes* argument enumeration values are as follows:

Value	Constant	Description
Normal	**vbnormal**	Default. Specifies files with no attributes.
ReadOnly	**vbReadOnly**	Specifies read-only files in addition to files with no attributes.
Hidden	**vbHidden**	Specifies hidden files in addition to files with no attributes.
System	**vbSystem**	Specifies system files in addition to files with no attributes.
Volume	**vbVolume**	Specifies volume label; if any other attribute is specified, **vbVolume** is ignored.
Directory	**vbDirectory**	Specifies directories or folders in addition to files with no attributes.
Archive	**vbArchive**	File has changed since last backup.
Alias	**vbAlias**	File has a different name.

Note These enumerations are specified by the Visual Basic language and can be used anywhere in your code in place of the actual values.

Remarks

The **Dir** function supports the use of multiple-character (*) and single-character (?) wildcards to specify multiple files.

You must supply a **PathName** the first time you call the **Dir** function. Subsequent calls to the **Dir** function may be made with no parameters to retrieve the next item.

Example

This example uses the **Dir** function to check if certain files and directories exist.

```
Dim MyFile, MyPath, MyName
' Returns "WIN.INI" if it exists.
MyFile = Dir("C:\WINDOWS\WIN.INI")

' Returns filename with specified extension. If more than one *.INI
' file exists, the first file found is returned.
MyFile = Dir("C:\WINDOWS\*.INI")

' Call Dir again without arguments to return the next *.INI file in the
' same directory.
MyFile = Dir()

' Return first *.TXT file, including files with a set hidden attribute.
MyFile = Dir("*.TXT", vbHidden)

' Display the names in C:\ that represent directories.
MyPath = "c:\"   ' Set the path.
MyName = Dir(MyPath, vbDirectory)   ' Retrieve the first entry.
Do While MyName <> ""   ' Start the loop.
      ' Use bitwise comparison to make sure MyName is a directory.
      If (GetAttr(MyPath & MyName) And vbDirectory) = vbDirectory Then
         ' Display entry only if it's a directory.
         Debug.WriteLine(MyName)
      End If
   MyName = Dir()   ' Get next entry.
Loop
```

See Also

ChDir Function, CurDir Function

DirectCast

The **DirectCast** keyword introduces a type conversion operation. You use it the same way you use the **CType** keyword, as the following example shows:

```
Dim Q As Object = 2.37   ' Requires Option Strict to be Off.
Dim I As Integer = CType(Q, Integer)   ' Succeeds.
Dim J As Integer = DirectCast(Q, Integer)   ' Fails.
```

Both keywords take an expression to be converted as the first argument, and the type to convert it to as the second argument. Both conversions fail if there is no conversion defined between the data type of the expression and the data type specified as the second argument.

The difference between the two keywords is that **CType** succeeds as long as there is a valid conversion defined between the expression and the type, whereas **DirectCast** requires the run-time type of an object variable to be the same as the specified type. If the specified type and the run-time type of the expression are the same, however, the run-time performance of **DirectCast** is better than that of **CType**.

In the preceding example, the run-time type of `Q` is **Double**. **CType** succeeds because **Double** can be converted to **Integer**, but **DirectCast** fails because the run-time type of `Q` is not already **Integer**.

DirectCast throws an **InvalidCastException** error if the argument types do not match.

Do...Loop Statements

Repeats a block of statements while a **Boolean** condition is **True** or until the condition becomes **True**.

```
Do { While | Until } condition
   [ statements ]
[ Exit Do ]
   [ statements ]
Loop
```

-or-

```
Do
   [ statements ]
[ Exit Do ]
   [ statements ]
Loop { While | Until } condition
```

Parts

While
Required unless **Until** is used. Keyword. Repeat the loop until *condition* is **False**.

Until
Required unless **While** is used. Keyword. Repeat the loop until *condition* is **True**.

condition
Optional. **Boolean**. Expression that evaluates to a value of **True** or **False**.

statements
Optional. One or more statements that are repeated while, or until, *condition* is **True**.

Remarks

The **Exit Do** statement transfers control immediately to the statement following the **Loop** statement. Any number of **Exit Do** statements can be placed anywhere in the **Do** loop. **Exit Do** is often used after evaluating some condition, for example with **If...Then...Else**.

Example

This example shows how **Do...Loop** statements can be used. The inner **Do...Loop** statement loops 10 times, sets the value of the flag to **False**, and exits prematurely using the **Exit Do** statement. The outer loop exits immediately upon checking the value of the flag.

```
Dim Check As Boolean = True
Dim Counter As Integer = 0
Do   ' Outer loop.
   Do While Counter < 20   ' Inner loop.
      Counter += 1   ' Increment Counter.
      If Counter = 10 Then   ' If condition is True,
         Check = False   ' Set value of flag to False.
         Exit Do   ' Exit inner loop.
      End If
   Loop
Loop Until Check = False   ' Exit outer loop immediately.
```

See Also

Exit Statement, For...Next Statements, Do...Loop Statements (Conceptual), While...End While Statements

Double Data Type

Double variables are stored as signed IEEE 64-bit (8-byte) double-precision floating-point numbers ranging in value from –1.79769313486231570E+308 through –4.94065645841246544E–324 for negative values and from 4.94065645841246544E–324 through 1.79769313486231570E+308 for positive values.

> **Note** The **Double** data type can be converted to the **Decimal** data type without encountering a **System.OverflowException** error.

Appending the literal type character **R** to a literal forces it to the **Double** data type. Appending the identifier type character **#** to any identifier forces it to **Double**.

The equivalent .NET data type is **System.Double**.

See Also

Data Type Summary, Single Data Type, Type Conversion Functions, Conversion Summary, Efficient Use of Data Types

DueDate Enumeration

When you call date-related functions, you can use enumeration members in your code in place of the actual values.

The **DueDate** enumeration defines constants used to identify where a due date falls within a date interval. The following table lists the **DueDate** enumeration members.

Member	Description
DueDate.BegOfPeriod	Falls at the beginning of the date interval.
DueDate.EndOfPeriod	Falls at the end of the date interval.

See Also

DateInterval Enumeration, DatePart Function, DateAdd Function, DateDiff Function

Each

The **Each** keyword specifies the loop variable to be used in a **For Each** loop.

The **Each** keyword is used in this context:

For Each...Next Statements

See Also

Visual Basic Language Keywords

Else

The **Else** keyword introduces a group of statements to be executed if no other conditional group of statements has been executed.

The **Else** keyword is used in these contexts:

If...Then...Else Statements

Select...Case Statements

See Also

Visual Basic Language Keywords

ElseIf

The **ElseIf** keyword introduces a condition to be tested if the previous conditional test has failed.

The **ElseIf** keyword is used in this context:

If...Then...Else Statements

See Also

Visual Basic Language Keywords

End

When used with an additional keyword, **End** indicates the end of the definition of a procedure or block.

```
End Class
End Enum
End Function
End Get
End If
End Interface
End Module
End Namespace
End Property
End Select
End Set
End Structure
End Sub
End SyncLock
End Try
End While
End With
```

Parts

End
Required. Terminates the definition of the procedure or block.

Class
Required to end a **Class** definition.

Enum
Required to end an **Enum** definition.

Function
Required to end a **Function** procedure definition. If execution encounters an **End Function** statement, control is returned to the calling code.

Get
Required to end a **Property** procedure definition to retrieve the property's value. If execution encounters an **End Get** statement, control is returned to the statement requesting the value.

If
Required to end the definition of the **If…Then…Else** statements.

Interface
Required to end an **Interface** definition.

Module
Required to end a **Module** definition.

Namespace
Required to end a **Namespace** definition.

Property
Required to end a **Property** definition.

Select
Required to end the definition of the **Select...Case** statements.

Set
Required to end a **Property** procedure definition to set the property's value. If execution encounters an **End Set** statement, control is returned to the statement setting the value.

Structure
Required to end a **Structure** definition.

Sub
Required to end a **Sub** procedure definition. If execution encounters an **End Sub** statement, control is returned to the calling code.

SyncLock
Required to end the definition of the **SyncLock...End SyncLock** statements.

Try
Required to end the definition of the **Try…Catch…Finally** statements.

While
Required to end the definition of the **While** statement.

With
Required to end the definition of the **With...End With** statements.

Remarks

The **End** statement, without an additional keyword, terminates execution immediately.

See Also

End Statement, Class Statement, Enum Statement, Function Statement, If...Then...Else Statements, Interface Statement, Module Statement, Namespace Statement, Property Statement, Select...Case Statements, Structure Statement, Sub Statement, SyncLock Statement, Try...Catch...Finally Statements, While...End While Statements, With...End With Statements

End Statement

Terminates execution immediately.

```
End
```

Remarks

The **End** statement can be placed anywhere in a procedure to end code execution, close files opened with an **Open** statement, and clear variables. The **End** statement calls the **Exit** method of the **Environment** class in the **System** namespace. **System.Environment.Exit** requires that you have **SecurityPermissionFlag.UnmanagedCode** permissions. If you do not, a **SecurityException** error occurs.

When executed, the **End** statement clears all variables at module and class level and all static local variables in all modules.

> **Note** The **End** statement stops code execution abruptly, without invoking the **Finalize** method or any other Visual Basic code. Object references held by other programs are invalidated.

The **End** statement provides a way to force your program to halt. For normal termination of a Visual Basic program, you should unload all forms. Your program closes as soon as there are no other programs holding references to objects created and no code executing.

With an additional keyword, **End** delineates the end of the definition of the appropriate procedure or block.

Example

This example uses the **End** Statement to end code execution if the user enters an invalid password.

```
Sub Form_Load()
   Dim Password, Pword As String
   PassWord = "Swordfish"
   Pword = InputBox("Type in your password")
   If Pword <> PassWord Then
      MsgBox ("Sorry, incorrect password")
      End
   End If
End Sub
```

See Also

End

Enum Statement

Used at module, class, or structure level to declare an enumeration and define the values of its members.

```
[ <attrlist> ] [{ Public | Protected | Friend | Protected Friend |
Private }] [ Shadows ] Enum name [ As type ]
   [<attrlist1>] membname1 [ = initexpr1 ]
   [<attrlist2>] membname2 [ = initexpr2 ]
...
   [<attrlistn>] membnamen [ = initexprn ]
End Enum
```

Parts

attrlist
: Optional. List of attributes that apply to the enumeration or to this member. Multiple attributes are separated by commas.

Public
: Optional. Enumerations declared with the **Public** keyword have public access. There are no restrictions on the accessibility of public enumerations.

Protected
: Optional. Enumerations declared with the **Protected** keyword have protected access. They are accessible only from within their own class or from a derived class. Protected access can be specified only on members of classes. It is not a superset of friend access.

Friend
: Optional. Enumerations declared with the **Friend** keyword have friend access. They are accessible from within the program that contains their declaration and from anywhere else in the same assembly.

Protected Friend
: Optional. Enumerations declared with the **Protected Friend** keywords have the union of protected and friend access. They can be used by code in the same assembly, as well as by code in derived classes. Protected friend access can be specified only on members of classes.

Private
: Optional. Enumerations declared with the **Private** keyword have private access. They are accessible only from within their declaration context, including from members of any nested types such as procedures.

Shadows

Optional. Indicates that this enumeration shadows an identically named programming element, or set of overloaded elements, in a base class. You can shadow any kind of declared element with any other kind. A shadowed element is unavailable in the derived class that shadows it.

name

Required. Name of the enumeration. Must be a valid Visual Basic identifier. When you subsequently declare variables or arguments to be of this **Enum** type, you specify *name* for their data type.

type

Optional, even if **Option Strict** is **On**. Data type of the enumeration and all of its members. Can be **Byte**, **Integer**, **Long**, or **Short**. If you do not specify *type*, it defaults to **Integer**.

membname

Required. Name of this member of the enumeration. Must be a valid Visual Basic identifier.

The accessibility of every member is **Public**, and you cannot declare it otherwise. However, if the enumeration itself is declared with **Protected**, **Friend**, **Protected Friend**, or **Private** access, this limits the accessibility of the members.

initexpr

Optional. Expression that is evaluated and assigned to this member when the enumeration is created. Can consist of a literal; a constant that is already defined; another enumeration member; or any combination of literals, constants, and enumeration members. You can use arithmetic and logical operators to combine such elements.

You cannot use variables or functions in *initexpr*. However, you can use conversion keywords such as **CByte** and **CShort**. You can also use **AscW** if you call it with a constant **String** or **Char** argument, since that can be evaluated at compile time.

If you do not specify *initexpr*, the value assigned is either zero (if it is the first *membname*), or greater by one than the value of the immediately preceding *membname*.

End Enum

Terminates an **Enum** block.

Each attribute in the *attrlist* part has the following syntax and parts:

```
attrname [({ attrargs | attrinit })]
```

attrlist Parts

attrname

Required. Name of the attribute. Must be a valid Visual Basic identifier.

attrargs

Optional. List of positional arguments for this attribute. Multiple arguments are separated by commas.

attrinit

Optional. List of field or property initializers for this attribute. Multiple initializers are separated by commas.

Remarks

The **Enum** statement can appear only at module, namespace, or file level. This means you can declare enumerations in a source file or inside a module, class, or structure, but not inside a procedure. Once the **Enum** type is defined, it can be used to declare the type of variables, procedure arguments, and **Function** returns.

Enumerations can be accessed from anywhere within the module, class, or structure in which they are declared. An enumeration and all its members are **Public** by default. To specify the accessibility in more detail, include **Public**, **Protected**, **Friend**, **Protected Friend**, or **Private** in the **Enum** statement. The accessibility you specify applies to all the members as well as to the enumeration itself.

An enumeration is a related set of constants. The enumeration members between the **Enum** and **End Enum** statements are initialized to constant values. The defined values cannot be modified at run time. Values can include both positive and negative numbers, as the following example shows:

```
Enum SecurityLevel
   IllegalEntry = -1
   MinimumSecurity = 0
   MaximumSecurity = 1
End Enum
```

If the value of a member exceeds the allowable range for the underlying data type, or if you initialize any member to the maximum value allowed by the underlying data type, the compiler reports an error.

Enumeration variables are variables declared to be of an **Enum** type. Declaring a variable in this way helps you to control the values you assign to it. If **Option Strict** is **On**, you can assign only enumeration members to the enumeration variable. In this case, you can use the **CType** keyword to explicitly convert a numeric data type to an **Enum** type.

You must qualify every reference to an enumeration member, either with the name of an enumeration variable or with the enumeration name itself. For example, in the preceding example, you can refer to the first member as `SecurityLevel.IllegalEntry`, but not as `IllegalEntry`.

Example

This example uses the **Enum** statement to define a set of named constants. In this case, the constants are colors you might choose to design data entry forms for a database.

```
Public Enum InterfaceColors
   MistyRose   = &HE1E4FF&
   SlateGray   = &H908070&
   DodgerBlue  = &HFF901E&
   DeepSkyBlue = &HFFBF00&
   SpringGreen = &H7FFF00&
   ForestGreen = &H228B22&
   Goldenrod   = &H20A5DA&
   Firebrick   = &H2222B2&
End Enum
```

See Also

Const Statement, Dim Statement, Type Conversion Functions, Asc, AscW Functions

Environ Function

Returns the string associated with an operating system environment variable.

```
Overloads Function Environ(ByVal Expression As Integer) As String
```

-or-

```
Overloads Function Environ(ByVal Expression As String) As String
```

Parameter

Expression

Required. Expression that evaluates to either a string containing the name of an environment variable, or an integer corresponding to the numeric order of an environment string in the environment-string table.

Exceptions/Errors

Exception type	Error number	Condition
ArgumentException	5	*Expression* is missing.

Remarks

If *Expression* contains a string, the **Environ** function returns the text assigned to the specified environment string; that is, the text following the equal sign (=) in the environment-string table for that environment variable. If the string in *Expression* cannot be found in the environment-string table, a zero-length string (" ") is returned.

If *Expression* contains an integer, the string occupying that numeric position in the environment-string table is returned. In this case, **Environ** returns all of the text, including the name of the environment variable. If there is no environment string in the specified position, **Environ** returns a zero-length string.

Example

This example uses the **Environ** function to supply the entry number and length of the PATH statement from the environment-string table.

```
Sub tenv()
   Dim envString As String
   Dim found As Boolean = False
   Dim index As Integer = 1
   Dim pathLength As Integer
   Dim message As String

   envString = Environ(index)
   While Not found And (envString <> "")
      If (envString.Substring(0, 5) = "Path=") Then
         found = True
      Else
         index += 1
         envString = Environ(index)
      End If
   End While

   If found Then
      pathLength = Environ("PATH").Length
      message = "PATH entry = " & index & " and length = " & pathLength
   Else
      message = "No PATH environment variable exists."
   End If

   MsgBox(message)
End Sub
```

See Also

Visual Basic Run-Time Library Members

EOF Function

Returns a Boolean value **True** when the end of a file opened for **Random** or sequential **Input** has been reached.

```
Public Function EOF(ByVal FileNumber As Integer) As Boolean
```

Parameter

FileNumber

Required. An **Integer** containing any valid file number.

Exceptions/Errors

Exception type	Error number	Condition
IOException	52	*FileNumber* does not exist.
IOException	54	File mode is invalid.

Remarks

Use **EOF** to avoid the error generated by attempting to get input past the end of a file.

The **EOF** function returns **False** until the end of the file has been reached. With files opened for **Random** or **Binary** access, **EOF** returns **False** until the last executed **FileGet** function is unable to read an entire record.

With files opened for **Binary** access, an attempt to read through the file using the **Input** function until **EOF** returns **True** generates an error. Use the **LOF** and **Loc** functions instead of **EOF** when reading binary files with **Input**, or use **Get** when using the **EOF** function. With files opened for **Output**, **EOF** always returns **True**.

Example

This example uses the **EOF** function to detect the end of a file. This example assumes that `TESTFILE` is a text file with a few lines of text.

```
Dim TextLine As String
FileOpen(1, "TESTFILE", OpenMode.Input)   ' Open file.
Do While Not EOF(1)   ' Loop until end of file.
   TextLine = LineInput(1)   ' Read line into variable.
   Debug.WriteLine(TextLine)   ' Print to the Command window.
Loop
FileClose(1)   ' Close file.
```

See Also

FileGet Function, Loc Function, LOF Function, FileOpen Function

Erase Statement

Used to release array variables and deallocate the memory used for their elements.

```
Erase arraylist
```

Parts

arraylist

Required. List of array variables to be erased. Multiple variables are separated by commas.

Remarks

The **Erase** statement can appear only at procedure level. This means you can release arrays inside a procedure but not at class or module level.

The **Erase** statement is equivalent to assigning **Nothing** to each array variable.

Example

This example uses the **Erase** statement to clear two arrays and free their memory (1000 and 100 storage elements respectively). The **ReDim** statement then assigns a new array instance to the three-dimensional array.

```
Dim Int3DArray(9, 9, 9), Int2DArray(9, 9) As Integer
' ...
Erase Int3DArray, Int2DArray
' ...
ReDim Int3DArray(4, 4, 9)
```

See Also

Nothing, ReDim Statement

Erl Property

Returns an integer indicating the line number of the last executed statement. Read-only.

```
Public ReadOnly Property Erl() As Integer
```

Remarks

If Visual Basic encounters no line numbers, it returns 0.

Example

This example uses the **Erl** property to indicate the line number.

```
10:      On Error Resume Next
20:      Err.Raise(60000)
' Returns 20.
30:      MsgBox(Erl())
```

See Also

ErrorToString Function

Applies To

Err Object

Err Object

Contains information about run-time errors.

Remarks

The properties of the **Err** object are set by the generator of an error—Visual Basic, an object, or the programmer.

When a run-time error occurs, the properties of the **Err** object are filled with information that uniquely identifies the error, and information you can use to handle it. To generate a run-time error in your code, use the **Raise** method.

The **Err** object's properties are reset to zero or zero-length strings (" ") after an **Exit Sub**, **Exit Function**, **Exit Property**, or **Resume Next** statement within an error-handling routine. Using any form of the **Resume** statement outside of an error-handling routine will not reset the **Err** object's properties. You can use the **Clear** method to explicitly reset **Err**.

Use the **Raise** method rather than the **Error** statement to generate run-time errors for system errors and class modules. Whether you use the **Raise** method in other code depends on the richness of the information you want to return.

The **Err** object is an intrinsic object with global scope. Therefore, you do not need to create an instance of it in your code.

Example

This example uses the properties of the **Err** object in constructing an error-message dialog box. Note that if you use the **Clear** method first, when you generate a Visual Basic error with the **Raise** method, Visual Basic's default values become the properties of the **Err** object.

```
Dim Msg As String
' If an error occurs, construct an error message.
On Error Resume Next   ' Defer error handling.
Err.Clear
Err.Raise(6)   ' Generate an "Overflow" error.
' Check for error, then show message.
If Err.Number <> 0 Then
   Msg = "Error # " & Str(Err.Number) & " was generated by " _
      & Err.Source & ControlChars.CrLf & Err.Description
   MsgBox(Msg, MsgBoxStyle.Information, "Error")
End If
```

See Also

Error Statement; On Error Statement; Exit Statement; Resume Statement

Error

The **Error** keyword either simulates or responds to a run-time error.

The **Error** keyword is used in these contexts:

Error Statement

On Error Statement

See Also

Visual Basic Language Keywords

Error Statement

Simulates the occurrence of an error.

```
Error errornumber
```

Parts

errornumber
Required. Can be any valid error number.

Remarks

The **Error** statement is supported for backward compatibility. In new code, especially when creating objects, use the **Err** object's **Raise** method to generate run-time errors.

If *errornumber* is defined, the **Error** statement calls the error handler after the properties of the **Err** object are assigned the following default values:

Property	Value
Number	Value specified as argument to **Error** statement. Can be any valid error number.
Source	Name of the current Visual Basic project.
Description	String expression corresponding to the return value of the **Error** function for the specified **Number**, if this string exists. If the string doesn't exist, **Description** contains a zero-length string (" ").
HelpFile	The fully qualified drive, path, and file name of the appropriate Visual Basic Help file.
HelpContext	The appropriate Visual Basic Help file context ID for the error corresponding to the **Number** property.
LastDLLError	Zero.

If no error handler exists or if none is enabled, an error message is created and displayed from the **Err** object properties.

> **Note** Some Visual Basic host applications cannot create objects. See your host application's documentation to determine whether it can create classes and objects.

Example

This example uses the **Error** statement to generate error number 11.

```
On Error Resume Next   ' Defer error handling.
Error 11   ' Simulate the "Division by zero" error.
```

See Also

Clear Method, Err Object, On Error Statement, Raise Method, Resume Statement

ErrorToString Function

Returns the error message that corresponds to a given error number.

```
ErrorToString(errornumber)
```

Parameter

errornumber
: Optional. Any valid error number.

Exceptions/Errors

Exception type	Error number	Condition
ArgumentException	5	*ErrorNumber* is out of range.

Remarks

The **ErrorToString** function examines the property settings of the **Err** object to identify the most recent run-time error. The return value of the **ErrorToString** function corresponds to the **Description** property of the **Err** object. If *errornumber* is a valid error number but is not defined, **ErrorToString** returns the string, "Application-defined or object-defined error." If *errornumber* is not valid, an error occurs. If *errornumbe*r is omitted, the message corresponding to the most recent run-time error is returned. If no run-time error has occurred, or *errornumber* is 0, **ErrorToString** returns a zero-length string (" ").

In Visual Basic version 6.0 and earlier, this functionality was provided by the **Error** function.

Example

The following code uses the **ErrorToString** function to display error messages that correspond to the specified error numbers:

```
Dim ErrorNumber As Integer
For ErrorNumber = 61 To 64   ' Loop through values 61 - 64.
   MsgBox(ErrorToString(ErrorNumber))   ' Display error names in message box.
Next ErrorNumber
```

See Also

Err Object, Description Property

Event Statement

Declares a user-defined event.

```
[ <attrlist> ] [ Public | Private | Protected | Friend | Protected Friend ] _
[ Shadows ] Event eventname[(arglist)] _
[ Implements interfacename.interfaceeventname ]
```

Parts

attrlist
Optional. List of attributes that apply to this event. Multiple attributes are separated by commas.

Public
Optional. Entities declared with the **Public** modifier have public access. There are no restrictions on the use of public entities. Events that do not specify an access modifier are declared as **Public** by default.

Private
Optional. Entities declared with the **Private** modifier have private access. A private entity is accessible only within its declaration context, including any nested entities.

Protected
Optional. Entities declared with the **Protected** keyword have protected access. They are accessible only from within their own class or from a derived class. Protected access can be specified only on members of classes. It is not a superset of friend access.

Friend
Optional. Entities declared with the **Friend** modifier have friend access. An entity with friend access is accessible only within the program that contains the entity declaration.

Protected Friend
Optional. Entities declared with the **Protected Friend** modifiers have the union of protected and friend accessibility.

Shadows
Optional. Indicates that this event shadows an identically named programming element in a base class. You can shadow any kind of declared element with any other kind. A shadowed element is unavailable in the derived class that shadows it

eventname
Required. Name of the event; follows standard variable naming conventions.

Implements
Optional. Indicates that this event implements an event of an interface.

interfacename
The name of an interface.

interfaceeventname
The name of the event being implemented.

Each attribute in the *attrlist* part has the following syntax and parts:

```
attrname [({ attrargs | attrinit })]
```

attrlist Parts

attrname
Required. Name of the attribute. Must be a valid Visual Basic identifier.

attrargs
Optional. List of positional arguments for this attribute. Multiple arguments are separated by commas.

attrinit
Optional. List of field or property initializers for this attribute. Multiple initializers are separated by commas.

The *arglist* argument has the following syntax and parts:

```
[ <attrlist> ] [ ByVal | ByRef ] varname[ ( ) ] [ As type ]
```

arglist Parts

attrlist
Optional. List of attributes that apply to this argument. Multiple attributes are separated by commas.

ByVal
Optional. Indicates that the argument is passed by value. **ByVal** is the default in Visual Basic.

ByRef
Optional. Indicates that the argument is passed by reference.

varname
Required. Name of the variable representing the argument being passed to the procedure; follows standard variable naming conventions.

type

Optional. Data type of the argument passed to the procedure; may be **Byte**, **Boolean**, **Char**, **Short**, **Integer**, **Long**, **Single**, **Double**, **Decimal**, **Date**, **String** (variable length only), **Object**, a user-defined type, or an object type.

Remarks

Once the event has been declared, use the **RaiseEvent** statement to raise the event. A typical event might be declared and raised as shown in the following fragments:

```
Public Class EventSource
   ' Declare an event.
   Public Event LogonCompleted(ByVal UserName As String)
   Sub CauseEvent()
      ' Raise an event on successful logon.
      RaiseEvent LogonCompleted("AustinSteele")
   End Sub
End Class
```

> **Note** You can declare event arguments just as you do arguments of procedures, with the following exceptions: events cannot have named arguments, or **Optional** arguments. Events do not have return values.

Example

The following example uses events to count off seconds during a demonstration of the fastest 100 meter race. The code illustrates all of the event-related methods, properties, and statements, including the **RaiseEvent** statement.

The class that raises an event is the event source, and the methods that process the event are the event handlers. An event source can have multiple handlers for the events it generates. When the class raises the event, that event is raised on every class that has elected to handle events for that instance of the object.

The example also uses a form (`Form1`) with a button (`Command1`), a label (`Label1`), and two text boxes (`Text1` and `Text2`). When you click the button, the first text box displays "From Now" and the second starts to count seconds. When the full time (9.84 seconds) has elapsed, the first text box displays "Until Now" and the second displays "9.84".

The code for `Form1` specifies the initial and terminal states of the form. It also contains the code executed when events are raised.

To use this example, open a new Windows Forms project, add a button named `Button1`, a label named `Label1` and two text boxes, named `TextBox1` and `TextBox2`, to the main form, named `form1`. Then right click the form and click **View Code** to open the code editor.

To simplify access to the **Timer** property, add an **Imports** statement as the first line of code above the `Class Form1` statement.

```
Imports Microsoft.VisualBasic.DateAndTime
```

Add a **WithEvents** variable to the declarations section of the `Form1` class.

```
Private WithEvents mText As TimerState
```

Add the following code to the code for `Form1`. Replace any duplicate procedures that may exist, such as `Form_Load`, or `Button_Click`.

```
Private Sub Form1_Load(ByVal sender As Object, _
                       ByVal e As System.EventArgs) _
                       Handles MyBase.Load
   Button1.Text = "Click to Start Timer"
   TextBox1.Text = ""
   TextBox2.Text = ""
   Label1.Text = "The fastest 100 meters ever run took this long:"
   mText = New TimerState()
End Sub
Private Sub Button1_Click(ByVal sender As System.Object, _
                          ByVal e As System.EventArgs) _
                          Handles Button1.Click
   TextBox1.Text = "From Now"
   TextBox1.Refresh()
   TextBox2.Text = "0"
   TextBox2.Refresh()
   mText.TimerTask(9.84)
End Sub

Private Sub mText_ChangeText() Handles mText.ChangeText
   TextBox1.Text = "Until Now"
   TextBox2.Text = "9.84"
End Sub

Private Sub mText_UpdateTime(ByVal Jump As Double) _
      Handles mText.UpdateTime
   TextBox2.Text = Format(Jump, "##0.00")
   Application.DoEvents()
End Sub

Class TimerState
   Public Event UpdateTime(ByVal Jump As Double)
   Public Event ChangeText()
   Public Sub TimerTask(ByVal Duration As Double)
      Dim Start As Double
      Dim Second As Double
      Dim SoFar As Double
      Start = Timer
      SoFar = Start
```

```
      Do While Timer < Start + Duration
         If Timer - SoFar >= 0.1 Then
            SoFar = SoFar + 0.1
            RaiseEvent UpdateTime(Timer - Start)
         End If
      Loop
      RaiseEvent ChangeText()
   End Sub
End Class
```

Press F5 To run this example, and click the button labeled **Click to start timer**. The first text box displays "From Now" and the second starts to count seconds. When the full time (9.84 seconds) has elapsed, the first text box displays "Until Now" and the second displays "9.84".

See Also

RaiseEvent Statement, Implements Statement

Exit Statement

Exits a procedure or block and transfers control immediately to the statement following the procedure call or the block definition.

```
Exit { Do | For | Function | Property | Select | Sub | Try | While }
```

Parts

Do

Immediately exits the **Do** loop in which it appears. Execution continues with the statement following the **Loop** statement. **Exit Do** can be used only inside a **Do** loop. When used within nested **Do** loops, **Exit Do** transfers control to the loop that is one nested level above the loop where **Exit Do** occurs.

For

Immediately exits the **For** loop in which it appears. Execution continues with the statement following the **Next** statement. **Exit For** can be used only inside a **For...Next** or **For Each...Next** loop. When used within nested **For** loops, **Exit For** transfers control to the loop that is one nested level above the loop where **Exit For** occurs.

Function

Immediately exits the **Function** procedure in which it appears. Execution continues with the statement following the statement that called the **Function** procedure. **Exit Function** can be used only inside a **Function** procedure.

Property

Immediately exits the **Property** procedure in which it appears. Execution continues with the statement that called the **Property** procedure, that is, with the statement requesting or setting the property's value. **Exit Property** can be used only inside a **Property** procedure.

Select

Immediately exits the **Select Case** in which it appears. Execution continues with the statement following the **End Select** statement. **Exit Select** can be used only inside a **Select Case** statement.

Sub

Immediately exits the **Sub** procedure in which it appears. Execution continues with the statement following the statement that called the **Sub** procedure. **Exit Sub** can be used only inside a **Sub** procedure.

Try

Immediately exits the **Try** or **Catch** block in which it appears. Execution continues with the **Finally** block if there is one, or with the statement following the **End Try** statement otherwise. **Exit Try** can be used only inside a **Try...Catch...Finally** statement.

While

Immediately exits the **While** loop in which it appears. Execution continues with the statement following the **End While** statement. **Exit While** can be used only inside a **While** loop. When used within nested **While** loops, **Exit While** transfers control to the loop that is one nested level above the loop where **Exit While** occurs.

Remarks

Do not confuse **Exit** statements with **End** statements. **Exit** does not define the end of a statement.

Example

This example uses the **Exit** statement to exit a **For...Next** loop, a **Do...Loop**, and a **Sub** procedure.

```
Sub ExitStatementDemo()
Dim I, MyNum As Integer
   Do    ' Set up infinite loop.
      For I = 1 To 1000    ' Loop 1000 times.
         MyNum = Int(Rnd * 1000)    ' Generate random numbers.
         Select Case MyNum    ' Evaluate random number.
            Case 7: Exit For    ' If 7, exit For...Next.
            Case 29: Exit Do    ' If 29, exit Do...Loop.
            Case 54: Exit Sub    ' If 54, exit Sub procedure.
         End Select
      Next I
   Loop
End Sub
```

See Also

Do...Loop Statements, End Statement, For Each...Next Statements, For...Next Statements, Function Statement, Stop Statement, Sub Statement, Try...Catch...Finally Statements

Explicit

The **Explicit** keyword is used in this context:

Option Explicit Statement

See Also

Visual Basic Language Keywords

False

The **False** keyword represents a Boolean value that fails a conditional test.

See Also

Boolean Data Type, True, Visual Basic Language Keywords

FileAttr Function

Returns an enumeration representing the file mode for files opened using the **FileOpen** function.

```
Public Function FileAttr(ByVal FileNumber As Integer) As OpenMode
```

Parameter

FileNumber
Required. **Integer**. Any valid file number.

Exceptions/Errors

Exception type	Error number	Condition
IOException	52	*FileNumber* does not exist.
IOException	54	File mode is invalid.

Return Values

The following enumeration values indicate the file access mode:

Value	Mode
1	**OpenMode.Input**
2	**OpenMode.Output**
4	**OpenMode.Random**

(continued)

(continued)

Value	Mode
8	**OpenMode.Append**
32	**OpenMode.Binary**

Example

This example uses the **FileAttr** function to return the file mode of an open file.

```
Dim mode As OpenMode
FileOpen(1, "c:\MYFILE.TXT", OpenMode.Input)
mode = FileAttr(1)
MsgBox("The file mode is " & mode.ToString())
FileClose(1)
```

See Also

GetAttr Function, FileOpen Function, SetAttr Function

FileAttribute Enumeration

When you call the **Dir**, **GetAttr**, or **SetAttr** functions, you can use the **FileAttribute** enumeration in your code in place of the actual values.

FileAttribute Enumeration Members

The *Attributes* argument takes the following **FileAttribute** enumeration members:

Member	Constant	Description
Normal	**vbNormal**	Normal (default for **Dir** and **SetAttr**).
ReadOnly	**vbReadOnly**	Read only.
Hidden	**vbHidden**	Hidden.
System	**vbSystem**	System file.
Volume	**vbVolume**	Volume label.
Directory	**vbDirectory**	Directory or folder.
Archive	**vbArchive**	File has changed since last backup.

See Also

Dir Function, GetAttr Function, SetAttr Function

FileClose Function

Concludes input/output (I/O) to a file opened using the **FileOpen** function.

```
Public Sub FileClose(ParamArray FileNumbers() As Integer)
```

Parameter

FileNumbers()

Optional. Parameter array of 0 or more channels to be closed.

Exceptions/Errors

Exception type	Error number	Condition
IOException	52	*FileNumber* does not exist.

Remarks

If you omit *FileNumbers()*, all active files opened by the **FileOpen** function are closed.

When you close files that were opened for **Output** or **Append**, the final buffer of output is written to the operating system buffer for that file. All buffer space associated with the closed file is released.

When the **FileClose** function is executed, the association of a file with its file number ends.

Example

This example uses the **FileClose** function to close a file opened for **Input**.

```
Dim TextLine As String
FileOpen(1, "TESTFILE", OpenMode.Input)   ' Open file.
Do While Not EOF(1)   ' Loop until end of file.
   TextLine = LineInput(1)   ' Read line into variable.
   Debug.WriteLine(TextLine)   ' Print to the Immediate window.
Loop
FileClose(1)   ' Close file.
```

See Also

End Statement, FileOpen Function, Reset Function, Stop Statement

FileCopy Function

Copies a file.

```
Public Sub FileCopy( _
   ByVal Source As String, _
   ByVal Destination As String _
)
```

Parameters

Source

Required. **String** expression that specifies the name of the file to be copied. *Source* may include the directory or folder, and drive, of the source file.

Destination

Required. **String** expression that specifies the target file name. *Destination* may include the directory or folder, and drive, of the destination file.

Exceptions/Errors

Exception type	Error number	Condition
ArgumentException	52	*Source* or *Destination* is invalid or not specified.
IOException	55	File is already open.
FileNotFoundException	53	File does not exist.

Remarks

If you try to use the **FileCopy** function on a currently open file, an error occurs.

Example

This example uses the **FileCopy** function to copy one file to another. For purposes of this example, assume that `SRCFILE` is a file containing some data.

```
Dim SourceFile, DestinationFile As String
SourceFile = "SRCFILE"   ' Define source file name.
DestinationFile = "DESTFILE"   ' Define target file name.
FileCopy(SourceFile, DestinationFile)   ' Copy source to target.
```

See Also

Kill Function

FileDateTime Function

Returns a **Date** value that indicates the date and time when a file was created or last modified.

```
Public Function FileDateTime(ByVal PathName As String) As DateTime
```

Parameter

PathName

Required. **String** expression that specifies a file name. *PathName* may include the directory or folder, and the drive.

Exceptions/Errors

Exception type	Error number	Condition
ArgumentException	52	*PathName* is invalid or contains wildcards.
FileNotFoundException	53	Target file does not exist.

Example

This example uses the **FileDateTime** function to determine the date and time a file was created or last modified. The format of the date and time displayed is based on the locale settings of your system.

```
Dim MyStamp As Date
' Assume TESTFILE was last modified on October 12, 2001 at 4:35:47 PM.
' Assume English/U.S. locale settings.
' Returns "10/12/2001 4:35:47 PM".
MyStamp = FileDateTime("C:\TESTFILE.txt")
```

See Also

FileLen Function, GetAttr Function

FileGet Function

Reads data from an open disk file into a variable.

```
Public Overloads Sub FileGet( _
   ByVal FileNumber As Integer, _
   ByRef Value As Object, _
   Optional RecordNumber As Integer = -1 _
)
```

-or-

```
Public Overloads Sub FileGet( _
   ByVal FileNumber As Integer, _
   ByRef Value As Short, _
   Optional RecordNumber As Integer = -1 _
)
```

-or-

```
Public Overloads Sub FileGet( _
   ByVal FileNumber As Integer, _
   ByRef Value As Integer, _
   Optional RecordNumber As Integer = -1 _
)
```

-or-

```
Public Overloads Sub FileGet( _
   ByVal FileNumber As Integer, _
   ByRef Value As Single, _
   Optional RecordNumber As Integer = -1 _
)
```

-or-

```
Public Overloads Sub FileGet( _
   ByVal FileNumber As Integer, _
   ByRef Value As Double, _
   Optional RecordNumber As Integer = -1 _
)
```

-or-

```
Public Overloads Sub FileGet( _
   ByVal FileNumber As Integer, _
   ByRef Value As Decimal, _
   Optional RecordNumber As Integer = -1 _
)
```

-or-

```
Public Overloads Sub FileGet( _
   ByVal FileNumber As Integer, _
   ByRef Value As Byte, _
   Optional RecordNumber As Integer = -1 _
)
```

-or-

```
Public Overloads Sub FileGet( _
   ByVal FileNumber As Integer, _
   ByRef Value As Boolean, _
   Optional RecordNumber As Integer = -1 _
)
```

-or-

```
Public Overloads Sub FileGet( _
   ByVal FileNumber As Integer, _
   ByRef Value As Date, _
   Optional RecordNumber As Integer = -1 _
)
```

-or-

```
Public Overloads Sub FileGet( _
   ByVal FileNumber As Integer, _
   ByRef Value As System.Array, _
   Optional RecordNumber As Integer = -1, _
   Optional ArrayIsDynamic as Boolean = False _
)
```

-or-

```
Public Overloads Sub FileGet(
   ByVal FileNumber As Integer, _
   ByRef Value As String, _
   Optional RecordNumber As Integer = -1, _
   Optional StringIsFixedLength as Boolean = False _
)
```

Parameters

FileNumber
Required. Any valid file number.

Value
Required. Valid variable name into which data is read.

RecordNumber
Optional. Record number (**Random** mode files) or byte number (**Binary** mode files) at which reading begins.

ArrayIsDynamic
Optional. Applies only when writing an array. Specifies whether the array is to be treated as dynamic and so whether to write an array descriptor describing the size and bounds of the array.

StringIsFixedLength

Optional. Applies only when writing a string. Specifies whether to write a two-byte descriptor for the string describing the length. The default is **False**.

Exceptions/Errors

Exception type	Error number	Condition
ArgumentException	63	*RecordNumber* < 1 and not equal to –1.
IOException	52	*FileNumber* does not exist.
IOException	54	File mode is invalid.

Remarks

FileGet is only valid in **Random** and **Binary** mode.

Data read with **FileGet** is usually written to a file with **FilePut**.

The first record or byte in a file is at position 1, the second record or byte at position 2, and so on. If you omit *RecordNumber*, the next record or byte following the last **FileGet** or **FilePut** function (or pointed to by the last **Seek** function) is read.

For files opened in **Random** mode, the following rules apply:

- If the length of the data being read is less than the length specified in the *RecordLength* clause of the **FileOpen** function, **FileGet** reads subsequent records on record-length boundaries. The space between the end of one record and the beginning of the next record is padded with the existing contents of the file buffer. Because the amount of padding data can't be determined with any certainty, it is generally a good idea to have the record length match the length of the data being read.
- If the variable being read into is a string, by default **FileGet** reads a two-byte descriptor containing the string length and then reads the data that goes into the variable. Therefore, the record length specified by the *RecordLength* clause of the **FileOpen** function must be at least two bytes greater than the actual length of the string. Visual Basic 6 and earlier versions supported fixed-length strings and when put to a file, the length descriptor would not be written. If you wish to read a string without the descriptor, you should pass **True** to the *StringIsFixedLength* parameter, and the string you read into should be the correct length.
- If the variable being read into is an array, then you have a choice as to whether to read a descriptor for the size and dimension of the array. To write the descriptor, set the *ArrayIsDynamic* parameter to **True**. When reading the array, you need to match the way the array was written. If it was written with the descriptor, then you need to read the descriptor. If the descriptor is not used, then the size and bounds of the array passed into **FileGet** will be used to determine what to read.

The descriptor specifies the rank of the array, the size, and the lower bounds for each rank. Its length equals 2 plus 8 times the number of dimensions, that is, 2 + 8 * *NumberOfDimensions*. The record length specified by the *RecordLength* parameter in the **FileOpen** function must be greater than or equal to the sum of all the bytes required to write the array data and the array descriptor. For example, the following array declaration requires 118 bytes when the array is written to disk.

```
Dim MyArray(4,9) As Integer
```

The 118 bytes are distributed as follows: 18 bytes for the descriptor (2 + 8 * 2), and 100 bytes for the data (5 * 10 * 2).

- If the variable being read into is any other type of variable (not a variable-length string or an object), **FileGet** reads only the variable data. The record length specified by the *RecordLength* clause in the **FileOpen** function must be greater than or equal to the length of the data being read.
- **FileGet** reads elements of structures as if each were being read individually, except that there is no padding between elements. On disk, a dynamic array in a user-defined type (written with **FilePut**) is prefixed by a descriptor whose length equals 2 plus 8 times the number of dimensions, that is, 2 + 8 * *NumberOfDimensions*. The record length specified by the *RecordLength* clause in the **FileOpen** function must be greater than or equal to the sum of all the bytes required to read the individual elements, including any arrays and their descriptors. The **VBFixedString** attribute can be applied to string fields in the structures to indicate the size of string when written to disk.

For files opened in **Binary** mode, all of the **Random** mode rules apply, except:

- The *RecordLength* clause in the **FileOpen** function has no effect. **FileGet** reads all variables from disk contiguously; that is, with no padding between records.
- For any array other than an array in a structure, **FileGet** reads only the data. No descriptor is read.
- **FileGet** reads variable-length strings that aren't elements of structures without expecting the two-byte length descriptor. The number of bytes read equals the number of characters already in the string. For example, the following statements read 11 bytes from file number 1:

```
Dim hellow As New String(" ", 11)
FileOpen(1, "C:\TESTFILE.txt", OpenMode.Binary)
FileGet(1, hellow)
Console.WriteLine(hellow)
FileClose(1)
```

See Also

FileOpen Function, FilePut Function, Seek Function, FileGetObject Function

FileGetObject Function

Reads data from an open disk file into a variable.

```
Public Sub FileGetObject( _
   ByVal FileNumber As Integer, _
   ByRef Value As Object, _
   Optional RecordNumber As Integer = -1 _
)
```

-or-

```
Overloads Public Sub FileGetObject( _
   ByVal FileNumber As Integer, _
   ByRef Value As Short, _
   Optional RecordNumber As Integer = -1 _
)
```

-or-

```
Overloads Public Sub FileGetObject( _
   ByVal FileNumber As Integer, _
   ByRef Value As Integer, _
   Optional RecordNumber As Integer = -1 _
)
```

-or-

```
Overloads Public Sub FileGetObject( _
   ByVal FileNumber As Integer, _
   ByRef Value As Single, _
   Optional RecordNumber As Integer = -1 _
)
```

-or-

```
Overloads Public Sub FileGetObject( _
   ByVal FileNumber As Integer, _
   ByRef Value As Double, _
   Optional RecordNumber As Integer = -1 _
)
```

-or-

```
Overloads Public Sub FileGetObject( _
   ByVal FileNumber As Integer, _
   ByRef Value As Decimal, _
   Optional RecordNumber As Integer = -1 _
)
```

-or-

```
Overloads Public Sub FileGetObject( _
   ByVal FileNumber As Integer, _
   ByRef Value As Byte, _
   Optional RecordNumber As Integer = -1 _
)
```

-or-

```
Overloads Public Sub FileGetObject( _
   ByVal FileNumber As Integer, _
   ByRef Value As Boolean, _
   Optional RecordNumber As Integer = -1 _
)
```

-or-

```
Overloads Public Sub FileGetObject( _
   ByVal FileNumber As Integer, _
   ByRef Value As Date, _
   Optional RecordNumber As Integer = -1 _
)
```

-or-

```
Overloads Public Sub FileGetObject( _
   ByVal FileNumber As Integer, _
   ByRef Value As System.Array, _
   Optional RecordNumber As Integer = -1, _
   Optional ArrayIsDynamic as Boolean = False _
)
```

-or-

```
Overloads Public Sub FileGetObject( _
   ByVal FileNumber As Integer, _
   ByRef Value As String, _
   Optional RecordNumber As Integer = -1, _
   Optional StringIsFixedLength as Boolean = False _
)
```

Parameters

FileNumber
Required. Any valid file number.

Value
Required. Valid variable name into which data is read.

RecordNumber

Optional. Record number (**Random** mode files) or byte number (**Binary** mode files) at which reading begins.

ArrayIsDynamic

Optional. Applies only when writing an array. Specifies whether the array is to be treated as dynamic and so whether to write an array descriptor describing the size and bounds of the array.

StringIsFixedLength

Optional. Applies only when writing a string. Specifies whether to write a two-byte descriptor for the string describing the length. The default is **False**.

Remarks

The **FileGetObject** function is used in place of **FileGet** to avoid ambiguities at compile time if type **Object** is returned rather than another type, such as **Integer**, **Long**, **Short**, and so forth.

If you intend to write out the **Variant** type, **FileGetObject** is required. When in doubt, if you are using an object for the second parameter, it is always safer to use **FilePutObject** and **FileGetObject**.

FileGetObject is only valid in **Random** and **Binary** mode.

Data read with **FileGetObject** is usually written with **FilePutObject**.

The first record or byte in a file is at position 1, the second record or byte is at position 2, and so on. If you omit *RecordNumber*, **FileGetObject** reads the record or byte after the last **FileGetObject** or **FilePutObject** function (or pointed to by the last **Seek** function).

For files opened in **Random** mode, the following rules apply:

- If the length of the data being read is less than the length specified in the *RecordLength* clause of the **FileOpen** function, **FileGetObject** reads subsequent records on record-length boundaries. The space between the end of one record and the beginning of the next record is padded with the existing contents of the file buffer. Because the amount of padding data can't be precisely determined, it is a good idea to have the record length match the length of the data being read.

- If the variable being read into is a string, by default **FileGetObject** reads a two-byte descriptor containing the string length and then reads the data that goes into the variable. Therefore, the record length specified by the *RecordLength* clause of the **FileOpen** function must be at least two bytes greater than the actual length of the string. Visual Basic 6 and earlier versions supported fixed-length strings and when read to a file, the length descriptor would not be written. If you wish to read a string without the descriptor, you should pass **True** to the *StringIsFixedLength* parameter, and the string you read into should be the correct length.

- If the variable being read into is an array, then you can choose to read a descriptor for the size and dimension of the array. To read the descriptor, set the *ArrayIsDynamic* parameter to **True**. When reading the array, you need to match the way the array was written. If it was written with the descriptor, you need to read the descriptor. If the descriptor is not used, the size and bounds of the array passed into **FileGetObject** is used to determine what to read.

  The descriptor specifies the rank of the array, the size, and the lower bounds for each rank. Its length equals 2 plus 8 times the number of dimensions, that is, 2 + 8 * *NumberOfDimensions*. The record length specified by the *RecordLength* parameter in the **FileOpen** function must be greater than or equal to the sum of all the bytes required to write the array data and the array descriptor. For example, the following array declaration requires 118 bytes when the array is written to disk:

  ```
  Dim MyArray(4,9) As Integer
  ```

  The 118 bytes are distributed as follows: 18 bytes for the descriptor (2 + 8 * 2), and 100 bytes for the data (5 * 10 * 2).

- **FileGetObject** reads elements of structures as if each were being read individually, except that there is no padding between elements. On disk, a dynamic array in a user-defined type (written with **FilePutObject**) is prefixed by a descriptor whose length equals 2 plus 8 times the number of dimensions, that is, 2 + 8 * *NumberOfDimensions*. The record length specified by the *RecordLength* clause in the **FileOpen** function must be greater than or equal to the sum of all the bytes required to read the individual elements, including any arrays and their descriptors. The **VBFixedString** attribute can be applied to string fields in the structures to indicate the size of string when written to disk.

For files opened in **Binary** mode, all of the **Random** rules apply, except:

- The *RecordLength* clause in the **FileOpen** function has no effect. **FileGetObject** reads all variables from disk contiguously; that is, with no padding between records.

- For any array other than an array in a structure, **FileGetObject** reads only the data. No descriptor is read.

FileGetObject reads variable-length strings that aren't elements of structures without expecting the two-byte length descriptor. The number of bytes read equals the number of characters already in the string.

Example

The following example reads a record into a test file and then retrieves it.

```
Dim c As String
FileSystem.FileOpen(1, "test.dat", OpenMode.Binary)
FileSystem.FilePutObject(1, "ABCDEF")
FileSystem.Seek(1, 1)
FileSystem.FileGetObject(1, c)
System.Console.WriteLine(c)
FileSystem.FileClose(1)
```

See Also

FilePut Function; FileOpen Function; Seek Function; FileGet Function

FileLen Function

Returns a **Long** value specifying the length of a file in bytes.

```
Public Function FileLen(ByVal PathName As String) As Long
```

Parameter

PathName
: Required. **String** expression that specifies a file. *PathName* may include the directory or folder, and the drive.

Exceptions/Errors

Exception type	Error number	Condition
FileNotFoundException	53	File does not exist.

Remarks

If the specified file is open when the **FileLen** function is called, the value returned represents the size of the file at the time it was opened.

> **Note** To obtain the current length of an open file, use the **LOF** function.

Example

This example uses the **FileLen** function to return the length of a file in bytes. For purposes of this example, assume that `TESTFILE` is a file containing some data.

```
Dim MySize As Long
MySize = FileLen("TESTFILE")   ' Returns file length (bytes).
```

See Also

FileDateTime Function, GetAttr Function, LOF Function

FileOpen Function

Opens a file for input or output.

```
Public Sub FileOpen( _
   ByVal FileNumber As Integer, _
   ByVal FileName As String, _
   ByVal Mode As OpenMode, _
   Optional ByVal Access As OpenAccess = OpenAccess.Default, _
   Optional ByVal Share As OpenShare = OpenShare.Default, _
   Optional ByVal RecordLength As Integer = -1 _
)
```

Parameters

FileNumber
Required. Any valid file number. Use the **FreeFile** function to obtain the next available file number.

FileName
Required. **String** expression that specifies a file name—may include directory or folder, and drive.

Mode
Required. **Enum** specifying the file mode: **Append**, **Binary**, **Input**, **Output**, or **Random**.

Access
Optional. Keyword specifying the operations permitted on the open file: **Read**, **Write**, or **ReadWrite**. Defaults to **ReadWrite**.

Share
Optional. **Enum** specifying the operations restricted on the open file by other processes: **Shared**, **Lock Read**, **Lock Write**, and **Lock Read Write**. Defaults to **Shared**.

RecordLength
Optional. Number less than or equal to 32,767 (bytes). For files opened for random access, this value is the record length. For sequential files, this value is the number of characters buffered.

Exceptions/Errors

Exception type	Error number	Condition
ArgumentException	5	Invalid **Access, Share,** or **Mode.**
ArgumentException	5	**WriteOnly** file is opened for **Input.**
ArgumentException	5	**ReadOnly** file is opened for **Output.**
ArgumentException	5	**ReadOnly** file is opened for **Append.**

(continued)

(continued)

Exception type	Error number	Condition
ArgumentException	5	Record length is negative (and not equal to –1).
IOException	52	*FileNumber* is invalid (<–1 or >255), or *FileNumber* is already in use.
IOException	55	*FileName* is already open, or *FileName* is invalid.

Remarks

You must open a file before any I/O operation can be performed on it. **FileOpen** allocates a buffer for I/O to the file and determines the mode of access to use with the buffer.

If the file specified by *FileName* doesn't exist, it is created when a file is opened for **Append**, **Binary**, **Output**, or **Random** modes.

The channel to open can be found using the **FreeFile()** function.

Example

This example illustrates various uses of the **FileOpen** function to enable input and output to a file.

The following code opens the file `TESTFILE` in **Input** mode.

```
FileOpen(1, "TESTFILE", OpenMode.Input)
' Close before reopening in another mode.
FileClose(1)
```

This example opens the file in **Binary** mode for writing operations only.

```
FileOpen(1, "TESTFILE", OpenMode.Binary,OpenAccess.Write)
' Close before reopening in another mode.
FileClose(1)
```

The following example opens the file in **Random** mode. The file contains records of the structure `Person`.

```
Structure Person
   <VBFixedString(30)> Dim Name As String
   Dim ID As Integer
End Structure
' Count 30 for the string, plus 4 for the integer.
FileOpen(1, "TESTFILE", OpenMode.Random, , , 34)
' Close before reopening in another mode.
FileClose(1)
```

This code example opens the file in **Output** mode; any process can read or write to file.

```
FileOpen(1, "TESTFILE", OpenMode.Output, OpenShare.Shared)
' Close before reopening in another mode.
FileClose(1)
```

This code example opens the file in **Binary** mode for reading; other processes can't read file.

```
FileOpen(1, "TESTFILE", OpenMode.Binary, OpenAccess.Read, _
   OpenShare.LockRead)
```

See Also
FileClose Function, FreeFile Function

FilePut Function

Writes data from a variable to a disk file.

```
Public Overloads Sub FilePut( _
   FileNumber As Integer, _
   Value As Short, _
   Optional RecordNumber As Integer = -1 _
)
```

-or-

```
Public Overloads Sub FilePut( _
   FileNumber As Integer, _
   Value As Integer, _
   Optional RecordNumber As Integer = -1 _
)
```

-or-

```
Public Overloads Sub FilePut( _
   FileNumber As Integer, _
   Value As Single, _
   Optional RecordNumber As Integer = -1 _
)
```

-or-

```
Public Overloads Sub FilePut( _
   FileNumber As Integer, _
   Value As Double, _
   RecordNumber As Integer = -1 _
)
```

-or-

```
Public Overloads Sub FilePut( _
   FileNumber As Integer, _
   Value As Decimal, _
   Optional RecordNumber As Integer = -1 _
)
```

-or-

```
Public Overloads Sub FilePut( _
   FileNumber As Integer, _
   Value As Byte, _
   Optional RecordNumber As Integer = -1 _
)
```

-or-

```
Public Overloads Sub FilePut( _
   FileNumber As Integer, _
   Value As Boolean, _
   Optional RecordNumber As Integer = -1 _
)
```

-or-

```
Public Overloads Sub FilePut( _
   FileNumber As Integer, _
   Value As Date, _
   Optional RecordNumber As Integer = -1 _
)
```

-or-

```
Public Overloads Sub FilePut( _
   FileNumber As Integer, _
   Value As System.Array, _
   Optional RecordNumber As Integer = -1, _
   Optional ArrayIsDynamic As Boolean = False _
)
```

-or-

```
Public Overloads Sub FilePut (
   FileNumber As Integer,
   Value As String, _
   Optional RecordNumber As Integer = -1,
   Optional StringIsFixedLength As Boolean = False
)
```

Parameters

FileNumber
  Required. Any valid file number.

Value
  Required. Valid variable name containing data written to disk.

RecordNumber
Optional. Record number (**Random** mode files) or byte number (**Binary** mode files) at which writing begins.

ArrayIsDynamic
Optional. Applies only when writing an array. Specifies whether the array is to be treated as dynamic, and whether to write an array descriptor for the string describing the length.

StringIsFixedLength
Optional. Applies only when writing a string. Specifies whether to write a two-byte string length descriptor for the string to the file. The default is **False**.

Exceptions/Errors

Exception type	Error number	Condition
ArgumentException	63	*RecordNumber* < 1 and not equal to –1.
IOException	52	*FileNumber* does not exist.
IOException	54	File mode is invalid.

Remarks

FilePut is only valid in **Random** and **Binary** mode.

Data written with **FilePut** is usually read from a file with **FileGet**.

The first record or byte in a file is at position 1, the second record or byte at position 2, and so on. If you omit *RecordNumber*, the next record or byte after the last **FileGet** or **FilePut** function or pointed to by the last **Seek** function is written.

The *StringIsFixedLength* argument controls whether the function interprets strings as variable or fixed length. **FilePut** does not write the length descriptor when the argument is **True**. If you use *StringIsFixedLength* = **True** with **FilePut**, you will need to do the same with **FileGet**, and also make sure the string is initialized to the length expected.

For files opened in **Random** mode, the following rules apply:

- If the length of the data being written is less than the length specified in the *RecordLength* clause of the **FileOpen** function, **FilePut** writes subsequent records on record-length boundaries. The space between the end of one record and the beginning of the next record is padded with the existing contents of the file buffer. Because the amount of padding data can't be determined with any certainty, it is generally a good idea to have the record length match the length of the data being written. If the length of the data being written is greater than the length specified in the *RecordLength* clause of the **FileOpen** function, an exception will be thrown.

- If the variable being written is a string, **FilePut** writes a two-byte descriptor containing the string length, and then writes the data that goes into the variable. Therefore, the record length specified by the *RecordLength* clause in the **FileOpen** function must be at least two bytes greater than the actual length of the string.

- If the variable being written is an object containing a numeric type, **FilePut** writes two bytes identifying the **VarType** of the object and then writes the variable. For example, when writing an object containing an integer, **FilePut** writes six bytes: two bytes identifying the object as **VarType(3)** (**Integer**) and four bytes containing the data. The record length specified by the *RecordLength* parameter in the **FileOpen** function must be at least two bytes greater than the actual number of bytes required to store the variable.
- If the variable being written is an object containing a string, **FilePut** writes a two byte descriptor identifying the **VarType(8)** of the object, a two-byte descriptor indicating the length of the string, and then writes the string data. The record length specified by the *RecordLength* parameter in the **FileOpen** function must be at least four bytes greater than the actual length of the string. If you wish to put a string without the descriptor, then you should pass **True** to the *StringIsFixedLength* parameter, and the string you read into should be the correct length.
- If the variable being written is an array, then you have a choice as to whether or not to write a descriptor for the size and dimensions of the array. Visual Basic 6 and earlier versions would write the file descriptor for a dynamic array, but not for a fixed-size array. Visual Basic .NET defaults to not writing the descriptor. To write the descriptor, set the *ArrayIsDynamic* parameter to **True**. When writing the array, you need to match the way the array will be read; if it will be read with the descriptor, then you need to write the descriptor. The descriptor specifies the rank of the array, the size, and the lower bounds for each rank. Its length equals 2 plus 8 times the number of dimensions, that is, 2 + 8 * *NumberOfDimensions*. The record length specified by the *RecordLength* clause in the **FileOpen** function must be greater than or equal to the sum of all the bytes required to write the array data and the array descriptor. For example, the following array declaration requires 118 bytes when the array is written to disk.

  ```
  Dim MyArray(4,9) As Integer
  ```

- If the variable being written is any other type of variable (not a variable-length string or an object), **FilePut** writes only the variable data. The record length specified by the *RecordLength* clause in the **FileOpen** function must be greater than or equal to the length of the data being written.
- **FilePut** writes elements of structures as if each were written individually, except there is no padding between elements. The **VBFixedString** attribute can be applied to string fields in the structures to indicate the size of the string when written to disk.

For files opened in **Binary** mode, all of the **Random** mode rules apply, except:

- The *RecordLength* clause in the **FileOpen** function has no effect. **FilePut** writes all variables to disk contiguously; that is, with no padding between records.
- For any array other than an array in a structure, **FilePut** writes only the data. No descriptor is written.

- **FilePut** writes variable-length strings that are not elements of structures without the two-byte length descriptor. The number of bytes written equals the number of characters in the string. For example, the following statements write 11 bytes to file number 1:

```
Dim hellow As String = "Hello World"
FilePut(1,hellow)
```

Example

This example uses the **FilePut** function to write data to a file. Five records of the structure `Person` are written to the file.

```
Structure Person
   Public ID As Integer
   Public Name As String
End Structure

Sub WriteData()
   Dim MyRecord As Person
   Dim recordNumber As Integer
'    Open file for random access.
   FileOpen(1, "C:\TESTFILE.txt", OpenMode.Binary)
   For recordNumber = 1 To 5   ' Loop 5 times.
      MyRecord.ID = recordNumber   ' Define ID.
      MyRecord.Name = "My Name" & recordNumber   ' Create a string.
      FilePut(1, MyRecord)   ' Write record to file.
   Next recordNumber
   FileClose(1)
End Sub
```

See Also

FileGet Function, FileOpen Function, Seek Function, FileGetObject Function

FilePutObject Function

Writes data from a variable to a disk file.

```
Public Sub FilePutObject( _
   FileNumber As Integer, _
   Value As Object, _
   RecordNumber As Integer = -1 _
)
```

-or-

```
Overloads Public Sub FilePutObject( _
   FileNumber As Integer, _
   Value As Short, _
   Optional RecordNumber As Integer = -1 _
)
```

-or-

```
Overloads Public Sub FilePutObject( _
   FileNumber As Integer, _
   Value As Integer, _
   Optional RecordNumber As Integer = -1 _
)
```

-or-

```
Overloads Public Sub FilePutObject( _
   FileNumber As Integer, _
   Value As Single, _
   Optional RecordNumber As Integer = -1 _
)
```

-or-

```
Overloads Public Sub FilePutObject( _
   FileNumber As Integer, _
   Value As Double, _
   RecordNumber As Integer = -1 _
)
```

-or-

```
Overloads Public Sub FilePutObject( _
   FileNumber As Integer, _
   Value As Decimal, _
   Optional RecordNumber As Integer = -1 _
)
```

-or-

```
Overloads Public Sub FilePutObject( _
   FileNumber As Integer, _
   Value As Byte, _
   Optional RecordNumber As Integer = -1 _
)
```

-or-

```
Overloads Public Sub FilePutObject( _
   FileNumber As Integer, _
   Value As Boolean, _
   Optional RecordNumber As Integer = -1 _
)
```

-or-

```
Overloads Public Sub FilePutObject( _
   FileNumber As Integer, _
   Value As Date, _
   Optional RecordNumber As Integer = -1 _
)
```

-or-

```
Overloads Public Sub FilePutObject( _
   FileNumber As Integer, _
   Value As System.Array, _
   Optional RecordNumber As Integer = -1, _
   Optional ArrayIsDynamic As Boolean = False _
)
```

-or-

```
Overloads Public Sub FilePutObject( _
   FileNumber As Integer, _
   Value As String, _
   Optional RecordNumber As Integer = -1, _
   Optional StringIsFixedLength as Boolean = False _
)
```

Parameters

FileNumber
: Required. Any valid file number.

Value
: Required. Valid variable name containing data written to disk.

RecordNumber
: Optional. Record number (**Random** mode files) or byte number (**Binary** mode files) at which writing begins.

ArrayIsDynamic
: Optional. Applies only when writing an array. Specifies whether the array is to be treated as dynamic, and whether to write an array descriptor for the string describing the length.

StringIsFixedLength
: Optional. Applies only when writing a string. Specifies whether to write a descriptor for the string describing the length. The default is **False**.

Remarks

The **FilePutObject** function is used in place of **FilePut** to avoid ambiguities at compile time if type **Object** is passed rather than another type, such as **Integer**, **Long**, **Short**, and so forth.

FilePutObject writes and reads descriptors that describe the object. If you intend to write out the **Variant** type, **FilePutObject** is required. When in doubt, if you are using an object for the second parameter, it is always safer to use **FilePutObject** and **FileGetObject**.

FilePutObject is only valid in **Random** and **Binary** mode.

Data written with **FilePutObject** is usually read from a file with **FileGetObject**.

The first record or byte in a file is at position 1, the second record or byte is at position 2, and so on. If you omit *RecordNumber*, **FilePutObject** writes the next record or byte after the last **FileGetObject** or **FilePutObject** function (or the record or byte pointed to by the last **Seek** function).

The *StringIsFixedLength* argument controls whether the function interprets strings as variable or fixed length. **FilePutObject** does not write the length descriptor when the argument is **True**. If you use *StringIsFixedLength* = **True** with **FilePutObject**, you need to do the same with **FileGetObject**, and must also make sure that the string is initialized to the length expected.

For files opened in **Random** mode, the following rules apply:

- If the length of the data being written is less than the length specified in the *RecordLength* clause of the **FileOpen** function, **FilePutObject** writes subsequent records on record-length boundaries. The space between the end of one record and the beginning of the next record is padded with the existing contents of the file buffer. Because the amount of padding data can't be precisely determined, it is generally a good idea to have the record length match the length of the data being written. If the length of the data being written is greater than the length specified in the *RecordLength* clause of the **FileOpen** function, an exception is thrown.
- If the variable being written is an object containing a numeric type, **FilePutObject** writes two bytes identifying the **VarType** of the object and then writes the variable. For example, when writing an object containing an integer, **FilePutObject** writes six bytes: two bytes identifying the object as **VarType**(3) (**Integer**) and four bytes containing the data. The record length specified by the *RecordLength* parameter in the **FileOpen** function must be at least two bytes greater than the actual number of bytes required to store the variable.
- If the variable being written is an object containing a string, **FilePutObject** writes a two-byte descriptor identifying the **VarType**(8) of the object, a two-byte descriptor indicating the length of the string, and then writes the string data. The record length specified by the *RecordLength* parameter in the **FileOpen** function must be at least four bytes greater than the actual length of the string. If you wish to put a string without the descriptor, then you should pass **True** to the *StringIsFixedLength* parameter, and the string you read into should be the correct length.

- If the variable being written is an array, you can choose to write a descriptor for the size and dimensions of the array. Visual Basic 6 and earlier versions would write the file descriptor for a dynamic array, but not for a fixed-size array; Visual Basic .NET defaults to not writing the descriptor. To write the descriptor, set the *ArrayIsDynamic* parameter to **True**. When writing the array, you need to match the way the array is read; if it is read with the descriptor, you need to write the descriptor. The descriptor specifies the rank of the array, the size, and the lower bounds for each rank. Its length equals 2 plus 8 times the number of dimensions, that is, 2 + 8 * *NumberOfDimensions*. The record length specified by the *RecordLength* clause in the **FileOpen** function must be greater than or equal to the sum of all the bytes required to write the array data and the array descriptor.

For files opened in **Binary** mode, all of the **Random** mode rules apply, except:

- The *RecordLength* clause in the **FileOpen** function has no effect. **FilePutObject** writes all variables to disk contiguously, that is, with no padding between records.

Example

This example uses the **FilePutObject** function to write data to a file. Five records of the structure `Person` are written to the file.

```
Sub WriteData()
    Dim Person As String
    Dim recordNumber As Integer
    '    Open file for random access.
    FileOpen(1, "C:\TESTFILE.txt", OpenMode.Binary)
    For recordNumber = 1 To 5    ' Loop 5 times.
        Person = "My Name" & recordNumber    ' Create a string.
        FilePutObject(1, Person)    ' Write record to file.
    Next recordNumber
    FileClose(1)
End Sub
```

See Also

FileGet Function, FileOpen Function, Seek Function, File Access with Visual Basic Run-Time Functions, FilePut Function

FileWidth Function

Assigns an output line width to a file opened using the **FileOpen** function.

```
Public Sub FileWidth( _
   FileNumber As Integer, _
   RecordWidth As Integer _
)
```

Parameters

FileNumber

Required. Any valid file number.

RecordWidth

Required. Numeric expression in the range 0–255, inclusive, which indicates how many characters appear on a line before a new line is started. If *RecordWidth* equals 0, there is no limit to the length of a line. The default value for *RecordWidth* is 0.

Exceptions/Errors

Exception type	Error number	Condition
IOException	52	*FileNumber* does not exist.
IOException	54	File mode is invalid.

Example

This example uses the **FileWidth** function to set the output line width for a file.

```
Dim i As Integer
FileOpen(1, "TESTFILE", OpenMode.Output) ' Open file for output.
FileWidth(1, 5)    ' Set output line width to 5.
For i = 0 To 9    ' Loop 10 times.
   Print(1, Chr(48 + I))    ' Prints five characters per line.
Next
FileClose(1)    ' Close file.
```

See Also

FileOpen Function; Print, PrintLine Functions

Filter Function

Returns a zero-based array containing a subset of a **String** array based on specified filter criteria.

```
Function Filter(
   ByVal Source() As { Object | String },
   ByVal Match As String,
   Optional ByVal Include As Boolean = True,
   Optional ByVal Compare As CompareMethod = CompareMethod.Binary
) As String()
```

Parameters

Source
Required. One-dimensional array of strings to be searched.

Match
Required. String to search for.

Include
Optional. **Boolean** value indicating whether to return substrings that include or exclude *Match*. If *Include* is **True**, the **Filter** function returns the subset of the array that contains *Match* as a substring. If *Include* is **False**, the **Filter** function returns the subset of the array that does not contain *Match* as a substring.

Compare
Optional. Numeric value indicating the kind of string comparison to use. See "Settings" for values.

Settings

The *Compare* argument can have the following values:

Constant	Description
CompareMethod.Binary	Performs a binary comparison
CompareMethod.Text	Performs a textual comparison

Exceptions/Errors

Exception type	Error number	Condition
ArgumentException	5	*Source* is **Nothing** or is not a one-dimensional array.

Remarks

If no matches of *Match* are found within *Source*, the **Filter** function returns an empty array. An error occurs if *Source* is set to **Nothing** or is not a one-dimensional array.

The array returned by the **Filter** function contains only enough elements to contain the number of matched items.

Example

This example demonstrates the use of the **Filter** function.

```
Dim myStrings(2) As String
MyStrings(0) = "This"
MyStrings(1) = "Is"
MyStrings(2) = "It"
' Returns ["This", "Is"].
Dim subStrings() As String = Filter(myStrings, "is", True, _
   CompareMethod.Text)
' Returns ["This"].
Dim subStrings() As String = Filter(myStrings, "is", True, _
   CompareMethod.Binary)
' Returns ["Is", "It"].
Dim subStrings() As String = Filter(myStrings, "is", False, _
   CompareMethod.Binary)
```

See Also

Replace Function

FirstDayOfWeek Enumeration

When you call date-related functions, you can use the following enumeration members in your code in place of the actual values.

Some date-related functions take a *DayOfWeek* argument, a *WeekOfYear* argument, or both. The **FirstDayOfWeek** enumeration specifies the valid values for the *DayOfWeek* arguments, as well as the possible return values from the functions.

FirstDayOfWeek Enumeration Members

The *DayOfWeek* argument takes the following **FirstDayOfWeek** enumeration members:

Member	Constant	Description
System	**vbUseSystemDayOfWeek**	The first day of the week as specified in your system settings
Sunday	**vbSunday**	Sunday (default)
Monday	**vbMonday**	Monday
Tuesday	**vbTuesday**	Tuesday
Wednesday	**vbWednesday**	Wednesday
Thursday	**vbThursday**	Thursday
Friday	**vbFriday**	Friday
Saturday	**vbSaturday**	Saturday

Date-related functions also return **FirstDayOfWeek** values (except **System**).

See Also

FirstWeekOfYear Enumeration, DateFormat Enumeration, DateDiff Function, DatePart Function, Format Function, Weekday Function

FirstWeekOfYear Enumeration

When you call date-related functions, you can use the following enumeration members in your code in place of the actual values.

Some date-related functions take a *DayOfWeek* argument, a *WeekOfYear* argument, or both. The **FirstWeekOfYear** enumeration specifies the valid values for the *WeekOfYear* arguments, as well as the possible return values from the functions.

FirstWeekOfYear Enumeration Members

The *WeekOfYear* argument takes the following **FirstWeekOfYear** enumeration members:

Member	Constant	Description
System	**vbUseSystem**	The day of the week specified in your system settings as the first day of the week
Jan1	**vbFirstJan1**	The week in which January 1 occurs (default)
FirstFourDays	**vbFirstFourDays**	The first week that has at least four days in the new year
FirstFullWeek	**vbFirstFullWeek**	The first full week of the year

See Also

FirstDayOfWeek Enumeration, DateFormat Enumeration, DateDiff Function, DatePart Function, Format Function, Weekday Function

For

The **For** keyword introduces a loop that is iterated with different values of a loop variable.

The **For** keyword is used in these contexts:

For...Next Statements

For Each...Next Statements

See Also

Visual Basic Language Keywords

For Each...Next Statements

Repeats a group of statements for each element in an array or collection.

```
For Each element In group
   [ statements ]
[ Exit For ]
   [ statements ]
Next [ element ]
```

Parts

element

Required. Variable. Used to iterate through the elements of the collection or array. The data type of *element* must be such that the data type of the elements of *group* can be implicitly converted to it.

group

Required. Object variable. Must refer to an object collection or array.

statements

Optional. One or more statements between **For Each** and **Next** that are executed on each item in *group*.

Remarks

The **For Each...Next** loop is entered if there is at least one element in *group*. Once the loop has been entered, the statements are executed for the first element in *group*; if there are more elements in *group*, the statements in the loop continue to execute for each element. When there are no more elements, the loop is terminated and execution continues with the statement following the **Next** statement.

Any number of **Exit For** statements may be placed anywhere in the loop as an alternative way to exit. **Exit For** is often used after evaluating some condition, for example with an **If...Then...Else** statement, and transfers control to the statement immediately following **Next**.

You can nest **For Each...Next** loops by placing one loop within another. Each loop must have a unique *element* variable.

Example

This example uses the **For Each...Next** statement to search the **Text** property of all elements in a collection for the existence of the string "Hello". In the example, `MyObject` is a text-related object and is an element of the collection `MyCollection`. Both are generic names used for illustration purposes only.

```
Dim Found As Boolean = False
Dim MyObject, MyCollection As Object
For Each MyObject In MyCollection   ' Iterate through elements.
   If CStr(MyObject.Text) = "Hello" Then   ' If Text equals "Hello"
      Found = True   ' Set Found to True.
      Exit For   ' Exit loop.
   End If
Next
```

See Also

Do...Loop Statements, Exit Statement, For...Next Statements, While...End While Statements

For...Next Statements

Repeats a group of statements a specified number of times.

```
For counter = start To end [ Step step ]
   [ statements ]
[ Exit For ]
   [ statements ]
Next [ counter ]
```

Parts

counter
: Required. Variable. The type of *counter* is usually **Integer** but can be any elementary numeric type that supports the greater than (>), less than (<), and addition (+) operators.

start
: Required. Expression. The initial value of *counter*. The *start* expression usually evaluates to type **Integer** but can evaluate to any data type that widens to the type of *counter*.

end
: Required. Expression. The final value of *counter*. The *end* expression usually evaluates to type **Integer** but can evaluate to any data type that widens to the type of *counter*.

step
: Optional. Expression. The amount by which *counter* is incremented each time through the loop. The *step* expression usually evaluates to type **Integer** but can evaluate to any data type that widens to the type of *counter*. If not specified, *step* defaults to 1.

statements
: Optional. One or more statements between **For** and **Next** that are executed the specified number of times.

Remarks

The *step* argument can be either positive or negative. The value of the *step* argument determines loop processing as follows:

Step value	Loop executes if
Positive or zero	*counter* <= *end*
Negative	*counter* >= *end*

The expressions *start*, *end*, and *step* are all evaluated only once, when the **For** statement is first encountered. They are not evaluated again, even if the loop statements change their constituent parts.

The *counter* variable is compared to *end* every time before the loop is entered. This includes the first time the **For** statement is executed. Therefore, if the value of *start* is past the value of *end* when the loop is entered, the loop is not executed, and execution passes immediately to the statement following the **Next** statement.

After the loop statements have executed, *step* is added to *counter*. At this point, the **For** statement again compares *counter* to *end*. As a result of this comparison, either the statements in the loop execute again, or the loop is terminated and execution continues with the statement following the **Next** statement.

> **Note** Changing the value of *counter* while inside a loop can make it more difficult to read and debug your code.

The **Exit For** statement transfers control immediately to the statement following the **Next** statement. Any number of **Exit For** statements can be placed anywhere in the **For...Next** loop. **Exit For** is often used after evaluating some condition, for example with an **If...Then...Else** statement.

You can *nest* **For...Next** loops by placing one loop within another. Each loop must have a unique *counter* variable. The following construction is correct:

```
For I = 1 To 10
   For J = 1 To 10
      For K = 1 To 10
         ' Statements to operate with current values of I, J, and K.
      Next K
   Next J
Next I
```

> **Note** If a **Next** statement is encountered before its corresponding **For** statement, or if a **Next** statement of an outer nesting level is encountered before the **Next** of an inner level, an error occurs.

Example

This example uses the **For...Next** statement to create a string that contains 10 instances of the numbers 0 through 9, each string separated from the other by a single space. The outer loop uses a loop counter variable that is decremented each time through the loop.

```
Dim Words, Digit As Integer
Dim MyString As String
For Words = 10 To 1 Step -1     ' Set up 10 repetitions.
   For Digit = 0 To 9    ' Set up 10 repetitions.
      MyString = MyString & CStr(Digit)    ' Append number to string.
   Next Digit    ' Increment counter.
   MyString = MyString & " "    ' Append a space.
Next Words
```

See Also

Do...Loop Statements, Exit Statement, For Each...Next Statements, While...End While Statements

Format Function

Returns a string formatted according to instructions contained in a format **String** expression.

```
Public Shared Function Format( _
   ByVal Expression As Object, _
   Optional ByVal Style As String = "" _
) As String
```

Parameters

Expression
Required. Any valid expression.

Style
Optional. A valid named or user-defined format **String** expression.

Settings

For information on how to create the *Style* argument, see the appropriate topic listed below:

To format	Do this
Numbers	Use predefined numeric formats or create user-defined numeric formats.
Dates and times	Use predefined date/time formats or create user-defined date/time formats.
Date and time serial numbers	Use date and time formats or numeric formats.

If you try to format a number without specifying *Style*, the **Format** function provides functionality similar to the **Str** function, although it is internationally aware. However, positive numbers formatted as strings using the **Format** function don't include a leading space reserved for the sign of the value; those converted using the **Str** function retain the leading space.

Remarks

If you are formatting a nonlocalized numeric string, you should use a user-defined numeric format to ensure that you get the look you want.

The **String.Format** method also provides similar functionality.

Example

This example shows various uses of the **Format** function to format values using both **String** formats and user-defined formats. For the date separator (**/**), time separator (**:**), and the AM/PM indicators (**t** and **tt**), the actual formatted output displayed by your system depends on the locale settings the code is using. When times and dates are displayed in the development environment, the short time format and short date format of the code locale are used.

```
Dim MyDateTime As Date = #1/27/2001 5:04:23 PM#
Dim MyStr As String
' Returns current system time in the system-defined long time format.
MyStr = Format(Now(), "Long Time")
' Returns current system date in the system-defined long date format.
MyStr = Format(Now(), "Long Date")
' Also returns current system date in the system-defined long date
' format, using the single letter code for the format.
MyStr = Format(Now(), "D")
' Returns the value of MyDateTime in user-defined date/time formats.
MyStr = Format(MyDateTime, "h:m:s")   ' Returns "5:4:23".
MyStr = Format(MyDateTime, "hh:mm:ss tt")   ' Returns "05:04:23 PM".
MyStr = Format(MyDateTime, "dddd, MMM d yyyy")   ' Returns "Saturday,
   ' Jan 27 2001".
MyStr = Format(MyDateTime, "HH:mm:ss")   ' Returns "17:04:23"
MyStr = Format(23)   ' Returns "23".
' User-defined numeric formats.
MyStr = Format(5459.4, "##,##0.00")   ' Returns "5,459.40".
MyStr = Format(334.9, "###0.00")   ' Returns "334.90".
MyStr = Format(5, "0.00%")   ' Returns "500.00%".
```

See Also

Different Formats for Different Numeric Values (Format Function), Predefined Date/Time Formats (Format Function), Predefined Numeric Formats (Format Function), Str Function, Type Conversion Functions, User-Defined Date/Time Formats (Format Function), User-Defined Numeric Formats (Format Function)

FormatCurrency Function

Returns an expression formatted as a currency value using the currency symbol defined in the system control panel.

```
Function FormatCurrency(
   ByVal Expression As Object,
   Optional ByVal NumDigitsAfterDecimal As Integer = -1,
   Optional ByVal IncludeLeadingDigit As TriState = TriState.UseDefault,
   Optional ByVal UseParensForNegativeNumbers As TriState = TriState.UseDefault,
   Optional ByVal GroupDigits As TriState = TriState.UseDefault
) As String
```

Parameters

Expression
: Required. Expression to be formatted.

NumDigitsAfterDecimal
: Optional. Numeric value indicating how many places are displayed to the right of the decimal. Default value is –1, which indicates that the computer's regional settings are used.

IncludeLeadingDigit
: Optional. Tristate enumeration that indicates whether or not a leading zero is displayed for fractional values. See "Settings" for values.

UseParensForNegativeNumbers
: Optional. Tristate enumeration that indicates whether or not to place negative values within parentheses. See "Settings" for values.

GroupDigits
: Optional. Tristate enumeration that indicates whether or not numbers are grouped using the group delimiter specified in the computer's regional settings. See "Settings" for values.

Settings

The *IncludeLeadingDigit*, *UseParensForNegativeNumbers*, and *GroupDigits* arguments take the following Tristate enumeration values:

Value	Description
TriState.True	True
TriState.False	False
TriState.UseDefault	The computer's regional settings

Exceptions/Errors

Exception type	Error number	Condition
ArgumentException	5	Number of digits after decimal point is greater than 99.
InvalidCastException	13	Type is not numeric.

Remarks

When one or more optional arguments are omitted, the computer's matching regional-settings values are used instead.

The position of the currency symbol relative to the currency value is determined by the system's regional settings.

> **Note** All settings information comes from the locale of the application. By default, that will be the locale set in the control panel. However, it may be changed programmatically by using the .NET Framework, except leading zero, which comes from the **Number** tab.

Example

The following example illustrates the use of the **FormatCurrency** function.

```
Dim myDebt As Double = -4456.43
Dim myString As String
' Returns"($4,456.43)".
MyString = FormatCurrency(myDebt,,, TriState.True, TriState.True)
```

See Also

FormatDateTime Function, FormatNumber Function, FormatPercent Function, Tristate Enumeration

FormatDateTime Function

Returns an expression formatted as a date or time.

```
Function FormatDateTime(
   ByVal Expression As DateTime,
   Optional ByVal NamedFormat As DateFormat = DateFormat.GeneralDate
) As String
```

Parameters

Expression
: Required. Date expression to be formatted.

NamedFormat
: Optional. Numeric value that indicates the date or time format used. If omitted, **GeneralDate** is used.

Settings

The *NamedFormat* argument has the following settings:

Constant	Description
DateFormat.GeneralDate	Display a date and/or time. If there is a date part, display it as a short date. If there is a time part, display it as a long time. If present, both parts are displayed.
DateFormat.LongDate	Display a date using the long date format specified in your computer's regional settings.
DateFormat.ShortDate	Display a date using the short date format specified in your computer's regional settings.
DateFormat.LongTime	Display a time using the time format specified in your computer's regional settings.
DateFormat.ShortTime	Display a time using the 24-hour format (hh:mm).

Exceptions/Errors

Exception type	Error number	Condition
ArgumentException	5	*NamedFormat* setting is invalid.

Example

This example demonstrates the use of the **FormatDateTime** function.

```
Dim myDate As DateTime = #2/14/89#
Dim myString As String
' Returns "Tuesday, February 14, 1989".
myString = FormatDateTime(myDate, DateFormat.LongDate)
```

See Also

FormatCurrency Function, FormatNumber Function, FormatPercent Function

FormatNumber Function

Returns an expression formatted as a number.

```
Function FormatNumber(
   ByVal Expression As Object,
   Optional ByVal NumDigitsAfterDecimal As Integer = -1,
   Optional ByVal IncludeLeadingDigit As TriState = TriState.UseDefault,
   Optional ByVal UseParensForNegativeNumbers As TriState = TriState.UseDefault,
   Optional ByVal GroupDigits As TriState = TriState.UseDefault
) As String
```

Parameters

Expression

Required. Expression to be formatted.

NumDigitsAfterDecimal

Optional. Numeric value indicating how many places are displayed to the right of the decimal. The default value is –1, which indicates that the computer's regional settings are used.

IncludeLeadingDigit

Optional. Tristate constant that indicates whether a leading zero is displayed for fractional values. See "Settings" for values.

UseParensForNegativeNumbers

Optional. Tristate constant that indicates whether to place negative values within parentheses. See "Settings" for values.

GroupDigits

Optional. Tristate constant that indicates whether or not numbers are grouped using the group delimiter specified in the locale settings. See "Settings" for values.

Settings

The *IncludeLeadingDigit*, *UseParensForNegativeNumbers*, and *GroupDigits* arguments have the following settings:

Constant	Description
TriState.True	True
TriState.False	False
TriState.UseDefault	The computer's regional settings

Exceptions/Errors

Exception type	Error number	Condition
InvalidCastException	13	Type is not numeric.

Remarks

When one or more optional arguments are omitted, the values for omitted arguments are provided by the locale settings.

Note All settings information comes from the locale of the application. by default, that will be the locale set in the control panel. However, it may be changed programmatically by using the .NET Framework.

Example

This example demonstrates the **FormatNumber** function.

```
Dim myNumber As Integer = 45600
Dim myString As String
' Returns "45,600.00".
myString = FormatNumber(myNumber, 2, , ,TriState.True)
```

See Also

FormatCurrency Function, FormatDateTime Function, FormatPercent Function, Tristate Enumeration

FormatPercent Function

Returns an expression formatted as a percentage (that is, multiplied by 100) with a trailing % character.

```
Function FormatPercent(
    ByVal Expression As Object,
    Optional ByVal NumDigitsAfterDecimal As Integer = -1,
    Optional ByVal IncludeLeadingDigit As TriState = TriState.UseDefault,
    Optional ByVal UseParensForNegativeNumbers As TriState = TriState.UseDefault,
    Optional ByVal GroupDigits As TriState = TriState.UseDefault
) As String
```

Parameters

Expression
: Required. Expression to be formatted.

NumDigitsAfterDecimal
: Optional. Numeric value indicating how many places to the right of the decimal are displayed. Default value is –1, which indicates that the locale settings are used.

IncludeLeadingDigit
: Optional. Tristate constant that indicates whether or not a leading zero is displayed for fractional values. See "Settings" for values.

UseParensForNegativeNumbers
: Optional. Tristate constant that indicates whether or not to place negative values within parentheses. See "Settings" for values.

GroupDigits
: Optional. Tristate constant that indicates whether or not numbers are grouped using the group delimiter specified in the locale settings. See "Settings" for values.

Settings

The *IncludeLeadingDigit*, *UseParensForNegativeNumbers*, and *GroupDigits* arguments have the following settings:

Constant	Description
TriState.True	True
TriState.False	False
TriState.Default	The computer's regional settings

Exceptions/Errors

Exception type	Error number	Condition
InvalidCastException	13	Type is not numeric.

Remarks

When one or more optional arguments are omitted, the values for omitted arguments are provided by the locale settings.

> **Note** All settings information comes from the locale of the application. by default, that will be the locale set in the control panel. However, it may be changed programmatically by using the .NET Framework.

Example

This example illustrates the use of the **FormatPercent** function:

```
Dim myNumber As Single = 0.76
Dim myString As String
' Returns "76.00%".
myString = FormatPercent(myNumber)
```

See Also

FormatCurrency Function, FormatDateTime Function, FormatNumber Function, Tristate Enumeration

FreeFile Function

Returns an **Integer** value representing the next file number available for use by the **FileOpen** function.

```
Public Function FreeFile() As Integer
```

Exceptions/Errors

Exception type	Error number	Condition
IOException	67	More than 255 files are in use.

Remarks

Use **FreeFile** to supply a file number that is not already in use.

Example

This example uses the **FreeFile** function to return the next available file number. Five files are opened for output within the loop, and some sample data is written to each.

```
Dim count As Integer
Dim fileNumber As Integer
For count = 1 To 5
   fileNumber = FreeFile()
   FileOpen(fileNumber, "TEST" & count & ".TXT", OpenMode.Output)
   PrintLine(fileNumber, "This is a sample.")
   FileClose(fileNumber)
Next
```

See Also

FileOpen Function

Friend

The **Friend** keyword confers friend access on one or more declared programming elements. Friend elements are accessible from within the program that contains their declaration and from anywhere else in the same assembly.

The **Friend** keyword can be used in conjunction with the **Protected** keyword in the same declaration. This combination confers both friend and protected access on the declared elements, so they are accessible from the same assembly, from their own class, and from any derived classes.

The **Friend** keyword is used in these contexts:

- Class Statement
- Const Statement
- Declare Statement
- Delegate Statement
- Dim Statement
- Enum Statement
- Event Statement
- Function Statement
- Interface Statement
- Module Statement
- Property Statement
- Structure Statement
- Sub Statement

See Also

Protected

Function Statement

Declares the name, arguments, and code that define a **Function** procedure.

```
[ <attrlist> ] [{ Overloads | Overrides | Overridable |
NotOverridable | MustOverride | Shadows | Shared }]
[{ Public | Protected | Friend | Protected Friend | Private }]
Function name[(arglist)] [ As type ] [ Implements interface.definedname ]
   [ statements ]
   [ Exit Function ]
   [ statements ]
End Function
```

Parts

attrlist

Optional. List of attributes that apply to this procedure. Multiple attributes are separated by commas.

Overloads

Optional. Indicates that this **Function** procedure overloads one or more procedures defined with the same name in a base class. The argument list in this declaration must be different from the argument list of every overloaded procedure. The lists must differ in the number of arguments, their data types, or both. This allows the compiler to distinguish which version to use.

You do not have to use the **Overloads** keyword when you are defining multiple overloaded procedures in the same class. However, if you use **Overloads** in one of the declarations, you must use it in all of them.

You cannot specify both **Overloads** and **Shadows** in the same procedure declaration.

Overrides

Optional. Indicates that this **Function** procedure overrides an identically named procedure in a base class. The number and data types of the arguments, and the data type of the return value, must exactly match those of the base class procedure.

Overridable

Optional. Indicates that this **Function** procedure can be overridden by an identically named procedure in a derived class. **Overridable** is the default setting for a procedure that itself overrides a base class procedure.

NotOverridable

Optional. Indicates that this **Function** procedure cannot be overridden in a derived class. **NotOverridable** is the default setting for a procedure that does not itself override a base class procedure.

MustOverride

Optional. Indicates that this **Function** procedure is not implemented in this class, and must be implemented in a derived class for that class to be creatable.

Shadows

Optional. Indicates that this **Function** procedure shadows an identically named programming element, or set of overloaded elements, in a base class. You can shadow any kind of declared element with any other kind. If you shadow a procedure with another procedure, the arguments and the return type do not have to match those in the base class procedure. A shadowed element is unavailable in the derived class that shadows it.

You cannot specify both **Overloads** and **Shadows** in the same procedure declaration.

Shared

Optional. Indicates that this **Function** procedure is a shared procedure. This means it is not associated with a specific instance of a class or structure. You can call a shared procedure by qualifying it either with the class or structure name, or with the variable name of a specific instance of the class or structure.

Public

Optional. Procedures declared with the **Public** keyword have public access. There are no restrictions on the accessibility of public procedures.

Protected

Optional. Procedures declared with the **Protected** keyword have protected access. They are accessible only from within their own class or from a derived class. Protected access can be specified only on members of classes. It is not a superset of friend access.

Friend

Optional. Procedures declared with the **Friend** keyword have friend access. They are accessible from within the program that contains their declaration and from anywhere else in the same assembly.

Protected Friend

Optional. Procedures declared with the **Protected Friend** keywords have the union of protected and friend access. They can be used by code in the same assembly, as well as by code in derived classes. Protected friend access can be specified only on members of classes.

Private

Optional. Procedures declared with the **Private** keyword have private access. They are accessible only from within their declaration context, including from members of any nested types such as procedures.

name

Required. Name of the **Function** procedure. Must be a valid Visual Basic identifier.

arglist

Optional. List of variables or expressions representing arguments that are passed to the **Function** procedure when it is called. Multiple arguments are separated by commas. If you supply an argument list, you must enclose it in parentheses.

type

Optional unless **Option Strict** is **On**. Data type of the value returned by the **Function** procedure. Can be **Boolean**, **Byte**, **Char**, **Date**, **Decimal**, **Double**, **Integer**, **Long**, **Object**, **Short**, **Single**, or **String**; or the name of an enumeration, structure, class, or interface.

Implements

Optional. Indicates that this **Function** procedure implements a **Function** procedure defined by an interface.

interface

Required if **Implements** is supplied. The interface implemented by the class or structure containing this **Function** procedure. The class or structure must specify *interface* in an **Implements** statement immediately following the **Class** or **Structure** statement.

definedname

Required if **Implements** is supplied. The name by which the **Function** procedure is defined in *interface*. The name of this **Function** procedure (in *name*) does not have to be the same as *definedname*.

statements

Optional. A block of statements to be executed within the **Function** procedure.

End Function

Terminates the definition of this **Function** procedure.

Each argument in the *arglist* part has the following syntax and parts:

```
[ <attrlist> ] [ Optional ] [{ ByVal | ByRef }] [ ParamArray ]
argname[( )] [ As argtype ] [ = defaultvalue ]
```

arglist Parts

attrlist
: Optional. List of attributes that apply to this argument. Multiple attributes are separated by commas.

Optional
: Optional. Indicates that this argument is not required when the procedure is called. If this keyword is used, all subsequent arguments in *arglist* must also be optional and be declared using the **Optional** keyword. Every optional argument declaration must supply the *defaultvalue* clause. **Optional** cannot be used for any argument if **ParamArray** is used.

ByVal
: Optional. Indicates that the procedure cannot replace or reassign the underlying variable element in the calling code. However, if the argument is a reference type, the procedure can modify the contents or members of the underlying object. **ByVal** is the default in Visual Basic.

ByRef
: Optional. Indicates that the procedure can modify the underlying variable in the calling code the same way the calling code itself can.

ParamArray
: Optional. Used only as the last argument in *arglist* to indicate that the final argument is an optional array of elements of the specified type. The **ParamArray** keyword allows you to pass an arbitrary number of arguments to the procedure. A **ParamArray** argument is always passed using **ByVal**.

argname
: Required. Name of the variable representing the argument. Must be a valid Visual Basic identifier.

argtype
: Optional unless **Option Strict** is **On**. Data type of the argument passed to the procedure. Can be **Boolean**, **Byte**, **Char**, **Date**, **Decimal**, **Double**, **Integer**, **Long**, **Object**, **Short**, **Single**, or **String**; or the name of an enumeration, structure, class, or interface.

defaultvalue
: Required for **Optional** arguments. Any constant or constant expression that evaluates to the data type of the argument. If the type is **Object**; or a class, interface, array, or structure, the default value can only be **Nothing**.

Each attribute in the *attrlist* part has the following syntax and parts:

```
attrname [({ attrargs | attrinit })]
```

attrlist Parts

attrname
: Required. Name of the attribute. Must be a valid Visual Basic identifier.

attrargs
: Optional. List of positional arguments for this attribute. Multiple arguments are separated by commas.

attrinit
: Optional. List of field or property initializers for this attribute. Multiple initializers are separated by commas.

Remarks

All executable code must be in procedures. You can define a **Function** procedure inside a module, class, interface, or structure, but not inside another procedure.

Function procedures are **Public** by default. To specify a different accessibility, include **Protected**, **Friend**, **Protected Friend**, or **Private** in the declaration.

When the **Function** procedure returns to the calling program, execution continues with the statement following the statement that called it.

The **Exit Function** statement causes an immediate exit from a **Function** procedure. Any number of **Exit Function** statements can appear anywhere in the procedure.

To return a value from a function, you can either assign the value to the function name or include it in a **Return** statement. The following example assigns the return value to the function name `MyFunction` and then uses the **Exit Function** statement to return:

```
Function MyFunction(ByVal J As Integer) As Double
   ' ...
   MyFunction = 3.87
   ' ...
   Exit Function
   ' ...
End Function
```

If you use **Exit Function** without assigning a value to *name*, the function returns the default value appropriate to *argtype*. This is 0 for **Byte**, **Char**, **Decimal**, **Double**, **Integer**, **Long**, **Short**, and **Single**; **Nothing** for **Object**, **String**, and all arrays; **False** for **Boolean**; and #1/1/0001 12:00 AM# for **Date**.

The **Return** statement simultaneously assigns the return value and exits the function, as in the following example:

```
Function MyFunction(ByVal J As Integer) As Double
   ' ...
   Return 3.87
   ' ...
End Function
```

Any number of **Return** statements can appear anywhere in the procedure. You can also mix **Exit Function** and **Return** statements.

You can use a **Function** procedure on the right side of an expression when you want to use the value returned by the function. You use the **Function** procedure the same way you use any library function such as **Sqrt**, **Cos**, or **ChrW**.

You call a **Function** procedure by using the procedure name, followed by the argument list in parentheses, in an expression. You can omit the parentheses only if you are not supplying any arguments. A function can also be called using the **Call** statement, in which case the return value is ignored.

Note Visual Basic sometimes rearranges arithmetic expressions to increase internal efficiency. For that reason, avoid using a **Function** procedure in an arithmetic expression when the function changes the value of variables in the same expression.

Example

This example uses the **Function** statement to declare the name, arguments, and code that form the body of a **Function** procedure. The last example uses hard-typed, initialized **Optional** arguments.

```
' The following user-defined function returns the square root of the
' argument passed to it.
Function CalculateSquareRoot(ByVal NumberArg As Double) As Double
   If NumberArg < 0 Then    ' Evaluate argument.
      Exit Function    ' Exit to calling procedure.
   Else
      CalculateSquareRoot = Sqrt(NumberArg)    ' Return square root.
   End If
End Function
```

Using the **ParamArray** keyword enables a function to accept a variable number of arguments.

```
' If a function's arguments are defined as follows:
Function CalcSum(ByVal ParamArray Args() As Double) As Object
' The function can be invoked as follows:
Dim ReturnedValue As Object
ReturnedValue = CalcSum(4, 3, 2, 1)
' Local variables are assigned the following values:
' Args(0) = 4, Args(1) = 3, and so on.
```

Optional arguments can have default values and types, as long as the types are specified within the function.

```
' If a function's arguments are defined as follows:
Function MyFunc(MyStr As String, Optional MyArg1 As Integer = 5, _
                Optional MyArg2 As String = "Dolly") As Object
' The function can be invoked as follows:
Dim RetVal As Object
RetVal = MyFunc("Hello", 2, "World") ' All 3 arguments supplied.
RetVal = MyFunc("Test", , 5) ' Second argument omitted.
' Arguments one and three passing arguments by name.
RetVal = MyFunc(MyStr:="Hello", MyArg2:="World")
```

See Also

Sub Statement, Dim Statement, Implements Statement

FV Function

Returns a **Double** specifying the future value of an annuity based on periodic, fixed payments and a fixed interest rate.

```
Function FV( _
   ByVal Rate As Double, _
   ByVal NPer As Double, _
   ByVal Pmt As Double, _
   Optional ByVal PV As Double = 0, _
   Optional ByVal Due As DueDate = DueDate.EndOfPeriod _
) As Double
```

Parameters

Rate

Required. **Double** specifying interest rate per period. For example, if you get a car loan at an annual percentage rate (APR) of 10 percent and make monthly payments, the rate per period is 0.1/12, or 0.0083.

NPer

Required. **Double** specifying total number of payment periods in the annuity. For example, if you make monthly payments on a four-year car loan, your loan has a total of 4 * 12 (or 48) payment periods.

Pmt

Required. **Double** specifying payment to be made each period. Payments usually contain principal and interest that doesn't change over the life of the annuity.

PV

Optional. **Double** specifying present value (or lump sum) of a series of future payments. For example, when you borrow money to buy a car, the loan amount is the present value to the lender of the monthly car payments you will make. If omitted, 0 is assumed.

Due

Optional. Object of type `Microsoft.VisualBasic.DueDate` that specifies when payments are due. This argument must be either `DueDate.EndOfPeriod` if payments are due at the end of the payment period, or `DueDate.BegOfPeriod` if payments are due at the beginning of the period. If omitted, `DueDate.EndOfPeriod` is assumed.

Remarks

An annuity is a series of fixed cash payments made over a period of time. An annuity can be a loan (such as a home mortgage) or an investment (such as a monthly savings plan).

The *Rate* and *NPer* arguments must be calculated using payment periods expressed in the same units. For example, if *Rate* is calculated using months, *NPer* must also be calculated using months.

For all arguments, cash paid out (such as deposits to savings) is represented by negative numbers; cash received (such as dividend checks) is represented by positive numbers.

Example

This example uses the **FV** function to return the future value of an investment given the percentage rate that accrues per period (`APR / 12`), the total number of payments (`TotPmts`), the payment (`Payment`), the current value of the investment (`PVal`), and a number that indicates whether the payment is made at the beginning or end of the payment period (`PayType`). Note that because `Payment` represents cash paid out, it is a negative number.

```
Sub TestFV()
   Dim Fmt As String
   Dim TotPmts As Integer
   Dim Payment, APR, PVal, Fval As Double
   Dim PayType As DueDate
   Dim Response As MsgBoxResult
   Fmt = "###,###,##0.00"    ' Define money format.
   Payment = CDbl(InputBox("How much do you plan to save each month?"))
   APR = CDbl(InputBox("Enter the expected interest annual percentage rate."))
   If APR > 1 Then APR = APR / 100 ' Ensure proper form.
   TotPmts = CInt(InputBox("For how many months do you expect to save?"))
   Response = MsgBox("Do you make payments at the end of month?", MsgBoxStyle.YesNo)
   If Response = MsgBoxResult.No Then
      PayType = DueDate.BegOfPeriod
   Else
      PayType = DueDate.EndOfPeriod
   End If
   PVal = CDbl(InputBox("How much is in this savings account now?"))
   Fval = FV(APR / 12, TotPmts, -Payment, -PVal, PayType)
   MsgBox("Your savings will be worth " & Format(Fval, Fmt) & ".")
End Sub
```

See Also

DDB Function, IPmt Function, IRR Function, MIRR Function, NPer Function, NPV Function, Pmt Function, PPmt Function, PV Function, Rate Function, SLN Function, SYD Function

Get Statement

Declares a **Get** property procedure used to assign a value to a property.

```
[ <attrlist> ] Get()
   [ block ]
End Get
```

Parts

attrlist

Optional. List of attributes that apply to this **Get** block. Multiple attributes are separated by commas.

block

Optional. The body of the **Get** property procedure contains code to return the property value.

End Get

Terminates a **Get** property procedure.

Each attribute in the *attrlist* part has the following syntax and parts:

```
attrname [({ attrargs | attrinit })]
```

attrlist Parts

attrname

Required. Name of the attribute. Must be a valid Visual Basic identifier.

attrargs

Optional. List of positional arguments for this attribute. Multiple arguments are separated by commas.

attrinit

Optional. List of field or property initializers for this attribute. Multiple initializers are separated by commas.

Remarks

Get property procedures can return a value using either the **Return** keyword or by assigning the return value to the property where the get procedure is declared. The value returned by a **Get** property procedure is usually a private class level variable that stored the property value after a property set operation.

Example

This example uses the **Get** statement to return the value of a property.

```
Class PropClass
   ' Define a local variable to store the property value.
   Private CurrentTime As String
   ' Define the property.
   Public ReadOnly Property DateAndTime() As String
      Get
         ' Get procedure is called when the value
         ' of a property is retrieved.
         CurrentTime = CStr(Now)
         Return CurrentTime    ' Returns the date and time As a string.
      End Get
   End Property
End Class
```

See Also

Set Statement, Property Statement

GetAllSettings Function

Returns a list of key settings and their respective values (originally created with **SaveSetting**) from an application's entry in the Windows registry.

```
Public Function GetAllSettings( _
   ByVal AppName As String, _
   ByVal Section As String _
) As String(,)
```

Parameters

AppName
: Required. **String** expression containing the name of the application or project whose key settings are requested.

Section
: Required. **String** expression containing the name of the section whose key settings are requested. **GetAllSettings** returns an object that contains a two-dimensional array of strings. The strings contain all the key settings in the specified section plus their corresponding values.

Exceptions/Errors

Exception type	Error number	Condition
ArgumentException	5	User is not logged in.

Remarks

GetAllSettings returns an uninitialized **Object** if either *AppName* or *Section* does not exist.

GetAllSettings requires that a user be logged on since it operates under the HKEY_LOCAL_USER registry key, which is not active until a user logs on interactively.

Registry settings that are to be accessed from a non-interactive process (such as mtx.exe) should be stored under either the HKEY_LOCAL_MACHINE\Software\ or the HKEY_USER\DEFAULT\Software registry keys.

Example

This example first uses the **SaveSetting** statement to make entries in the Windows registry for the application specified as *AppName*, then uses the **GetAllSettings** function to display the settings. Note that application names and *Section* names can't be retrieved with **GetAllSettings**. Finally, the **DeleteSetting** statement removes the application's entries.

```
' Object to hold 2-dimensional array returned by GetAllSettings.
' Integer to hold counter.
Dim MySettings(,) As String
Dim intSettings As Integer
' Place some settings in the registry.
SaveSetting("MyApp", "Startup", "Top", "75")
SaveSetting("MyApp", "Startup", "Left", "50")
' Retrieve the settings.
MySettings = GetAllSettings("MyApp", "Startup")
For intSettings = LBound(MySettings, 1) To UBound(MySettings, 1)
   Debug.WriteLine(MySettings(intSettings, 0))
   Debug.WriteLine(MySettings(intSettings, 1))
Next intSettings
DeleteSetting("MyApp")
```

See Also

DeleteSetting Function, GetSetting Function, SaveSetting Function

GetAttr Function

Returns a **FileAttribute** value representing the attributes of a file, directory, or folder.

```
Public Function GetAttr(ByVal PathName As String) As FileAttribute
```

Parameter

PathName

Required. **String** expression that specifies a file, directory, or folder name. *PathName* may include the directory or folder, and the drive.

Return Values

The value returned by **GetAttr** is the sum of the following enumeration values:

Value	Constant	Description
Normal	**VbNormal**	Normal.
ReadOnly	**VbReadOnly**	Read-only.
Hidden	**VbHidden**	Hidden.
System	**VbSystem**	System file.
Directory	**VbDirectory**	Directory or folder.
Archive	**VbArchive**	File has changed since last backup.
Alias	**VbAlias**	File has a different name.

Note These enumerations are specified by the Visual Basic language. The names can be used anywhere in your code in place of the actual values.

Exceptions/Errors

Exception type	Error number	Condition
IOException	52	*Pathname* is invalid or contains wildcards.
FileNotFoundException	53	Target file does not exist.

Remarks

To determine which attributes are set, use the **And** operator to perform a bitwise comparison of the value returned by the **GetAttr** function and the value of the individual file attribute you want. If the result is not zero, that attribute is set for the named file. For example, the return value of the following **And** expression is zero if the Archive attribute is not set:

```
Result = GetAttr(FName) And vbArchive
```

A nonzero value is returned if the **Archive** attribute is set.

Example

This example uses the **GetAttr** function to determine the attributes of a file and directory or folder.

```
Dim MyAttr As FileAttribute
' Assume file TESTFILE is normal and readonly.
MyAttr = GetAttr("C:\TESTFILE.txt")   ' Returns VbNormal.

' Test for normal.
If (MyAttr And FileAttribute.Normal) = FileAttribute.Normal Then
   MsgBox("This file is normal.")
End If
```

(continued)

(continued)

```
' Test for normal and readonly.
Dim normalReadonly As FileAttribute
normalReadonly = FileAttribute.Normal Or FileAttribute.ReadOnly
If (MyAttr And normalReadonly) = normalReadonly Then
   MsgBox("This file is normal and readonly.")
End If

' Assume MYDIR is a directory or folder.
MyAttr = GetAttr("C:\MYDIR")
If (MyAttr And FileAttribute.Directory) = FileAttribute.Directory Then
   MsgBox("MYDIR is a directory")
End If
```

See Also

And Operator, FileAttr Function, SetAttr Function

GetChar Function

Returns a **Char** value representing the character from the specified index in the supplied string.

```
Public Shared Function GetChar( _
   ByVal Str As String, _
   ByVal Index As Integer _
) As Char
```

Parameters

Str
: Required. Any valid **String** expression.

Index
: Required. **Integer** expression. The (1-based) index of the character in *Str* to be returned.

Exceptions/Errors

Exception type	Error number	Condition
ArgumentException	5	*Str* is **Nothing**, *Index* < 1, or *Index* is greater than index of last character of *Str*.

Remarks

If *Index* is less than 1 or greater than the index of the last character in *Str*, an **ArgumentException** is thrown.

Example

This example shows how to use the **GetChar** function to return a character from a specified index in a **String**.

```
Dim myString As String = "ABCDE"
Dim myChar As Char
myChar = GetChar(myString, 4)    ' myChar = "D"
```

See Also

Mid Function

GetEnumerator Method

Returns a reference to an **IEnumerator** interface, whose purpose is to grant access to an enumeration's items.

```
Public Function GetEnumerator() As IEnumerator
```

Remarks

When **GetEnumerator** is called, it constructs an enumerator object containing the current version number in the collection and a reference to the collection's items. Every time the enumerator is accessed, it compares the version of the enumerator with the version of the collection. If the versions do not match, it means that the collection has changed; an exception then occurs.

Example

The following example shows how to use **GetEnumerator** to retrieve a member of an enumeration.

```
Public Sub GetEnumerator() As IEnumerator
Implements IEnumerable.GetEnumerator
GetEnumerator = MyCollection.GetEnumerator
End Function
```

GetException Function

Returns the exception representing the error that occurred.

```
Overridable Public Function GetException() As Exception
```

Remarks

The **GetException** function is available only from the **Err** object class. It works with the **Exception** property of the **Err** object to display the error that has occurred.

Example

The following code displays the message assigned to the exception in the **Err** object:

```
On Error Resume Next
Dim myError As System.Exception
' Generate an overflow exception.
Err.Raise(6)
' Assigns the exception from the Err object to myError.
myError = Err.GetException()
' Displays the message associated with the exception.
MsgBox(myError.Message)
```

See Also

Err Object

GetObject Function

Returns a reference to an object provided by a COM component.

```
Public Function GetObject( _
   Optional ByVal PathName As String = Nothing, _
   Optional ByVal Class As String = Nothing _
) As Object
```

Parameters

PathName

Optional; **String**. The full path and name of the file containing the object to retrieve. If *pathname* is omitted, *class* is required.

Class

Optional; **String**. A string representing the class of the object.

The *Class* argument has the following syntax and parts:

```
appname.objecttype
```

Class Parameters

appname

Required; **String**. The name of the application providing the object.

objecttype

Required; **String**. The type or class of object to create.

Exceptions/Errors

Exception type	Error number	Condition
Exception	429	No object with the specified pathname exists.
FileNotFoundException	432	No object of the specified type exists.

Remarks

Use the **GetObject** function to load an instance of a COM component from a file. For example:

```
Dim CADObject As Object
CADObject = GetObject("C:\CAD\SCHEMA.CAD")
```

When this code is executed, the application associated with the specified *pathname* is started and the object in the specified file is activated.

If *PathName* is a zero-length string (" "), **GetObject** returns a new object instance of the specified type. If the *PathName* argument is omitted, **GetObject** returns a currently active object of the specified type. If no object of the specified type exists, an error occurs.

Some applications allow you to activate a sub-object associated with a file. Add an exclamation point (!) to the end of the file name and follow it with a string that identifies the part of the file you want to activate. For information on how to create this string, see the documentation for the application that created the object.

For example, in a drawing application you might have multiple layers to a drawing stored in a file. You could use the following code to activate a layer within a drawing called `SCHEMA.CAD`:

```
LayerObject = GetObject("C:\CAD\SCHEMA.CAD!Layer3")
```

If you don't specify the object's *Class*, Automation determines the application to start and the object to activate, based on the file name you provide. Some files, however, may support more than one class of object. For example, a drawing might support three different types of objects: an Application object, a Drawing object, and a Toolbar object, all of which are part of the same file. To specify which object in a file you want to activate, use the optional *Class* argument. For example:

```
Dim MyObject As Object
MyObject = GetObject("C:\DRAWINGS\SAMPLE.DRW", "FIGMENT.DRAWING")
```

In the example, `FIGMENT` is the name of a drawing application and `DRAWING` is one of the object types it supports.

Once an object is activated, you reference it in code using the object variable you defined. In the preceding example, you access properties and methods of the new object using the object variable `MyObject`. For example:

```
MyObject.Line (9, 90)
MyObject.InsertText (9, 100, "Hello, world.")
MyObject.SaveAs ("C:\DRAWINGS\SAMPLE.DRW")
```

Note Use the **GetObject** function when there is a current instance of the object or if you want to create the object with a file already loaded. If there is no current instance, and you do not want the object started with a file loaded, use the **CreateObject** function. If an object has registered itself as an ActiveX® single-instance object, only one instance of the object is created, no matter how many times **CreateObject** is executed. With a single-instance object, **GetObject** always returns the same instance when called with the zero-length string (" ") syntax, and it causes an error if the *PathName* argument is omitted. You cannot use **GetObject** to obtain a reference to a class created with Visual Basic.

Example

This example uses the **GetObject** function to get a reference to a specific Microsoft Excel worksheet (`MyXL`). It uses the worksheet's Application property to make Microsoft Excel visible, to close it, and so on. Using two API calls, the `DetectExcel` sub procedure looks for Microsoft Excel, and if it is running, enters it in the running object table. The first call to **GetObject** causes an error if Microsoft Excel isn't already running. In the example, the error causes the `ExcelWasNotRunning` flag to be set to `True`. The second call to **GetObject** specifies a file to open. If Microsoft Excel isn't already running, the second call starts it and returns a reference to the worksheet represented by the specified file, `test.xls`. The file must exist in the specified location; otherwise, the Visual Basic error Automation error is generated. Next the example code makes both Microsoft Excel and the window containing the specified worksheet visible.

Option Strict Off is required because this example uses late binding, where objects are assigned to generic object variables. You can specify **Option Strict On** and declare objects of specific object types if you add a reference to the Excel type library from the **COM** tab of the **Add Reference** dialog box of the **Project** menu in Visual Studio .NET.

```
' Add Option Strict Off to the top of your program.
Option Strict Off
 ' Declare necessary API routines:
   Declare Function FindWindow Lib "user32" Alias _
      "FindWindowA" (ByVal lpClassName As String, _
      ByVal lpWindowName As Long) As Long

   Declare Function SendMessage Lib "user32" Alias _
   "SendMessageA" (ByVal hWnd As Long, ByVal wMsg As Long, _
      ByVal wParam As Long, ByVal lParam As Long) As Long

Sub GetExcel()
   Dim MyXL As Object   ' Variable to hold reference
   ' to Microsoft Excel.
   Dim ExcelWasNotRunning As Boolean   ' Flag for final release.
```

```
    ' Test to see if there is a copy of Microsoft Excel already running.
    On Error Resume Next    ' Defer error trapping.
    ' Getobject function called without the first argument returns a
    ' reference to an instance of the application.
    ' If the application is not running, an error occurs.
    MyXL = GetObject(, "Excel.Application")
    If Err().Number <> 0 Then ExcelWasNotRunning = True
    Err().Clear() ' Clear Err object in case error occurred.

    ' Check for Microsoft Excel. If Microsoft Excel is running,
    ' enter it into the Running Object table.
    DetectExcel()

    ' Set the object variable to reference the file you want to see.
    MyXL = GetObject("c:\vb\TEST.XLS")

    ' Show Microsoft Excel through its Application property. Then
    ' show the actual window containing the file using the Windows
    ' collection of the MyXL object reference.
    MyXL.Application.Visible = True
    MyXL.Parent.Windows(1).Visible = True
    '  Do manipulations of your  file here.
    '
End Sub

Sub DetectExcel()
    ' Procedure dectects a running Excel and registers it.
    Const WM_USER = 1024
    Dim hWnd As Long
    ' If Excel is running this API call returns its handle.
    hWnd = FindWindow("XLMAIN", 0)
    If hWnd = 0 Then    ' 0 means Excel not running.
        Exit Sub
    Else
        ' Excel is running so use the SendMessage API
        ' function to enter it in the Running Object Table.
        SendMessage(hWnd, WM_USER + 18, 0, 0)
    End If
End Sub
```

When you call the `GetExcel` function, a check is made to see if Excel is already running. If it is not, then an instance of Excel is created.

See Also

CreateObject Function, Declare Statement

GetSetting Function

Returns a key setting value from an application's entry in the Windows registry.

```
Public Function GetSetting( _
   ByVal AppName As String, _
   ByVal Section As String, _
   ByVal Key As String, _
   Optional ByVal Default As String = "" _
) As String
```

Parameters

AppName
Required. **String** expression containing the name of the application or project whose key setting is requested.

Section
Required. **String** expression containing the name of the section in which the key setting is found.

Key
Required. **String** expression containing the name of the key setting to return.

Default
Optional. Expression containing the value to return if no value is set in the *Key* setting. If omitted, *Default* is assumed to be a zero-length string (" ").

Exceptions/Errors

Exception type	Error number	Condition
ArgumentException	5	One or more arguments are not **String** expressions, or user is not logged in.

Remarks

If any of the items named in the **GetSetting** arguments do not exist, **GetSetting** returns a value of *Default*.

GetSetting requires that a user be logged on since it operates under the HKEY_LOCAL_USER registry key, which is not active until a user logs on interactively.

Registry settings that are to be accessed from a non-interactive process (such as mtx.exe) should be stored under either the HKEY_LOCAL_MACHINE\Software\ or the HKEY_USER\DEFAULT\Software registry keys.

Example

This example first uses the **SaveSetting** statement to make entries in the Windows registry for the application specified as *AppName*, and then uses the **GetSetting** function to display one of the settings. Because the *Default* argument is specified, some value is guaranteed to be returned. Note that *Section* names can't be retrieved with **GetSetting**. Finally, the **DeleteSetting** statement removes all the application's entries.

```
' Place some settings in the registry.
SaveSetting("MyApp", "Startup", "Top", "75")
SaveSetting("MyApp", "Startup", "Left", "50")
Console.WriteLine(GetSetting("MyApp", "Startup", "Left", "25"))
DeleteSetting("MyApp")
```

See Also

DeleteSetting Function, GetAllSettings Function, SaveSetting Function

GetType Operator

Returns the type object of the specified type. The type object can be used to retrieve various information about the type such as its properties, methods, and events.

```
GetType(typename)
```

Parameters

typename
The name of the type within the class object.

Remarks

The **GetType** operator returns the type object for the specified *typename*. If you want to get the type object of an object variable, use Type.GetType Method.

Example

The following examples show the **GetType** operator in use.

```
GetType(Integer)   ' Returns the integer class object.
GetType(Project1.Type1)   ' Returns the class object for Project1.Type1.
GetType(String())   ' Returns the class object for 1D string arrays.
```

See Also

Operator Precedence in Visual Basic, Operators Listed by Functionality, Operators

GoTo Statement

Branches unconditionally to a specified line within a procedure.

```
GoTo line
```

Part

line

Required. Any line label.

Remarks

GoTo can branch only to lines within the procedure where it appears.

You cannot use a **GoTo** to branch from outside a **For...Next**, **For Each...Next**, **SyncLock...End SyncLock**, **Try...Catch...Finally**, or **With...End With** block to a label inside.

Within a **Try...Catch...Finally** block, you cannot use **GoTo** to branch into or out of a **Catch** or **Finally** block.

> **Note** **GoTo** statements can make code difficult to read and maintain. Whenever possible, use **Do...Loop**, **For...Next**, **If...Then...Else**, **Select Case**, **Try...Catch...Finally**, **While**, and **With...End With** structures instead.

Example

This example uses the **GoTo** statement to branch to line labels within a procedure.

```
Sub GotoStatementDemo()
Dim Number As Integer
dim MyString As String
   Number = 1   ' Initialize variable.
   ' Evaluate Number and branch to appropriate label.
   If Number = 1 Then GoTo Line1 Else GoTo Line2

Line1:
   MyString = "Number equals 1"
   GoTo LastLine   ' Go to LastLine.
Line2:
   ' The following statement never gets executed because Number = 1.
   MyString = "Number equals 2"
LastLine:
   ' Print "Number equals 1" in the Output window.
   Debug.WriteLine (MyString)
End Sub
```

See Also

Do...Loop Statements, For...Next Statements, If...Then...Else Statements, Select...Case Statements

Handles

The **Handles** keyword is used to declare that a procedure handles a specified event.

```
proceduredeclaration Handles event
```

Parts

proceduredeclaration
The **Sub** procedure declaration for the procedure that will handle the event.

event
The name of the event being handled. This event must be raised by either the base class for the current class, or by an object declared using the **WithEvents** keyword.

Remarks

Use the **Handles** keyword at the end of a procedure declaration to cause it to handle events raised by an object variable declared using the **WithEvents** keyword. The **Handles** keyword can also be used in a derived class to handle events from a base class.

Example

```
WithEvents Obj As New Class2()   ' Module or class level declaration.
Sub EventHandler() Handles Obj.Ev_Event
   MsgBox("EventHandler caught event.")   ' Handle the event.
End Sub

Public Class Class2
   Public Event Ev_Event()     ' Declare an event.
   Sub CauseSomeEvent()
      RaiseEvent Ev_Event()    ' Raise an event.
   End Sub
End Class

Public Class Class3
   Sub TestEvents()
      Obj.CauseSomeEvent()    ' Ask the object to raise an event.
   End Sub
End Class
```

The following example demonstrates how a derived class can use the **Handles** statement to handle an event from a base class.

```
Public Class BaseClass
   Event Ev1() ' Declare an event.
End Class
Class DerivedClass
   Inherits BaseClass
   Sub TestEvents() Handles MyBase.Ev1
      ' Add code to handle this event.
   End Sub
End Class
```

See Also

WithEvents, AddHandler Statement, RemoveHandler Statement

HelpContext Property

Returns or sets an **Integer** containing the context ID for a topic in a Help file. Read/write.

```
Public Property HelpContext() As Integer
```

Remarks

The **HelpContext** property is used to display context-sensitive help for an application. If a help file is specified in **HelpFile**, the **HelpContext** property is used to automatically display the help file identified. If both the **HelpFile** and **HelpContext** properties are empty, the value of the Number property is checked. If the value of the **Number** property corresponds to a Visual Basic run-time error value, then the Visual Basic Help context ID for the error is used. If the value of the **Number** property doesn't correspond to a Visual Basic error, the contents screen for the Visual Basic Help file is displayed.

> **Note** You should write routines in your application to handle typical errors. When programming with an object, you can use the object's Help file to improve the quality of your error handling, or to display a meaningful message to your user if the error isn't recoverable.

Example

This example uses the **HelpContext** property of the **Err** object to show the Visual Basic Help topic for the `Overflow` error.

```
Dim Msg As String
Err.Clear
On Error Resume Next
Err.Raise(6)   ' Generate "Overflow" error.
If Err.Number <> 0 Then
   Msg = "Press F1 or HELP to see " & Err.HelpFile & " topic for" & _
   " the following HelpContext: " & Err.HelpContext
   MsgBox(Msg, , "Error:" )
End If
```

See Also

Description Property, ErrorToString Function, HelpFile Property, LastDLLError Property, Number Property, Source Property

Applies To

Err Object

HelpFile Property

Returns or sets a **String** expression containing the fully qualified path to a Help file. Read/write.

```
Public Property HelpFile() As String
```

Remarks

If a Help file is specified by the **HelpFile** property, it is automatically called when the user presses the Help key (or the F1 key) in the error message dialog box. If the **HelpContext** property contains a valid context ID for the specified file, that topic is automatically displayed. If no **HelpFile** is specified, the Visual Basic Help file is displayed.

> **Note** You should write routines in your application to handle typical errors. When programming with an object, you can use the object's Help file to improve the quality of your error handling, or to display a meaningful message to your user if the error isn't recoverable.

Example

This example uses the **HelpFile** property of the **Err** object to start the Help system. By default, the **HelpFile** property contains the name of the Visual Basic Help file.

```
Dim Msg As String
Err.Clear
On Error Resume Next   ' Suppress errors for demonstration purposes.
Err.Raise(6)   ' Generate "Overflow" error.
Msg = "Press F1 or HELP to see " & Err.HelpFile & _
" topic for this error"
MsgBox (Msg, , "Error: ")
```

See Also

Description Property, HelpContext Property, LastDLLError Property, Number Property, Source Property

Applies To

Err Object

Hex Function

Returns a string representing the hexadecimal value of a number.

```
Public Shared Function Hex( _
   ByVal Number As { Byte | Short | Integer | Long | Object } _
) As String
```

Parameter

Number

Required. Any valid numeric expression or **String** expression.

Exceptions/Errors

Exception type	Error number	Condition
ArgumentNullException	5	*Number* is not specified.
ArgumentException	5	*Number* is not a numeric type.

Remarks

If *Number* is not already a whole number, it is rounded to the nearest whole number before being evaluated.

If *Number* is	Hex returns
Empty	Zero (0)
Any numeric value	Up to sixteen hexadecimal characters

You can represent hexadecimal numbers directly by preceding numbers in the proper range with **&H**. For example, `&H10` represents decimal 16 in hexadecimal notation.

Example

This example uses the **Hex** function to return the hexadecimal value of a number.

```
Dim MyHex As String
MyHex = Hex(5)   ' Returns 5.
MyHex = Hex(10)   ' Returns A.
MyHex = Hex(459)   ' Returns 1CB.
```

See Also

Oct Function, Type Conversion Functions

Hour Function

Returns an **Integer** value from 0 through 23 representing the hour of the day.

```
Public Function Hour(ByVal TimeValue As DateTime) As Integer
```

Parameter

TimeValue
Required. **Date** value from which you want to extract the hour.

You can also obtain the hour of the day by calling **DatePart** and specifying **DateInterval.Hour** for the *Interval* argument.

Example

This example uses the **Hour** function to obtain the hour from a specified time. In the development environment, the time literal is displayed in short time format using the locale settings of your code.

```
Dim MyTime As Date
Dim MyHour As Integer
MyTime = #4:35:17 PM#    ' Assign a time.
MyHour = Hour(MyTime)    ' MyHour contains 16.
```

See Also

Day Function, Minute Function, Now Property, Second Function, TimeOfDay Property, DatePart Function

If...Then...Else Statements

Conditionally executes a group of statements, depending on the value of an expression.

```
If condition [ Then ]
   [ statements ]
[ ElseIf elseifcondition [ Then ]
   [ elseifstatements ] ]
[ Else
   [ elsestatements ] ]
End If
```

-or-

```
If condition Then [ statements] [ Else elsestatements ]
```

Parts

condition

Required. Expression. The expression you supply for *condition* must evaluate to **True** or **False**, or to a data type that is implicitly convertible to **Boolean**.

statements

Optional in multiple-line form; required in single-line form that has no **Else** clause. One or more statements following **If...Then** that are executed if *condition* is **True**.

elseifcondition

Required if **ElseIf** is present. Same as *condition*.

elseifstatements

Optional. One or more statements following **ElseIf...Then** that are executed if the associated *elseifcondition* is **True**.

elsestatements

Optional in multiple-line form; required in single-line form that has an **Else** clause. One or more statements that are executed if no previous *condition* or *elseifcondition* expression is **True**.

End If

Terminates **If...Then** block.

Remarks

You can use the single-line form for short, simple tests. However, the multiple-line form provides more structure and flexibility than the single-line form and is usually easier to read, maintain, and debug.

With the single-line form, it is possible to have multiple statements executed as the result of an **If...Then** decision. All statements must be on the same line and be separated by colons, as in the following example:

```
If A > 10 Then A = A + 1 : B = B + A : C = C + B
```

In the multiple-line form, the **If** statement must be the only statement on the first line. The **Else**, **ElseIf**, and **End If** statements can be preceded only by a line label. The multiple-line **If...Then...Else** must end with an **End If** statement.

To determine whether or not an **If** statement introduces a multiple-line form, examine what follows the **Then** keyword. If anything other than a comment appears after **Then** in the same statement, the statement is treated as a single-line **If** statement. If **Then** is absent, it must be the beginning of a multiple-line **If...Then...Else**.

The **ElseIf** and **Else** clauses are both optional. You can have as many **ElseIf** clauses as you want in a multiple-line **If...Then...Else**, but none can appear after an **Else** clause. Multiple-line forms can be nested within one another.

When a multiple-line **If...Then...Else** is encountered, *condition* is tested. If *condition* is **True**, the statements following **Then** are executed. If *condition* is **False**, each **ElseIf** statement is evaluated in order. When a **True** *elseifcondition* is found, the statements immediately following the associated **Then** are executed. If no *elseifcondition* evaluates to **True**, or if there are no **ElseIf** statements, the statements following **Else** are executed. After executing the statements following **Then**, **ElseIf**, or **Else**, execution continues with the statement following **End If**.

Tip **Select Case** might be more useful when evaluating a single expression that has several possible values.

Example

This example shows both the multiple- and single-line forms of the **If...Then...Else** statement.

```
Dim Number, Digits As Integer
Dim MyString As String
Number = 53   ' Initialize variable.
If Number < 10 Then
   Digits = 1
ElseIf Number < 100 Then
' Condition evaluates to True so the next statement is executed.
   Digits = 2
Else
   Digits = 3
End If

' Assign a value using the single-line form of syntax.
If Digits = 1 Then MyString = "One" Else MyString = "More than one"
```

Use the **TypeOf** keyword to determine whether the **Control** object passed into a procedure is a text box.

```
Sub ControlProcessor(ByVal MyControl As Control)
   If TypeOf MyControl Is ComboBox Then
      Debug.WriteLine ("You passed in a " & TypeName(MyControl))
   ElseIf TypeOf MyControl Is CheckBox Then
      Debug.WriteLine ("You passed in a " & TypeName(MyControl))
   ElseIf TypeOf MyControl Is TextBox Then
      Debug.WriteLine ("You passed in a " & TypeName(MyControl))
   End If
End Sub
```

See Also

#If...Then...#Else Directives, Choose Function, Select...Case Statements, Switch Function

IIf Function

Returns one of two objects, depending on the evaluation of an expression.

```
Public Function IIf( _
   ByVal Expression As Boolean, _
   ByVal TruePart As Object, _
   ByVal FalsePart As Object _
) As Object
```

Parameters

Expression

Required. **Boolean**. The expression you want to evaluate.

TruePart

Required. **Object**. Returned if *Expression* evaluates to **True**.

FalsePart

Required. **Object**. Returned if *Expression* evaluates to **False**.

Remarks

Note The expressions in the argument list can include function calls. As part of preparing the argument list for the call to **IIf**, the Visual Basic compiler calls every function in every expression. This means that you cannot rely on a particular function not being called if the other argument is selected by *Expression*.

Example

This example uses the **IIf** function to evaluate the `TestMe` parameter of the `CheckIt` procedure and returns the word "Large" if the amount is greater than 1000; otherwise, it returns the word "Small".

```
Function CheckIt (ByVal TestMe As Integer) As String
   CheckIt = IIf(TestMe > 1000, "Large", "Small")
End Function
```

See Also

Choose Function, If...Then...Else Statements, Select...Case Statements, Switch Function

Implements

The **Implements** keyword indicates that a class or structure member is providing the implementation for a member defined in an interface. The **Implements** keyword is not the same as the **Implements** statement.

If a class or structure implements an interface, it must include the **Implements** statement immediately after the **Class** or **Structure** statement, and it must implement all the members defined by the interface.

The **Implements** keyword is used in these contexts:

Event Statement

Function Statement

Property Statement

Sub Statement

See Also

Implements Statement, Interface Statement, Class Statement, Structure Statement

Implements Statement

Specifies one or more interfaces, or interface members, that will be implemented in the class or structure definition in which it appears.

```
Implements interfacename [, ...]
```

-or-

```
Implements interfacename.interfacemember [, ...]
```

Parts

interfacename
Required. An interface whose properties, methods, and events will be implemented by corresponding members in the class or structure.

interfacemember
Required. The member of an interface that is being implemented.

Remarks

An interface is a collection of prototypes representing the members (properties, methods and events) the interface encapsulates. Interfaces contain only the declarations for members; classes and structures implement these members.

When you implement an interface, you must implement all the members declared in the interface. Omitting any member is considered to be a syntax error. Classes can use **Private** implementations of properties and methods, but these members are only accessible by casting an instance of the implementing class into a variable declared to be of the type of the interface.

Example

The following example shows how to use the **Implements** statement to implement the properties, methods and events of an interface.

This example defines an interface named **ICustomerInfo** with a property, method, and an event. The Class **CustomerInfo** implements all the members defined in the interface.

```
Interface IcustomerInfo
' Declare an interface.
   Property CustomerName() As String
   Sub UpdateCustomerStatus()
   Event UpdateComplete()
End Interface

Public Class CustomerInfo
' The CustomerInfo class implements the IcustomerInfo interface.
   Implements ICustomerInfo
   Private CustomerNameValue As String ' Used to store the property value.
   Public Event UpdateComplete() Implements ICustomerInfo.UpdateComplete
   Public Property CustomerName() As String Implements _
      ICustomerInfo.CustomerName
      Get
         Return CustomerNameValue
      End Get
      Set(ByVal Value As String)
         ' The Value parameter is passed to the Set procedure
         ' when the contents of this property is modified.
         CustomerNameValue = Value ' Save the new value.
      End Set
   End Property
   Public Sub UpdateCustomerStatus() Implements _
      ICustomerInfo.UpdateCustomerStatus
      ' Add code here to update the status of this account.
      ' Raise an event to indicate that this method is done.
      RaiseEvent UpdateComplete()
   End Sub
End Class
```

The following two procedures show how you could use the implemented interface. To test the interface implementation, add these procedures to your project and call the `TestImplements` procedure.

```
Public Sub TestImplements()
'  This procedure tests the interface implementation by
'  creating an instance of the class that implements ICustomerInfo.
   Dim Cust As New CustomerInfo()
   ' Associate an event handler with the event
   ' that is raised by the Cust object.
   AddHandler Cust.UpdateComplete, AddressOf HandleUpdateComplete
   ' Set the CustomerName Property
   Cust.CustomerName = "Fred"
   ' Retrieve and display the CustomerName property.
   MsgBox("Customer name is: " & Cust.CustomerName)
   ' Call the update CustomerStatus method that
   ' raises the UpdateComplete event.
   Cust.UpdateCustomerStatus()
End Sub

Sub HandleUpdateComplete()
   ' This is the event handler for the UpdateComplete event.
   MsgBox("Update is complete.")
End Sub
```

See Also

Interface Statement

Imports Statement

Imports namespace names from referenced projects and assemblies. Also imports namespace names defined within the same project as the file in which the statement appears.

```
Imports [ aliasname = ] namespace [ . element ]
```

Parts

aliasname

Optional. The name by which *namespace* may also be known or referred to. When the **Imports** statement does not include *aliasname*, the elements defined within the specified *namespace* can be accessed within the file without qualification. When *aliasname* is specified, it must be used as a qualifier for the names contained in the namespace. Aliases are useful when you need to use items with the same name that are declared in one or more namespaces.

namespace
: Required. The name of the namespace being imported. The namespace can be any number of nesting levels deep.

element
: Optional. The name of an element declared in the namespace. The element can be an enumeration, structure, class, or module.

Remarks

Each file can contain any number of **Imports** statements. **Imports** statements must be placed before any declarations, including **Module** or **Class** statements, and before any references to identifiers.

The scope of the elements made available by an **Imports** statement depends on how specific you are when using the **Imports** statement. For example, if only a namespace is specified, all uniquely named members of that namespace, and members of modules within that namespace, are available without qualification. If both a namespace and the name of an element of that namespace are specified, only the members of that element are available without qualification.

It is not permitted to define a member at module level with the same name as an import alias.

Example

The following example imports the **Microsoft.VisualBasic.Strings** class and assigns an alias, `Str`, that can be used to access the **Left** method.

```
Imports Str = Microsoft.VisualBasic.Strings
' Place Imports statements at the top of your program
Class MyClass1
   Sub ShowHello()
      MsgBox(Str.Left("Hello World", 5)) ' Displays the word "Hello"
   End Sub
End Class
```

See Also

Namespace Statement

In

The **In** keyword specifies the group the loop variable is to traverse in a **For Each** loop.

The **In** keyword is used in this context:

For Each...Next Statements

See Also

Visual Basic Language Keywords

Inherits Statement

Causes the current class or interface to inherit the attributes, fields, properties, methods, and events from another class or interface.

```
Inherits typename
```

Parts

typename
Required. The name of a class or interface being inherited by the class or interface in which the **Inherits** statement is used.

Remarks

If used, the **Inherits** statement must be the first non-blank, non-comment line in a class definition.

An interface may inherit from more than one interface, but a class may only inherit from one other class.

Example

This example uses the **Inherits** statement to show how a class named `ThisClass` can inherit the fields, properties, methods and events from another class named `AnotherClass`.

```
Public Class ThisClass
   Inherits AnotherClass
   ' Add code to override, overload, or extend members
   ' inherited from the base class.
   ...' Variable, property, method, and event declarations here.
End Class
```

See Also

MustInherit, NotInheritable, MyBase, MyClass

Input Function

Reads data from an open sequential file and assigns the data to variables.

```
Public Sub Input( _
   FileNumber As Integer, _
   ByRef Value As Object _
)
```

Parameters

FileNumber

Required. Any valid file number.

Value

Required. Variable that is assigned the values read from the file—can't be an array or object variable.

Exceptions/Errors

Exception type	Error number	Condition
IOException	52	*FileNumber* does not exist.
IOException	54	File mode is invalid.

Remarks

Data read with **Input** is usually written to a file with **Write**. Use this function only with files opened in **Input** or **Binary** mode.

When read, standard string or numeric data is assigned to variables without modification. The following table illustrates how other input data are treated:

Data	Value assigned to variable
Delimiting comma or blank line	Empty
#NULL#	**DBNull**
#TRUE# or #FALSE#	**True** or **False**
#*yyyy-mm-dd hh:mm:ss*#	The date and/or time represented by the expression
#ERROR *errornumber*#	*errornumber* (variable is an object tagged as an error)

If you reach the end of the file while you are inputting a data item, the input is terminated and an error occurs.

Note The **Input** function is not localized. For example, in the German version, if you input 3,14159, it will return only 3, since the comma is treated as a variable separator, rather than a decimal point.

Example

This example uses the **Input** function to read data from a file into two variables. This example assumes that TESTFILE is a file with a few lines of data written to it using the **Write** function; that is, each line contains a string in quotations and a number separated by a comma, for example, ("Hello", 234).

```
FileOpen(1, "TESTFILE", OpenMode.Output)
Write(1, "hello")
Write(1, 14)
FileClose(1)

Dim s As String
Dim i As Integer
FileOpen(1, "TESTFILE", OpenMode.Input)
Input(1, s)
Debug.WriteLine(s)
Input(1, i)
Debug.WriteLine(i)
FileClose(1)
```

See Also

InputString Function, FileOpen Function, Print, PrintLine Functions, Write, WriteLine Functions

InputBox Function

Displays a prompt in a dialog box, waits for the user to input text or click a button, and then returns a string containing the contents of the text box.

```
Public Function InputBox( _
   ByVal Prompt As String, _
   Optional ByVal Title As String = "", _
   Optional ByVal DefaultResponse As String = "", _
   Optional ByVal XPos As Integer = -1, _
   Optional ByVal YPos As Integer = -1 _
) As String
```

Parameters

Prompt

Required. **String** expression displayed as the message in the dialog box. The maximum length of *Prompt* is approximately 1024 characters, depending on the width of the characters used. If *Prompt* consists of more than one line, you can separate the lines using a carriage return character (**Chr**(13)), a linefeed character (**Chr**(10)), or a carriage return—linefeed character combination (**Chr**(13) & **Chr**(10)) between each line.

Title

Optional. **String** expression displayed in the title bar of the dialog box. If you omit *Title*, the application name is placed in the title bar.

DefaultResponse

Optional. **String** expression displayed in the text box as the default response if no other input is provided. If you omit *DefaultResponse*, the displayed text box is empty.

XPos

Optional. Numeric expression that specifies, in twips, the distance of the left edge of the dialog box from the left edge of the screen. If you omit *XPos*, the dialog box is centered horizontally.

YPos

Optional. Numeric expression that specifies, in twips, the distance of the upper edge of the dialog box from the top of the screen. If you omit *YPos*, the dialog box is positioned vertically approximately one-third of the way down the screen.

Remarks

To specify more than the first argument, you must use the **InputBox** function in an expression. If you omit any positional arguments, you must retain the corresponding comma delimiter.

Example

This example shows various ways to use the **InputBox** function to prompt the user to enter a value. If the x and y positions are omitted, the dialog box is automatically centered for the respective axes. The variable `MyValue` contains the value entered by the user if the user clicks OK or presses the ENTER key. If the user clicks Cancel, a zero-length string is returned.

```
Dim message, title, defaultValue As String
Dim myValue As Object
message = "Enter a value between 1 and 3"   ' Set prompt.
title = "InputBox Demo"   ' Set title.
DefaultValue = "1"   ' Set default value.

' Display message, title, and default value.
myValue = InputBox(message, title, defaultValue)

' Display dialog box at position 100, 100.
myValue = InputBox(message, title, defaultValue, 100, 100)
```

See Also

MsgBox Function, Chr, ChrW Functions

InputString Function

Returns **String** value containing characters from a file opened in **Input** or **Binary** mode.

```
InputString(_
   ByVal FileNumber As Integer, _
   ByVal CharCount As Integer _
) As String
```

Parameters

FileNumber

Required. Any valid file number.

CharCount

Required. Any valid numeric expression specifying the number of characters to read.

Exceptions/Errors

Exception type	Error number	Condition
IOException	52	*FileNumber* does not exist.
ArgumentException	5	*CharCount* < 0 or > 2^{14}.

Remarks

Data read with the **InputString** function is usually written to a file with **Print** or **FilePut**. Use this function only with files opened in **Input** or **Binary** mode.

Unlike the **Input** function, the **InputString** function returns all of the characters it reads, including commas, carriage returns, linefeeds, quotation marks, and leading spaces.

With files opened for **Binary** access, an attempt to read through the file using the **InputString** function until **EOF** returns **True** generates an error. Use the **LOF** and **Loc** functions instead of **EOF** when reading binary files with **InputString**, or use File**Get** when using the **EOF** function.

Example

This example uses the **InputString** function to read one character at a time from a file and print it to the **Output** window. This example assumes that `MYFILE` is a text file with a few lines of sample data.

```
Dim oneChar As Char
FileOpen(1, "MYFILE.TXT", OpenMode.Input) ' Open file.
While Not EOF(1)   ' Loop until end of file.
oneChar = (InputString(1, 1))   ' Get one character.
System.Console.Out.WriteLine(oneChar)   ' Print to the output window.
End While
FileClose(1)
```

See Also

Input Function

InStr Function

Returns an integer specifying the start position of the first occurrence of one string within another.

```
Public Shared Function InStr(_
   ByVal Start As Integer, _
   ByVal String1 As String, _
   ByVal String2 As String, _
   Optional ByVal Compare As Microsoft.VisualBasic.CompareMethod _
) As Integer
```

Parameters

Start

Required. Numeric expression that sets the starting position for each search. If omitted, search begins at the first character position. The start index is 1 based.

String1

Required. **String** expression being searched.

String2

Required. **String** expression sought.

Compare

Optional. Specifies the type of string comparison. If *Compare* is omitted, the **Option Compare** setting determines the type of comparison. Specify a valid LCID (**LocaleID**) to use locale-specific rules in the comparison.

Settings

The *compare* argument settings are:

Constant	Value	Description
Binary	0	Performs a binary comparison
Text	1	Performs a text comparison

Return Values

If	InStr returns
String1 is zero length or **Nothing**	0
String2 is zero length or **Nothing**	*start*
String2 is not found	0
String2 is found within *String1*	Position where match begins
Start > *String2*	0

Exceptions/Errors

Exception type	Error number	Condition
ArgumentException	5	*Start* < 1.

Example

This example uses the **InStr** function to return the position of the first occurrence of one string within another.

```
Dim SearchString, SearchChar As String
Dim MyPos As Integer

SearchString ="XXpXXpXXPXXP"   ' String to search in.
SearchChar = "P"   ' Search for "P".

' A textual comparison starting at position 4. Returns 6.
MyPos = InStr(4, SearchString, SearchChar, CompareMethod.Text)

' A binary comparison starting at position 1. Returns 9.
MyPos = InStr(1, SearchString, SearchChar, CompareMethod.Binary)

' Comparison is binary by default (last argument is omitted).
MyPos = InStr(SearchString, SearchChar)   ' Returns 9.

MyPos = InStr(1, SearchString, "W")   ' Returns 0.
```

See Also

InStrRev Function, Option Compare Statement, StrComp Function

InStrRev Function

Returns the position of the first occurrence of one string within another, starting from the right side of the string.

```
Public Function InStrRev(
   ByVal StringCheck As String,
   ByVal StringMatch As String,
   Optional ByVal Start As Integer = -1,
   Optional ByVal Compare As CompareMethod = CompareMethod.Binary
) As Integer
```

Parameters

StringCheck
Required. String expression being searched.

StringMatch
Required. String expression being searched for.

Start
Optional. Numeric expression that sets the one-based starting position for each search, starting from the left side of the string. If *Start* is omitted, –1 is used, which means that the search begins at the last character position. Search then proceeds from right to left.

Compare
Optional. Numeric value indicating the kind of comparison to use when evaluating substrings. If omitted, a binary comparison is performed. See "Settings" for values.

Settings

The *Compare* argument can have the following values:

Constant	Description
Binary	Performs a binary comparison
Text	Performs a textual comparison

Return Values

InStrRev returns the following values:

If	InStrRev returns
StringCheck is zero-length	0
StringMatch is zero-length	*start*
StringMatch is not found	0
StringMatch is found within *StringCheck*	Position at which the first match is found, starting with the left side of the string.
Start is greater than length of *StringMatch*	0

Exceptions/Errors

Exception type	Error number	Condition
ArgumentException	5	*Start* = 0 or *Start* < –1.

Remarks

Note that the syntax for the **InStrRev** function is not the same as the syntax for the **InStr** function.

Example

This example demonstrates the use of the **InStrRev** function:

```
Dim myString As String = "the quick brown fox jumps over the lazy dog"
Dim myNumber As Integer
MyNumber = InStrRev(myString, "the")    ' Returns 32.
MyNumber = InStrRev(myString, "the", 16)    ' Returns 1
```

See Also

InStr Function

Int, Fix Functions

Return the integer portion of a number.

```
Int(number)
Fix(number)
```

Parameter

number

Required. A number of type **Double** or any valid numeric expression. If *number* contains Nothing, **Nothing** is returned.

Exceptions/Errors

Exception type	Error number	Condition
ArgumentNullException	5	*Number* is not specified.
ArgumentException	5	*Number* is not a numeric type.

Remarks

Both the **Int** and **Fix** functions remove the fractional part of *number* and return the resulting integer value.

The difference between **Int** and **Fix** functions is that if *number* is negative, **Int** returns the first negative integer less than or equal to *number*, whereas **Fix** returns the first negative integer greater than or equal to *number*. For example, **Int** converts –8.4 to –9, and **Fix** converts –8.4 to –8.

`Fix(number)` is equivalent to `Sign(number) * Int(Abs(number))`.

Example

This example illustrates how the **Int** and **Fix** functions return integer portions of numbers. In the case of a negative number argument, the **Int** function returns the first negative integer less than or equal to the number; the **Fix** function returns the first negative integer greater than or equal to the number. The following example requires you to specify **Option Strict Off** because implicit conversions from type **Double** to type **Integer** are not allowed under **Option Strict On**:

```
Option Strict Off
...
Dim MyNumber As Integer
MyNumber = Int(99.8)    ' Returns 99.
MyNumber = Fix(99.8)    ' Returns 99.

MyNumber = Int(-99.8)   ' Returns -100.
MyNumber = Fix(-99.8)   ' Returns -99.

MyNumber = Int(-99.2)   ' Returns -100.
MyNumber = Fix(-99.2)   ' Returns -99.
```

You can use the **CInt** function to explicitly convert other data types to type **Integer** with **Option Strict Off**. However, **Cint** rounds to the nearest integer instead of truncating the fractional part of numbers. For example:

```
MyNumber = CInt(99.8)    ' Returns 100.
MyNumber = CInt(-99.8)   ' Returns -100.
MyNumber = CInt(-99.2)   ' Returns -99.
```

You can use the **CInt** function on the result of a call to **Fix** or **Int** to perform explicit conversion to integer without rounding. For example:

```
MyNumber = CInt(Fix(99.8))   ' Returns 99.
MyNumber = CInt(Int(99.8))   ' Returns 99.
```

See Also

Integer Data Type, Math Summary, Math Functions

Integer Data Type

Integer variables are stored as signed 32-bit (4-byte) integers ranging in value from –2,147,483,648 through 2,147,483,647.

The **Integer** data type provides optimal performance on a 32-bit processor, as the smaller integral types are slower to load and store from and to memory.

Note The **Integer** data type can be converted to the **Long**, **Single**, **Double**, or **Decimal** data type without encountering a **System.OverflowException** error.

Appending the literal type character **I** to a literal forces it to the **Integer** data type. Appending the identifier type character % to any identifier forces it to **Integer**.

The equivalent .NET data type is **System.Int32**.

See Also

Data Type Summary, Long Data Type, Short Data Type, Type Conversion Functions, Conversion Summary

Interface Statement

Declares the name of an interface, as well as the properties, methods and events that comprise the interface.

```
[ <attrlist> ] [ Public | Private | Protected | Friend | Protected Friend ] _
[ Shadows ] Interface name
   [ Inherits interfacename[, interfacename ]]
   [ [ Default ] Property proname ]
   [ Function memberame ]
   [ Sub memberame ]
   [ Event memberame ]
End Interface
```

Parts

attrlist

Optional. List of attributes that apply to this interface. Multiple attributes are separated by commas.

Public

Optional. Entities declared with the **Public** modifier have public access. There are no restrictions on the use of public entities.

Private

Optional. Entities declared with the **Private** modifier have private access. A private entity is accessible only within its declaration context, including any nested entities.

Protected

Optional. Entities declared with the **Protected** keyword have protected access. They are accessible only from within their own class or from a derived class. Protected access can be specified only on members of classes. It is not a superset of friend access.

Friend

Optional. Entities declared with the **Friend** modifier have friend access. An entity with friend access is accessible only within the program that contains the entity declaration. Interfaces that do not specify an access modifier are declared as **Friend** by default.

Protected Friend

Optional. Entities declared with the **Protected Friend** modifiers have the union of protected and friend accessibility.

Shadows

Optional. Indicates that this interface shadows an identically named programming element in a base class. You can shadow any kind of declared element with any other kind. A shadowed element is unavailable in the derived class that shadows it

name

Required. Name of the interface; follows standard variable naming conventions.

Inherits

Optional. Specifies that the interface being declared inherits the properties and methods from the interface specified by *interfacename*.

interfacename

Required if optional **Inherits** statement is present. Indicates the name of one or more interfaces being inherited.

Default

Optional. Indicates that the property with which the **Default** keyword is associated is the default property for the interface.

Property

Optional. Indicates a **Property** procedure that is a member of the interface.

Function

Optional. Indicates a **Function** procedure that is a member of the interface.

Sub

Optional. Indicates a **Sub** procedure that is a member of the interface.

Event

Optional. Indicates an **Event** that is a member of the interface.

memberame

Required if optional **Property**, **Event**, **Function**, or **Sub** statements exist. Indicates the name of the property, procedure, or event.

End Interface

Terminates an **Interface** block.

Each attribute in the *attrlist* part has the following syntax and parts:

```
attrname [({ attrargs | attrinit })]
```

attrlist Parts

attrname
: Required. Name of the attribute. Must be a valid Visual Basic identifier.

attrargs
: Optional. List of positional arguments for this attribute. Multiple arguments are separated by commas.

attrinit
: Optional. List of field or property initializers for this attribute. Multiple initializers are separated by commas.

Remarks

The methods and properties of an interface are implemented in a class. When methods are implemented, the return data type and the argument data types must exactly match those of the method described in the **Interface** block. The method name, however, need not be the same as that described in the **Interface** block. Methods being implemented in a class cannot be designated as **Shared,** nor can they be **Private**, except in a non-inheritable class.

The **Interface** statement can appear in the declaration section of any module. Interfaces are implicitly **Friend** by default but can be explicitly declared **Public**, **Friend**, **Protected**, **Protected Friend** or **Private**.

An interface can have, at most, one default property. This implies that an interface can either inherit only one interface containing a default property, or its definition block can contain one property that is marked as default.

An interface cannot inherit from another interface whose access level is more restrictive than its own. For example, a public interface cannot inherit a friend interface.

Example

This example uses the **Interface** statement to define a `MyInterface` interface, which must be implemented with a **Property** statement and a **Function** statement.

```
Public Interface MyInterface
   Property MyProp(ByVal MyStr As String)
   Function MyFunc(ByVal MyInt As Integer) As Integer
End Interface
```

See Also

Class Statement, Function Statement, Inherits Statement, Implements Statement, Sub Statement

IPmt Function

Returns a **Double** specifying the interest payment for a given period of an annuity based on periodic, fixed payments and a fixed interest rate.

```
Function IPmt( _
   ByVal Rate As Double, _
   ByVal Per As Double, _
   ByVal NPer As Double, _
   ByVal PV As Double, _
   Optional ByVal FV As Double = 0, _
   Optional ByVal Due As DueDate = DueDate.EndOfPeriod _
) As Double
```

Parameters

Rate

Required. **Double** specifying interest rate per period. For example, if you get a car loan at an annual percentage rate (APR) of 10 percent and make monthly payments, the rate per period is 0.1/12, or 0.0083.

Per

Required. **Double** specifying payment period in the range 1 through *NPer*.

NPer

Required. **Double** specifying total number of payment periods in the annuity. For example, if you make monthly payments on a four-year car loan, your loan has a total of 4 * 12 (or 48) payment periods.

PV

Required. **Double** specifying present value, or value today, of a series of future payments or receipts. For example, when you borrow money to buy a car, the loan amount is the present value to the lender of the monthly car payments you will make.

FV

Optional. **Double** specifying future value or cash balance you want after you've made the final payment. For example, the future value of a loan is $0 because that's its value after the final payment. However, if you want to save $50,000 over 18 years for your child's education, then $50,000 is the future value. If omitted, 0 is assumed.

Due

Optional. Object of type `Microsoft.VisualBasic.DueDate` that specifies when payments are due. This argument must be either `DueDate.EndOfPeriod` if payments are due at the end of the payment period, or `DueDate.BegOfPeriod` if payments are due at the beginning of the period. If omitted, `DueDate.EndOfPeriod` is assumed.

Exceptions/Errors

Exception type	Error number	Condition
ArgumentException	5	*Per* is invalid.

Remarks

An annuity is a series of fixed cash payments made over a period of time. An annuity can be a loan (such as a home mortgage) or an investment (such as a monthly savings plan).

The *Rate* and *NPer* arguments must be calculated using payment periods expressed in the same units. For example, if *Rate* is calculated using months, *NPer* must also be calculated using months.

For all arguments, cash paid out (such as deposits to savings) is represented by negative numbers; cash received (such as dividend checks) is represented by positive numbers.

Example

This example uses the **IPmt** function to calculate how much of a payment is interest when all the payments are of equal value. Given are the interest percentage rate per period (`APR / 12`), the payment period for which the interest portion is desired (`Period`), the total number of payments (`TotPmts`), the present value or principal of the loan (`PVal`), the future value of the loan (`FVal`), and a number that indicates whether the payment is due at the beginning or end of the payment period (`PayType`).

```
Sub TestIPMT()
   Dim Fmt, Msg As String
   Dim APR, PVal, Fval, Period, IntPmt, TotInt, TotPmts As Double
   Dim PayType As DueDate
   Dim Response As MsgBoxResult

   Fval = 0   ' Usually 0 for a loan.
   Fmt = "###,###,##0.00"   ' Define money format.
   PVal = CDbl(InputBox("How much do you want to borrow?"))
   APR = CDbl(InputBox("What is the annual percentage rate of your loan?"))
   If APR > 1 Then APR = APR / 100 ' Ensure proper form.
   TotPmts = CInt(InputBox("How many monthly payments?"))
   Response = MsgBox("Do you make payments at end of the month?", MsgBoxStyle.YesNo)
   If Response = MsgBoxResult.No Then
      PayType = DueDate.BegOfPeriod
   Else
      PayType = DueDate.EndOfPeriod
   End If
   For Period = 1 To TotPmts   ' Total all interest.
      IntPmt = IPmt(APR / 12, Period, TotPmts, -PVal, Fval, PayType)
      TotInt = TotInt + IntPmt
   Next Period
   Msg = "You'll pay a total of " & Format(TotInt, Fmt)
   Msg = Msg & " in interest for this loan."
   MsgBox(Msg)    ' Display results.
End Sub
```

See Also

DDB Function, IRR Function, MIRR Function, NPer Function, NPV Function, Pmt Function, PPmt Function, PV Function, Rate Function, SLN Function, SYD Function

IRR Function

Returns a **Double** specifying the internal rate of return for a series of periodic cash flows (payments and receipts).

```
Function IRR( _
    ByRef ValueArray() As Double, _
   Optional ByVal Guess As Double = 0.1 _
) As Double
```

Parameters

ValueArray()

Required. Array of **Double** specifying cash flow values. The array must contain at least one negative value (a payment) and one positive value (a receipt).

Guess

Optional. Object specifying value you estimate will be returned by **IRR**. If omitted, *Guess* is 0.1 (10 percent).

Exceptions/Errors

Exception type	Error number	Condition
ArgumentException	5	Array argument values are invalid.

Remarks

The internal rate of return is the interest rate received for an investment consisting of payments and receipts that occur at regular intervals.

The **IRR** function uses the order of values within the array to interpret the order of payments and receipts. Be sure to enter your payment and receipt values in the correct sequence. The cash flow for each period doesn't need to be fixed, as it is for an annuity.

IRR is calculated by iteration. Starting with the value of *Guess*, **IRR** cycles through the calculation until the result is accurate to within 0.00001 percent. If **IRR** can't find a result after 20 tries, it fails.

Example

In this example, the **IRR** function returns the internal rate of return for a series of 5 cash flows contained in the array `Values()`. The first array element is a negative cash flow representing business start-up costs. The remaining 4 cash flows represent positive cash flows for the subsequent 4 years. `Guess` is the estimated internal rate of return.

```
Sub TestIRR()
   Dim Guess, RetRate, Values(4) As Double
   Dim Fmt, Msg As String
   Guess = 0.1  ' Guess starts at 10 percent.
   Fmt = "#0.00"   ' Define percentage format.
   Values(0) = -70000   ' Business start-up costs.
   ' Positive cash flows reflecting income for four successive years.
   Values(1) = 22000 : Values(2) = 25000
   Values(3) = 28000 : Values(4) = 31000
   RetRate = IRR(Values, Guess) * 100   ' Calculate internal rate.
   Msg = "The internal rate of return for these five cash flows is "
   Msg = Msg & Format(RetRate, CStr(Fmt)) & " percent."
   MsgBox(Msg)    ' Display internal return rate.
End Sub
```

See Also

DDB Function, FV Function, IPmt Function, MIRR Function, NPer Function, NPV Function, Pmt Function, PPmt Function, PV Function, Rate Function, SLN Function, SYD Function

Is

The **Is** keyword introduces an **Is** clause that makes a comparison.

The **Is** keyword is used in these contexts:

Is Operator

Select...Case Statements

See Also

Visual Basic Language Keywords

Is Operator

Compares two object reference variables.

```
result = object1 Is object2
```

Parts

result
    Required. Any **Boolean** value.

object1
    Required. Any **Object** name.

object2
    Required. Any **Object** name.

Remarks

The **Is** operator determines if two object references refer to the same object. However, it does not perform value comparisons. If *object1* and *object2* both refer to the same object, *result* is **True**; if they do not, *result* is **False**.

Example

This example uses the **Is** operator to compare two object references. The object variable names are generic and used for illustration purposes only. The result is a **Boolean** value representing whether the two objects are identical.

```
Dim myObject, otherObject As New Object
Dim yourObject, thisObject, thatObject As Object
Dim myCheck As Boolean
yourObject = myObject
thisObject = myObject
thatObject = otherObject
myCheck = yourObject Is thisObject   ' Returns True.
myCheck = thatObject Is thisObject   ' Returns False.
myCheck = myObject Is thatObject ' Returns False, if myObject is not thatObject.
```

See Also

Comparison Operators, Operator Precedence in Visual Basic, Operators Listed by Functionality, Operators

IsArray Function

Returns a **Boolean** value indicating whether a variable points to an array.

```
Public Function IsArray(ByVal VarName As Object) As Boolean
```

Parameter

VarName

Required. **Object** variable.

Remarks

IsArray returns **True** if the variable points to an array; otherwise, it returns **False**. **IsArray** is especially useful with objects containing arrays.

Example

This example uses the **IsArray** function to check if several variables refer to an array.

```
Dim MyArray(4), YourArray(3) As Integer   ' Declare array variables.
Dim MyString As String
Dim MyCheck As Boolean
MyCheck = IsArray(MyArray)    ' Returns True.
MyCheck = IsArray(YourArray)    ' Returns True.
MyCheck = IsArray(MyString)    ' Returns False.
```

See Also

IsDate Function, IsDBNull Function, IsError Function, IsNothing Function, IsNumeric Function, IsReference Function, Object Data Type, TypeName Function

IsDate Function

Returns a **Boolean** value indicating whether an expression can be converted to a date.

```
Public Function IsDate(ByVal Expression As Object) As Boolean
```

Parameter

Expression

Required. **Object** expression.

Remarks

IsDate returns **True** if the expression is of type **Date** or is a string convertible to type **Date**; otherwise, it returns **False**.

Example

This example uses the **IsDate** function to determine if several variables can be converted to dates.

```
Dim MyDate, YourDate As Date
Dim NoDate As String
Dim MyCheck As Boolean
MyDate = "February 12, 1969"
YourDate = #2/12/1969#
NoDate = "Hello"
MyCheck = IsDate(MyDate)   ' Returns True.
MyCheck = IsDate(YourDate)   ' Returns True.
MyCheck = IsDate(NoDate)   ' Returns False.
```

See Also

IsArray Function, IsDBNull Function, IsError Function, IsNothing Function, IsNumeric Function, IsReference Function, Object Data Type, Date Data Type, TypeName Function

IsDBNull Function

Returns a **Boolean** value indicating whether an expression evaluates to the **System.DBNull** class.

```
Public Function IsDBNull(ByVal Expression As Object) As Boolean
```

Parameter

Expression
  Required. **Object** expression.

Remarks

IsDBNull returns **True** if the data type of *Expression* evaluates to the **DBNull** type; otherwise, **IsDBNull** returns **False**.

The **System.DBNull** value indicates that the **Object** represents missing or nonexistent data. **DBNull** is not the same as **Nothing**, which indicates that a variable has not yet been initialized. It is also not the same as a zero-length string (" "), which is sometimes referred to as a null string.

Example

This example uses the **IsDBNull** function to determine if a variable evaluates to **DBNull**.

```
Dim MyVar As Object
Dim MyCheck As Boolean
MyCheck = IsDBNull(MyVar)   ' Returns False.
MyVar = ""
MyCheck = IsDBNull(MyVar)   ' Returns False.
MyVar = System.DBNull.Value
MyCheck = IsDBNull(MyVar)   ' Returns True.
MsgBox(MyCheck)
```

See Also

IsArray Function, IsDate Function, IsError Function, IsNothing Function, IsNumeric Function, IsReference Function, Object Data Type, TypeName Function

IsError Function

Returns a **Boolean** value indicating whether an expression is an exception type.

```
Public Function IsError(ByVal Expression As Object) As Boolean
```

Parameter

Expression
Required. **Object** expression.

Remarks

IsError returns **True** if the expression represents an **Object** variable that derives from the **Exception** class in the **System** namespace.

An exception that derives from **System.Exception** can be caught with the **Try...Catch...Finally** statements.

Example

This example uses the **IsError** function to check if an expression represents a system exception.

```
Dim ReturnVal As Object
Dim BadArg As String    ' Name of out-of-range argument.
Dim MyCheck As Boolean
' ...
ReturnVal = New System.ArgumentOutOfRangeException(BadArg)
' ...
MyCheck = IsError(ReturnVal)    ' Returns True.
```

See Also

IsArray Function, IsDate Function, IsDBNull Function, IsNothing Function, IsNumeric Function, IsReference Function, Object Data Type, TypeName Function

IsNothing Function

Returns a **Boolean** value indicating whether an expression has no object assigned to it.

```
Public Function IsNothing(ByVal Expression As Object) As Boolean
```

Parameter

Expression
Required. **Object** expression.

Remarks

IsNothing returns **True** if the expression represents an **Object** variable that currently has no object assigned to it; otherwise, it returns **False**.

Example

This example uses the **IsNothing** function to determine if an object variable is associated with any object instance.

```
Dim MyVar As Object   ' No instance assigned to this variable yet.
Dim MyCheck As Boolean
' ...
MyCheck = IsNothing(MyVar)   ' Returns True.
' ...
MyVar = "ABCDEF"   ' Assign a string instance to the variable.
MyCheck = IsNothing(MyVar)   ' Returns False.
' ...
MyVar = Nothing   ' Disassociate the variable from any instance.
MyCheck = IsNothing(MyVar)   ' Returns True.
```

See Also

IsArray Function, IsDate Function, IsDBNull Function, IsError Function, IsNumeric Function, IsReference Function, Object Data Type, TypeName Function, Nothing

IsNumeric Function

Returns a **Boolean** value indicating whether an expression can be evaluated as a number.

```
Public Function IsNumeric(ByVal Expression As Object) As Boolean
```

Parameter

Expression
Required. **Object** expression.

Remarks

IsNumeric returns **True** if the entire *Expression* is recognized as a number; otherwise, it returns **False**.

IsNumeric returns **True** if the data type of *Expression* is **Short**, **Integer**, **Long**, **Decimal**, **Single**, or **Short**. It also returns **True** if *Expression* is a **String** that can be successfully converted to a **Double**. It returns **False** if *Expression* is of data type **Date**.

Example

This example uses the **IsNumeric** function to determine if the contents of a variable can be evaluated as a number.

```
Dim MyVar As Object
Dim MyCheck As Boolean
' ...
MyVar = "53"    ' Assign value.
MyCheck = IsNumeric(MyVar)    ' Returns True.
' ...
MyVar = "459.95"    ' Assign value.
MyCheck = IsNumeric(MyVar)    ' Returns True.
' ...
MyVar = "45 Help"    ' Assign value.
MyCheck = IsNumeric(MyVar)    ' Returns False.
```

See Also

IsArray Function, IsDate Function, IsDBNull Function, IsError Function, IsNothing Function, IsReference Function, Object Data Type, TypeName Function

IsReference Function

Returns a **Boolean** value indicating whether an expression evaluates to a reference type.

```
Public Function IsReference(ByVal Expression As Object) As Boolean
```

Parameter

Expression

Required. **Object** expression.

Remarks

IsReference returns **True** if the expression represents a reference type, such as a class instance, a **String** type, or an array of any type; otherwise, it returns **False**.

A reference type contains a pointer to data stored elsewhere in memory. A value type contains its own data.

Example

This example uses the **IsReference** function to check if several variables refer to reference types.

```
Dim MyArray(3) As Boolean
Dim MyString As String
Dim MyObject As Object
Dim MyNumber As Integer
MyArray(0) = IsReference(MyArray)    ' Returns True.
MyArray(1) = IsReference(MyString)    ' Returns True.
MyArray(2) = IsReference(MyObject)    ' Returns True.
MyArray(2) = IsReference(MyNumber)    ' Returns False.
```

See Also

IsArray Function, IsDate Function, IsDBNull Function, IsError Function, IsNothing Function, IsNumeric Function, Object Data Type, TypeName Function

Item Property

Returns a specific member of a **Collection** object either by position or by key.

```
ReadOnly Public Default Overloads Property Item( _
   ByVal Index As { Integer | Object } _
) As Object
```

Parameters

Object

An object expression that evaluates to an object in the **Collection** object.

Index

An expression that specifies the position of a member of the collection. If a numeric expression, *Index* must be a number from 1 to the value of the collection's **Count** property. If *Index* is a **String** expression, it must correspond to the key value specified when the member referred to was added to the collection.

Exceptions/Errors

Exception type	Error number	Condition
IndexOutOfRangeException	9	Index doesn't match an existing member of the collection.

Remarks

If *Index* doesn't match any existing member of the collection, an error occurs.

The **Item** property is the default property for a collection. Therefore, the following lines of code are equivalent:

```
Print MyCollection(1)
Print MyCollection.Item(1)
```

Example

This example uses the **Item** property to retrieve a reference to an object in a collection. Given that `birthdays` is a **Collection** object, the following code retrieve a reference to the objects representing Bill's birthday from the collection, using the key "Bill" as the *Index* arguments.

```
Dim birthdays As New Collection()
Dim aBirthday As DateTime
birthdays.Add(New DateTime(2001, 1, 12), "Bill")
aBirthday = birthdays("Bill")
MsgBox(aBirthday.ToString())
aBirthday = birthdays.Item("Bill")
MsgBox(aBirthday.ToString())
```

Note that the first call explicitly specifies the **Item** property, but the second does not. Both calls work because the **Item** property is the default for a **Collection** object. The reference, assigned to `aBirthday`, can be used to access the properties and methods of the specified object.

See Also

Add Method, Count Property, Remove Method

Applies To

Collection Object

Join Function

Returns a string created by joining a number of substrings contained in an array.

```
Function Join(
   ByVal SourceArray() As { Object | String },
   Optional ByVal Delimiter As String = " "
) As String
```

Parameters

SourceArray()
Required. One-dimensional array containing substrings to be joined.

Delimiter
Optional. String used to separate the substrings in the returned string. If omitted, the space character (" ") is used. If *Delimiter* is a zero-length string (" "), all items in the list are concatenated with no delimiters.

Exceptions/Errors

Exception type	Error number	Condition
ArgumentException	5	*SourceArray()* is not one dimensional.

Example

The following example demonstrates use of the **Join** function.

```
Dim myItem(2) As String
Dim myShoppingList As String
myItem(0) = "Pickle"
myItem(1) = "Pineapple"
myItem(2) = "Papaya"
' Returns "Pickle, Pineapple, Papaya"
myShoppingList = Join(myItem, ", ")
```

See Also

Split Function

Kill Function

Deletes files from a disk.

```
Public Sub Kill(ByVal PathName As String)
```

Parameter

PathName

Required. **String** expression that specifies one or more file names to be deleted. *PathName* may include the directory or folder, and the drive.

Exceptions/Errors

Exception type	Error number	Condition
IOException	55	Target file(s) open.
FileNotFoundException	53	Target file(s) not found.

Remarks

Kill supports the use of multiple-character (*) and single-character (?) wildcards to specify multiple files.

Example

This example uses the **Kill** function to delete a file from a disk.

```
' Assume TESTFILE is a file containing some data.
Kill("TestFile")    ' Delete file.

' Delete all *.TXT files in current directory.
Kill("*.TXT")
```

See Also

RmDir Function

LastDLLError Property

Returns a system error code produced by a call to a dynamic-link library (DLL). Read-only.

```
ReadOnly Property LastDLLError() As Integer
```

Remarks

The **LastDLLError** property applies only to DLL calls made from Visual Basic code. When such a call is made, the called function usually returns a code indicating success or failure, and the **LastDLLError** property is filled. Check the documentation for the DLL's functions to determine the return values that indicate success or failure. Whenever the failure code is returned, the Visual Basic application should immediately check the **LastDLLError** property. No exception is raised when the **LastDLLError** property is set.

Example

When pasted into a **UserForm** module, the following code causes an attempt to call a DLL function. The call fails because the argument that is passed in (a null pointer) generates an error, and in any event, SQL can't be cancelled if it isn't running. The code following the call checks the return of the call, and then prints at the **LastDLLError** property of the **Err** object to reveal the error code. On systems without DLLs, **LastDLLError** always returns zero.

```
Private Declare Function SQLCancel Lib "ODBC32.dll" _
(ByVal hstmt As Long) As Integer

Private Sub Update()
   Dim RetVal As Integer
   Dim myhandle As Long
   ' Call with invalid argument.
   RetVal = SQLCancel(myhandle)
   ' Check for SQL error code.
   If RetVal = -2 Then
      ' Display the information code.
      MsgBox("Error code is :" & Err.LastDllError)
    End If
End Sub
```

See Also

Declare Statement, Description Property, Err Object, ErrorToString Function, HelpContext Property, HelpFile Property, Number Property, Source Property

Applies To

Err Object

LBound Function

Returns the lowest available subscript for the indicated dimension of an array.

```
Public Function LBound( _
   ByVal Array As System.Array, _
   Optional ByVal Rank As Integer = 1 _
) As Integer
```

Parameters

Array

Required. Array of any data type. The array in which you want to find the lowest possible subscript of a dimension.

Rank

Optional. **Integer**. The dimension for which the lowest possible subscript is to be returned. Use 1 for the first dimension, 2 for the second, and so on. If *Rank* is omitted, 1 is assumed.

Exceptions/Errors

Exception type	Error number	Condition
ArgumentNullException	9	*Array* is **Nothing.**
RankException	9	*Rank* < 1 or *Rank* is greater than the rank of *Array*.

Remarks

Since array subscripts start at 0, the lowest available subscript for every dimension is always 0.

For an array with the following dimensions, **LBound** returns the values in the following table:

```
Dim A(100, 5, 4) As Byte
```

Call to LBound	Return value
`LBound(A, 1)`	0
`LBound(A, 2)`	0
`LBound(A, 3)`	0

Example

This example uses the **LBound** function to determine the lowest available subscript for the indicated dimension of an array.

```
Dim Lowest, MyArray(10, 15, 20), AnyArray(6) as Integer
Lowest = LBound(MyArray, 1)    ' Returns 0.
Lowest = LBound(MyArray, 3)    ' Returns 0.
Lowest = LBound(AnyArray)    ' Returns 0.
```

See Also

UBound Function, Dim Statement, ReDim Statement

LCase Function

Returns a string or character converted to lowercase.

```
Public Shared Function LCase(ByVal Value As Char) As Char
```

-or-

```
Public Shared Function LCase(ByVal Value As String) As String
```

Parameter

Value

Required. Any valid **String** or **Char** expression.

Remarks

Only uppercase letters are converted to lowercase; all lowercase letters and nonletter characters remain unchanged.

Example

This example uses the **LCase** function to return a lowercase version of a string.

```
Dim UpperCase, LowerCase As String
Uppercase = "Hello World 1234"    ' String to convert.
Lowercase = LCase(UpperCase)    ' Returns "hello world 1234".
```

See Also

UCase Function

Left Function

Returns a string containing a specified number of characters from the left side of a string.

```
Public Shared Function Left( _
   ByVal Str As String, _
   ByVal Length As Integer _
) As String
```

Parameters

Str

Required. **String** expression from which the leftmost characters are returned.

Length

Required. **Integer** expression. Numeric expression indicating how many characters to return. If 0, a zero-length string ("") is returned. If greater than or equal to the number of characters in *Str*, the entire string is returned.

Exceptions/Errors

Exception type	Error number	Condition
ArgumentException	5	*Length* < 0.

Remarks

To determine the number of characters in *Str*, use the **Len** function. If used in a Windows Form, or any other class that has a **Left** property, you must fully qualify the function with `Microsoft.VisualBasic.Left`.

Example

This example demonstrates the use of the **Left** function to return a substring of a given **String**. In a class that has a **Left** property, it may be necessary to fully qualify the **Left** function.

```
Dim myString As String = "Hello World!"
Dim subString As String
subString = Microsoft.VisualBasic.Left(myString, 5)   ' Returns "Hello"
```

See Also

Right Function, Len Function, Mid Function

Len Function

Returns an integer containing either the number of characters in a string or the number of bytes required to store a variable.

```
Public Shared Function Len( _
   ByVal Expression As { Boolean | Byte | Char | Double | Integer | Long |
   Object | Short | Single | String | DateTime | Decimal } _
) As Integer
```

Parameters

Expression

Any valid **String** expression or variable name. If *Expression* is of type **Object**, the **Len** function returns the size as it will be written to the file.

Remarks

With user-defined types and **Object** variables, the **Len** function returns the size as it will be written to the file. If an **Object** contains a **String**, it will return the length of the string. If an **Object** contains any other type, it will return the size of the object as it will be written to the file.

Note The **Len** function may not be able to determine the actual number of storage bytes required when used with variable-length strings in user-defined data types.

Example

This example uses **Len** to return the number of characters in a string.

```
Dim MyString As String
Dim MyLen As Integer
MyString = "Hello World"    ' Initializes variable.
MyLen = Len(MyString)    ' Returns 11.
```

See Also

Data Type Summary, InStr Function

Lib

The **Lib** keyword identifies the library containing an external procedure.

The **Lib** keyword is used in this context:

Declare Statement

See Also

Visual Basic Language Keywords

Like Operator

Compares two strings.

```
result = string Like pattern
```

Parts

result
Required. Any **Boolean** variable. The result is a **Boolean** value indicating whether or not the *string* matches the *pattern*.

string
Required. Any **String** expression.

pattern
Required. Any **String** expression conforming to the pattern-matching conventions described in Remarks.

Remarks

If *string* matches *pattern*, *result* is **True**; if there is no match, *result* is **False**. If both *string* and *pattern* are an empty string. the result is **True**. Otherwise, if either *string* or *pattern* is an empty string, the result is **False**.

The behavior of the **Like** operator depends on the **Option Compare** statement. The default string-comparison method for each module is **Option Compare Binary**.

Built-in pattern matching provides a versatile tool for string comparisons. The pattern-matching features allow you to match strings using wildcard characters, character lists, or character ranges, in any combination. The following table shows the characters allowed in *pattern* and what they match:

Characters in *pattern*	Matches in *string*
?	Any single character
*	Zero or more characters
#	Any single digit (0–9)
[*charlist*]	Any single character in *charlist*
[!*charlist*]	Any single character not in *charlist*

A group of one or more characters (*charlist*) enclosed in brackets ([ ]) can be used to match any single character in *string* and can include almost any character code, including digits.

Note To match the special characters left bracket ([), question mark (?), number sign (#), and asterisk (*), enclose them in brackets. The right bracket (]) can't be used within a group to match itself, but it can be used outside a group as an individual character.

By using a hyphen (-) to separate the upper and lower bounds of the range, *charlist* can specify a range of characters. For example, `[A-Z]` results in a match if the corresponding character position in *string* contains any uppercase letters in the range *A–Z*. Multiple ranges are included within the brackets without delimiters.

The meaning of a specified range depends on the character ordering valid at run time (as determined by **Option Compare** and the locale setting of the system the code is running on). Using **Option Compare Binary**, the range `[A-E]` matches *A*, *B*, *C*, *D*, and *E*. With **Option Compare Text**, `[A-E]` matches *A*, *a*, *À*, *à*, *B*, *b*, *C*, *c*, *D*, *d*, *E*, and *e*. The range does not match *Ê* or *ê* because accented characters fall after unaccented characters in the sort order.

Other important rules for pattern matching include the following:

- An exclamation point (**!**) at the beginning of *charlist* means that a match is made if any character except the characters in *charlist* is found in *string*. When used outside brackets, the exclamation point matches itself.
- A hyphen (-) can appear either at the beginning (after an exclamation point if one is used) or at the end of *charlist* to match itself. In any other location, the hyphen identifies a range of characters delimited by the characters on either side of the hyphen.
- When a range of characters is specified, they must appear in ascending sort order (that is, from lowest to highest). Thus, `[A-Z]` is a valid pattern, but `[Z-A]` is not.
- The character sequence `[]` is considered a zero-length string (" ").

In some languages, there are special characters in the alphabet that represent two separate characters. For example, several languages use the character *æ* to represent the characters *a* and *e* when they appear together. The **Like** operator recognizes that the single special character and the two individual characters are equivalent.

When a language that uses a special character is specified in the system locale settings, an occurrence of the single special character in either *pattern* or *string* matches the equivalent two-character sequence in the other string. Similarly, a single special character in *pattern* enclosed in brackets (by itself, in a list, or in a range) matches the equivalent two-character sequence in *string*.

Example

This example uses the **Like** operator to compare a string to a pattern. The result is a **Boolean** value representing whether the string fits the pattern.

```
Dim myCheck As Boolean
myCheck = "F" Like "F"    ' Does "F" match "F"? Returns True.
myCheck = "F" Like "f"    ' Does "F" match "f"? Returns False.
myCheck = "F" Like "FFF"    ' Does "F" match "FFF"? Returns False.
myCheck = "aBBBa" Like "a*a"    ' Does "aBBBa" have a "a" at the
   ' beginning, an "a" at the end, and any number of characters in
   ' between? Returns True.
myCheck = "F" Like "[A-Z]"    ' Does "F" occur in the set of
   ' characters from A to Z? Returns True.
```

```
myCheck = "F" Like "[!A-Z]"      ' Does "F" NOT occur in the set of
    ' characters from A to Z? Returns False.
myCheck = "a2a" Like "a#a"      ' Does "a2a" begin and end with an
    ' "a" and have any single-digit number inbetween? Returns True.
myCheck = "aM5b" Like "a[L-P]#[!c-e]" ' Does "aM5b" fit the following
    ' pattern: Begins with "a", has and character from the set L through
    ' P, followed byb any single-digit number, and finally contains any
    ' character excluded from the character set c through e. Returns True.
myCheck = "BAT123khg" Like "B?T*"  ' Does "BAT123khg" fit the
    ' following pattern: Begins with "B", followed by any single
    ' character, followed by a "T" and finally zero or more characters
    ' of any type. Returns True.
myCheck = "CAT123khg" Like "B?T*"  ' Does "CAT123khg" fit the
    ' following pattern: Begins with "B", followed by any single
    ' character, followed by a "T" and finally zero or more characters
    ' of any type. Returns False.
```

See Also

Comparison Operators, InStr Function, Operator Precedence in Visual Basic, Operators Listed by Functionality, Option Compare Statement, StrComp Function, Operators

LineInput Function

Reads a single line from an open sequential file and assigns it to a **String** variable.

```
Public Function LineInput(ByVal FileNumber As Integer) As String
```

Parameters

FileNumber

Required. Any valid file number.

Exceptions/Errors

Exception type	Error number	Condition
EndOfStreamException	62	End of file reached.
IOException	52	*FileNumber* does not exist.

Remarks

Data read with **LineInput** is usually written to a file with **Print**.

The **LineInput** function reads from a file one character at a time until it encounters a carriage return (**Chr**(13)) or carriage return-linefeed (**Chr**(13) + **Chr**(10)) sequence. Carriage return-linefeed sequences are skipped rather than appended to the character string.

Example

This example uses the **LineInput** function to read a line from a sequential file and assign it to a variable. This example assumes that `TESTFILE` is a text file with a few lines of sample data.

```
Dim TextLine As String
FileOpen(1, "TESTFILE", OpenMode.Input)   ' Open file.
While Not EOF(1)   ' Loop until end of file.
   TextLine = LineInput(1)   ' Read line into variable.
   Debug.WriteLine(TextLine)   ' Print to the console.
End While
FileClose(1)   ' Close file.
```

See Also

Chr, ChrW Functions, Input Function

Loc Function

Returns a **Long** value specifying the current read/write position within an open file.

```
Public Function Loc(ByVal FileNumber As Integer) As Long
```

Parameter

FileNumber
: Required. Any valid **Integer** file number.

Exceptions/Errors

Exception type	Error number	Condition
IOException	52	*FileNumber* does not exist.
IOException	54	File mode is invalid.

Remarks

The following describes the return value for each file access mode:

Mode	Return value
Random	Number of the last record read from or written to the file.
Sequential	Current byte position in the file divided by 128. However, information returned by **Loc** for sequential files is neither used nor required.
Binary	Position of the last byte read or written.

Example

This example uses the **Loc** function to return the current read/write position within an open file. This example assumes that `MYFILE` is a text file with a few lines of sample data.

```
Dim location As Long
Dim oneLine As String
Dim oneChar As Char
FileOpen(1, "C:\MYFILE.TXT", OpenMode.Binary)
While location < EOF(1)
   Input(1, oneChar)
   location = Loc(1)
   Debug.WriteLine(location & ControlChars.CrLf)
End While
FileClose(1)
```

See Also

EOF Function, LOF Function, Seek Function

Lock, Unlock Functions

Controls access by other processes to all or part of a file opened using the **Open** function.

```
Public Overloads Sub Lock(ByVal FileNumber As Integer)
. . .
Public Overloads Sub Unlock(ByVal FileNumber As Integer)
```

-or-

```
Public Overloads Sub Lock(_
   ByVal FileNumber As Integer, _
   ByVal FromRecord As Long _
)
. . .
Public Overloads Sub Unlock( _
   ByVal FileNumber As Integer, _
   ByVal FromRecord As Long _
)
```

-or-

```
Public Overloads Sub Lock( _
   ByVal FileNumber As Integer, _
   ByVal FromRecord As Long, _
   ByVal ToRecord As Long _
)
. . .
Public Overloads Sub Unlock( _
   ByVal FileNumber As Integer, _
   ByVal FromRecord As Long, _
   ByVal ToRecord As Long _
)
```

Parameters

FileNumber
Required. Any valid file number.

FromRecord
Optional. Number of the first record or byte to lock or unlock.

ToRecord
Optional. Number of the last record or byte to lock or unlock.

Exceptions/Errors

Exception type	Error number	Condition
IOException	52	*FileNumber* does not exist.
IOException	54	File mode is invalid.

Remarks

The **Lock** and **Unlock** functions are used in environments where several processes might need access to the same file.

Lock and **Unlock** functions are always used in pairs. The arguments to **Lock** and **Unlock** must match exactly.

If *FromRecord* and *ToRecord* are not supplied, the lock will be for the entire file. If *FromRecord* is specified but not *ToRecord*, the single record will be locked/unlocked.

If the file has been opened for sequential input or output, **Lock** and **Unlock** affect the entire file, regardless of the range specified by *FromRecord* and *ToRecord*.

Example

This example illustrates the use of the **Lock** and **Unlock** functions. This example assumes that `people.txt` is a file containing records of the structure `Person`.

```
Structure Person
   Dim Name As String
   Dim ID As Integer
End Structure

Sub PutInLockedFile(ByVal index As Integer, ByVal onePerson As Person)
   Try
      FileOpen(1, "c:\people.txt", OpenMode.Binary)
      Lock(1)
      FilePut(index, onePerson)
      Unlock(1)
      FileClose(1)
   Catch
      ' Error recovery code here.
   End Try
End Sub
```

See Also

FileOpen Function

LOF Function

Returns a **Long** representing the size, in bytes, of a file opened using the **FileOpen** function.

```
Public Function LOF(ByVal FileNumber As Integer) As Long
```

Parameter

FileNumber
 Required. An **Integer** containing a valid file number.

Exceptions/Errors

Exception type	Error number	Condition
IOException	52	*FileNumber* does not exist.
IOException	54	File mode is invalid.

Remarks

Use the **FileLen** function to obtain the length of a file that is not open.

Example

This example uses the **LOF** function to determine the size of an open file. This example assumes that TESTFILE is a text file containing sample data.

```
Dim length As Integer
FileOpen(1, "C:\TESTFILE.TXT", OpenMode.Input) ' Open file.
length = LOF(1)   ' Get length of file.
Debug.WriteLine(length)
FileClose(1)   ' Close file.
```

See Also

EOF Function, FileLen Function, Loc Function, FileOpen Function

Long Data Type

Long variables are stored as signed 64-bit (8-byte) integers ranging in value from –9,223,372,036,854,775,808 through 9,223,372,036,854,775,807.

> **Note** The **Long** data type can be converted to the **Single**, **Double**, or **Decimal** data type without encountering a **System.OverflowException** error.

Appending the literal type character **L** to a literal forces it to the **Long** data type. Appending the identifier type character **&** to any identifier forces it to **Long**.

The equivalent .NET data type is **System.Int64**.

See Also

Data Type Summary, Integer Data Type, Short Data Type, Type Conversion Functions, Conversion Summary

Loop

The **Loop** keyword terminates a loop introduced with a **Do** statement.

The **Loop** keyword is used in this context:

Do...Loop Statements

See Also

Visual Basic Language Keywords

LSet Function

Returns a left-aligned string containing the specified string adjusted to the specified length.

```
Public Shared Function LSet( _
   ByVal Source As String, _
   ByVal Length As Integer _
) As String
```

Parameters

Source
: Required. **String** expression. Name of string variable.

Length
: Required. **Integer** expression. Length of returned string.

Remarks

If the specified string is longer than the specified length, the returned string is shortened to the specified length. If the specified string is shorter than the specified length, spaces are added to the right end of the returned string to produce the appropriate length.

Example

This example demonstrates the use of the **LSet** function.

```
Dim myString As String = "Left"
Dim lString As String
LString = LSet(myString, 10)   ' Returns "Left      "
```

See Also

Data Type Summary, RSet Function

LTrim, RTrim, and Trim Functions

Returns a string containing a copy of a specified string with no leading spaces (**LTrim**), no trailing spaces (**RTrim**), or no leading or trailing spaces (**Trim**).

```
Public Shared Function LTrim(ByVal Str As String) As String
Public Shared Function RTrim(ByVal Str As String) As String
Public Shared Function Trim(ByVal Str As String) As String
```

Parameter

Str
: Required. Any valid **String** expression.

Example

This example uses the **LTrim** function to strip leading spaces and the **RTrim** function to strip trailing spaces from a string variable. It uses the **Trim** function to strip both types of spaces.

```
Dim MyString, TrimString As String
MyString = "  <-Trim->  "   ' Initializes string.
TrimString = LTrim(MyString)   ' TrimString = "<-Trim->  ".
TrimString = RTrim(MyString)   ' TrimString = "  <-Trim->".
TrimString = LTrim(RTrim(MyString))   ' TrimString = "<-Trim->".
' Using the Trim function alone achieves the same result.
TrimString = Trim(MyString)   ' TrimString = "<-Trim->".
```

See Also

Left Function, Right Function

Math Functions

The math functions in Visual Basic 6 have been replaced by equivalent methods in the **System.Math** class of the .NET Framework.

Remarks

The .NET Framework math methods are functionally identical to their Visual Basic 6 counterparts, although some have slightly different names. For example, the .NET Framework equivalent of the Visual Basic 6 Atn function is **Atan**. The following table lists the Visual Basic 6 math function names and the equivalent .NET Framework methods.

Visual Basic 6 function	Visual Basic .NET method	Description
Abs	Math.Abs Method	Returns the absolute value of a specified number.
Atn	Math.Atan Method	Returns a **Double** value containing the angle whose tangent is the specified number.
Cos	Math.Cos Method	Returns a **Double** value containing the cosine of the specified angle.
Exp	Math.Exp Method	Returns a **Double** value containing e (the base of natural logarithms) raised to the specified power.
Log	Math.Log Method	Returns a **Double** value containing the logarithm of a specified number. This method is overloaded and can return either the natural (base e) logarithm of a specified number or the logarithm of a specified number in a specified base.
Round	Math.Round Method	Returns a **Double** value containing the number nearest the specified value. Additional round functions are available as methods of the intrinsic types such as Decimal.Round Method.

Visual Basic 6 function	Visual Basic .NET method	Description
Sgn	Math.Sign Method	Returns an **Integer** value indicating the sign of a number.
Sin	Math.Sin Method	Returns a **Double** value specifying the sine of an angle.
Sqr	Math.Sqrt Method	Returns a **Double** value specifying the square root of a number.
Tan	Math.Tan Method	Returns a **Double** value containing the tangent of an angle.

In addition, the .NET Framework math class provides constants and other static methods for trigonometric, logarithmic, and other common mathematical functions. All of these can be used in a Visual Basic program.

To use these functions without qualification, import the **System.Math** namespace into your project by adding the following code to the top of the source code:

```
Imports System.Math
```

Requirements

Class: Math Class

Abs Example

This example uses the **Abs** method of the **Math** class to compute the absolute value of a number.

```
Imports System.Math
...
Dim MyNumber As Double
MyNumber = Abs(50.3)     ' Returns 50.3.
MyNumber = Abs(-50.3)    ' Returns 50.3.
```

Atan Example

This example uses the **Atan** method of the **Math** class to calculate the value of pi.

```
Imports System.Math
...
Dim pi As Double
pi = 4 * Atan(1)    ' Calculate the value of pi.
```

Cos Example

This example uses the **Cos** method of the **Math** class to return the cosine of an angle.

```
Imports System.Math
...
Dim MyAngle, MySecant As Double
MyAngle = 1.3    ' Define angle in radians.
MySecant = 1 / Cos(MyAngle)    ' Calculate secant.
```

Exp Example

This example uses the **Exp** method of the **Math** class to return *e* raised to a power.

```
Imports System.Math
...
Dim MyAngle, MyHSin As Double
' Define angle in radians.
MyAngle = 1.3
' Calculate hyperbolic sine.
MyHSin = (Exp(MyAngle) - Exp(-1 * MyAngle)) / 2
```

Log Example

This example uses the **Log** method of the **Math** class to return the natural logarithm of a number.

```
Imports System.Math
...
Dim MyAngle, MyLog As Double
' Define angle in radians.
MyAngle = 1.3
' Calculate inverse hyperbolic sine.
MyLog = Log(MyAngle + Sqrt(MyAngle * MyAngle + 1))
```

Round Example

This example uses the **Round** method of the **Math** class to round a number to the nearest integer.

```
Imports System.Math
...
Dim MyVar1 As Double = 2.8
Dim MyVar2 As Double
MyVar2 =Round(MyVar1)    ' Returns 3.
```

Sign Example

This example uses the **Sign** method of the **Math** class to determine the sign of a number.

```
Imports System.Math
...
Dim MyVar1, MyVar2, MyVar3 As Double
Dim MySign As Integer
MyVar1 = 12
MyVar2 = -2.4
MyVar3 = 0
MySign = Sign(MyVar1)    ' Returns 1.
MySign = Sign(MyVar2)    ' Returns -1.
MySign = Sign(MyVar3)    ' Returns 0.
```

Sin Example

This example uses the **Sin** method of the **Math** class to return the sine of an angle.

```
Imports System.Math
...
Dim MyAngle, MyCosecant As Double
MyAngle = 1.3   ' Define angle in radians.
MyCosecant = 1 / Sin(MyAngle)   ' Calculate cosecant.
```

Sqrt Example

This example uses the **Sqrt** method of the **Math** class to calculate the square root of a number.

```
Imports System.Math
...
Dim MySqr As Double
MySqr = Sqrt(4)    ' Returns 2.
MySqr = Sqrt(23)   ' Returns 4.79583152331272.
MySqr = Sqrt(0)    ' Returns 0.
MySqr = Sqrt(-4)   ' Generates an OverFlow Exception error.
```

Tan Example

This example uses the **Tan** method of the **Math** class to return the tangent of an angle.

```
Imports System.Math
...
Dim MyAngle, MyCotangent As Double
MyAngle = 1.3   ' Define angle in radians.
MyCotangent = 1 / Tan(MyAngle)   ' Calculate cotangent.
```

See Also

Rnd Function, Randomize Statement, Derived Math Functions

Me

The **Me** keyword behaves like an object variable referring to the current instance of a class. When a class can have more than one instance, **Me** provides a way to refer to the specific instance of the class where the code is currently executing. Using **Me** is particularly useful for passing information about the currently executing instance of a class to a procedure in another class or module. For example, suppose you have the following procedure in a module:

```
Sub ChangeFormColor(FormName As Form)
   FormName.BackColor = RGB(Rnd() * 256, Rnd() * 256, Rnd() * 256)
End Sub
```

You can call this procedure and pass the current instance of the **Form** class as an argument using the following statement:

```
ChangeFormColor(Me)
```

See Also

MyBase, MyClass

Mid Function

Returns a string containing a specified number of characters from a string.

```
Public Shared Function Mid( _
   ByVal Str As String, _
   ByVal Start As Integer, _
   Optional ByVal Length As Integer _
) As String
```

Parameters

Str

Required. **String** expression from which characters are returned.

Start

Required. **Integer** expression. Character position in *Str* at which the part to be taken starts. If *Start* is greater than the number of characters in *Str*, the **Mid** function returns a zero-length string (" "). *Start* is one based.

Length

Optional. **Integer** expression. Number of characters to return. If omitted or if there are fewer than *Length* characters in the text (including the character at position *Start*), all characters from the start position to the end of the string are returned.

Exceptions/Errors

Exception type	Error number	Condition
ArgumentException	5	*Start* <= 0 or *Length* < 0.

Remarks

To determine the number of characters in *Str*, use the **Len** function.

Example

This example uses the **Mid** function to return a specified number of characters from a string.

```
Dim MyString, FirstWord, LastWord, MidWords As String
MyString = "Mid Function Demo"    ' Creates text string.
FirstWord = Mid(MyString, 1, 3)    ' Returns "Mid".
LastWord = Mid(MyString, 14, 4)    ' Returns "Demo".
MidWords = Mid(MyString, 5)    ' Returns "Function Demo".
```

See Also

Left Function; Len Function; LTrim, RTrim, and Trim Functions; Mid Statement; Right Function

Mid Statement

Replaces a specified number of characters in a **String** variable with characters from another string.

```
Mid( _
   ByRef Target As String, _
   ByVal Start As Integer, _
   Optional ByVal Length As Integer _
) = StringExpression
```

Parts

Target
Required. Name of the **String** variable to modify.

Start
Required. **Integer** expression. Character position in *Target* where the replacement of text begins. *Start* uses a one based index.

Length
Optional. **Integer** expression. Number of characters to replace. If omitted, all of *String* is used.

StringExpression
Required. **String** expression that replaces part of *Target*.

Remarks

The number of characters replaced is always less than or equal to the number of characters in *Target*.

Example

This example uses the **Mid** statement to replace a specified number of characters in a string variable with characters from another string.

```
Dim MyString As String
MyString = "The dog jumps"   ' Initializes string.
Mid(MyString, 5, 3) = "fox"   ' MyString = "The fox jumps".
Mid(MyString, 5) = "cow"   ' MyString = "The cow jumps".
Mid(MyString, 5) = "cow jumped over"   ' MyString = "The cow jumpe".
Mid(MyString, 5, 3) = "duck"   ' MyString = "The duc jumpe".
```

See Also

Mid Function

Minute Function

Returns an **Integer** value from 0 through 59 representing the minute of the hour.

```
Public Function Minute(ByVal TimeValue As DateTime) As Integer
```

Parameter

TimeValue
Required. **Date** value from which you want to extract the minute.

You can also obtain the minute of the hour by calling **DatePart** and specifying **DateInterval.Minute** for the *Interval* argument.

Example

This example uses the **Minute** function to obtain the minute of the hour from a specified time. In the development environment, the time literal is displayed in short time format using the locale settings of your code.

```
Dim MyTime As Date
Dim MyMinute As Integer
MyTime = #4:35:17 PM#    ' Assign a time.
MyMinute = Minute(MyTime)    ' MyMinute contains 35.
```

See Also

Day Function, Hour Function, Now Property, Second Function, TimeOfDay Property, DatePart Function

MIRR Function

Returns a **Double** specifying the modified internal rate of return for a series of periodic cash flows (payments and receipts).

```
Function MIRR( _
   ByRef ValueArray() As Double, _
   ByVal FinanceRate As Double, _
   ByVal ReinvestRate As Double _
) As Double
```

Parameters

ValueArray()
Required. Array of **Double** specifying cash flow values. The array must contain at least one negative value (a payment) and one positive value (a receipt).

FinanceRate
Required. **Double** specifying interest rate paid as the cost of financing.

ReinvestRate

Required. **Double** specifying interest rate received on gains from cash reinvestment.

Exceptions/Errors

Exception type	Error number	Condition
ArgumentException	5	Rank of *ValueArray* does not equal 1.
ArgumentException	5	*FinanceRate* = –1
ArgumentException	5	*ReinvestRate* = –1
DivideByZeroException	11	Division by zero has occurred.

Remarks

The modified internal rate of return is the internal rate of return when payments and receipts are financed at different rates. The **MIRR** function takes into account both the cost of the investment (*FinanceRate*) and the interest rate received on reinvestment of cash (*ReinvestRate*).

The *FinanceRate* and *ReinvestRatearguments* are percentages expressed as decimal values. For example, 12 percent is expressed as 0.12.

The **MIRR** function uses the order of values within the array to interpret the order of payments and receipts. Be sure to enter your payment and receipt values in the correct sequence.

Example

This example uses the **MIRR** function to return the modified internal rate of return for a series of cash flows contained in the array `Values()`. `LoanAPR` represents the financing interest, and `InvAPR` represents the interest rate received on reinvestment.

```
Sub TestMIRR()
   Dim LoanAPR, InvAPR, RetRate, Values(4) As Double
   Dim Msg, Fmt As String
   LoanAPR = 0.1  ' Loan rate.
   InvAPR = 0.12  ' Reinvestment rate.
   Fmt = "#0.00"   ' Define money format.
   Values(0) = -70000   ' Business start-up costs.
   ' Positive cash flows reflecting income for four successive years.
   Values(1) = 22000 : Values(2) = 25000
   Values(3) = 28000 : Values(4) = 31000
   RetRate = MIRR(Values, LoanAPR, InvAPR)   ' Calculate internal rate.
   Msg = "The modified internal rate of return for these five cash flows is "
   Msg = Msg & Format(Math.Abs(RetRate) * 100, CStr(Fmt)) & "%."
   MsgBox(Msg)    ' Display internal return rate.
End Sub
```

See Also

DDB Function, FV Function, IPmt Function, IRR Function, NPer Function, NPV Function, Pmt Function, PPmt Function, PV Function, Rate Function, SLN Function, SYD Function

MkDir Function

Creates a new directory or folder.

```
Public Sub MkDir(ByVal Path As String)
```

Parameter

Path

Required. **String** expression that identifies the directory or folder to be created. The *Path* may include the drive. If no drive is specified, **MkDir** creates the new directory or folder on the current drive.

Exceptions/Errors

Exception type	Error number	Condition
ArgumentException	52	*Path* is not specified or is empty.
IOException	75	Directory already exists.

Example

This example uses the **MkDir** function to create a directory or folder. If the drive is not specified, the new directory or folder is created on the current drive.

```
MkDir("C:\MYDIR")    ' Make new directory or folder.
```

See Also

ChDir Function, CurDir Function, RmDir Function, ArgumentException, IOException

Mod Operator

Divides two numbers and returns only the remainder.

```
number1 Mod number2
```

Parts

number1

Required. Any numeric expression.

number2

Required. Any numeric expression.

Result

The result is the remainder left after division is performed on *number1* and *number2*.

Supported Types

Byte, Short, Integer, Long, Single, Double, Decimal

Remarks

The **Mod** operator divides *number1* by *number2* and returns only the remainder as *result*. For example, in the following expression, A (*result*) equals 2.

```
A = 8 Mod 3
```

If *number1* or *number2* are floating-point values, then division is carried out and the floating-point remainder is returned. The data type of the result is the same as that of the data type with the greatest range. The order of range, from least to greatest range, is Byte, Short, Integer, Long, Single, Double, and Decimal.

If any expression is stated as Nothing, or Empty, it is treated as zero. If division by zero occurs, the **Mod** operation returns **NaN (Not a Number)**.

`A Mod B` is the equivalent of `A - Int(A / B) * B + CLng(Math.Sign(A) <> Math.Sign(B)) * B`.

Example

This example uses the **Mod** operator to divide two numbers and return only the remainder. If either number is a floating-point number, the result is a floating-point number representing the remainder.

```
Dim myResult As Double
myResult = 10 Mod 5   ' Returns 0.
myResult = 10 Mod 3   ' Returns 1.
myResult = 12 Mod 4.3   ' Returns 3.4.
myResult = 12.6 Mod 5   ' Returns 2.6.
myResult = 47.9 Mod 9.35   ' Returns 1.15.
```

See Also

Arithmetic Operators, Operator Precedence in Visual Basic, Operators Listed by Functionality

Module

The **Module** keyword indicates that an attribute block at the beginning of a source file applies only to the current module and not to the entire assembly. The **Module** keyword is not the same as the **Module** statement.

See Also

Module Statement

Module Statement

Declares a module block.

```
[ <attrilist> ] [ Public | Friend ] Module name
   [ statements ]
End Module
```

Parts

attrlist
: Optional. List of attributes that apply to this module. Multiple attributes are separated by commas.

Public
: Optional. Modules declared with the **Public** keyword have public access. There are no restrictions on the accessibility of public modules.

Friend
: Optional. Modules declared with the **Friend** keyword have friend access. They are accessible from within the program that contains their declaration and from anywhere else in the same assembly. Modules that do not specify an access modifier are declared as **Friend** by default.

name
: Required. Name of the module. Must be a valid Visual Basic identifier.

statements
: Optional. Statements that comprise the variables, properties, events, and methods of the module.

End Module
: Terminates a **Module** block.

Each attribute in the *attrlist* part has the following syntax and parts:

```
attrname [({ attrargs | attrinit })]
```

attrlist Parts

attrname
: Required. Name of the attribute. Must be a valid Visual Basic identifier.

attrargs
: Optional. List of positional arguments for this attribute. Multiple arguments are separated by commas.

attrinit
: Optional. List of field or property initializers for this attribute. Multiple initializers are separated by commas.

Remarks

Modules are a reference type similar to classes, but with some important distinctions. The members of a module are implicitly **Shared** and scoped to the declaration space of the standard module's containing namespace, rather than just to the module itself. Unlike classes, modules can never be instantiated, do not support inheritance, and cannot implement interfaces. A module can only be declared in a namespace and cannot be nested in another type.

You can have multiple modules in a project, but members with the same name defined in two or more modules must be qualified with their module name when accessed outside of their module.

Example

```
Public Module Module1
   ' Add classes, properties, methods, fields, and events for this module.
End Module
```

See Also

Class Statement, Namespace Statement, Property Statement

Month Function

Returns an **Integer** value from 1 through 12 representing the month of the year.

```
Public Function Month(ByVal DateValue As DateTime) As Integer
```

Parameter

DateValue
   Required. **Date** value from which you want to extract the month.

You can also obtain the month of the year by calling **DatePart** and specifying **DateInterval.Month** for the *Interval* argument.

Example

This example uses the **Month** function to obtain the month from a specified date. In the development environment, the date literal is displayed in short date format using the locale settings of your code.

```
Dim MyDate As Date
Dim MyMonth As Integer
MyDate = #2/12/1969#    ' Assign a date.
MyMonth = Month(MyDate)   ' MyMonth contains 2.
```

See Also

Day Function, Now Property, Weekday Function, Year Function, DatePart Function

MonthName Function

Returns a **String** value containing the name of the specified month.

```
Public Function MonthName( _
   ByVal Month As Integer, _
   Optional ByVal Abbreviate As Boolean = False _
) As String
```

Parameters

Month

Required. **Integer**. The numeric designation of the month, from 1 through 13; 1 indicates January and 12 indicates December. You can use the value 13 with a 13-month calendar. If your system is using a 12-month calendar and *Month* is 13, **MonthName** returns an empty string.

Abbreviate

Optional. **Boolean** value that indicates if the month name is to be abbreviated. If omitted, the default is **False**, which means the month name is not abbreviated.

Exceptions/Errors

Exception type	Error number	Condition
ArgumentException	5	*Month* is less than 1 or greater than 13.

Remarks

The string returned by **MonthName** depends not only on the input arguments, but also on the Regional Options settings specified in the Windows Control Panel.

If *Month* is less than 1 or more than 13, an **ArgumentException** error occurs.

Note **MonthName** uses the current calendar setting from the **CurrentCulture** property of the **CultureInfo** class in the **System.Globalization** namespace. The default **CurrentCulture** values are determined by **Control Panel** settings.

Example

This example uses the **MonthName** function to determine the name of the month, by the integer given. The Boolean value will determine whether the full name (**False**) or the abbreviated name (**True**) will be displayed.

```
Dim MyMonth As Integer
Dim Name As String
MyMonth = 4
Name = MonthName(MyMonth, True)    ' "True" returns an abbreviated name.
Msgbox(Name)   ' Name contains "Apr".
```

See Also

WeekdayName Function

MsgBox Function

Displays a message in a dialog box, waits for the user to click a button, and then returns an integer indicating which button the user clicked.

```
Public Function MsgBox( _
   ByVal Prompt As Object, _
   Optional ByVal Buttons As MsgBoxStyle = MsgBoxStyle.OKOnly, _
   Optional ByVal Title As Object = Nothing _
) As MsgBoxResult
```

Parameters

Prompt

Required. **String** expression displayed as the message in the dialog box. The maximum length of *Prompt* is approximately 1024 characters, depending on the width of the characters used. If *Prompt* consists of more than one line, you can separate the lines using a carriage return character (**Chr**(13)), a linefeed character (**Chr**(10)), or a carriage return/linefeed character combination (**Chr**(13) & **Chr**(10)) between each line.

Buttons

Optional. Numeric expression that is the sum of values specifying the number and type of buttons to display, the icon style to use, the identity of the default button, and the modality of the message box. If you omit *Buttons*, the default value is zero.

Title

Optional. **String** expression displayed in the title bar of the dialog box. If you omit *Title*, the application name is placed in the title bar.

Settings

The **MsgBoxStyle** enumeration values are listed in the following table.

Enumeration	Value	Description
OKOnly	0	Displays OK button only.
OKCancel	1	Displays OK and Cancel buttons.
AbortRetryIgnore	2	Displays Abort, Retry, and Ignore buttons.
YesNoCancel	3	Displays Yes, No, and Cancel buttons.
YesNo	4	Displays Yes and No buttons.
RetryCancel	5	Displays Retry and Cancel buttons.

(continued)

(continued)

Enumeration	Value	Description
Critical	16	Displays Critical Message icon.
Question	32	Displays Warning Query icon.
Exclamation	48	Displays Warning Message icon.
Information	64	Displays Information Message icon.
DefaultButton1	0	First button is default.
DefaultButton2	256	Second button is default.
DefaultButton3	512	Third button is default.
ApplicationModal	0	Application is modal. The user must respond to the message box before continuing work in the current application.
SystemModal	4096	System is modal. All applications are suspended until the user responds to the message box.
MsgBoxSetForeground	65536	Specifies the message box window as the foreground window.
MsgBoxRight	524288	Text is right-aligned.
MsgBoxRtlReading	1048576	Specifies text should appear as right-to-left reading on Hebrew and Arabic systems.

The first group of values (0–5) describes the number and type of buttons displayed in the dialog box; the second group (16, 32, 48, 64) describes the icon style; the third group (0, 256, 512) determines which button is the default; the fourth group (0, 4096) determines the modality of the message box, and the fifth group specifies whether or not the message box window is the foreground window, along with the alignment and direction of the text. When adding numbers to create a final value for the *Buttons* argument, use only one number from each group.

Return Values

Constant	Value
OK	1
Cancel	2
Abort	3
Retry	4
Ignore	5
Yes	6
No	7

Exceptions/Errors

Exception type	Error number	Condition
ArgumentException	5	*Prompt* is not a **String** expression, or *Title* is invalid.
InvalidOperationException	5	Process is not running in User Interactive mode.
InvalidEnumArgumentException	5	One or more parameters not a member of **MsgBoxResult** or **MsgBoxStyle** enumerations.

Remarks

If the dialog box displays a **Cancel** button, pressing the ESC key has the same effect as clicking **Cancel**. If the dialog box contains a **Help** button, context-sensitive Help is provided for the dialog box. However, no value is returned until one of the other buttons is clicked.

Note To specify more than the first argument, you must use the **MsgBox** function in an expression. If you omit any positional arguments, you must retain the corresponding comma delimiter.

Example

This example uses the **MsgBox** function to display a critical-error message in a dialog box with Yes and No buttons. The No button is specified as the default response. This is done by combining the **MsgBox** constant values into one numeric expression. In this case, adding 4 (the Yes/No button combination) and 16 (the Critical Message window) and 256 (the second button as default button) gives a total of 276. The value returned by the **MsgBox** function depends on the button chosen by the user: Yes returns a value of 6; No returns a value of 7.

```
Dim msg As String
Dim title As String
Dim style As MsgBoxStyle
Dim response As MsgBoxResult
msg = "Do you want to continue?"   ' Define message.
style = MsgBoxStyle.DefaultButton2 Or _
   MsgBoxStyle.Critical Or MsgBoxStyle.YesNo
title = "MsgBox Demonstration"   ' Define title.
' Display message.
response = MsgBox(msg, style, title)
If response = MsgBoxResult.Yes Then   ' User chose Yes.
   ' Perform some action.
Else
   ' Perform some other action.
End If
```

See Also

InputBox Function

MsgBoxResult Enumeration

When you call the **MsgBox** function, you can use the **MsgBoxResult** enumeration in your code in place of the actual values.

MsgBoxResult Enumeration Members

The **MsgBox** function returns the following **MsgBoxResult** enumeration values:

Member	Constant	Description
OK	**vbOK**	**OK** button was pressed.
Cancel	**vbCancel**	**Cancel** button was pressed.
Abort	**vbAbort**	**Abort** button was pressed.
Retry	**vbRetry**	**Retry** button was pressed.
Ignore	**vbIgnore**	**Ignore** button was pressed.
Yes	**vbYes**	**Yes** button was pressed.
No	**vbNo**	**No** button was pressed.

See Also

MsgBoxStyle Enumeration, MsgBox Function

MsgBoxStyle Enumeration

When you call the **MsgBox** function, you can use the **MsgBoxStyle** enumeration in your code in place of the actual values.

MsgBoxStyle Enumeration Members

The *Buttons* argument takes the following **MsgBoxStyle** enumeration members:

Member	Constant	Description
OKOnly	**vbOKOnly**	**OK** button only (default).
OKCancel	**vbOKCancel**	**OK** and **Cancel** buttons.
AbortRetryIgnore	**vbAbortRetryIgnore**	**Abort**, **Retry**, and **Ignore** buttons.
YesNoCancel	**vbYesNoCancel**	**Yes**, **No**, and **Cancel** buttons.
YesNo	**vbYesNo**	**Yes** and **No** buttons.
RetryCancel	**vbRetryCancel**	**Retry** and **Cancel** buttons.

Member	Constant	Description
Critical	**vbCritical**	Critical message.
Question	**vbQuestion**	Warning query.
Exclamation	**vbExclamation**	Warning message.
Information	**vbInformation**	Information message.
DefaultButton1	**vbDefaultButton1**	First button is default (default).
DefaultButton2	**vbDefaultButton2**	Second button is default.
DefaultButton3	**vbDefaultButton3**	Third button is default.
ApplicationModal	**vbApplicationModal**	Application modal message box (default).
SystemModal	**vbSystemModal**	System modal message box.
MsgBoxSetForeground	**vbMsgBoxSetForeground**	Foreground message box window.
MsgBoxRight	**vbMsgBoxRight**	Right-aligned text.
MsgBoxRtlReading	**vbMsgBoxRtlReading**	Right-to-left reading text (Hebrew and Arabic systems).
MsgBoxHelp	**vbMsgBoxHelp**	Help text.

See Also

MsgBoxResult Enumeration, MsgBox Function

MustInherit

The **MustInherit** keyword specifies that a class cannot be instantiated and can be used only as a base class.

The **MustInherit** keyword is used in this context:

Class Statement

See Also

Visual Basic Language Keywords

MustOverride

The **MustOverride** keyword specifies that a property or procedure in a base class must be overridden in a derived class before it can be used.

The **MustOverride** keyword is used in these contexts:

Function Statement

Property Statement

Sub Statement

See Also

Visual Basic Language Keywords

MyBase

The **MyBase** keyword behaves like an object variable referring to the base class of the current instance of a class. **MyBase** is commonly used to access base class members that are overridden or shadowed in a derived class. In particular, **MyBase.New** is used to explicitly call a base class constructor from a derived class constructor.

It is invalid to use **MyBase** to call **MustOverride** base methods.

See Also

Me, MyClass, New

MyClass

MyClass behaves like an object variable referring to the current instance of a class as originally implemented. **MyClass** is similar to **Me**, but all method calls on it are treated as if the method were **NotOverridable**. Therefore, the method being called is not affected by overriding in a derived class. The following example compares **Me** and **MyClass**.

```
Class BaseClass
   Public Overridable Sub MyMethod()
      MsgBox("Base class string")
   End Sub
   Public Sub UseMe()
      Me.MyMethod()    ' Use calling class's version, even if an override.
   End Sub
   Public Sub UseMyClass()
      MyClass.MyMethod()    ' Use this version and not any override.
   End Sub
End Class
```

```
Class DerivedClass : Inherits BaseClass
   Public Overrides Sub MyMethod()
      MsgBox("Derived class string")
   End Sub
End Class
Class TestClasses
   Sub StartHere()
      Dim TestObj As DerivedClass = New DerivedClass()
      TestObj.UseMe()   ' Displays "Derived class string".
      TestObj.UseMyClass()   ' Displays "Base class string".
   End Sub
End Class
```

Even though `DerivedClass` overrides `MyMethod`, the **MyClass** keyword in `UseMyClass` nullifies the effects of overriding, and the compiler resolves the call to the base class version of `MyMethod`.

MyClass cannot not be used inside a **Shared** method, but you can use it inside an instance method to access a shared member of a class.

See Also

Me, MyBase

Namespace Statement

Declares the name of a namespace.

```
Namespace { name | name.name }
   [ componenttypes ]
End Namespace
```

Parts

name
  Required. A unique name that identifies the namespace.

componenttypes
  Optional. Elements that make up the namespace. These include (but are not limited to) enumerations, structures, interfaces, classes, modules, delegates, and other namespaces.

End Namespace
  Terminates a **Namespace** block.

Remarks

Namespaces are used as an organizational system—a way of presenting program components that are exposed to other programs and applications.

Namespaces are always **Public;** therefore the declaration of a namespace cannot include an access modifiers. However, the components within the namespace may have **Public** or **Friend** access. If it is not stated, the default access type is **Friend**.

Example

The following example declares two namespaces.

```
Namespace N1   ' Declares a namespace named N1.
   Namespace N2   ' Declares a namespace named N2 within N1.
      Class A   ' Declares a class within N1.N2.
      ' Add class statements here.
      End Class
   End Namespace
End Namespace
```

The next example declares multiple nested namespaces on a single line, and is equivalent to the previous example.

```
Namespace N1.N2 ' Declares two namespaces; N1 and N2.
   Class A   ' Declares a class within N1.N2.
      ' Add class statements here.
   End Class
End Namespace
```

See Also

Imports Statement, Namespaces

New

The **New** keyword introduces a **New** clause, which creates a new object instance. The **New** clause must specify a defined class from which the instance can be created. You can use **New** in a declaration statement or an assignment statement. When the statement is executed, it calls the constructor of the specified class, passing any arguments you have supplied:

```
Dim Obj As Object
Obj = New SomeClass("String required by constructor")
' ...
Dim MyLabel As New Label()
```

Since arrays are classes, **New** can create a new array instance:

```
Dim MyArray As Integer()
MyArray = New Integer() {0, 1, 2, 3}
```

The **New** keyword is used in this context:

Dim Statement

See Also

Visual Basic Language Keywords

Next

The **Next** keyword either terminates a loop that is iterated with different values of a loop variable, or specifies that execution should continue with the statement following the statement that generated an error.

The **Next** keyword is used in these contexts:

For...Next Statements

For Each...Next Statements

On Error Statement

Resume Statement

See Also

Visual Basic Language Keywords

Not Operator

Performs logical negation on a **Boolean** expression, or bitwise negation on a numeric expression.

```
result = Not expression
```

Parts

result
Required. Any **Boolean** or numeric expression.

expression
Required. Any **Boolean** or numeric expression.

Remarks

For **Boolean** expressions, the following table illustrates how *result* is determined:

If *expression* is	Then *result* is
True	**False**
False	**True**

For numeric expressions, the **Not** operator inverts the bit values of any numeric expression and sets the corresponding bit in *result* according to the following table:

If bit in *expression* is	Then bit in *result* is
0	1
1	0

Note Since the logical/bitwise operators have a lower precedence than other arithmetic and relational operators, any bitwise operations should be enclosed in parentheses to insure accurate execution.

Example

This example uses the **Not** operator to perform logical negation on a **Boolean** expression. The result is a **Boolean** value representing whether the expression is false. That is, if the expression is false, the result of the **Not** operator is true.

```
Dim A As Integer = 10
Dim B As Integer = 8
Dim C As Integer = 6
Dim myCheck As Boolean
myCheck = Not(A > B)   ' Returns False.
myCheck = Not(B > A)   ' Returns True.
```

This example uses the **Not** operator to perform logical negation of the individual bits of two numeric expressions. The bit in the result pattern is set to the reverse of the corresponding bit in the operand pattern, including the sign bit.

```
Dim A As Integer = 10
Dim B As Integer = 8
Dim C As Integer = 6
Dim myCheck As Integer
myCheck = (Not A)   ' Returns -11.
myCheck = (Not B)   ' Returns -9.
myCheck = (Not C)   ' Returns -7.
```

See Also

Logical/Bitwise Operators, Operator Precedence in Visual Basic, Operators Listed by Functionality, Logical Operators

Nothing

The **Nothing** keyword represents the default value of any data type. Assigning **Nothing** to a variable sets it to the default value for its declared type. If that type contains variable members, they are all set to their default values. The following example illustrates this:

```
Public Structure MyStruct
   Public Name As String
   Public Number As Short
End Structure
Dim S As MyStruct, I As Integer, B As Boolean
S = Nothing   ' Sets S.Name to Nothing, S.Number to 0.
I = Nothing   ' Sets I to 0.
B = Nothing   ' Sets B to False.
```

If the variable is of a reference type—that is, an object variable—**Nothing** means the variable is not associated with any object. For example:

```
Dim MyObject As Object
MyObject = Nothing   ' No object currently referred to.
```

When you assign **Nothing** to an object variable, it no longer refers to any object instance. If the variable had previously referred to an instance, setting it to **Nothing** does not terminate the instance itself. The instance is terminated, and the memory and system resources associated with it are released, only after the garbage collector detects there are no active references remaining.

See Also

Dim Statement

NotInheritable

The **NotInheritable** keyword specifies that a class cannot be used as a base class.

The **NotInheritable** keyword is used in this context:

Class Statement

See Also

Visual Basic Language Keywords

NotOverridable

The **NotOverridable** keyword specifies that a property or procedure cannot be overridden in a derived class.

The **NotOverridable** keyword is used in these contexts:

Function Statement

Property Statement

Sub Statement

See Also

Visual Basic Language Keywords

Now Property

Returns a **Date** value containing the current date and time according to your system.

```
ReadOnly Public Property Now() As DateTime
```

Remarks

To set the system date, use the **Today** property. To set the system time, use the **TimeOfDay** property.

Example

This example uses the **Now** property to return the current system date and time.

```
Dim ThisMoment As Date
ThisMoment= Now   ' Assign current system date and time.
```

See Also

Day Function, Hour Function, Minute Function, Month Function, Second Function, TimeOfDay Property, Weekday Function, Year Function, TimeOfDay Property, Today Property

NPer Function

Returns a **Double** specifying the number of periods for an annuity based on periodic, fixed payments and a fixed interest rate.

```
Function NPer( _
    ByVal Rate As Double, _
   ByVal Pmt As Double, _
   ByVal PV As Double, _
   Optional ByVal FV As Double = 0, _
   Optional ByVal Due As DueDate = DueDate.EndOfPeriod _
) As Double
```

Parameters

Rate

Required. **Double** specifying interest rate per period. For example, if you get a car loan at an annual percentage rate (APR) of 10 percent and make monthly payments, the rate per period is 0.1/12, or 0.0083.

Pmt

Required. **Double** specifying payment to be made each period. Payments usually contain principal and interest that doesn't change over the life of the annuity.

PV

Required. **Double** specifying present value, or value today, of a series of future payments or receipts. For example, when you borrow money to buy a car, the loan amount is the present value to the lender of the monthly car payments you will make.

FV

Optional. **Double** specifying future value or cash balance you want after you've made the final payment. For example, the future value of a loan is $0 because that's its value after the final payment. However, if you want to save $50,000 over 18 years for your child's education, then $50,000 is the future value. If omitted, 0 is assumed.

Due

Optional. Object of type `Microsoft.VisualBasic.DueDate` that specifies when payments are due. This argument must be either `DueDate.EndOfPeriod` if payments are due at the end of the payment period, or `DueDate.BegOfPeriod` if payments are due at the beginning of the period. If omitted, `DueDate.EndOfPeriod` is assumed.

Exceptions/Errors

Exception type	Error number	Condition
ArgumentException	5	*Rate* <= –1.
ArgumentException	5	*Rate* = 0 and *Pmt* = 0

Remarks

An annuity is a series of fixed cash payments made over a period of time. An annuity can be a loan (such as a home mortgage) or an investment (such as a monthly savings plan).

For all arguments, cash paid out (such as deposits to savings) is represented by negative numbers; cash received (such as dividend checks) is represented by positive numbers.

Example

This example uses the **NPer** function to return the number of periods during which payments must be made to pay off a loan whose value is contained in `PVal`. Also provided are the interest percentage rate per period (`APR / 12`), the payment (`Payment`), the future value of the loan (`FVal`), and a number that indicates whether the payment is due at the beginning or end of the payment period (`PayType`).

```
Sub TestNPer()
   Dim FVal, TotPmts As Double
   Dim PVal, APR, Payment As Double
   Dim PayType As DueDate
   Dim Response As MsgBoxResult
   FVal = 0   ' Usually 0 for a loan.
   PVal = CDbl(InputBox("How much do you want to borrow?"))
   APR = CDbl(InputBox("What is the annual percentage rate of your loan?"))
   If APR > 1 Then APR = APR / 100 ' Ensure proper form.
   Payment = CDbl(InputBox("How much do you want to pay each month?"))
   Response = MsgBox("Do you make payments at the end of month?", MsgBoxStyle.YesNo)
   If Response = MsgBoxResult.No Then
      PayType = DueDate.BegOfPeriod
   Else
      PayType = DueDate.EndOfPeriod
   End If
   TotPmts = NPer(APR / 12, -Payment, PVal, FVal, PayType)
   If Int(TotPmts) <> TotPmts Then TotPmts = Int(TotPmts) + 1
      MsgBox("It will take you " & TotPmts & " months to pay off your loan.")
End Sub
```

See Also

DDB Function, FV Function, IPmt Function, IRR Function, MIRR Function, NPV Function, Pmt Function, PPmt Function, PV Function, Rate Function, SLN Function, SYD Function

NPV Function

Returns a **Double** specifying the net present value of an investment based on a series of periodic cash flows (payments and receipts) and a discount rate.

```
Function NPV( _
   ByVal Rate As Double, _
   ByRef ValueArray() As Double _
) As Double
```

Parameters

Rate
: Required. **Double** specifying discount rate over the length of the period, expressed as a decimal.

ValueArray()
: Required. Array of **Double** specifying cash flow values. The array must contain at least one negative value (a payment) and one positive value (a receipt).

Exceptions/Errors

Exception type	Error number	Condition
ArgumentException	5	*ValueArray* is **Nothing,** rank of *ValueArray* <> 1, or *Rate* = –1

Remarks

The net present value of an investment is the current value of a future series of payments and receipts.

The **NPV** function uses the order of values within the array to interpret the order of payments and receipts. Be sure to enter your payment and receipt values in the correct sequence.

The **NPV** investment begins one period before the date of the first cash flow value and ends with the last cash flow value in the array.

The net present value calculation is based on future cash flows. If your first cash flow occurs at the beginning of the first period, the first value must be added to the value returned by **NPV** and must not be included in the cash flow values of *ValueArray()*.

The **NPV** function is similar to the **PV** function (present value) except that the **PV** function allows cash flows to begin either at the end or the beginning of a period. Unlike the variable **NPV** cash flow values, **PV** cash flows must be fixed throughout the investment.

Example

This example uses the **NPV** function to return the net present value for a series of cash flows contained in the array `Values()`. `RetRate` represents the fixed internal rate of return.

```
Sub TestNPV()
   Dim Guess, RetRate, NetPVal, values(4) As Double
   Dim Fmt, Msg As String
   Fmt = "###,##0.00"   ' Define money format.
   Guess = 0.1  ' Guess starts at 10 percent.
   RetRate = 0.0625  ' Set fixed internal rate.
   values(0) = -70000   ' Business start-up costs.
   ' Positive cash flows reflecting income for four successive years.
   values(1) = 22000 : values(2) = 25000
   values(3) = 28000 : values(4) = 31000
   NetPVal = NPV(RetRate, values)   ' Calculate net present value.
   Msg = "The net present value of these cash flows is "
   Msg = Msg & Format(NetPVal, Fmt) & "."
   MsgBox(Msg)    ' Display net present value.
End Sub
```

See Also

DDB Function, FV Function, IPmt Function, IRR Function, MIRR Function, NPer Function, Pmt Function, PPmt Function, PV Function, Rate Function, SLN Function, SYD Function

Number Property

Returns or sets a numeric value specifying an error. Read/write.

```
Public Property Number() As Integer
```

Remarks

When returning a user-defined error from an object, set **Err.Number** by adding the number you selected as an error code to the **VbObjectError** constant. For example, you use the following code to return the number 1051 as an error code:

```
Err.Raise(Number := VbObjectError + 1051, Source:= "SomeClass")
```

Example

This example illustrates a typical use of the **Number** property in an error-handling routine.

```
' Typical use of Number property.
Sub test()
   On Error GoTo out

   Dim x, y As Integer
   x = 1 / y    ' Create division by zero error.
   Exit Sub
   out:
   MsgBox(Err.Number)
   MsgBox(Err.Description)
   ' Check for division by zero error.
   If Err.Number = 11 Then
      y = y + 1
   End If
   Resume Next
End Sub
```

See Also

Description Property, ErrorToString Function, HelpContext Property, HelpFile Property, LastDLLError Property, Source Property

Applies To

Err Object

Object Data Type

Object variables are stored as 32-bit (4-byte) addresses that refer to objects. You can assign any reference type (string, array, class, or interface) to a variable declared as an **Object**.

An **Object** variable can also refer to data of any value type (numeric, **Boolean**, **Char**, **Date**, structure, or enumeration).

> **Note** Although a variable declared with **Object** type is flexible enough to contain a reference to any object, the invocation of a method of an instance using an **Object** variable is always late (run-time) binding. To force early (compile-time) binding, assign the object reference to a variable declared with a specific class name or cast to the specific data type.

The equivalent .NET data type is **System.Object**.

See Also

Data Type Summary, Type Conversion Functions, Conversion Summary

Objects

In This Section

Collection Object

Collection Object Properties, Methods, and Events

Err Object

Err Object Properties, Methods, and Events

Related Sections

Visual Basic Language and Run-Time Reference

Visual Basic Language

Oct Function

Returns a string representing the octal value of a number.

```
Public Shared Function Oct( _
   ByVal Number As { Byte | Short | Integer | Long | Object } _
) As String
```

Parameter

Number
Required. Any valid numeric expression or **String** expression.

Exceptions/Errors

Exception type	Error number	Condition
ArgumentNullException	5	*Number* is not specified.
ArgumentException	5	*Number* is not a numeric type.

Remarks

If *Number* is not already a whole number, it is rounded to the nearest whole number before being evaluated.

If *Number* is	Oct returns
Empty	Zero (0)
Any other number	Up to 22 octal characters

You can represent octal numbers directly by preceding numbers in the proper range with **&O**. For example, `&O10` is the octal notation for decimal 8.

Example

This example uses the **Oct** function to return the octal value of a number.

```
Dim MyOct As String
MyOct = Oct(4)     ' Returns 4.
MyOct = Oct(8)    ' Returns 10.
MyOct = Oct(459)    ' Returns 713.
```

See Also

Hex Function, Type Conversion Functions

Off

The **Off** keyword turns a compiler option off.

The **Off** keyword is used in these contexts:

Option Explicit Statement

Option Strict Statement

See Also

Visual Basic Language Keywords

On

The **On** keyword either introduces a response to a run-time error or turns a compiler option on.

The **On** keyword is used in these contexts:

On Error Statement

Option Explicit Statement

Option Strict Statement

See Also

Visual Basic Language Keywords

On Error Statement

Enables an error-handling routine and specifies the location of the routine within a procedure; can also be used to disable an error-handling routine. Without an **On Error** statement, any run-time error that occurs is fatal: an error message is displayed, and execution stops.

```
On Error { GoTo [ line | 0 | -1 ] | Resume Next }
```

Parts

GoTo *line*

Enables the error-handling routine that starts at the line specified in the required *line* argument. The *line* argument is any line label or line number. If a run-time error occurs, control branches to the specified line, making the error handler active. The specified line must be in the same procedure as the **On Error** statement, or a compile-time error will occur.

GoTo 0

Disables enabled error handler in the current procedure and resets it to **Nothing**.

GoTo -1

Disables enabled exception in the current procedure and resets it to **Nothing**.

Resume Next

Specifies that when a run-time error occurs, control goes to the statement immediately following the statement where the error occurred and execution continues from that point. Use this form rather than **On Error GoTo** when accessing objects.

Remarks

An "enabled" error handler is one that is turned on by an **On Error** statement; an "active" error handler is an enabled handler that is in the process of handling an error. If an error occurs while an error handler is active (between the occurrence of the error and a **Resume**, **Exit Sub**, **Exit Function**, or **Exit Property** statement), the current procedure's error handler can't handle the error. Control returns to the calling procedure. If the calling procedure has an enabled error handler, it is activated to handle the error. If the calling procedure's error handler is also active, control passes back through previous calling procedures until an enabled, but inactive, error handler is found. If no such error handler is found, the error is fatal at the point at which it actually occurred.

Each time the error handler passes control back to a calling procedure, that procedure becomes the current procedure. Once an error is handled by an error handler in any procedure, execution resumes in the current procedure at the point designated by the **Resume** statement.

Note An error-handling routine is not a **Sub** procedure or a **Function** procedure. It is a section of code marked by a line label or a line number.

Error-handling routines rely on the value in the **Number** property of the **Err** object to determine the cause of the error. The routine should test or save relevant property values in the **Err** object before any other error can occur or before a procedure that might cause an error is called. The property values in the **Err** object reflect only the most recent error. The error message associated with **Err.Number** is contained in **Err.Description**.

An error that is raised with the **Err.Raise** method will set the **Exception** property to a newly created instance of the **Exception** class. In order to support the raising of exceptions of derived exception types, a **Throw** statement is supported in the language. This takes a single parameter that is the exception instance to be thrown. The following example shows how these features can be used with the existing exception handling support:

```
   On Error Goto Handler
   Throw New DivideByZeroException()
Handler:
   If (TypeOf Err.GetException() Is DivideByZeroException) Then
   ' Code for handling the error is entered here.
   End If
```

Note that the **On Error GoTo** statement traps all errors regardless of the exception class.

On Error Resume Next causes execution to continue with the statement immediately following the statement that caused the run-time error, or with the statement immediately following the most recent call out of the procedure containing the **On Error Resume Next** statement. This statement allows execution to continue despite a run-time error. You can place the error-handling routine where the error would occur rather than transferring control to another location within the procedure. An **On Error Resume Next** statement becomes inactive when another procedure is called, so you should execute an **On Error Resume Next** statement in each called routine if you want inline error handling within that routine.

> **Note** The **On Error Resume Next** construct may be preferable to **On Error GoTo** when handling errors generated during access to other objects. Checking **Err** after each interaction with an object removes ambiguity about which object was accessed by the code. You can be sure which object placed the error code in **Err.Number**, as well as which object originally generated the error (the object specified in **Err.Source**).

On Error GoTo 0 disables error handling in the current procedure. It doesn't specify line 0 as the start of the error-handling code, even if the procedure contains a line numbered 0. Without an **On Error GoTo 0** statement, an error handler is automatically disabled when a procedure is exited.

On Error GoTo -1 disables the exception in the current procedure. It doesn't specify line –1 as the start of the error-handling code, even if the procedure contains a line numbered –1. Without an **On Error GoTo -1** statement, an exception is automatically disabled when a procedure is exited.

To prevent error-handling code from running when no error has occurred, place an **Exit Sub**, **Exit Function**, or **Exit Property** statement immediately before the error-handling routine, as in the following fragment:

```
Public Sub InitializeMatrix(Var1, Var2, Var3, Var4)
   On Error GoTo ErrorHandler
   ' Insert code that might generate an error here
   Exit Sub
ErrorHandler:
   ' Insert code to handle the error here
   Resume Next
End Sub
```

Here, the error-handling code follows the **Exit Sub** statement and precedes the **End Sub** statement to separate it from the procedure flow. You can place error-handling code anywhere in a procedure.

Untrapped errors in objects are returned to the controlling application when the object is running as an executable file. Within the development environment, untrapped errors are returned to the controlling application only if the proper options are set. See your host application's documentation for a description of which options should be set during debugging, how to set them, and whether the host can create classes.

If you create an object that accesses other objects, you should try to handle any unhandled errors they pass back. If you cannot, map the error codes in **Err.Number** to one of your own errors and then pass them back to the caller of your object. You should specify your error by adding your error code to the **VbObjectError** constant. For example, if your error code is 1052, assign it as follows:

```
Err.Number = VbObjectError + 1052
```

Caution System errors during calls to Windows dynamic-link libraries (DLL) do not raise exceptions and cannot be trapped with Visual Basic error trapping. When calling DLL functions, you should check each return value for success or failure (according to the API specifications), and in the event of a failure, check the value in the **Err** object's **LastDLLError** property.

Example

This example first uses the **On Error GoTo** statement to specify the location of an error-handling routine within a procedure. In the example, an attempt to divide by zero generates error number 6. The error is handled in the error-handling routine, and control is then returned to the statement that caused the error. The **On Error GoTo 0** statement turns off error trapping. Then the **On Error Resume Next** statement is used to defer error trapping so that the context for the error generated by the next statement can be known for certain. Note that **Err.Clear** is used to clear the **Err** object's properties after the error is handled.

```
Public Sub OnErrorDemo()
   On Error Goto ErrorHandler   ' Enable error-handling routine.
   Dim x As Integer = 32
   Dim y As Integer = 0
   Dim z As Integer
   z = x / y   ' Creates a divide by zero error
   On Error Goto 0   ' Turn off error trapping.
   On Error Resume Next   ' Defer error trapping.
   z = x / y   ' Creates a divide by zero error again
   If Err.Number = 6 Then
      ' Tell user what happened. Then clear the Err object.
      Dim Msg As String
      Msg = "There was an error attempting to divide by zero!"
      MsgBox(Msg, , "Divide by zero error")
      Err.Clear() ' Clear Err object fields.
   End If
Exit Sub      ' Exit to avoid handler.
ErrorHandler:  ' Error-handling routine.
   Select Case Err.Number   ' Evaluate error number.
      Case 6   ' Divide by zero error
         MsgBox("You attempted to divide by zero!")
         ' Insert code to handle this error
      Case Else
         ' Insert code to handle other situations here...
   End Select
   Resume Next  ' Resume execution at same line
                ' that caused the error.
End Sub
```

See Also

End Statement, Err Object, Exit Statement, LastDLLError Property, Resume Statement

OpenAccess Enumeration

When you call file access-related functions, you can use enumeration members in your code in place of the actual values.

The **OpenAccess** enumeration defines constants used to identify how a file can be accessed. The following table lists the **OpenAccess** enumeration members.

Member	Description
OpenAccess.Default	Read and write permitted. This is the default.
OpenAccess.Read	Read permitted.
OpenAccess.ReadWrite	Read and write permitted.
OpenAccess.Write	Write permitted.

See Also

OpenMode Enumeration, OpenShare Enumeration

OpenMode Enumeration

When you call file access-related functions, you can use enumeration members in your code in place of the actual values.

The **OpenMode** enumeration defines constants used to set file access modes. The following table lists the **OpenMode** enumeration members.

Member	Description
OpenMode.Append	Append mode.
OpenMode.Binary	Binary mode.
OpenMode.Input	Input mode.
OpenMode.Output	Output mode.
OpenMode.Random	Random mode.

See Also

OpenShare Enumeration, OpenAccess Enumeration

OpenShare Enumeration

When you call file access-related functions, you can use enumeration members in your code in place of the actual values.

The **OpenShare** enumeration defines constants that identify a file's sharing level. The following table lists the **OpenShare** enumeration members.

Member	Description
OpenShare.Default	Shared. This is the default.
OpenShare.LockRead	Cannot be read.
OpenShare.LockReadWrite	Cannot be read or written to.
OpenShare.LockWrite	Cannot be written to.
OpenShare.Shared	Shared.

See Also

OpenAccess Enumeration, OpenMode Enumeration

Operators Summary

Visual Basic language keywords and run-time library members are organized by purpose and use.

Action	Language element
Arithmetic.	^, –, *, /, \, Mod, +, =
Assignment.	=, ^=, *=, /=, \=, +=, -=, &=
Comparison.	=, <>, <, >, <=, >=, Like, Is
Concatenation.	&, +
Logical/bitwise operations.	Not, And, Or, Xor, AndAlso, OrElse
Miscellaneous operations.	AddressOf, GetType

See Also

Keywords and Members by Task, Visual Basic Language Keywords, Visual Basic Run-Time Library Members

Option

The **Option** keyword is used in these contexts:

Option Compare Statement

Option Explicit Statement

Option Strict Statement

See Also

Visual Basic Language Keywords

Option Compare Statement

Used at file level to declare the default comparison method to use when string data is compared.

```
Option Compare { Binary | Text }
```

Parts

Binary

Optional. Results in string comparisons based on a sort order derived from the internal binary representations of the characters.

Text

Optional. Results in string comparisons based on a case-insensitive text sort order determined by your system's locale.

Remarks

If used, the **Option Compare** statement must appear in a file before any other source statements.

The **Option Compare** statement specifies the string comparison method (**Binary** or **Text**) for a class, module or structure. If an **Option Compare** statement is not included, the default text comparison method is **Binary**.

In Microsoft Windows, sort order is determined by the code page. In the following example, characters are sorted using **Option Compare Binary**, which produces a typical binary sort order:

```
A < B < E < Z < a < b < e < z < À < Ê < Ø < à < ê < ø
```

When the same characters are sorted using **Option Compare Text**, the following text sort order is produced:

```
(A=a) < ( À=à) < (B=b) < (E=e) < (Ê=ê) < (Z=z) < (Ø=ø)
```

Example

This example uses the **Option Compare** statement to set the default string comparison method. The **Option Compare** statement is used at the module level only.

```
' Set the string comparison method to Binary.
Option Compare Binary   ' That is, "AAA" is less than "aaa".
' Set the string comparison method to Text.
Option Compare Text   ' That is, "AAA" is equal to "aaa".
```

See Also

Comparison Operators, InStr Function, InStrRev Function, Option Strict Statement, Option Explicit Statement, Replace Function, Split Function, StrComp Function

Option Explicit Statement

Used at file level to force explicit declaration of all variables in that file.

```
Option Explicit { On | Off }
```

Parts

On

Optional. Enables **Option Explicit** checking. If **On** or **Off** is not specified after the **Option Explicit** statement, the default is **Off**.

Off

Optional. Disables **Option Explicit** checking.

Remarks

If used, the **Option Explicit** statement must appear in a file before any other source statements.

When **Option Explicit** appears in a file, you must explicitly declare all variables using the **Dim**, **Private**, **Public**, or **ReDim** statements. If you attempt to use an undeclared variable name, an error occurs at compile time.

If you don't use the **Option Explicit** statement, all undeclared variables are of **Object** type.

> **Note** Use **Option Explicit** to avoid incorrectly typing the name of an existing variable or to avoid confusion in code where the scope of the variable is not clear.

Example

This example uses the **Option Explicit** statement to force explicit declaration of all variables. Attempting to use an undeclared variable causes an error at compile time. The **Option Explicit** statement is used at the module level only.

```
Option Explicit On    ' Force explicit variable declaration.
Dim MyVar As Integer    ' Declare variable.
MyInt = 10    ' Undeclared variable generates error.
MyVar = 10    ' Declared variable does not generate error.
```

See Also

Const Statement, Dim Statement, Function Statement, Option Compare Statement, Private, Public, ReDim Statement, Sub Statement

Option Strict Statement

Restricts implicit data type conversions to only *widening* conversions. This explicitly disallows any data type conversions in which data loss would occur and any conversion between numeric types and strings.

```
Option Strict { On | Off }
```

Parts

On

Optional. Enables **Option Strict** checking. If **On** or **Off** is not specified after the **Option Strict** statement, the default is **Off**.

Off

Optional. Disables **Option Strict** checking.

Remarks

When used, the **Option Strict** statement must appear before any other code.

Visual Basic .NET generally allows implicit conversions of any data type to any other data type. Data loss can occur when the value of one data type is converted to a data type with less precision or smaller capacity, however, a run-time error message will occur if data will be lost in such a conversion. **Option Strict** ensures compile-time notification of these types of conversions so they may be avoided.

In addition to the conditions described above, **Option Strict** generates an error for:

- Any undeclared variable since it is implied that **Option Strict** also means **Option Explicit**.
- Late-binding.

Example

This example uses the **Option Strict** statement to show how a declared variable can be converted to a data type of a larger capacity. Attempting to use an undeclared variable causes an error at compile time.

```
Option Strict On    ' Force explicit variable declaration.
Dim MyVar As Integer    ' Declare variables.
Dim Obj As Object
MyVar = 1000    ' Declared variable does not generate error.
MyVar = 1234567890.987654321    '
'Attempting to convert to an Integer will generate an error.
MyInt = 10    ' Undeclared variable generates error in Option Strict mode.
Call Obj.Method1()    ' Late-bound call generates an error
```

See Also

Option Explicit Statement, Option Compare Statement

Optional

The **Optional** keyword indicates that a procedure argument can be omitted when the procedure is called.

The **Optional** keyword is used in these contexts:

Declare Statement

Function Statement

Property Statement

Sub Statement

See Also

Visual Basic Language Keywords

Or Operator

Used to perform a logical disjunction on two **Boolean** expressions, or bitwise disjunction on two numeric values..

```
result = expression1 Or expression2
```

Parts

result
Required. Any **Boolean** or numeric expression. For **Boolean** comparison the result is the logical disjunction of two expressions. For bitwise operations the result is a numeric value resulting from the bitwise disjunction of two numeric expressions.

expression1
Required. Any **Boolean** or numeric expression.

expression2
Required. Any **Boolean** or numeric expression of the same type as *expression1*.

Remarks

For **Boolean** comparison, if either *expression1* or *expression2* evaluates to **True**, *result* is **True.** If *expression1* evaluates to **True**, and *expression2* evaluates to **False** the *result* is **True**. The following table illustrates how *result* is determined:

If *expression1* is	And *expression2* is	Then *result* is
True	**True**	**True**
True	**False**	**True**
False	**True**	**True**
False	**False**	**False**

For bitwise operations, the **Or** operator performs a bitwise comparison of identically positioned bits in two numeric expressions and sets the corresponding bit in *result* according to the following table:

If bit in *expression1* is	And bit in *expression2* is	Then *result* is
0	0	0
0	1	1
1	0	1
1	1	1

Note Since the logical/bitwise operators have a lower precedence than other arithmetic and relational operators, any bitwise operations should be enclosed in parentheses to insure accurate execution.

If the operands consist of one **Boolean** expression and one numeric expression, the result **Boolean** expression will be converted to a numeric value (–1 for True, and 0 for False) and the bitwise operation will result.

Example

This example uses the **Or** operator to perform logical disjunction on two expressions. The result is a **Boolean** value that represents whether either of the two expressions is true.

```
Dim A As Integer = 10
Dim B As Integer = 8
Dim C As Integer = 6
Dim myCheck As Boolean
myCheck = A > B Or B > C    ' Returns True.
myCheck = B > A Or B > C    ' Returns True.
myCheck = B > A Or C > B    ' Returns False.
```

This example uses the **Or** operator to perform logical disjunction of the individual bits of two numeric expressions. The bit in the result pattern is set if either of the corresponding bits in the operands are set.

```
Dim A As Integer = 10
Dim B As Integer = 8
Dim C As Integer = 6
Dim myCheck As Integer
myCheck = (A Or B)    ' Returns 10.
myCheck = (A Or C)    ' Returns 14.
myCheck = (B Or C)    ' Returns 14.
```

See Also

Logical/Bitwise Operators, Operator Precedence in Visual Basic, Operators Listed by Functionality, OrElse Operator, Logical Operators

OrElse Operator

Used to perform short-circuiting logical disjunction on two expressions.

```
result = expression1 OrElse expression2
```

Parts

result
Required. Any **Boolean** expression.

expression1
Required. Any **Boolean** expression.

expression2
Required. Any **Boolean** expression.

Remarks

If either *expression1* or *expression2* evaluates to **True**, *result* is **True.** If *expression1* evaluates to **True**, *expression2* is not evaluated, and *result* is **True** (the operator is said to have short-circuited the expression). The following table illustrates how *result* is determined:

If *expression1* is	And *expression2* is	Then *result* is
True	(not evaluated)	**True**
False	**True**	**True**
False	**False**	**False**

Example

This example uses the **OrElse** operator to perform logical disjunction on two expressions. The result is a **Boolean** value that represents whether either of the two expressions is true. If the first expression is **True**, the second is not evaluated.

```
Dim A As Integer = 10
Dim B As Integer = 8
Dim C As Integer = 6
Dim myCheck As Boolean
myCheck = A > B OrElse B > C    ' True. Second expression is not evaluated.
myCheck = B > A OrElse B > C    ' True. Second expression is evaluated.
myCheck = B > A OrElse C > B    ' False.

' This example demonstrates the use of the OrElse operator. If the first
' function call returns true, the second function call is not made.
If MyFunction(5) = True OrElse MyOtherFunction(4) = True Then
'    Insert code to be executed.
End If
```

See Also

Logical/Bitwise Operators, Operator Precedence in Visual Basic, Operators Listed by Functionality, Logical Operators

Overloads

The **Overloads** keyword declares a property or method with the same name as an existing member, but with an argument list different from the original member.

Overloads can also be used to shadow an existing member, or set of overloaded members, in a base class. When you use **Overloads** in this way, you declare the property or method with the same name and the same argument list as the base class member, and you do not supply the **Shadows** keyword.

The **Overloads** keyword is used in these contexts:

Function Statement

Property Statement

Sub Statement

See Also

Shadows

Overridable

The **Overridable** keyword specifies that a property or method can be overridden in a derived class.

The **Overridable** keyword is used in these contexts:

Function Statement

Property Statement

Sub Statement

See Also

Visual Basic Language Keywords

Overrides

The **Overrides** keyword specifies that a property or method overrides a member inherited from a base class.

The **Overrides** keyword is used in these contexts:

Function Statement

Property Statement

Sub Statement

See Also

Visual Basic Language Keywords

ParamArray

The **ParamArray** keyword indicates that a procedure argument is an optional array of elements of the specified type. **ParamArray** can be used only on the last argument of an argument list. It allows you to pass an arbitrary number of arguments to the procedure. A **ParamArray** argument is always passed using **ByVal**.

The **ParamArray** keyword is used in these contexts:

Declare Statement

Function Statement

Property Statement

Sub Statement

See Also

Visual Basic Language Keywords

Partition Function

Returns a string representing the calculated range that contains a number.

```
Public Function Partition( _
   ByVal Number As Long, _
   ByVal Start As Long, _
   ByVal Stop As Long, _
   ByVal Interval As Long _
) As String
```

Parameters

Number

Required. **Long**. Whole number that you want to locate within one of the calculated ranges.

Start

Required. **Long**. Whole number that indicates the start of the set of calculated ranges. *Start* cannot be less than 0.

Stop

Required. **Long**. Whole number that indicates the end of the set of calculated ranges. *Stop* cannot be less than or equal to *Start*.

Interval

Required. **Long**. Whole number that indicates the size of each range calculated between *Start* and *Stop*. *Interval* cannot be less than 1.

Exceptions/Errors

Exception type	Error number	Condition
ArgumentException	5	*Start* < 0, *Stop* <= *Start,* or *Interval* < 1.

Remarks

The **Partition** function calculates a set of numeric ranges, each containing the number of values specified by *Interval*. The first range begins at *Start*, and the last range ends at *Stop*. The **Partition** function then identifies which range contains *Number* and returns a string describing that range. The range is represented in the string as "*lowervalue*:*uppervalue*", where the low end of the range (*lowervalue*) is separated from the high end (*uppervalue*) by a colon (:).

If necessary, the **Partition** function inserts leading spaces before *lowervalue* and *uppervalue* so that they both have the same number of characters as the string representation of the value (*Stop* + 1). This ensures that if you use the output of the **Partition** function with several values of *Number*, the resulting text will be handled properly during any subsequent sort operation.

The following table shows some sample strings for ranges calculated using three sets of *Start*, *Stop*, and *Interval*. The "First range" and "Last range" columns show the lowest and highest ranges possible given the values of *Start* and *Stop*. The "Before first range" and "After last range" columns show the strings returned for values of *Number* less than *Start* and greater than *Stop*, respectively.

Start	*Stop*	*Interval*	Before first range	First range	Last range	After last range
0	99	5	" : -1"	" 0: 4"	" 95: 99"	"100: "
20	199	10	" : 19"	" 20: 29"	"190:199"	"200: "
100	1010	20	" : 99"	" 100: 119"	"1000:1010"	"1011: "

In the preceding table, the third line shows the result when *Start* and *Stop* define a set of numbers that cannot be evenly divided by *Interval*. The last range ends at *Stop*, making it only 11 numbers long, even though *Interval* is 20.

If *Interval* is 1, the range is "*Number*:*Number*", regardless of the *Start* and *Stop* arguments. For example, if *Number* is 267, *Stop* is 1000, and *Interval* is 1, **Partition** returns " 267: 267".

Partition is useful in database queries. You can create a select query that shows how many orders occur within various value ranges, for example with invoice values from 1 to 1000, 1001 to 2000, and so on.

Example

This example assumes you have an **Orders** table that contains a `Freight` field. It creates a SELECT procedure that counts the number of orders for which freight cost is within each of several ranges. The **Partition** function first establishes these ranges, and then the SQL **Count** function counts the number of orders in each range. In this example, the arguments to the **Partition** function are *Start* = 0, *Stop* = 500, *Interval* = 50. The first range is therefore 0:49, and so on up to 450:499 and 500:500.

```
SELECT DISTINCTROW Partition([Freight],0, 500, 50) As Range,
Count(Orders.Freight) As Count
FROM Orders
GROUP BY Partition([Freight],0,500,50);
```

Pmt Function

Returns a **Double** specifying the payment for an annuity based on periodic, fixed payments and a fixed interest rate.

```
Function Pmt( _
   ByVal Rate As Double, _
   ByVal NPer As Double, _
   ByVal PV As Double, _
   Optional ByVal FV As Double = 0, _
   Optional ByVal Due As DueDate = DueDate.EndOfPeriod _
) As Double
```

Parameters

Rate

Required. **Double** specifying interest rate per period. For example, if you get a car loan at an annual percentage rate (APR) of 10 percent and make monthly payments, the rate per period is 0.1/12, or 0.0083.

NPer

Required. **Double** specifying total number of payment periods in the annuity. For example, if you make monthly payments on a four-year car loan, your loan has a total of 4 * 12 (or 48) payment periods.

PV

Required. **Double** specifying present value (or lump sum) that a series of payments to be paid in the future is worth now. For example, when you borrow money to buy a car, the loan amount is the present value to the lender of the monthly car payments you will make.

FV

Optional. **Double** specifying future value or cash balance you want after you've made the final payment. For example, the future value of a loan is $0 because that's its value after the final payment. However, if you want to save $50,000 over 18 years for your child's education, then $50,000 is the future value. If omitted, 0 is assumed.

Due

Optional. Object of type `Microsoft.VisualBasic.DueDate` that specifies when payments are due. This argument must be either `DueDate.EndOfPeriod` if payments are due at the end of the payment period, or `DueDate.BegOfPeriod` if payments are due at the beginning of the period. If omitted, `DueDate.EndOfPeriod` is assumed.

Exceptions/Errors

Exception type	Error number	Condition
ArgumentException	5	*NPer* = 0.

Remarks

An annuity is a series of fixed cash payments made over a period of time. An annuity can be a loan (such as a home mortgage) or an investment (such as a monthly savings plan).

The *Rate* and *NPer* arguments must be calculated using payment periods expressed in the same units. For example, if *Rate* is calculated using months, *NPer* must also be calculated using months.

For all arguments, cash paid out (such as deposits to savings) is represented by negative numbers; cash received (such as dividend checks) is represented by positive numbers.

Example

This example uses the **Pmt** function to return the monthly payment for a loan over a fixed period. Given are the interest percentage rate per period (`APR / 12`), the total number of payments (`TotPmts`), the present value or principal of the loan (`PVal`), the future value of the loan (`FVal`), and a number that indicates whether the payment is due at the beginning or end of the payment period (`PayType`).

```
Sub TestPMT()
   Dim PVal, APR, FVal, Payment, TotPmts As Double
   Dim PayType As DueDate
   Dim Fmt As String
   Dim Response As MsgBoxResult
   Fmt = "###,###,##0.00"    ' Define money format.
   FVal = 0   ' Usually 0 for a loan.
   PVal = CDbl(InputBox("How much do you want to borrow?"))
   APR = CDbl(InputBox("What is the annual percentage rate of your loan?"))
   If APR > 1 Then APR = APR / 100 ' Ensure proper form.
   TotPmts = CDbl(InputBox("How many monthly payments will you make?"))
   Response = MsgBox("Do you make payments at the end of month?", MsgBoxStyle.YesNo)
```

```
   If Response = MsgBoxResult.No Then
      PayType = DueDate.BegOfPeriod
   Else
      PayType = DueDate.BegOfPeriod
   End If
   Payment = Pmt(APR / 12, TotPmts, -PVal, FVal, PayType)
   MsgBox("Your payment will be " & Format(Payment, Fmt) & " per month.")
End Sub
```

See Also

DDB Function, FV Function, IPmt Function, IRR Function, MIRR Function, NPer Function, NPV Function, PPmt Function, PV Function, Rate Function, SLN Function, SYD Function

PPmt Function

Returns a **Double** specifying the principal payment for a given period of an annuity based on periodic, fixed payments and a fixed interest rate.

```
Function PPmt( _
    ByVal Rate As Double, _
   ByVal Per As Double, _
   ByVal NPer As Double, _
   ByVal PV As Double, _
   Optional ByVal FV As Double = 0, _
   Optional ByVal Due As DueDate = DueDate.EndOfPeriod _
) As Double
```

Parameters

Rate

Required. **Double** specifying interest rate per period. For example, if you get a car loan at an annual percentage rate (APR) of 10 percent and make monthly payments, the rate per period is 0.1/12, or 0.0083.

Per

Required. **Double** specifying payment period in the range 1 through *NPer*.

NPer

Required. **Double** specifying total number of payment periods in the annuity. For example, if you make monthly payments on a four-year car loan, your loan has a total of 4 * 12 (or 48) payment periods.

PV

Required. **Double** specifying present value, or value today, of a series of future payments or receipts. For example, when you borrow money to buy a car, the loan amount is the present value to the lender of the monthly car payments you will make.

FV

Optional. **Double** specifying future value or cash balance you want after you've made the final payment. For example, the future value of a loan is $0 because that's its value after the final payment. However, if you want to save $50,000 over 18 years for your child's education, then $50,000 is the future value. If omitted, 0 is assumed.

Due

Optional. Object of type `Microsoft.VisualBasic.DueDate` that specifies when payments are due. This argument must be either `DueDate.EndOfPeriod` if payments are due at the end of the payment period, or `DueDate.BegOfPeriod` if payments are due at the beginning of the period. If omitted, `DueDate.EndOfPeriod` is assumed.

Exceptions/Errors

Exception type	Error number	Condition
ArgumentException	5	*Per* value invalid: must be > 1 and < *NPer*.

Remarks

An annuity is a series of fixed cash payments made over a period of time. An annuity can be a loan (such as a home mortgage) or an investment (such as a monthly savings plan).

The *Rate* and *NPer* arguments must be calculated using payment periods expressed in the same units. For example, if *Rate* is calculated using months, *NPer* must also be calculated using months.

For all arguments, cash paid out (such as deposits to savings) is represented by negative numbers; cash received (such as dividend checks) is represented by positive numbers.

Example

This example uses the **PPmt** function to calculate how much of a payment for a specific period is principal when all the payments are of equal value. Given are the interest percentage rate per period (`APR / 12`), the payment period for which the principal portion is desired (`Period`), the total number of payments (`TotPmts`), the present value or principal of the loan (`PVal`), the future value of the loan (`FVal`), and a number that indicates whether the payment is due at the beginning or end of the payment period (`PayType`).

```
Sub TestPPMT()
   Dim PVal, APR, TotPmts, MakeChart, FVal, Payment, Period, P, I As Double
   Dim PayType As DueDate
   Dim Msg, Fmt As String
   Dim Response As MsgBoxResult

   Fmt = "###,###,##0.00"    ' Define money format.
   FVal = 0   ' Usually 0 for a loan.
   PVal = CDbl(InputBox("How much do you want to borrow?"))
   APR = CDbl(InputBox("What is the annual percentage rate of your loan?"))
   If APR > 1 Then APR = APR / 100 ' Ensure proper form.
   TotPmts = CDbl(InputBox("How many monthly payments do you have to make?"))
   Response = MsgBox("Do you make payments at the end of month?", MsgBoxStyle.YesNo)
   If Response = MsgBoxResult.No Then
      PayType = DueDate.BegOfPeriod
   Else
      PayType = DueDate.EndOfPeriod
   End If
   Payment = Math.Abs(-Pmt(APR / 12, TotPmts, PVal, FVal, PayType))
   Msg = "Your monthly payment is " & Format(Payment, Fmt) & ". "
   Msg = Msg & "Would you like a breakdown of your principal and "
   Msg = Msg & "interest per period?"
   MakeChart = MsgBox(Msg, MsgBoxStyle.YesNo)   ' See if chart is desired.
   If Response <> MsgBoxResult.No Then
      If TotPmts > 12 Then MsgBox("Only first year will be shown.")
      Msg = "Month  Payment  Principal  Interest" & vbNewLine
      For Period = 1 To TotPmts
         If Period > 12 Then Exit For ' Show only first 12.
         P = PPmt(APR / 12, Period, TotPmts, -PVal, FVal, PayType)
         P = (Int((P + 0.005) * 100) / 100)   ' Round principal.
         I = Payment - P
         I = (Int((I + 0.005) * 100) / 100)   ' Round interest.
         Msg = Msg & Period & vbTab & Format(Payment, Fmt)
         Msg = Msg & vbTab & Format(P, Fmt) & vbTab & Format(I, Fmt) & vbNewLine
      Next Period
      MsgBox(Msg)    ' Display amortization table.
   End If
End Sub
```

See Also

DDB Function, FV Function, IPmt Function, IRR Function, MIRR Function, NPer Function, NPV Function, Pmt Function, PV Function, Rate Function, SLN Function, SYD Function

Predefined Date/Time Formats (Format Function)

The following table identifies the predefined date and time format names. These may be used by name as the style argument for the **Format** function:

Format Name	Description
General Date, or **G**	Displays a date and/or time. For real numbers, display a date and time; for example, `4/3/93 05:34 PM`. If there is no fractional part, display only a date, for example, `4/3/93`. If there is no integer part, display time only, for example, `05:34 PM`. Date display is determined by your system's **LocaleID** value.
Long Date, or **D**	Displays a date according to your locale's long date format.
Medium Date	Displays a date using the medium date format appropriate for the language version of the host application.
Short Date, or **d**	Displays a date using your locale's short date format.
Long Time, or **T**	Displays a time using your locale's long time format; includes hours, minutes, seconds.
Medium Time	Displays time in 12-hour format using hours and minutes and the AM/PM designator.
Short Time, or **t**	Displays a time using the 24-hour format, for example, `17:45`.
f	Displays the long date and short time according to your locale's format.
F	Displays the long date and long time according to your locale's format.
g	Displays the short date and short time according to your locale's format.
M, m	Displays the month and the day of a date.
R, r	Formats the date and time as Greenwich Mean Time (GMT).
s	Formats the date and time as a sortable index.
u	Formats the date and time as a GMT sortable index.
U	Formats the date and time with the long date and long time as GMT.
y	Formats the date as the year and month.

See Also

Format Function, Predefined Numeric Formats (Format Function), User-Defined Date/Time Formats (Format Function)

Predefined Numeric Formats (Format Function)

The following table identifies the predefined numeric format names. These may be used by name as the style argument for the **Format** function:

Format name	Description
General Number, **G**, or **g**	Displays number with no thousand separator.
Currency, **C**, or **c**	Displays number with thousand separator, if appropriate; display two digits to the right of the decimal separator. Output is based on system locale settings.
Fixed, **F**, or **f**	Displays at least one digit to the left and two digits to the right of the decimal separator.
Standard, **N**, or **n**	Displays number with thousand separator, at least one digit to the left and two digits to the right of the decimal separator.
Percent, **P**, or **p**	Displays number multiplied by 100 with a percent sign (%) appended to the right; always display two digits to the right of the decimal separator.
Scientific, **E**, or **e**	Uses standard scientific notation
D, or **d**	Displays number as a string that contains the value of the number in Decimal (base 10) format. This option is supported for integral types (**Byte**, **Short**, **Integer**, **Long**) only.
X, or **x**	Displays number as a string that contains the value of the number in Hexadecimal (base 16) format. This option is supported for integral types (**Byte**, **Short**, **Integer**, **Long**) only.
Yes/No	Displays `No` if number is 0; otherwise, displays `Yes`.
True/False	Displays `False` if number is 0; otherwise, displays `True`.
On/Off	Displays `Off` if number is 0; otherwise, displays `On`.

See Also

Format Function, Predefined Date/Time Formats (Format Function), User-Defined Numeric Formats (Format Function)

Preserve

The **Preserve** keyword prevents the contents of an array from being cleared when the array is redimensioned.

The **Preserve** keyword is used in this context:

ReDim Statement

See Also

Visual Basic Language Keywords

Print and Display Constants

When you call print and display functions, you can use the following constants in your code in place of the actual values.

ControlChars Module Members

Member	Constant	Equivalent	Description
CrLf	**vbCrLf**	**Chr**(13) + **Chr**(10)	Carriage return/linefeed character combination.
Cr	**vbCr**	**Chr**(13)	Carriage return character.
Lf	**vbLf**	**Chr**(10)	Linefeed character.
NewLine	**vbNewLine**	**Chr**(13) + **Chr**(10)	New line character.
NullChar	**vbNullChar**	**Chr**(0)	Character having value 0.
na	**vbNullString**	String having value 0	Not the same as a zero-length string (" "); used for calling external procedures.
na	**vbObjectError**	–2147221504	Error number. User-defined error numbers should be greater than this value. For example: `Err.Raise(Number) = vbObjectError + 1000`
Tab	**vbTab**	**Chr**(9)	Tab character.
Back	**vbBack**	**Chr**(8)	Backspace character.
FormFeed	**vbFormFeed**	**Chr**(12)	Not useful in Microsoft Windows.
VerticalTab	**vbVerticalTab**	**Chr**(11)	Not useful in Microsoft Windows.
Quote	na	**Chr**(34)	Quotation mark character (" or ') used to enclose values.

See Also

Print, Printline Functions; Write, WriteLine Functions

Print, PrintLine Functions

Writes display-formatted data to a sequential file.

```
Public Sub Print( _
   ByVal FileNumber As Integer, _
   ByVal ParamArray Output() As Object _
)
```

-or-

```
Public Sub PrintLine( _
   ByVal FileNumber As Integer, _
   ByVal ParamArray Output() As Object _
)
```

Parameters

FileNumber
Required. Any valid file number.

Output
Optional. One or more comma-delimited expressions to write to a file.

Output argument settings

The *Output* argument settings are:

Setting	Description
SPC(*n*)	Used to insert space characters in the output, where *n* is the number of space characters to insert.
TAB(*n*)	Used to position the insertion point to an absolute column number, where *n* is the column number. Use **TAB** with no argument to position the insertion point at the beginning of the next print zone.
expression	Numeric expressions or string expressions to print.

Exceptions/Errors

Exception type	Error number	Condition
IOException	54	File mode is invalid.
IOException	52	*FileNumber* does not exist.

Remarks

Print will not include a linefeed at the end of a line; **PrintLine,** however, will include a linefeed.

Data written with **Print** is usually read from a file with **LineInput** or **Input**.

If you omit *Output* for **PrintLine**, a blank line is printed to the file; for **Print,** nothing is output. Multiple expressions separated with a comma will be aligned on tab boundaries, but mixing commas and **TAB** may result in inconsistent results.

For **Boolean** data, either `True` or `False` is printed. The **True** and **False** keywords are not translated, regardless of the locale.

Date data is written to the file using the standard short date format recognized by your system. When either the date or the time component is missing or zero, only the part provided is written to the file.

Nothing is written to the file if *Output* data is empty. However, if *Output* list data is **DBNull**, `Null` is written to the file.

For **Error** data, the output appears as `Error errorcode`. The **Error** keyword is not translated regardless of the locale.

All data written to the file using **Print** is internationally aware; that is, the data is properly formatted using the appropriate decimal separator. If the user wishes to output data for use by multiple locales, then **Write** should be used.

Example

This example uses the **Print** and **PrintLine** functions to write data to a file.

```
FileOpen(1, "c:\trash.txt", OpenMode.Output)   ' Open file for output.
Print(1, "This is a test.")   ' Print text to file.
PrintLine(1)   ' Print blank line to file.
PrintLine(1, "Zone 1", TAB(), "Zone 2")   ' Print in two print zones.
PrintLine(1, "Hello", " ", "World")   ' Separate strings with space.
PrintLine(1, SPC(5), "5 leading spaces ")   ' Print five leading spaces.
PrintLine(1, TAB(10), "Hello")   ' Print word at column 10.

' Assign Boolean, Date, and Error values.
Dim aBool As Boolean
Dim aDate As DateTime
aBool = False
aDate = DateTime.Parse("February 12, 1969")

' Dates and booleans are translated using locale settings of your system.
PrintLine(1, aBool, " is a Boolean value")
PrintLine(1, aDate, " is a date")
FileClose(1)   ' Close file.
```

See Also

FileOpen Function; SPC Function; TAB Function; Write, WriteLine Functions

Private

The **Private** keyword confers private access on one or more declared programming elements. Private elements are accessible only from within their declaration context, including from members of any nested types, for example from within a nested procedure or from an assignment expression in a nested enumeration.

The **Private** keyword is used in these contexts:

- Class Statement
- Const Statement
- Declare Statement
- Delegate Statement
- Dim Statement
- Enum Statement
- Event Statement
- Function Statement
- Interface Statement
- Property Statement
- Structure Statement
- Sub Statement

Property Statement

Declares the name of a property, and the property procedures used to store and retrieve the value of the property.

```
[ <attrlist> ] [ Default ] [ Public | Private | Protected | Friend | Protected
Friend ] _
[[ ReadOnly | WriteOnly ] [ Overloads | Overrides ] _
[ Overridable | NotOverridable ] | MustOverride | Shadows | Shared ] _
Property varname([ ByVal parameter list ]) [ As typename ]
[ Implements interfacemember ]
   [ <attrlist> ] Get
      [ block ]
   End Get
   [ <attrlist> ] Set(ByVal value As typename )
      [ block ]
   End Set
End Property
```

Parts

attrlist
: Optional. List of attributes that apply to this property. Multiple attributes are separated by commas.

Default
: Optional. Declares a default property. Default properties must accept parameters and can be set and retrieved without specifying the property name.

Overloads

Optional. Indicates that this property overloads one or more properties defined with the same name in a base class. The argument list in this declaration must be different from the argument list of every overloaded property. The lists must differ in the number of arguments, their data types, or both. This allows the compiler to distinguish which version to use.

You do not have to use the **Overloads** keyword when you are defining multiple overloaded properties in the same class. However, if you use **Overloads** in one of the declarations, you must use it in all of them.

You cannot specify both **Overloads** and **Shadows** in the same property declaration.

Overrides

Optional. Indicates that this property overrides an identically named property in a base class. The number and data types of the arguments, and the data type of the return value, must exactly match those of the base class property.

Overridable

Optional. Indicates that this property can be overridden by an identically named property in a derived class.

NotOverridable

Optional. Indicates that this property cannot be overridden in a derived class. Properties are **NotOverridable** by default but you cannot specify the **NotOverridable** modifier with properties or methods that do not override another member.

MustOverride

Optional. Indicates that this property is not implemented in this class, and must be implemented in a derived class for that class to be creatable.

Shadows

Optional. Indicates that this property shadows an identically named programming element, or set of overloaded elements, in a base class. You can shadow any kind of declared element with any other kind. If you shadow a property with another property, the arguments and the return type do not have to match those in the base class property. A shadowed element is unavailable in the derived class that shadows it.

Note You cannot specify both **Overloads** and **Shadows** in the same property declaration.

Shared

Optional. Indicates that this is a shared property. This means it is not associated with a specific instance of a class or structure. You can call a shared property by qualifying it either with the class or structure name, or with the variable name of a specific instance of the class or structure.

Public

Optional. Entities declared with the **Public** modifier have public access. There are no restrictions on the use of public entities. Properties that do not specify an access modifier are **Public** by default.

Private
Optional. Entities declared with the **Private** modifier have private access. A private entity is accessible only within its declaration context, including any nested entities.

Protected
Optional. Entities declared with the **Protected** keyword have protected access. They are accessible only from within their own class or from a derived class. Protected access can be specified only on members of classes. It is not a superset of friend access.

Friend
Optional. Entities declared with the **Friend** modifier have friend access. An entity with friend access is accessible only within the program that contains the entity declaration.

Protected Friend
Optional. Entities declared with the **Protected Friend** modifiers have the union of protected and friend accessibility.

ReadOnly
Optional. Indicates that a properties value can be retrieved, but it cannot be the modified. **ReadOnly** properties contain **Get** blocks but lack **Set** blocks.

WriteOnly
Optional. Indicates that a property can be the target of assignment but its value cannot be retrieved. **WriteOnly** properties contain **Set** blocks but lack **Get** blocks.

varname
Required. A unique name that identifies the property.

parameter list
Optional. This identifies the signature of the property. Parameters for properties must be passed **ByVal**.

typename
Optional. If no data type is specified, the default type is **Object**. If the property is implementing a property in an interface, *typename* must match the type declared in the interface.

Implements
Optional. Indicates that this property implements a property of an interface.

interfacemember
Optional. When a property is part of a class that implements an interface, this is the name of the property being implemented.

Get
Starts a **Get** property procedure used to return the value of a property. **Get** blocks are required unless the property is marked **WriteOnly**.

End Get
Terminates a **Get** property procedure.

Set

Starts a **Set** property procedure used to set the value of a property. **Set** blocks are required unless the property is marked **ReadOnly**. The new value of a property is passed to the **Set** property procedure in a parameter named *value* when the value of the property changes

End Set

Terminates a **Set** property procedure.

End Property

Terminates a **Property** definition.

Each attribute in the *attrlist* part has the following syntax and parts:

```
attrname [({ attrargs | attrinit })]
```

attrlist Parts

attrname

Required. Name of the attribute. Must be a valid Visual Basic identifier.

attrargs

Optional. List of positional arguments for this attribute. Multiple arguments are separated by commas.

attrinit

Optional. List of field or property initializers for this attribute. Multiple initializers are separated by commas.

Remarks

Visual Basic .NET passes a parameter to the **Set** block during property assignments. If you do not supply a parameter for **Set**, the integrated development environment (IDE) supplies a parameter named **Value**. The parameter contains the contents of the item that was assigned to the property when the Set block was called. The contents of the parameter are usually stored in a private local variable and returned whenever the **Get** block is called.

The declaration of the property determines what the user can do with that property:

- If the **ReadOnly** modifier is used, the property is known as a "Read-only property" and must only have a **Get**...**End Get** block. Therefore, the user is only able to retrieve the value of the property. An error will be raised if the user attempts to assign a value to that property.
- If the **WriteOnly** modifier is used, the property is known as a "Write-only property" and must only have a **Set**...**End Set** block. This allows the user to store a value to the property. An error will be raised if the user attempts to refer to the property, except in the assignment of a value to that property.
- If neither the **ReadOnly** nor the **WriteOnly** modifier is used, the property must have both a **Set**...**End Set** and a **Get**...**End Get** block. The property is said to be a read-write property.

Example

The following example declares a property in a class.

```
Class Class1
   ' Define a local variable to store the property value.
   Private PropertyValue As String
   ' Define the property.
   Public Property Prop1() As String
      Get
         ' The Get property procedure is called when the value
         ' of a property is retrieved.
         Return PropertyValue
      End Get
      Set(ByVal Value As String)
         ' The Set property procedure is called when the value
         ' of a property is modified.
         ' The value to be assigned is passed in the argument to Set.
         PropertyValue = Value
      End Set
   End Property
End Class
```

See Also

Get Statement, Set Statement

Protected

The **Protected** keyword confers protected access on one or more declared programming elements. Protected elements are accessible only from within their own class or from a derived class. Protected access is not a superset of friend access.

The **Protected** keyword can be used in conjunction with the **Friend** keyword in the same declaration. This combination confers both friend and protected access on the declared elements, so they are accessible from the same assembly, from their own class, and from any derived classes.

The **Protected** keyword is used in these contexts:

- Class Statement
- Const Statement
- Declare Statement
- Delegate Statement
- Dim Statement
- Enum Statement
- Event Statement
- Function Statement
- Interface Statement
- Property Statement
- Structure Statement
- Sub Statement

See Also

Friend

Public

The **Public** keyword confers public access on one or more declared programming elements. There are no restrictions on the accessibility of public elements.

The **Public** keyword is used in these contexts:

- Class Statement
- Const Statement
- Declare Statement
- Delegate Statement
- Dim Statement
- Enum Statement
- Event Statement
- Function Statement
- Interface Statement
- Module Statement
- Property Statement
- Structure Statement
- Sub Statement

PV Function

Returns a **Double** specifying the present value of an annuity based on periodic, fixed payments to be paid in the future and a fixed interest rate.

```
Function PV( _
   ByVal Rate As Double, _
   ByVal NPer As Double, _
   ByVal Pmt As Double, _
   Optional ByVal FV As Double = 0, _
   Optional ByVal Due As DueDate = DueDate.EndOfPeriod _
) As Double
```

Parameters

Rate

Required. **Double** specifying interest rate per period. For example, if you get a car loan at an annual percentage rate (APR) of 10 percent and make monthly payments, the rate per period is 0.1/12, or 0.0083.

NPer

Required. **Double** specifying total number of payment periods in the annuity. For example, if you make monthly payments on a four-year car loan, your loan has a total of 4 * 12 (or 48) payment periods.

Pmt

Required. **Double** specifying payment to be made each period. Payments usually contain principal and interest that doesn't change over the life of the annuity.

FV

Optional. **Double** specifying future value or cash balance you want after you've made the final payment. For example, the future value of a loan is $0 because that's its value after the final payment. However, if you want to save $50,000 over 18 years for your child's education, then $50,000 is the future value. If omitted, 0 is assumed.

Due

Optional. Object of type `Microsoft.VisualBasic.DueDate` that specifies when payments are due. This argument must be either `DueDate.EndOfPeriod` if payments are due at the end of the payment period, or `DueDate.BegOfPeriod` if payments are due at the beginning of the period. If omitted, `DueDate.EndOfPeriod` is assumed.

Remarks

An annuity is a series of fixed cash payments made over a period of time. An annuity can be a loan (such as a home mortgage) or an investment (such as a monthly savings plan).

The *Rate* and *NPer* arguments must be calculated using payment periods expressed in the same units. For example, if *Rate* is calculated using months, *NPer* must also be calculated using months.

For all arguments, cash paid out (such as deposits to savings) is represented by negative numbers; cash received (such as dividend checks) is represented by positive numbers.

Example

In this example, the **PV** function returns the present value of an $1,000,000 annuity that will provide $50,000 a year for the next 20 years. Provided are the expected annual percentage rate (`APR`), the total number of payments (`TotPmts`), the amount of each payment (`YrIncome`), the total future value of the investment (`FVal`), and a number that indicates whether each payment is made at the beginning or end of the payment period (`PayType`). Note that `YrIncome` is a negative number because it represents cash paid out from the annuity each year.

```
Sub TestPV()
   Dim Fmt As String = "###,##0.00"     ' Define money format.
   Dim APR, TotPmts, YrIncome, FVal, PVal As Double
   Dim PayType As DueDate
   APR = 0.0825  ' Annual percentage rate.
   TotPmts = 20   ' Total number of payments.
   YrIncome = 50000   ' Yearly income.
   FVal = 1000000   ' Future value.
   PayType = DueDate.BegOfPeriod   ' Payment at beginning of month.
   PVal = PV(APR, TotPmts, -YrIncome, FVal, PayType)
   MsgBox("The present value is " & Format(PVal, Fmt) & ".")
End Sub
```

See Also

DDB Function, FV Function, IPmt Function, IRR Function, MIRR Function, NPer Function, NPV Function, Pmt Function, PPmt Function, Rate Function, SLN Function, SYD Function

QBColor Function

Returns an **Integer** value representing the RGB color code corresponding to the specified color number.

```
QBColor(Color)
```

Parameter

Color

Required. A whole number in the range 0–15.

Settings

The *color* argument has these settings:

Number	Color	Number	Color
0	Black	8	Gray
1	Blue	9	Light blue
2	Green	10	Light green
3	Cyan	11	Light cyan
4	Red	12	Light red
5	Magenta	13	Light magenta
6	Yellow	14	Light yellow
7	White	15	Bright white

Exceptions/Errors

Exception type	Error number	Condition
ArgumentException	5	*Color* is outside of range 0 to 15, inclusive.

Remarks

Starting with the least-significant byte, the returned value specifies the red, green, and blue values used to set the appropriate color in the RGB system used by the Visual Basic language.

Example

This example uses the **QBColor** function to change to the color indicated by `colorInteger`. **QBColor** accepts integer values between 0 and 15.

```
Dim colorInteger As Integer
' Use 4 for red.
colorInteger = QBColor(4)
```

See Also

RGB Function

Raise Method

Generates a run-time error; can be used instead of the **Error** statement.

```
Public Sub Raise( _
    ByVal Number As Integer, _
    Optional ByVal Source As Object = Nothing, _
    Optional ByVal Description As Object = Nothing, _
    Optional ByVal HelpFile As Object = Nothing, _
    Optional ByVal HelpContext As Object = Nothing _
)
```

Parameter

Number
: Required. **Long** integer that identifies the nature of the error. Visual Basic errors are in the range 0–65535: the range 0–512 is reserved for system errors; the range 513–65535 is available for user-defined errors. When setting the **Number** property to your own error code in a class module, you add your error code number to the **vbObjectError** constant. For example, to generate the error number 513, assign `vbObjectError + 513` to the **Number** property.

Source
: Optional. **String** expression naming the object or application that generated the error. When setting this property for an object, use the form *project.class*. If *Source* is not specified, the process ID of the current Visual Basic project is used.

Description
: Optional. **String** expression describing the error. If unspecified, the value in the **Number** property is examined. If it can be mapped to a Visual Basic run-time error code, the string that would be returned by the **Error** function is used as the **Description** property. If there is no Visual Basic error corresponding to the **Number** property, the "Application-defined or object-defined error" message is used.

HelpFile
: Optional. The fully qualified path to the Help file in which help on this error can be found. If unspecified, Visual Basic uses the fully qualified drive, path, and file name of the Visual Basic Help file.

HelpContext
: Optional. The context ID identifying a topic within *HelpFile* that provides help for the error. If omitted, the Visual Basic Help file context ID for the error corresponding to the **Number** property is used, if it exists.

Exceptions/Errors

Exception type	Error number	Condition
ArgumentException	5	*Number* is greater than 65535.

Remarks

All of the **Raise** arguments except *Number* are optional. If you omit optional arguments, and the property settings of the **Err** object contain values that have not been cleared, those values serve as the values for your error.

Raise is useful for generating errors when writing class modules, because the **Err** object gives richer information than when you generate errors with the **Error** statement. For example, with the **Raise** method, the source that generated the error can be specified in the **Source** property, online Help for the error can be referenced, and so on.

Example

This example uses the **Err** object's **Raise** method to generate an error within a function written in Visual Basic. The calling function can catch the error and report it to the user with a message box.

```
Const WidthError = 1
Const WidthHelp = 101

Function TestWidth(ByVal width As Integer)
   If width > 1000 Then
      Err.Raise(vbObjectError + 512 + WidthError, "TestWidth", _
      "Width must be less than 1000.", "HelpFile.hlp", WidthHelp)
   End If
End Function

' Add to calling function.
Try
   TestWidth(2000)
Catch ex As Exception
   MsgBox(ex.Message)
End Try
```

See Also

Clear Method, Description Property, Err Object, Error Statement, HelpContext Property, HelpFile Property, LastDLLError Property, Number Property, On Error Statement, Source Property

Applies To

Err Object

RaiseEvent Statement

Triggers an event declared at module level within a class, form, or document.

```
RaiseEvent eventname[( argumentlist )]
```

The required *eventname* is the name of an event declared within the module. It follows Visual Basic variable naming conventions.

Parts

eventname
Required. Name of the event to trigger.

argumentlist
Optional. Comma-delimited list of variables, arrays, or expressions. The *argumentlist* argument must be enclosed by parentheses. If there are no arguments, the parentheses must be omitted.

Remarks

If the event has not been declared within the module in which it is raised, an error occurs. The following fragment illustrates an event declaration and a procedure in which the event is raised.

```
' Declare an event at module level of a class module.
Event LogonCompleted(UserName As String)

Sub
   ' Raise the event.
   RaiseEvent LogonCompleted("AustinSteele")
End Sub
```

You can't use **RaiseEvent** to raise events that are not explicitly declared in the module. For example, if a form has a Click event, you can't fire its Click event using **RaiseEvent**. If you declare a Click event in the form module, it shadows the form's own Click event. You can still invoke the form's Click event using normal syntax for calling the event, but not using the **RaiseEvent** statement.

Events are raised in the order that the connections are established. Since events can have **ByRef** parameters, a process that connects late may receive parameters that have been changed by an earlier event handler.

Example

The following example uses events to count off seconds during a demonstration of the fastest 100 meter race. The code illustrates all of the event-related methods, properties, and statements, including the **RaiseEvent** statement.

The class that raises an event is the event source, and the methods that process the event are the event handlers. An event source can have multiple handlers for the events it generates. When the class raises the event, that event is raised on every class that has elected to handle events for that instance of the object.

The example also uses a form (`Form1`) with a button (`Command1`), a label (`Label1`), and two text boxes (`Text1` and `Text2`). When you click the button, the first text box displays "From Now" and the second starts to count seconds. When the full time (9.84 seconds) has elapsed, the first text box displays "Until Now" and the second displays "9.84".

The code for `Form1` specifies the initial and terminal states of the form. It also contains the code executed when events are raised.

To use this example, open a new Windows Forms project, add a button named `Button1`, a label named `Label1` and two text boxes, named `TextBox1` and `TextBox2`, to the main form, named `form1`. Then right click the form and click **View Code** to open the code editor.

To simplify access to the Timer property, add an **Imports** statement as the first line of code above the `Class Form1` statement.

```
Imports Microsoft.VisualBasic.DateAndTime
```

Add a **WithEvents** variable to the declarations sectin of the `Form1` class.

```
Private WithEvents mText As TimerState
```

Add the following code to the code for `Form1`. Replace any duplicate procedures that may exist, such as `Form_Load`, or `Button_Click`.

```
Private Sub Form1_Load(ByVal sender As Object, _
                       ByVal e As System.EventArgs) _
                       Handles MyBase.Load
   Button1.Text = "Click to Start Timer"
   TextBox1.Text = ""
   TextBox2.Text = ""
   Label1.Text = "The fastest 100 meters ever run took this long:"
   mText = New TimerState()
End Sub
Private Sub Button1_Click(ByVal sender As System.Object, _
                          ByVal e As System.EventArgs) _
                          Handles Button1.Click
   TextBox1.Text = "From Now"
   TextBox1.Refresh()
   TextBox2.Text = "0"
   TextBox2.Refresh()
   mText.TimerTask(9.84)
End Sub

Private Sub mText_ChangeText() Handles mText.ChangeText
   TextBox1.Text = "Until Now"
   TextBox2.Text = "9.84"
End Sub
```

```
Private Sub mText_UpdateTime(ByVal Jump As Double) _
      Handles mText.UpdateTime
   TextBox2.Text = Format(Jump, "##0.00")
   Application.DoEvents()
End Sub

Class TimerState
   Public Event UpdateTime(ByVal Jump As Double)
   Public Event ChangeText()
   Public Sub TimerTask(ByVal Duration As Double)
      Dim Start As Double
      Dim Second As Double
      Dim SoFar As Double
      Start = Timer
      SoFar = Start
      Do While Timer < Start + Duration
         If Timer - SoFar >= 0.1 Then
            SoFar = SoFar + 0.1
            RaiseEvent UpdateTime(Timer - Start)
         End If
      Loop
      RaiseEvent ChangeText()
   End Sub
End Class
```

Press F5 to run this example, and click the button labeled **Click to start timer**. The text box will count up to 9.84 seconds.

See Also

Event Statement

Randomize Statement

Initializes the random-number generator.

```
Randomize [ number ]
```

Part

number

Optional. An **Object** or any valid numeric expression.

Remarks

Randomize uses *number* to initialize the **Rnd** function's random-number generator, giving it a new seed value. If you omit *number,* the value returned by the system timer is used as the new seed value.

If **Randomize** is not used, the **Rnd** function (with no arguments) uses the same number as a seed the first time it is called, and thereafter uses the last-generated number as a seed value.

Note To repeat sequences of random numbers, call **Rnd** with a negative argument immediately before using **Randomize** with a numeric argument. Using **Randomize** with the same value for *number* does not repeat the previous sequence.

Example

This example uses the **Randomize** statement to initialize the random-number generator. Because the number argument has been omitted, **Randomize** uses the return value from the **Timer** function as the new seed value.

```
Dim MyValue As Integer
Randomize   ' Initialize random-number generator.
MyValue = CInt(Int((6 * Rnd()) + 1)) ' Generate random value between 1 and 6.
```

See Also

Rnd Function

Rate Function

Returns a **Double** specifying the interest rate per period for an annuity.

```
Function Rate( _
   ByVal NPer As Double, _
   ByVal Pmt As Double, _
   ByVal PV As Double, _
   Optional ByVal FV As Double = 0, _
   Optional ByVal Due As DueDate = DueDate.EndOfPeriod, _
   Optional ByVal Guess As Double = 0.1 _
) As Double
```

Parameters

NPer

Required. **Double** specifying total number of payment periods in the annuity. For example, if you make monthly payments on a four-year car loan, your loan has a total of 4 * 12 (or 48) payment periods.

Pmt

Required. **Double** specifying payment to be made each period. Payments usually contain principal and interest that doesn't change over the life of the annuity.

PV

Required. **Double** specifying present value, or value today, of a series of future payments or receipts. For example, when you borrow money to buy a car, the loan amount is the present value to the lender of the monthly car payments you will make.

FV

Optional. **Double** specifying future value or cash balance you want after you make the final payment. For example, the future value of a loan is $0 because that's its value after the final payment. However, if you want to save $50,000 over 18 years for your child's education, then $50,000 is the future value. If omitted, 0 is assumed.

Due

Optional. Object of type `Microsoft.VisualBasic.DueDate` that specifies when payments are due. This argument must be either `DueDate.EndOfPeriod` if payments are due at the end of the payment period, or `DueDate.BegOfPeriod` if payments are due at the beginning of the period. If omitted, `DueDate.EndOfPeriod` is assumed.

Guess

Optional. **Double** specifying value you estimate will be returned by **Rate**. If omitted, *Guess* is 0.1 (10 percent).

Exceptions/Errors

Exception type	Error number	Condition
ArgumentException	5	*NPer* <= 0.

Remarks

An annuity is a series of fixed cash payments made over a period of time. An annuity can be a loan (such as a home mortgage) or an investment (such as a monthly savings plan).

For all arguments, cash paid out (such as deposits to savings) is represented by negative numbers; cash received (such as dividend checks) is represented by positive numbers.

Rate is calculated by iteration. Starting with the value of *Guess*, **Rate** cycles through the calculation until the result is accurate to within 0.00001 percent. If **Rate** can't find a result after 20 tries, it fails. If your guess is 10 percent and **Rate** fails, try a different value for *Guess*.

Example

This example uses the **Rate** function to calculate the interest rate of a loan given the total number of payments (`TotPmts`), the amount of the loan payment (`Payment`), the present value or principal of the loan (`PVal`), the future value of the loan (`FVal`), a number that indicates whether the payment is due at the beginning or end of the payment period (`PayType`), and an approximation of the expected interest rate (`Guess`).

```
Sub TestRate()
   Dim PVal, Payment, TotPmts, FVal, Guess, APR As Double
   Dim PayType As DueDate
   Dim Fmt As String = "##0.00"   ' Define percentage format.
   Dim Response As MsgBoxResult
   FVal = 0   ' Usually 0 for a loan.
   Guess = 0.1  ' Guess of 10 percent.
   PVal = CDbl(InputBox("How much did you borrow?"))
```

(continued)

(continued)

```
    Payment = CDbl(InputBox("What's your monthly payment?"))
    TotPmts = CDbl(InputBox("How many monthly payments do you have to make?"))
    Response = MsgBox("Do you make payments at the end of the month?", MsgBoxStyle.YesNo)
    If Response = MsgBoxResult.No Then
        PayType = DueDate.BegOfPeriod
    Else
        PayType = DueDate.EndOfPeriod
    End If
    APR = (Rate(TotPmts, -Payment, PVal, FVal, PayType, Guess) * 12) * 100
    MsgBox("Your interest rate is " & Format(CInt(APR), Fmt) & " percent.")
End Sub
```

See Also

DDB Function, FV Function, IPmt Function, IRR Function, MIRR Function, NPer Function, NPV Function, Pmt Function, PPmt Function, PV Function, SLN Function, SYD Function

ReadOnly

The **ReadOnly** keyword indicates that a variable or property can be read but not written.

The **ReadOnly** keyword is used in these contexts:

Dim Statement

Property Statement

See Also

Visual Basic Language Keywords

ReDim Statement

Used at procedure level to reallocate storage space for an array variable.

```
ReDim [ Preserve ] name[(boundlist)]
```

Parts

Preserve

Optional. Keyword used to preserve the data in the existing array when you change the size of only the last dimension.

name

Required. Name of the variable. Must be a valid Visual Basic identifier. You can redimension as many variables as you like in the same statement, specifying the *name* and *boundlist* parts for each one. Multiple variables are separated by commas.

boundlist

Required. List of non-negative integers representing the upper bounds of the dimensions of the redefined array. Multiple upper bounds are separated by commas. The number of dimensions in *boundlist* must match the original rank of the array.

Each value in *boundlist* specifies the upper bound of a dimension, not the length. The lower bound is always zero, so the subscript for each dimension can vary from zero through the upper bound.

It is possible to use –1 to declare the upper bound of an array dimension. This signifies that the array is empty but not **Nothing**, a distinction required by certain common language runtime functions. However, Visual Basic code cannot successfully access such an array. If you attempt to do so, an **IndexOutOfRangeException** error occurs during execution.

Remarks

The **ReDim** statement can appear only at procedure level. This means you can redefine arrays inside a procedure but not at class or module level.

The **ReDim** statement is used to change the size of one or more dimensions of an array that has already been formally declared. **ReDim** cannot change the rank (the number of dimensions) of the array.

The **ReDim** statement cannot change the data type of an array variable or provide new initialization values for the array elements.

ReDim releases the existing array and creates a new array with the same rank. The elements of the new array are initialized to the default value for their data type unless you specify **Preserve**.

If you include the **Preserve** keyword, Visual Basic copies the elements from the existing array to the new array. When you use **Preserve**, you can resize only the last dimension of the array, and for every other dimension you must specify the same size it already has in the existing array.

For example, if your array has only one dimension, you can resize that dimension and still preserve the contents of the array, because it is the last and only dimension. However, if your array has two or more dimensions, you can change the size of only the last dimension if you use **Preserve**.

The following example increases the size of the last dimension of a dynamic array without losing any existing data in the array, and then decreases the size with partial data loss:

```
Dim IntArray(10, 10, 10) As Integer
' ...
ReDim Preserve IntArray(10, 10, 20)
' ...
ReDim Preserve IntArray(10, 10, 15)
```

The first **ReDim** creates a new array, copying all the elements from the existing array. It also adds 10 more columns to the end of every row in every layer. The elements in these new columns are initialized to the default value of the element type of the array.

The second **ReDim** creates another new array, copying all the elements that fit. However, five columns are lost from the end of every row in every layer. This is not a problem if you have finished using these columns. Reducing the size of a large array can free up memory that you no longer need.

You can use **ReDim** on a property that holds an array of values.

Example

This example uses the **ReDim** statement to allocate and reallocate storage space for array variables.

```
Dim I, MyArray() As Integer   ' Declare variable and array variable.
ReDim MyArray(5) ' Allocate 6 elements.
For I = 0 To UBound(MyArray)
   MyArray(I) = I    ' Initialize array.
Next I
```

The next statement resizes the array without saving the contents of the elements.

```
ReDim MyArray(10) ' Resize to 11 elements.
For I = 0 To UBound(MyArray)
   MyArray(I) = I    ' Initialize array.
Next I
```

The following statement resizes the array but saves the contents of the elements.

```
ReDim Preserve MyArray(15) ' Resize to 16 elements.
```

See Also

Const Statement, Dim Statement, Erase Statement

REM Statement

Used to include explanatory remarks in a program.

```
REM comment
```

-or-

```
' comment
```

Parts

comment

Optional. The text of any comment you want to include. A space is required between the **REM** keyword and *comment*.

Remarks

You can put a **REM** statement alone on a line, or you can put it on a line following another statement. The **REM** statement must be the last statement on the line. If it follows another statement, the **REM** must be separated from that statement by a space.

You can use a single quote (') instead of **REM**. This is true whether your comment follows another statement on the same line or sits alone on a line.

Example

This example illustrates the **REM** statement, which is used to include explanatory remarks in a program. It also shows the alternative of using the single quote character (') instead of **REM**.

```
Dim MyStr1, MyStr2 as String
MyStr1 = "Hello" REM Comment after a statement using REM.
MyStr2 = "Goodbye"   ' Comment after a statement using the ' character.
REM This entire line is a comment.
' This entire line is also a comment.
```

Remove Method

Removes a member from a **Collection** object.

```
Public Overloads Sub Remove(ByVal { Key As String | Index As Integer })
```

Parameters

Key

A unique **String** expression that specifies a key string that can be used, instead of a positional index, to access a member of the collection.

Index

An expression that specifies the position of a member of the collection. If a numeric expression, *Index* must be a number from 1 to the value of the collection's **Count** property. If a **String** expression, *Index* must correspond to the *Key* argument specified when the member referred to was added to the collection.

Exceptions/Errors

Exception type	Error number	Condition
ArgumentException	5	*Key* is invalid or not specified.
IndexOutOfRangeException	9	*Index* does not match an existing member of the collection.

Remarks

If *Index* doesn't match an existing member of the collection, an error occurs.

Example

This example illustrates the use of the **Remove** method to remove objects from a **Collection** object, `birthdays`.

```
Dim birthdays As New Collection()
birthdays.Add(New DateTime(2001, 1, 12), "Bill")
birthdays.Add(New DateTime(2001, 1, 13), "Joe")
birthdays.Remove(1)
birthdays.Remove("Joe")
```

See Also

Add Method

Applies to

Collection Object

RemoveHandler Statement

Removes the association between an event and an event handler.

```
RemoveHandler event, AddressOf eventhandler
```

Parts

event
The name of the event being handled.

eventhandler
The name of the procedure currently handling the event.

Remarks

The **AddHandler** and **RemoveHandler** statements allow you to start and stop event handling for a specific event at any time during program execution.

Example

```
Sub TestEvents()
   Dim Obj As New Class1()
   ' Associate an event handler with an event.
   AddHandler Obj.Ev_Event, AddressOf EventHandler
   Obj.CauseSomeEvent() ' Ask the object to raise an event.
   RemoveHandler Obj.Ev_Event, AddressOf EventHandler ' Stop handling events.
   Obj.CauseSomeEvent() ' This event will not be handled.
End Sub
```

```
   Sub EventHandler()
      MsgBox("EventHandler caught event.") ' Handle the event.
   End Sub

Public Class Class1
   Public Event Ev_Event()  ' Declare an event.
   Sub CauseSomeEvent()
      RaiseEvent Ev_Event() ' Raise an event.
   End Sub
End Class
```

See Also

AddHandler Statement, Handles

Rename Function

Renames a disk file, directory, or folder.

```
Public Sub Rename( _
   ByVal OldPath As String, _
   ByVal NewPath As String _
)
```

Parameters

OldPath

Required. **String** expression that specifies the existing file name and location. *OldPath* may include the directory or folder, and drive, of the file.

NewPath

Required. **String** expression that specifies the new file name and location. *NewPath* may include directory or folder, and drive of the destination location. The file name specified by *NewPath* can't already exist.

Exceptions/Errors

Exception type	Error number	Condition
ArgumentException	5	Pathname is invalid.
FileNotFoundException	53	*OldPath* file does not exist.
IOException	58	*NewPath* file already exists.
IOException	75	Access is invalid.
IOException	74	Cannot rename to different device.

Remarks

The **Rename** function renames a file and moves it to a different directory or folder, if necessary. The **Rename** function can move a file across drives, but it can only rename an existing directory or folder when both *NewPath* and *OldPath* are located on the same drive. Name cannot create a new file, directory, or folder.

Using the **Rename** function on an open file produces an error. You must close an open file before renaming it. **Rename** arguments cannot include multiple-character (*) and single-character (?) wildcards.

Example

This example uses the **Rename** function to rename a file. For purposes of this example, assume that the directories or folders that are specified already exist.

```
Dim OldName, NewName As String
OldName = "OLDFILE"
NewName = "NEWFILE" ' Define file names.
Rename(OldName, NewName)   ' Rename file.

OldName = "C:\MYDIR\OLDFILE"
NewName = "C:\YOURDIR\NEWFILE"
Rename(OldName, NewName)   ' Move and rename file.
```

See Also

Kill Function

Replace Function

Returns a string in which a specified substring has been replaced with another substring a specified number of times.

```
Public Function Replace(
   ByVal Expression As String,
   ByVal Find As String,
   ByVal Replacement As String,
   Optional ByVal Start As Integer = 1,
   Optional ByVal Count As Integer = -1,
   Optional ByVal Compare As CompareMethod = CompareMethod.Binary
) As String
```

Parameters

Expression

Required. String expression containing substring to replace.

Find

Required. Substring being searched for.

Replacement
Required. Replacement substring.

Start
Optional. Position within *Expression* where substring search is to begin. If omitted, 1 is assumed.

Count
Optional. Number of substring substitutions to perform. If omitted, the default value is –1, which means make all possible substitutions.

Compare
Optional. Numeric value indicating the kind of comparison to use when evaluating substrings. See "Settings" for values.

Settings

The *Compare* argument can have the following values:

Constant	Description
Binary	Performs a binary comparison
Text	Performs a textual comparison

Return Values

Replace returns the following values:

If	Replace returns
Expression is zero-length	Zero-length string (" ")
Find is zero-length	Copy of *Expression*
Replace is zero-length	Copy of *Expression* with no occurrences of *Find*
Start is greater than length of *expression*	Zero-length string
Count is 0	Copy of *Expression*

Exceptions/Errors

Exception type	Error number	Condition
ArgumentException	5	*Count* < –1 or *Start* <= 0.

Remarks

The return value of the **Replace** function is a string that begins at the position specified by *Start* and concludes at the end of the *Expression* string, with the substitutions made as specified by the *Find* and *Replace* values.

Example

This example demonstrates the **Replace** function.

```
Dim myString As String = "Shopping List"
Dim aString As String
' Returns "Shipping List".
aString = Replace(myString, "o", "i")
```

See Also

Filter Function

Reset Function

Closes all disk files opened using the **FileOpen** function.

```
Public Sub Reset()
```

Remarks

The **Reset** function closes all active files opened by the **FileOpen** function and has the same function as **FileClose()** without any parameters.

Example

This example uses the **Reset** function to close all open files and write the contents of all file buffers to disk. Note the use of the **Object** variable `FileNumber` as both a string and a number.

```
' Open 5 files named TEST1, TEST2, etc.
Dim fileNumber As Integer
For fileNumber = 1 To 5    ' Open 5 files.
   FileOpen(fileNumber, "TEST" & fileNumber, OpenMode.Output)
   PrintLine(fileNumber, "Hello World")
Next fileNumber
Reset()   ' Close files and write contents to disk.
```

See Also

FileClose Function, End Statement, FileOpen Function

Resume

The **Resume** keyword indicates where execution should continue after an error has been handled.

The **Resume** keyword is used in these contexts:

- On Error Statement
- Resume Statement

See Also

Visual Basic Language Keywords

Resume Statement

Resumes execution after an error-handling routine is finished.

```
Resume [ Next | line ]
```

Parts

Resume

Required. If the error occurred in the same procedure as the error handler, execution resumes with the statement that caused the error. If the error occurred in a called procedure, execution resumes at the statement that last called out of the procedure containing the error-handling routine.

Next

Optional. If the error occurred in the same procedure as the error handler, execution resumes with the statement immediately following the statement that caused the error. If the error occurred in a called procedure, execution resumes with the statement immediately following the statement that last called out of the procedure containing the error-handling routine (or **On Error Resume Next** statement).

line

Optional. Execution resumes at the line specified in the required *line* argument. The *line* argument is a line label or line number and must be in the same procedure as the error handler.

Remarks

If you use a **Resume** statement anywhere except in an error-handling routine, an error will occur.

The **Resume** statement cannot be used in any procedure that contains a **Try...Catch...Finally** statement.

Example

This example uses the **Resume** statement to end error handling in a procedure, and then resume execution with the statement that caused the error. Error number 55 is generated to illustrate using the **Resume** statement.

```
Sub ResumeStatementDemo()
   On Error GoTo ErrorHandler   ' Enable error-handling routine.
   Dim x As Integer = 32
   Dim y As Integer = 0
   Dim z As Integer
   z = x / y   ' Creates a divide by zero error
   Exit Sub   ' Exit Sub to avoid error handler.
```

(continued)

(continued)

```
ErrorHandler:    ' Error-handling routine.
   Select Case Err.Number    ' Evaluate error number.
      Case 6    ' "Divide by zero" error.
         y = 1 ' Sets the value of y to 1 and tries the calculation again.
      Case Else
         ' Handle other situations here....
   End Select
   Resume    ' Resume execution at same line
   ' that caused the error.
End Sub
```

See Also

Try...Catch...Finally Statements, Error Statement, On Error Statement

Return Statement

Returns control to the code that called a **Sub**, **Function**, or **Property** procedure.

```
Return
```

-or-

```
Return expr
```

Part

expr

Required in a **Function** procedure or a **Property** procedure that retrieves the property's value. An expression that represents the value to be returned to the calling code.

Remarks

For a **Sub** procedure or a **Property** procedure that sets the property's value, the **Return** statement is equivalent to an **Exit Sub** statement, and *expr* must not be supplied.

For a **Function** procedure or a **Property** procedure that retrieves the property's value, *expr* must be present and must evaluate to a data type that is convertible to the return type of the function. In this form, **Return** is equivalent to assigning the expression to the function name as the return value and then executing an **Exit Function** statement.

Example

This example uses the **Return** statement several times to return to the calling code when the procedure does not need to do anything else.

```
Public Function GetAgePhrase(Age As Integer) As String
   If Age > 60 Then Return "Senior"
   If Age > 40 Then Return "Middle-aged"
   If Age > 20 Then Return "Adult"
   If Age > 12 Then Return "Teen-aged"
   If Age > 4 Then Return "School-aged"
   If Age > 1 Then Return "Toddler"
   Return "Infant"
End Function
```

See Also

Function Statement, Sub Statement

Returns for CStr

The following table describes the return values for **CStr** under different *expression* types:

If *expression* type is	CStr returns
Boolean	A string containing "True" or "False".
Date	A string containing a date in the short date format of your system.
Numeric	A string representing the number.

See Also

Type Conversion Functions

RGB Function

Returns an **Integer** value representing an RGB color value from a set of red, green and blue color components.

```
RGB( _
   Red As Integer, _
   Green As Integer, _
   Blue As Integer _
)
```

Parameters

Red

Required. **Integer** in the range 0–255, inclusive, that represents the intensity of the red component of the color.

Green

Required. **Integer** in the range 0–255, inclusive, that represents the intensity of the green component of the color.

Blue

Required. **Integer** in the range 0–255, inclusive, that represents the intensity of the blue component of the color.

Exceptions/Errors

Exception type	Error number	Condition
ArgumentException	5	*Green, Blue,* or *Red* outside of range 0 and 255, inclusive.

Remarks

Application methods and properties that accept a color specification expect that specification to be a number representing an RGB color value. An RGB color value specifies the relative intensity of red, green, and blue to cause a specific color to be displayed.

If the value for any argument to **RGB** is greater than 255, 255 is used.

The following table lists some standard colors and the red, green, and blue values they include:

Color	Red value	Green value	Blue value
Black	0	0	0
Blue	0	0	255
Green	0	255	0
Cyan	0	255	255
Red	255	0	0
Magenta	255	0	255
Yellow	255	255	0
White	255	255	255

Example

This example shows how the **RGB** function is used to return a whole number representing an **RGB** color value.

```
Dim red, rgbValue As Integer
Dim i As Integer = 75
red = RGB(255, 0, 0)    ' Return the value for red.
rgbValue = RGB(i, 64 + i, 128 + i)    ' Same as RGB(75, 139, 203).
```

See Also

QBColor Function

Right Function

Returns a string containing a specified number of characters from the right side of a string.

```
Public Shared Function Right( _
   ByVal Str As String, _
   ByVal Length As Integer _
) As String
```

Parameters

Str
Required. **String** expression from which the rightmost characters are returned.

Length
Required. **Integer**. Numeric expression indicating how many characters to return. If 0, a zero length string (" ") is returned. If greater than or equal to the number of characters in *Str*, the entire string is returned.

Exceptions/Errors

Exception type	Error number	Condition
ArgumentException	5	*Length* < 0.

Remarks

To determine the number of characters in *Str*, use the **Len** function. If used in a Windows Form, or any other class that has a **Right** property, you must fully qualify the function with `Microsoft.VisualBasic.Right`.

Example

This example demonstrates the use of the **Right** function to return a substring of a given **String**. In a class that has a **Right** property, it may be necessary to fully qualify the **Right** function.

```
Dim myString As String = "Hello World!"
Dim subString As String
subString = Microsoft.VisualBasic.Right(myString, 6)   ' Returns "World!"
```

See Also

Left Function, Len Function, Mid Function

RmDir Function

Removes an existing directory or folder.

```
Public Sub RmDir(ByVal Path As String)
```

Parameter

Path

Required. **String** expression that identifies the directory or folder to be removed. *Path* may include the drive. If no drive is specified, **RmDir** removes the directory or folder on the current drive.

Exceptions/Errors

Exception type	Error number	Condition
ArgumentException	52	*Path* is not specified or is empty.
IOException	75	Target directory contains files.
FileNotFoundException	76	Directory does not exist.

Remarks

An error occurs if you try to use **RmDir** on a directory or folder containing files. Use the **Kill** function to delete all files before attempting to remove a directory or folder.

Example

This example uses the **RmDir** function to remove an existing directory or folder.

```
' Assume that MYDIR is an empty directory or folder.
RmDir ("MYDIR")   ' Remove MYDIR.
```

See Also

ChDir Function, CurDir Function, Kill Function, MkDir Function

Rnd Function

Returns a random number of type **Single**.

```
Rnd[(number)]
```

Parameter

number

Optional. A **Single** value or any valid **Single** expression.

Return Values

If *number* is	Rnd generates
Less than zero	The same number every time, using *number* as the seed.
Greater than zero	The next random number in the sequence.
Equal to zero	The most recently generated number.
Not supplied	The next random number in the sequence.

Remarks

The **Rnd** function returns a value less than 1, but greater than or equal to zero.

The value of *number* determines how **Rnd** generates a random number:

For any given initial seed, the same number sequence is generated because each successive call to the **Rnd** function uses the previously generated number as a seed for the next number in the sequence.

Before calling **Rnd,** use the **Randomize** statement without an argument to initialize the random-number generator with a seed based on the system timer.

To produce random integers in a given range, use this formula:

```
Int((upperbound - lowerbound + 1) * Rnd + lowerbound)
```

Here, *upperbound* is the highest number in the range, and *lowerbound* is the lowest number in the range.

Note To repeat sequences of random numbers, call **Rnd** with a negative argument immediately before using **Randomize** with a numeric argument. Using **Randomize** with the same value for *number* does not repeat the previous sequence.

Example

This example uses the **Rnd** function to generate a random integer value from 1 to 6.

```
Dim MyValue As Integer
MyValue = CInt(Int((6 * Rnd()) + 1)) ' Generate random value between 1 and 6.
```

See Also

Math Summary, Randomize Statement

RSet Function

Returns a right-aligned string containing the specified string adjusted to the specified length.

```
Public Shared Function RSet( _
   ByVal Source As String, _
   ByVal Length As Integer _
) As String
```

Parameters

Source
: Required. **String** expression. Name of string variable.

Length
: Required. **Integer** expression. Length of returned string.

Remarks

If *Source* is longer than *Length*, **RSet** places only the leftmost characters, up to the length of *Source,* in the returned string. If the specified string is shorter than the specified length, spaces are added to the left end of the string to produce the appropriate length. If the specified string is longer than the specified length, it is shortened to the specified length.

Example

This example demonstrates the use of the **RSet** function.

```
Dim myString As String = "Right"
Dim rString As String
rString = RSet(myString, 11)   ' Returns "      Right"
```

See Also

Data Type Summary, LSet Function

SaveSetting Function

Saves or creates an application entry in the Windows registry.

```
Public Sub SaveSetting( _
   ByVal AppName As String, _
   ByVal Section As String, _
   ByVal Key As String, _
   ByVal Setting As String _
)
```

Parameters

AppName
Required. **String** expression containing the name of the application or project to which the setting applies.

Section
Required. **String** expression containing the name of the section in which the key setting is being saved.

Key
Required. **String** expression containing the name of the key setting being saved.

Setting
Required. Expression containing the value to which *Key* is being set.

Exceptions/Errors

Exception type	Error number	Condition
ArgumentException	5	Key registry could not be created, or user is not logged in.

Remarks

If the key setting can't be saved for any reason, an error occurs.

SaveSetting requires that a user be logged on since it operates under the HKEY_LOCAL_USER registry key, which is not active until a user logs on interactively.

Registry settings that are to be accessed from a non-interactive process (such as mtx.exe) should be stored under either the HKEY_LOCAL_MACHINE\Software\ or the HKEY_USER\DEFAULT\Software registry keys.

Example

The following example first uses the **SaveSetting** statement to make entries in the Windows registry for the `MyApp` application, and then uses the **DeleteSetting** statement to remove them.

```
' Place some settings in the registry.
SaveSetting("MyApp", "Startup", "Top", "75")
SaveSetting("MyApp","Startup", "Left", "50")
' Remove Startup section and all its settings from registry.
DeleteSetting ("MyApp", "Startup")
' Remove MyApp from the registry.
DeleteSetting ("MyApp")
```

See Also

DeleteSetting Function, GetAllSettings Function, GetSetting Function

ScriptEngine Property

Returns a string representing the runtime currently in use.

```
ReadOnly Public Property ScriptEngine As String
```

Remarks

The **ScriptEngine** property returns the string "VB".

You can use **ScriptEngine** when your application is running as a standalone program, in a script, or in a host application.

Example

The following example uses the **ScriptEngine** property and related properties to return a string describing the current run-time information:

```
Function GetRuntimeInfo() As String
   Dim Runtime As String = ""
   Runtime = ScriptEngine & " Version "
   Runtime = Runtime & CStr(ScriptEngineMajorVersion) & "."
   Runtime = Runtime & CStr(ScriptEngineMinorVersion) & "."
   Runtime = Runtime & CStr(ScriptEngineBuildVersion)
   Return Runtime    ' Return the current run-time information.
End Function
```

See Also

ScriptEngineBuildVersion Property, ScriptEngineMajorVersion Property, ScriptEngineMinorVersion Property

ScriptEngineBuildVersion Property

Returns an integer containing the build version number of the runtime currently in use.

```
ReadOnly Public Property ScriptEngineBuildVersion As Integer
```

Remarks

The returned value corresponds directly to the version information contained in the DLL for the current runtime.

You can use **ScriptEngineBuildVersion** when your application is running as a standalone program, in a script, or in a host application.

Example

The following example uses the **ScriptEngineBuildVersion** property and related properties to return a string describing the current run-time information:

```
Function GetRuntimeInfo() As String
   Dim Runtime As String = ""
   Runtime = ScriptEngine & " Version "
   Runtime = Runtime & CStr(ScriptEngineMajorVersion) & "."
   Runtime = Runtime & CStr(ScriptEngineMinorVersion) & "."
   Runtime = Runtime & CStr(ScriptEngineBuildVersion)
   Return Runtime   ' Return the current run-time information.
End Function
```

See Also

ScriptEngine Property, ScriptEngineMajorVersion Property, ScriptEngineMinorVersion Property

ScriptEngineMajorVersion Property

Returns an integer containing the major version number of the runtime currently in use.

```
ReadOnly Public Property ScriptEngineMajorVersion As Integer
```

Remarks

The returned value corresponds directly to the version information contained in the DLL for the current runtime.

You can use **ScriptEngineMajorVersion** when your application is running as a standalone program, in a script, or in a host application.

Example

The following example uses the **ScriptEngineMajorVersion** property and related properties to return a string describing the current run-time information:

```
Function GetRuntimeInfo() As String
   Dim Runtime As String = ""
   Runtime = ScriptEngine & " Version "
   Runtime = Runtime & CStr(ScriptEngineMajorVersion) & "."
   Runtime = Runtime & CStr(ScriptEngineMinorVersion) & "."
   Runtime = Runtime & CStr(ScriptEngineBuildVersion)
   Return Runtime   ' Return the current run-time information.
End Function
```

See Also

ScriptEngine Property, ScriptEngineBuildVersion Property, ScriptEngineMinorVersion Property

ScriptEngineMinorVersion Property

Returns an integer containing the minor version number of the runtime currently in use.

```
ReadOnly Public Property ScriptEngineMinorVersion As Integer
```

Remarks

The returned value corresponds directly to the version information contained in the DLL for the current runtime.

You can use **ScriptEngineMinorVersion** when your application is running as a standalone program, in a script, or in a host application.

Example

The following example uses the **ScriptEngineMinorVersion** property and related properties to return a string describing the current run-time information:

```
Function GetRuntimeInfo() As String
   Dim Runtime As String = ""
   Runtime = ScriptEngine & " Version "
   Runtime = Runtime & CStr(ScriptEngineMajorVersion) & "."
   Runtime = Runtime & CStr(ScriptEngineMinorVersion) & "."
   Runtime = Runtime & CStr(ScriptEngineBuildVersion)
   Return Runtime   ' Return the current run-time information.
End Function
```

See Also

ScriptEngine Property, ScriptEngineBuildVersion Property, ScriptEngineMajorVersion Property

Second Function

Returns an **Integer** value from 0 through 59 representing the second of the minute.

```
Public Function Second(ByVal TimeValue As DateTime) As Integer
```

Parameter

TimeValue
Required. **Date** value from which you want to extract the second.

You can also obtain the second of the minute by calling **DatePart** and specifying **DateInterval.Second** for the *Interval* argument.

Example

This example uses the **Second** function to obtain the second of the minute from a specified time. In the development environment, the time literal is displayed in short time format using the locale settings of your code.

```
Dim MyTime As Date
Dim MySecond As Integer
MyTime = #4:35:17 PM#    ' Assign a time.
MySecond = Second(MyTime)    ' MySecond contains 17.
```

See Also

Day Function, Hour Function, Minute Function, Now Property, TimeOfDay Property, DatePart Function

Seek Function

Returns a **Long** specifying the current read/write position within a file opened using the **FileOpen** function or sets the position for the next read/write operation within a file opened using the **FileOpen** function.

```
Public Overloads Function Seek( _
   ByVal FileNumber As Integer _
) As Long
```

-or-

```
Public Overloads Sub Seek( _
   ByVal FileNumber As Integer, _
   ByVal Position As Long _
)
```

Parameter

FileNumber

Required. An **Integer** containing a valid file number.

Position

Required. Number in the range 1–2,147,483,647, inclusive, that indicates where the next read/write operation should occur.

Exceptions/Errors

Exception type	Error number	Condition
IOException	52	*FileNumber* does not exist.
IOException	54	File mode is invalid.

Remarks

Seek returns a value between 1 and 2,147,483,647 (equivalent to 2^31 – 1), inclusive.

The following describes the return values for each file access mode:

Mode	Return Value
Random	Number of the next record read or written
Binary, **Input**, **Output**, **Append**	Byte position at which the next operation takes place. The first byte in a file is at position 1, the second byte is at position 2, and so on.

Example

This example uses the **Seek** function to return the current file position. The example assumes `TESTFILE` is a file containing records of the structure `Record`.

```
Structure Record   ' Define user-defined type.
   ID As Integer
   Name As String
End Structure
```

For files opened in **Random** mode, **Seek** returns the number of next record.

```
Dim MyRecord As Record
FileOpen(1, "TESTFILE", OpenMode.Random)
Do While Not EOF(1)
   Debug.WriteLine(Seek(1))   ' Print record number.
   FileGet(1, MyRecord)   ' Read next record.
Loop
FileClose(1)
```

For files opened in modes other than **Random** mode, **Seek** returns the byte position at which the next operation takes place. Assume TESTFILE is a file containing a few lines of text.

```
' Print character position at beginning of each line.
Dim TextLine As String
FileOpen(1, "TESTFILE", OpenMode.Input)   ' Open file for reading.
While Not EOF(1)
   TextLine = LineInput(1)   ' Read next line.
   Debug.WriteLine(Seek(1))   ' Position of next line.
End While
FileClose(1)
```

This example uses the **Seek** function to set the position for the next read or write within a file. This example assumes people.txt is a file containing records of the structure Record.

```
Structure Record
   Dim Name As String
   Dim ID As Integer
End Structure
```

For files opened in **Random** mode, **Seek** sets the next record.

```
Public Sub SeekAPerson(ByVal index As Integer)
   Try
      FileOpen(1, "c:\people.txt", OpenMode.Random)
      Dim onePerson As Record
      Seek(1, index)
      FileGet(1, onePerson)
      FileClose(1)
      Console.WriteLine(onePerson.Name & " " & onePerson.ID)
   Catch
      ' Error recovery code here.
   End Try
End Sub
```

For files opened in modes other than **Random** mode, **Seek** sets the byte position at which the next operation takes place. Assume TESTFILE is a file containing a few lines of text.

```
Dim someText As String
FileOpen(1, "TESTFILE", OpenMode.Input)   ' Open file for output.
Seek(1, 3)   ' Move to the third character.
Input(1, someText)
Console.WriteLine(someText)
FileClose(1)
```

See Also

FileGet Function, Loc Function, FileOpen Function, FilePut Function

Select...Case Statements

Executes one of several groups of statements, depending on the value of an expression.

```
Select [ Case ] testexpression
   [ Case expressionlist
      [ statements ] ]
   [ Case Else
      [ elsestatements ] ]
End Select
```

Parts

testexpression
Required. Expression. Must evaluate to one of the elementary data types (**Boolean**, **Byte**, **Char**, **Date**, **Double**, **Decimal**, **Integer**, **Long**, **Object**, **Short**, **Single**, and **String**).

expressionlist
Required in a **Case** statement. List of expression clauses representing match values for *testexpression*. Multiple expression clauses are separated by commas. Each clause can take one of the following forms:

- *expression1* **To** *expression2*
- [**Is**] *comparisonoperator expression*
- *expression*

Use the **To** keyword to specify the boundaries of a range of match values for *testexpression*. The value of *expression1* must be less than or equal to the value of *expression2*.

Use the **Is** keyword with a comparison operator (=, <>, <, <=, >, or >=) to specify a restriction on the match values for *testexpression*. If the **Is** keyword is not supplied, it is automatically inserted before *comparisonoperator*.

The form specifying only *expression* is treated as a special case of the **Is** form where *comparisonoperator* is the equal sign (=). This form is evaluated as *testexpression* = *expression*.

The expressions in *expressionlist* can be of any data type, provided they are implicitly convertible to the type of *testexpression* and the appropriate *comparisonoperator* is valid for the two types it is being used with.

statements
Optional. One or more statements following **Case** that are executed if *testexpression* matches any clause in *expressionlist*.

elsestatements
Optional. One or more statements following **Case Else** that are executed if *testexpression* does not match any clause in the *expressionlist* of any of the **Case** statements.

End Select
Terminates **Select...Case** block.

Remarks

If *testexpression* matches any **Case** *expressionlist* clause, the statements following that **Case** statement are executed up to the next **Case** statement or the **End Select** statement. Control then passes to the statement following **End Select**. If *testexpression* matches an *expressionlist* clause in more than one **Case** clause, only the statements following the first match are executed.

The **Case Else** statement is used to introduce the *elsestatements* to be executed if no match is found between the *testexpression* and an *expressionlist* clause in any of the other **Case** statements. Although not required, it is a good idea to have a **Case Else** statement in your **Select Case** block to handle unforeseen *testexpression* values. If no **Case** *expressionlist* clause matches *testexpression* and there is no **Case Else** statement, execution continues at the statement following **End Select**.

You can use multiple expressions or ranges in each **Case** clause. For example, the following line is valid:

```
Case 1 To 4, 7 To 9, 11, 13, Is > MaxNumber
```

Note The **Is** keyword used in the **Case** and **Case Else** statements is not the same as the **Is** comparison operator.

You also can specify ranges and multiple expressions for character strings. In the following example, **Case** matches strings that are exactly equal to "apples", strings with values between "nuts" and "soup" in alphabetical order, and the current value of `TestItem`:

```
Case "apples", "nuts" To "soup", TestItem
```

The setting of **Option Compare** can affect string comparisons. Under **Option Compare Text**, the strings "Apples" and "apples" compare as equal, but under **Option Compare Binary**, they do not.

Select Case statements can be nested. Each nested **Select Case** statement must have a matching **End Select** statement.

If you do not need to execute any more of the statements in a **Case** or **Case Else** statement block, you can exit the block by using the **Exit Select** statement. This transfers control immediately to the statement following **End Select**.

Example

This example uses the **Select Case** statements to evaluate the value of a variable. The second **Case** clause contains the value of the variable being evaluated, and therefore only the statement associated with it is executed.

```
Dim Number As Integer = 8
Select Number   ' Evaluate Number.
Case 1 To 5   ' Number between 1 and 5, inclusive.
   Debug.WriteLine("Between 1 and 5")
' The following is the only Case clause that evaluates to True.
Case 6, 7, 8   ' Number between 6 and 8.
   Debug.WriteLine("Between 6 and 8")
```

(continued)

(continued)

```
Case 9 To 10   ' Number is 9 or 10.
Debug.WriteLine("Greater than 8")
Case Else   ' Other values.
   Debug.WriteLine("Not between 1 and 10")
End Select
```

See Also

Choose Function, End Statement, If...Then...Else Statements, Option Compare Statement, Exit Statement

Set Statement

Declares a **Set** property procedure used to assign a value to a property.

```
[ <attrlist> ] Set(ByVal value [ As datatype ])
   [ block ]
End Set
```

Parts

attrlist
: Optional. List of attributes that apply to this **Set** block. Multiple attributes are separated by commas.

value
: Required. This parameter contains the new value for the property.

datatype
: Required if **Option Strict** is **On**. Declares the data type of the value parameter. The data type specified must be the same as the data type of the property where this **Set** statement is declared.

block
: Optional. The body of the **Set** procedure contains code to set the property value.

End Set
: Terminates a **Set** property procedure.

Each attribute in the *attrlist* part has the following syntax and parts:

```
attrname [({ attrargs | attrinit })]
```

attrlist Parts

attrname
: Required. Name of the attribute. Must be a valid Visual Basic identifier.

attrargs
: Optional. List of positional arguments for this attribute. Multiple arguments are separated by commas.

attrinit
: Optional. List of field or property initializers for this attribute. Multiple initializers are separated by commas.

Remarks

Visual Basic .NET calls the **Set** property procedure when the value of a property is changed in an assignment operation.

Example

This example uses the **Set** statement to set the value of a property.

```
Class PropClass
   Private PropVal As Integer
   Property Prop1() As Integer
      Get
         Return PropVal ' Same As Prop1 = PropVal
      End Get
      Set(ByVal Value As Integer)
         PropVal = Value
      End Set
   End Property
End Class
```

See Also

Get Statement, Property Statement

SetAttr Function

Sets attribute information for a file.

```
Public Sub SetAttr( _
   ByVal PathName As String, _
   ByVal Attributes As FileAttribute _
)
```

Parameters

PathName
: Required. **String** expression that specifies a file name. *PathName* may include directory or folder, and drive.

Attributes
: Required. Constant or numeric expression, whose sum specifies file attributes.

Settings

The *Attributes* argument enumeration values are:

Value	Constant	Description
Normal	**VbNormal**	Normal (default).
ReadOnly	**VbReadOnly**	Read-only.
Hidden	**VbHidden**	Hidden.
System	**VbSystem**	System file.
Volume	**VbVolume**	Volume label.
Directory	**VbDirectory**	Directory or folder.
Archive	**VbArchive**	File has changed since last backup.
Alias	**VbAlias**	File has a different name.

Note These enumerations are specified by the Visual Basic language. The names can be used anywhere in your code in place of the actual values.

Exceptions/Errors

Exception type	Error number	Condition
ArgumentException	52	*PathName* invalid or does not exist.
ArgumentException	5	*Attribute* type is invalid.

Remarks

A run-time error occurs if you try to set the attributes of an open file.

Example

This example uses the **SetAttr** function to set attributes for a file.

```
SetAttr("TESTFILE", vbHidden)   ' Set hidden attribute.
SetAttr("TESTFILE", vbHidden Or vbReadOnly)   ' Set hidden and read-only
   ' attributes.
```

See Also

FileAttr Function, GetAttr Function

Shadows

The **Shadows** keyword indicates that a declared programming element shadows an identically named element, or set of overloaded elements, in a base class. You can shadow any kind of declared element with any other kind. A shadowed element is unavailable in the derived class that shadows it.

The **Shadows** keyword is used in these contexts:

Class Statement

Const Statement

Declare Statement

Delegate Statement

Dim Statement

Enum Statement

Event Statement

Function Statement

Interface Statement

Property Statement

Structure Statement

Sub Statement

Shared

The **Shared** keyword indicates that one or more declared programming elements are shared. Shared elements are not associated with a specific instance of a class or structure. You can access them by qualifying them either with the class or structure name, or with the variable name of a specific instance of the class or structure.

The **Shared** keyword is used in these contexts:

Dim Statement

Event Statement

Function Statement

Property Statement

Sub Statement

Shell Function

Runs an executable program and returns an integer containing the program's process ID if it is still running.

```
Public Function Shell( _
   ByVal Pathname As String, _
   Optional ByVal Style As AppWinStyle = AppWinStyle.MinimizedFocus, _
   Optional ByVal Wait As Boolean = False, _
   Optional ByVal Timeout As Integer = -1 _
) As Integer
```

Parameters

Pathname

Required. **String**. Name of the program to execute, together with any required arguments and command-line switches. *Pathname* can also include the drive and the directory path or folder.

Style

Optional. **AppWinStyle**. A value chosen from the **AppWinStyle** enumeration corresponding to the style of the window in which the program is to be run. If *Style* is omitted, **Shell** uses **AppWinStyle.MinimizedFocus**, which starts the program minimized and with focus.

The *Style* argument can have one of the following settings:

Enumeration value	Description
AppWinStyle.Hide	The window is hidden and focus is given to the hidden window.
AppWinStyle.NormalFocus	The window is given focus and displayed in its most recent size and position.
AppWinStyle.MinimizedFocus	The window is given focus and displayed as an icon.
AppWinStyle.MaximizedFocus	The window is given focus and displayed using the entire screen.
AppWinStyle.NormalNoFocus	The window is set to its most recent size and position. The currently active window remains in focus.
AppWinStyle.MinimizedNoFocus	The window is displayed as an icon. The currently active window remains in focus.

Wait

Optional. **Boolean**. A value indicating whether the **Shell** function should wait for completion of the program. If *Wait* is omitted, **Shell** uses **False**.

Timeout

Optional. **Integer**. The number of milliseconds to wait for completion if *Wait* is **True**. If *Timeout* is omitted, **Shell** uses –1, which means there is no timeout and **Shell** does not return until the program completes. Therefore, if you omit *Timeout* or set it to –1, it is possible that **Shell** might never return control to your program.

Exceptions/Errors

Exception type	Error number	Condition
ArgumentException	5	*Style* is not within range 0 through 9, inclusive.
FileNotFoundException	53	**Shell** cannot start the named program.

Remarks

The return value of the **Shell** function depends on whether the program named in *Pathname* is still executing when **Shell** returns. If you set *Wait* to **True** and the program finishes before the timeout expires, **Shell** returns zero. If the timeout expires, or if you omit *Wait* or set it to **False**, **Shell** returns the process ID of the program. The process ID is a unique number that identifies the running program.

If the **Shell** function cannot start the named program, a **System.IO.FileNotFoundException** error occurs. This can happen, for example, when you attempt to run a 16-bit program, such as `command.com`, from an application using **System.Windows.Forms**. For a workaround, you can run a 32-bit program that calls the desired 16-bit program. In the case of `command.com`, you can run `cmd.exe` as an alternative.

By default, the **Shell** function runs the program asynchronously. This means that a program started with the **Shell** function might not finish executing before the statements following the **Shell** function are executed. If you want to wait for the program to finish before you continue, set *Wait* to **True**.

If the *Pathname* argument supplies the directory path as well as the file name, it is a good idea to enclose the entire specification in quotes, as the following example shows:

```
ID = Shell("""C:\Program Files\MyFile.exe"" -a -q", , True, 100000)
```

Each pair of adjacent double quotes (" ") within the string literal is interpreted as one double quote character in the string. Therefore, the preceding example presents the following string to the **Shell** function:

```
"C:\Program Files\MyFile.exe" -a -q
```

If you did not have the path enclosed in quotes, Windows would look for a file called Program.exe in the C:\ directory. If such a program had been installed at that location, for example by illicit tampering, it would be executed instead of MyFile.exe in the C:\Program Files directory.

Example

This example uses the **Shell** function to run an application specified by the user. Specifying **AppWinStyle.NormalFocus** as the second argument opens the application in normal size and gives it the focus.

```
Dim ProcID As Integer
   ' Run Calculator.
ProcID = Shell("C:\WINDOWS\CALC.EXE", AppWinStyle.NormalFocus)
```

See Also

AppActivate Function

Short Data Type

Short variables are stored as signed 16-bit (2-byte) integers ranging in value from –32,768 through 32,767.

> **Note** The **Short** data type can be converted to the **Integer**, **Long**, **Single**, **Double**, or **Decimal** data type without encountering a **System.OverflowException** error.

Appending the literal type character **S** to a literal forces it to the **Short** data type.

The equivalent .NET data type is **System.Int16**.

See Also

Data Type Summary, Type Conversion Functions, Conversion Summary, Byte Data Type, Integer Data Type, Long Data Type

Single Data Type

Single variables are stored as signed IEEE 32-bit (4-byte) single-precision floating-point numbers ranging in value from –3.4028235E+38 through –1.401298E–45 for negative values and from 1.401298E–45 through 3.4028235E+38 for positive values. Single-precision numbers store an approximation of a real number.

> **Note** The **Single** data type can be converted to the **Double** or **Decimal** data type without encountering a **System.OverflowException** error.

Appending the literal type character **F** to a literal forces it to the **Single** data type. Appending the identifier type character **!** to any identifier forces it to **Single**.

The equivalent .NET data type is **System.Single**.

See Also

Data Type Summary, Double Data Type, Type Conversion Functions, Conversion Summary

SLN Function

Returns a **Double** specifying the straight-line depreciation of an asset for a single period.

```
Function SLN( _
    ByVal Cost As Double, _
    ByVal Salvage As Double, _
    ByVal Life As Double _
) As Double
```

Parameters

Cost
Required. **Double** specifying initial cost of the asset.

Salvage
Required. **Double** specifying value of the asset at the end of its useful life.

Life
Required. **Double** specifying length of the useful life of the asset.

Exceptions/Errors

Exception type	Error number	Condition
ArgumentException	5	*Life* = 0.

Remarks

The depreciation period must be expressed in the same unit as the *Life* argument. All arguments must be positive numbers.

Example

This example uses the **SLN** function to return the straight-line depreciation of an asset for a single period given the asset's initial cost (`InitCost`), the salvage value at the end of the asset's useful life (`SalvageVal`), and the total life of the asset in years (`LifeTime`).

```
Sub TestSLN()
   Dim InitCost, SalvageVal, MonthLife As Double
   Dim LifeTime, Pdepr As Double
   Dim Fmt As String = "###,##0.00"    ' Define money format.
   Const YEARMONTHS As Integer = 12   ' Number of months in a year.

   InitCost = CDbl(InputBox("What's the initial cost of the asset?"))
   SalvageVal = CDbl(InputBox("What's the asset's value at the end of its useful life?"))
   MonthLife = CDbl(InputBox("What's the asset's useful life in months?"))
```

(continued)

(continued)

```
   Do While MonthLife < YEARMONTHS   ' Ensure period is >= 1 year.
      MsgBox("Asset life must be a year or more.")
      MonthLife = CDbl(InputBox("What's the asset's useful life in months?"))
   Loop
   LifeTime = MonthLife / YEARMONTHS   ' Convert months to years.
   If LifeTime <> Int(MonthLife / YEARMONTHS) Then
      LifeTime = Int(LifeTime + 1)   ' Round up to nearest year.
   End If
   Pdepr = SLN(InitCost, SalvageVal, LifeTime)
   MsgBox("The depreciation is " & Format(Pdepr, Fmt) & " per year.")
End Sub
```

See Also

DDB Function, FV Function, IPmt Function, IRR Function, MIRR Function, NPer Function, NPV Function, Pmt Function, PPmt Function, PV Function, Rate Function, SYD Function

Source Property

Returns or sets a **String** expression specifying the name of the object or application that originally generated the error. Read/write.

```
Public Property Source() As String
```

Remarks

The **Source** property specifies a **String** expression representing the object that generated the error; the expression is usually the object's class name or process ID. Use the **Source** property to provide information when your code is unable to handle an error generated in an accessed object. For example, if you access Microsoft Excel and it generates a `Division by zero` error, Microsoft Excel sets **Err.Number** to its error code for that error and sets **Source** to "Excel.Application".

When the application is generating an error from code, **Source** is your application's programmatic ID. Within a class, **Source** should contain a name having the form *project.class*. When an unexpected error occurs in your code, the **Source** property is automatically filled in. For errors in a module, **Source** contains the project name.

Example

This example demonstrates the use of the **Source** property in a typical error handling routine. When an error is raised from Class1, the string "Class1" is assigned to the **Source** property of the **Err** object. This string is then displayed in an informative message indicating the source and number of the error.

```
Public Class Class1
   Public Sub MySub()
      On Error Resume Next
      Err.Raise(60000, "Class1")
      MsgBox(Err.Source & " caused an error of type " & Err.Number)
   End Sub
End Class
```

See Also

Description Property, ErrorToString Function, GetObject Function, HelpContext Property, HelpFile Property, LastDLLError Property, Number Property, On Error Statement

Applies To

Err Object

Space Function

Returns a string consisting of the specified number of spaces.

```
Public Shared Function Space(ByVal Number As Integer) As String
```

Parameter

Number
Required. **Integer** expression. The number of spaces you want in the string.

Exceptions/Errors

Exception type	Error number	Condition
ArgumentException	5	*Number* < 0.

Remarks

The **Space** function is useful for formatting output and clearing data in fixed-length strings.

Example

This example uses the **Space** function to return a string consisting of a specified number of spaces.

```
Dim MyString As String
' Returns a string with 10 spaces.
MyString = Space(10)
' Inserts 10 spaces between two strings.
MyString = "Hello" & Space(10) & "World"
```

See Also

SPC Function

SPC Function

Used with the **Print** or **PrintLine** functions to position output.

```
Public Function SPC(ByVal Count As Short) As SPCInfo
```

Parameters

Count

Required. The number of spaces to insert before displaying or printing the next expression in a list.

Remarks

If *Count* is less than the output line width, the next print position immediately follows the number of spaces printed. If *Count* is greater than the output line width, **SPC** calculates the next print position using the formula:

```
currentprintposition + (Count Mod width)
```

For example, if the current print position is 24, the output line width is 80, and you specify **SPC**(90), the next print will start at position 34 (current print position + the remainder of 90/80). If the difference between the current print position and the output line width is less than *Count* (or *Count* **Mod** *width*), the **SPC** function skips to the beginning of the next line and generates spaces equal to *Count* - (*width* - *currentprintposition*).

Note Make sure your tabular columns are wide enough to accommodate wide letters.

Example

This example uses the **SPC** function to position output in a file and in the **Output** window.

```
' The SPC function can be used with the Print function.
FileOpen(1, "TESTFILE", OpenMode.Output)   ' Open file for output.
Print(1, "10 spaces between here", SPC(10), "and here.")
FileClose(1)   ' Close file.
```

The following statement causes the text to be printed in the **Output** window (using the **WriteLine** method), preceded by 30 spaces.

```
Debug.WriteLine(SPC(30), "Thirty spaces later...")
```

See Also

Mod Operator, Print, PrintLine Functions, Space Function, TAB Function, FileWidth Function

Split Function

Returns a zero-based, one-dimensional array containing a specified number of substrings.

```
Function Split(
   ByVal Expression As String,
   Optional ByVal Delimiter As String = " ",
   Optional ByVal Limit As Integer = -1,
   Optional ByVal Compare As CompareMethod = CompareMethod.Binary
) As String()
```

Parameters

Expression

Required. **String** expression containing substrings and delimiters. If *Expression* is a zero-length string (" "), *the* **Split** function returns an array with no elements and no data.

Delimiter

Optional. Single character used to identify substring limits. If *Delimiter* is omitted, the space character (" ") is assumed to be the delimiter. If *Delimiter* is a zero-length string, a single-element array containing the entire *Expression* string is returned.

Limit

Optional. Number of substrings to be returned; the default, –1, indicates that all substrings are returned.

Compare

Optional. Numeric value indicating the comparison to use when evaluating substrings. See "Settings" for values.

Settings

The *Compare* argument can have the following values:

Constant	Description
Binary	Performs a binary comparison
Text	Performs a textual comparison

Example

The following example demonstrates the **Split** function:

```
Dim myString As String = "Look at these!"
' Returns ["Look", "at", "these!"]
Dim myArray() As String = Split(myString)
```

See Also

Join Function

Static

The **Static** keyword indicates that one or more declared variables are static. Static variables remain in existence and retain their latest values after termination of the procedure in which they are declared.

The **Static** keyword is used in this context:

Dim Statement

Step

The **Step** keyword specifies an increment value for a loop counter.

The **Step** keyword is used in this context:

For...Next Statements

See Also

Visual Basic Language Keywords

Stop Statement

Suspends execution.

```
Stop
```

Remarks

You can place **Stop** statements anywhere in procedures to suspend execution. Using the **Stop** statement is similar to setting a breakpoint in the code.

The **Stop** statement suspends execution, but unlike **End**, it does not close any files or clear any variables, unless it is encountered in a compiled executable (.exe) file.

> **Note** If the **Stop** statement is encountered in code that is running outside of the integrated development environment (IDE), the debugger is invoked. This is true regardless of whether the code was compiled in debug or retail mode.

Example

This example uses the **Stop** statement to suspend execution for each iteration through the **For...Next** loop.

```
Dim I As Integer
For I = 1 To 10    ' Start For...Next loop.
   Debug.WriteLine (I)    ' Print I to the Output window.
   Stop    ' Stop during each iteration and wait for user to resume.
Next I
```

See Also

End Statement

Str Function

Returns a **String** representation of a number.

```
Public Shared Function Str(ByVal Number As Object) As String
```

Parameter

Number
Required. An **Object** containing any valid numeric expression.

Exceptions/Errors

Exception type	Error number	Condition
ArgumentNullException	5	*Number* is not specified.
InvalidCastException	5	*Number* is not a numeric type.

Remarks

When numbers are converted to strings, a leading space is always reserved for the sign of *Number*. If *Number* is positive, the returned string contains a leading space, and the plus sign is implied. A negative number will include the minus sign (–) and no leading space.

Use the **Format** function to convert numeric values you want formatted as dates, times, or currency or in other user-defined formats. Unlike the **Str** function, the **Format** function doesn't include a leading space for the sign of *Number*.

Note The **Str** function recognizes only the period (.) as a valid decimal separator. If different decimal separators are used (for example, in international applications), use the **CStr** function to convert a number to a string.

Example

This example uses the **Str** function to return a **String** representation of a number. When a positive number is converted to a string, a leading space is always reserved for its sign.

```
Dim MyString As String
MyString = Str(459)   ' Returns " 459".
MyString = Str(-459.65)   ' Returns "-459.65".
MyString = Str(459.001)   ' Returns " 459.001".
```

See Also

Format Function, Type Conversion Functions, Val Function, ArgumentNullException

StrComp Function

Returns –1, 0, or 1, based on the result of a string comparison.

```
Public Shared Function StrComp( _
   ByVal String1 As String, _
   ByVal String2 As String, _
   <Microsoft.VisualBasic.OptionCompareAttribute> _
   Optional ByVal Compare As Microsoft.VisualBasic.CompareMethod _
) As Integer
```

Parameters

String1
Required. Any valid **String** expression.

String2
Required. Any valid **String** expression.

Compare
Optional. Specifies the type of string comparison. If *compare* is omitted, the **Option Compare** setting determines the type of comparison.

Settings

The *Compare* argument settings are:

Constant	Description
Binary	Performs a binary comparison, based on a sort order derived from the internal binary representations of the characters.
Text	Performs a text comparison, based on a case-insensitive text sort order determined by your system's **LocaleID** value.

Return Values

The **StrComp** function has the following return values:

If	StrComp returns
String1 sorts ahead of *String2*	–1
String1 is equal to *String2*	0
String1 sorts after *String2*	1

Exceptions/Errors

Exception type	Error number	Condition
ArgumentException	5	*Compare* value is invalid.

Remarks

The strings are compared by alphanumeric sort values beginning with the first character. For further information on binary comparisons, textual comparisons, and sort order, see "Option Compare Statement."

Example

This example uses the **StrComp** function to return the results of a string comparison. If the third argument is omitted, a binary comparison is performed.

```
Dim MyStr1, MyStr2 As String
Dim MyComp As Integer
MyStr1 = "ABCD"
MyStr2 = "abcd"    ' Defines variables.
' The two strings sort equally. Returns 0
MyComp = StrComp(MyStr1, MyStr2, CompareMethod.Text)
' MyStr1 sorts after MyStr2. Returns -1.
MyComp = StrComp(MyStr1, MyStr2, CompareMethod.Binary)
' MyStr2 sorts before MyStr1. Returns 1.
MyComp = StrComp(MyStr2, MyStr1)
```

See Also

InStr Function

StrConv Function

Returns a string converted as specified.

```
Public Shared Function StrConv( _
   ByVal Str As String, _
   ByVal Conversion As Microsoft.VisualBasic.VbStrConv, _
   Optional ByVal LocaleID As Integer,
) As String
```

Parameters

Str

Required. **String** expression to be converted.

Conversion

Required. **Microsoft.VisualBasic.VbStrConv** member. The enumeration value specifying the type of conversion to perform.

LocaleID

Optional. The **LocaleID** value, if different from the system **LocaleID** value. (The system **LocaleID** value is the default.)

Settings

The *Conversion* argument settings are:

Enumeration member	Description
VbStrConv.None	Performs no conversion
VbStrConv.LinguisticCasing	Uses linguistic rules for casing, rather than File System (default). Valid with UpperCase and LowerCase only.
VbStrConv.UpperCase	Converts the string to uppercase characters.
VbStrConv.LowerCase	Converts the string to lowercase characters.
VbStrConv.ProperCase	Converts the first letter of every word in string to uppercase.
VbStrConv.Wide*	Converts narrow (half-width) characters in the string to wide (full-width) characters.
VbStrConv.Narrow*	Converts wide (full-width) characters in the string to narrow (half-width) characters.
VbStrConv.Katakana**	Converts Hiragana characters in the string to Katakana characters.

Enumeration member	Description
VbStrConv.Hiragana**	Converts Katakana characters in the string to Hiragana characters.
VbStrConv.SimplifiedChinese*	Converts Traditional Chinese characters to Simplified Chinese.
VbStrConv.TraditionalChinese*	Converts Simplified Chinese characters to Traditional Chinese.

* Applies to Asian locales.
** Applies to Japan only.

> **Note** These constants are specified in the .NET common language runtime. As a result, they may be used anywhere in your code in place of the actual values. Most can be combined, for example, `UpperCase + Wide`, except when they are mutually exclusive, for example, `VbStrConv.Wide + VbStrConv.Narrow`.

The following are valid word separators for proper casing: Null (**Chr$(0)**), horizontal tab (**Chr$(9)**), linefeed (**Chr$(10)**), vertical tab (**Chr$(11)**), form feed (**Chr$(12)**), carriage return (**Chr$(13)**), space (single-byte character set) (**Chr$(32)**). The actual value for a space varies by country/region for the double-byte character set.

Exceptions/Errors

Exception type	Error number	Condition
ArgumentException	5	Unsupported *LocaleID, Conversion* < 0 or > 2048, or unsupported conversion for specified locale.

Remarks

The constants **VbStrConv.Wide**, **VbStrConv.Narrow**, **VbStrConv.Simplified Chinese**, **VbStrConv.Traditional Chinese**, **VbStrConv.Katakana**, and **VbStrConv.Hiragana** can cause run-time errors when used in locales where they do not apply, but not always: the constants **VbStrConv.Katakana** and **VbStrConv.Hiragana** can be used in a non-Japanese system with the Japanese Language Pack installed. In addition, use of the constants **VbStrConv.Wide** and **VbStrConv.Narrow** is supported on any system with a double-byte character set (DBCS) language installed.

Example

This example converts text into all lowercase letters.

```
Dim sText, sNewText As String
sText = "Hello World"
sNewText = StrConv(sText, VbStrConv.LowerCase)
Debug.WriteLine (sNewText)   ' Outputs "hello world".
```

See Also

Chr, ChrW Functions, String Data Type, Type Conversion Functions

StrDup Function

Returns a string or object consisting of the specified character repeated the specified number of times.

```
Public Shared Function StrDup( _
   ByVal Number As Integer, _
   ByVal Character As { Char | String } _
) As String
```

-or-

```
Public Shared Function StrDup( _
   ByVal Number As Integer, _
   ByVal Character As Object _
) As Object
```

Parameters

Number

Required. **Integer** expression. The length to the string to be returned.

Character

Required. Any valid **Char**, **String**, or **Object** expression. Only the first character of the expression will be used. If Character is of type Object, it must contain either a **Char** or a **String** value.

Exceptions/Errors

Exception type	Error number	Condition
ArgumentException	5	*Number* < 0 or *Character* type is invalid.
ArgumentNullException	5	*Character* is **Nothing.**

Remarks

This function returns a **String** made up of repeated characters. The character that makes up the string is the first character in the *Character* argument, and it is duplicated *Number* number of times.

Example

This example uses the **StrDup** function to return a string of duplicated characters.

```
Dim aString As String = "Wow! What a string!"
Dim aObject As New Object()
Dim myString As String
aObject = "This is a String contained within an Object"
myString = StrDup(5, "P")   ' Returns "PPPPP"
myString = StrDup(10, aString)   ' Returns "WWWWWWWWWW"
myString = StrDup(6, aObject)   ' Returns "TTTTTT"
```

See Also

SPC Function

String Data Type

String variables are stored as sequences of unsigned 16-bit (2-byte) numbers ranging in value from 0 through 65535. Each number represents a single Unicode character. A string can contain up to approximately 2 billion (2 ^ 31) Unicode® characters.

The first 128 code points (0–127) of Unicode correspond to the letters and symbols on a standard U.S. keyboard. These first 128 code points are the same as those defined by the ASCII character set. The second 128 code points (128–255) represent special characters, such as Latin-based alphabet letters, accents, currency symbols, and fractions. The remaining code points are used for a wide variety of symbols, including worldwide textual characters, diacritics, and mathematical and technical symbols.

Appending the identifier type character **$** to any identifier forces it to the **String** data type.

The equivalent .NET data type is **System.String**.

See Also

Data Type Summary, Type Conversion Functions, Conversion Summary

StrReverse Function

Returns a string in which the character order of a specified string is reversed.

```
Public Function StrReverse(ByVal Expression As String) As String
```

Parameters

Expression
: Required. String expression whose characters are to be reversed. If *Expression* is a zero-length string (" "), a zero-length string is returned.

Example

```
Dim myString As String = "ABCDEFG"
Dim revString As String
' Returns "GFEDCBA"
revString = StrReverse(myString)
```

See Also

InStrRev Function

Structure Statement

Used at module or class level to declare a structure and define the characteristics of its members.

```
[ <attrlist> ] [{ Public | Protected | Friend | Protected Friend | Private }]
[ Shadows ]
Structure name
   [ Implements interfacenames ]
   variabledeclarations
   [ proceduredeclarations ]
End Structure
```

Parts

attrlist
  Optional. List of attributes that apply to this structure. Multiple attributes are separated by commas.

Public
  Optional. Structures declared with the **Public** keyword have public access. There are no restrictions on the accessibility of public structures.

Protected
  Optional. Structures declared with the **Protected** keyword have protected access. They are accessible only from within their own class or from a derived class. Protected access can be specified only on members of classes. It is not a superset of friend access.

Friend
  Optional. Structures declared with the **Friend** keyword have friend access. They are accessible from within the program that contains their declaration and from anywhere else in the same assembly.

Protected Friend
  Optional. Structures declared with the **Protected Friend** modifiers have the union of protected and friend access. They can be used by code in the same assembly, as well as by code in derived classes. Protected friend access can be specified only on members of classes.

Private
  Optional. Structures declared with the **Private** modifier have private access. They are accessible only from within their declaration context, including from members of any nested types such as procedures.

Shadows
  Optional. Indicates that this structure shadows an identically named programming element, or set of overloaded elements, in a base class. You can shadow any kind of declared element with any other kind. A shadowed element is unavailable in the derived class that shadows it.

name
  Required. Name of the structure. Must be a valid Visual Basic identifier.

Implements
Optional. Indicates that this structure implements the members of one or more interfaces.

interfacenames
Required if the **Implements** statement is used. The names of the interfaces implemented by this structure. If you use the **Implements** statement, it must immediately follow the **Structure** statement, and you must implement every member defined by every interface you specify.

variabledeclarations
Required. One or more **Dim**, **Event**, **Friend**, **Private**, or **Public** statements declaring variables and events that serve as data members of the structure. These declarations follow the same rules as they do outside of a structure.

You can also define constants and properties in the structure, but you must declare at least one nonshared variable or event.

proceduredeclarations
Optional. Zero or more declarations of **Function**, **Property**, or **Sub** procedures that serve as method members of the structure. These declarations follow the same rules as they do outside of a structure.

Each attribute in the *attrlist* part has the following syntax and parts:

```
attrname [({ attrargs | attrinit })]
```

attrlist Parts

attrname
Required. Name of the attribute. Must be a valid Visual Basic identifier.

attrargs
Optional. List of positional arguments for this attribute. Multiple arguments are separated by commas.

attrinit
Optional. List of field or property initializers for this attribute. Multiple initializers are separated by commas.

Remarks

The **Structure** statement can appear only at module, namespace, or file level. This means you can declare structures in a source file or inside a module, interface, or class, but not inside a procedure. You can also define one structure inside another, but you cannot access its members through the outer structure. Instead, you must declare a variable of the inner structure's data type.

Structures can be accessed from anywhere within the module or class in which they are declared. A structure is **Friend** by default. To specify the accessibility in more detail, include **Public**, **Protected**, **Friend**, **Protected Friend**, or **Private** in the **Structure** statement.

You must declare every data member of a structure. This means every statement in the *variabledeclarations* part must use **Dim**, **Friend**, **Private**, or **Public**. If **Option Strict** is **On**, you must also include the **As** clause in every statement. Members declared with **Dim** default to **Public** access, and members declared without the **As** clause default to the **Object** data type.

You must define at least one nonshared variable or event in a structure. You cannot have only constants, properties, and procedures, even if some of them are nonshared.

The scope of every structure member is the entire structure.

You cannot initialize the value of any data member of a structure as part of its declaration. You must either initialize a data member by means of a parameterized constructor on the structure, or assign a value to the member after you have created an instance of the structure.

Structures support many of the same features as classes. For example, structures can have properties and methods, they can implement interfaces, and they can have parameterized constructors. However, there are significant differences between structures and classes in areas such as inheritance, declarations, and usage.

Example

This example uses the **Structure** statement to define a set of related data for an employee. It shows the use of public, friend, and private members to reflect the sensitivity of the data items.

```
Public Structure Employee
   ' Public members, accessible throughout declaration region.
   Public FirstName As String
   Public MiddleName As String
   Public LastName As String
   ' Friend members, accessible anywhere within the same assembly.
   Friend EmployeeNumber As Integer
   Friend BusinessPhone As Long
   ' Private members, accessible only within the structure itself.
   Private HomePhone As Long
   Private Salary As Double
   Private Bonus As Double
   ' Procedure member, which can access structure's private members.
   Friend Sub CalculateBonus(ByVal Rate As Single)
      Bonus = Salary * CDbl(Rate)
   End Sub
End Structure
```

See Also

Dim Statement, Implements Statement

Sub Statement

Declares the name, arguments, and code that define a **Sub** procedure.

```
[ <attrlist> ] [{ Overloads | Overrides | Overridable |
NotOverridable | MustOverride | Shadows | Shared }]
[{ Public | Protected | Friend | Protected Friend | Private }]
Sub name [(arglist)] [ Implements interface.definedname ]
   [ statements ]
   [ Exit Sub ]
   [ statements ]
End Sub
```

Parts

attrlist
: Optional. List of attributes that apply to this procedure. Multiple attributes are separated by commas.

Overloads
: Optional. Indicates that this **Sub** procedure overloads one or more procedures defined with the same name in a base class. The argument list in this declaration must be different from the argument list of every overloaded procedure. The lists must differ in the number of arguments, their data types, or both. This allows the compiler to distinguish which version to use.

  You do not have to use the **Overloads** keyword when you are defining multiple overloaded procedures in the same class. However, if you use **Overloads** in one of the declarations, you must use it in all of them.

  You cannot specify both **Overloads** and **Shadows** in the same procedure declaration.

Overrides
: Optional. Indicates that this **Sub** procedure overrides an identically named procedure in a base class. The number and data types of the arguments must exactly match those of the base class procedure.

Overridable
: Optional. Indicates that this **Sub** procedure can be overridden by an identically named procedure in a derived class. **Overridable** is the default setting for a procedure that itself overrides a base class procedure.

NotOverridable
: Optional. Indicates that this **Sub** procedure cannot be overridden in a derived class. **NotOverridable** is the default setting for a procedure that does not itself override a base class procedure.

MustOverride
: Optional. Indicates that this **Sub** procedure is not implemented in this class and must be implemented in a derived class for that class to be creatable.

Shadows

Optional. Indicates that this **Sub** procedure shadows an identically named programming element, or set of overloaded elements, in a base class. You can shadow any kind of declared element with any other kind. If you shadow a procedure with another procedure, the arguments and the return type do not have to match those in the base class procedure. A shadowed element is unavailable in the derived class that shadows it.

You cannot specify both **Overloads** and **Shadows** in the same procedure declaration.

Shared

Optional. Indicates that this **Sub** procedure is a shared procedure. This means it is not associated with a specific instance of a class or structure. You can call a shared procedure by qualifying it either with the class or structure name, or with the variable name of a specific instance of the class or structure.

Public

Optional. Procedures declared with the **Public** keyword have public access. There are no restrictions on the accessibility of public procedures.

Protected

Optional. Procedures declared with the **Protected** keyword have protected access. They are accessible only from within their own class or from a derived class. Protected access can be specified only on members of classes. It is not a superset of friend access.

Friend

Optional. Procedures declared with the **Friend** keyword have friend access. They are accessible from within the program that contains their declaration and from anywhere else in the same assembly.

Protected Friend

Optional. Procedures declared with the **Protected Friend** keywords have the union of protected and friend access. They can be used by code in the same assembly, as well as by code in derived classes. Protected friend access can be specified only on members of classes.

Private

Optional. Procedures declared with the **Private** keyword have private access. They are accessible only from within their declaration context, including from members of any nested types such as procedures.

name

Required. Name of the **Sub** procedure. Must be a valid Visual Basic identifier.

arglist

Optional. List of variables or expressions representing arguments that are passed to the **Sub** procedure when it is called. Multiple arguments are separated by commas. If you supply an argument list, you must enclose it in parentheses.

Implements

Optional. Indicates that this **Sub** procedure implements a **Sub** procedure defined by an interface.

interface

Required if **Implements** is supplied. The interface implemented by the class or structure containing this **Sub** procedure. The class or structure must specify *interface* in an **Implements** statement immediately following the **Class** or **Structure** statement.

definedname

Required if **Implements** is supplied. The name by which the **Sub** procedure is defined in *interface*. The name of this **Sub** procedure (in *name*) does not have to be the same as *definedname*.

statements

Optional. A block of statements to be executed within the **Sub** procedure.

End Sub

Terminates the definition of this **Sub** procedure.

Each argument in the *arglist* part has the following syntax and parts:

```
[ <attrlist> ] [ Optional ] [{ ByVal | ByRef }] [ ParamArray ]
argname[( )] [ As argtype ] [ = defaultvalue ]
```

arglist Parts

attrlist

Optional. List of attributes that apply to this argument. Multiple attributes are separated by commas.

Optional

Optional. Indicates that this argument is not required when the procedure is called. If this keyword is used, all subsequent arguments in *arglist* must also be optional and be declared using the **Optional** keyword. Every optional argument declaration must supply the *defaultvalue* clause. **Optional** cannot be used for any argument if **ParamArray** is used.

ByVal

Optional. Indicates that the procedure cannot replace or reassign the underlying variable element in the calling code. However, if the argument is a reference type, the procedure can modify the contents or members of the underlying object. **ByVal** is the default in Visual Basic.

ByRef

Optional. Indicates that the procedure can modify the underlying variable in the calling code the same way the calling code itself can.

ParamArray

Optional. Used only as the last argument in *arglist* to indicate that the final argument is an optional array of elements of the specified type. The **ParamArray** keyword allows you to pass an arbitrary number of arguments to the procedure. A **ParamArray** argument is always passed **ByVal**.

argname

Required. Name of the variable representing the argument. Must be a valid Visual Basic identifier.

argtype

Optional unless **Option Strict** is **On**. Data type of the argument passed to the procedure. Can be **Boolean**, **Byte**, **Char**, **Date**, **Decimal**, **Double**, **Integer**, **Long**, **Object**, **Short**, **Single**, or **String**; or the name of an enumeration, structure, class, or interface.

defaultvalue

Required for **Optional** arguments. Any constant or constant expression that evaluates to the data type of the argument. If the type is **Object**, or a class, interface, array, or structure, the default value can only be **Nothing**.

Each attribute in the *attrlist* part has the following syntax and parts:

```
attrname [({ attrargs | attrinit })]
```

attrlist Parts

attrname

Required. Name of the attribute. Must be a valid Visual Basic identifier.

attrargs

Optional. List of positional arguments for this attribute. Multiple arguments are separated by commas.

attrinit

Optional. List of field or property initializers for this attribute. Multiple initializers are separated by commas.

Remarks

All executable code must be in procedures. You can define a **Sub** procedure inside a module, class, interface, or structure, but not inside another procedure.

Sub procedures are **Public** by default. To specify a different accessibility, include **Protected**, **Friend**, **Protected Friend**, or **Private** in the declaration.

When the **Sub** procedure returns to the calling program, execution continues with the statement following the statement that called it.

The **Exit Sub** statement causes an immediate exit from a **Sub** procedure. Any number of **Exit Sub** statements can appear anywhere in the procedure.

You can also use the **Return** statement to immediately exit the procedure, as the following example shows:

```
Sub MySub(ByVal Q As String)
   ' ...
   Return
   ' ...
End Sub
```

Any number of **Return** statements can appear anywhere in the procedure. You can also mix **Exit Sub** and **Return** statements.

A **Sub** procedure, like a **Function** procedure, is a separate procedure that can take arguments and perform a series of statements. However, unlike a **Function** procedure, which returns a value, a **Sub** procedure cannot be used in an expression.

You call a **Sub** procedure by using the procedure name, followed by the argument list in parentheses, in a statement. You can omit the parentheses only if you are not supplying any arguments. You can optionally use the **Call** statement to call a **Sub** procedure. This can improve the readability of your program.

Example

This example uses the **Sub** statement to define the name, arguments, and code that form the body of a **Sub** procedure.

```
' Sub procedure definition.
' Sub procedure with two arguments.
Sub SubComputeArea(ByVal Length As Double, ByVal Width As Double)
   Dim Area As Double   ' Declare local variable.
   If Length = 0 Or Width = 0 Then
      ' If either argument = 0.
      Exit Sub ' Exit Sub immediately.
   End If
   Area = Length * Width   ' Calculate area of rectangle.
   Debug.WriteLine(Area)   ' Print Area to Immediate window.
End Sub
```

See Also

Call Statement, Function Statement, Dim Statement, Implements Statement

Switch Function

Evaluates a list of expressions and returns an **Object** value of an expression associated with the first expression in the list that is **True**.

```
Public Function Switch( _
   ByVal ParamArray VarExpr() As Object _
) As Object
```

Parameter

VarExpr()

Required. **Object** parameter array. Must have an even number of elements. You can supply a list of **Object** variables or expressions separated by commas, or a single-dimensional array of **Object** elements.

Exceptions/Errors

Exception type	Error number	Condition
ArgumentException	5	Number of arguments is odd.

Remarks

The **Switch** function argument *VarExpr* consists of paired expressions and values. The **Switch** function evaluates the expressions from lowest to highest subscript in *VarExpr*, and returns the value associated with the first expression that evaluates to **True**. For example, if *VarExpr(0)* is **True**, **Switch** returns *VarExpr(1)*, and if *VarExpr(0)* is **False** but *VarExpr(2)* is **True**, **Switch** returns *VarExpr(3)*, and so on.

If you do not supply the *VarExpr* argument, **Switch** returns **Nothing**. If the number of elements in *VarExpr* is not divisible by two, an **ArgumentException** error occurs.

> **Note** The expressions in the argument list can include function calls. As part of preparing the argument list for the call to **Switch**, the Visual Basic compiler calls every function in every expression. This means that you cannot rely on a particular function not being called if an expression earlier in the argument list is **True**.

Example

This example uses the **Switch** function to return the name of a language that matches the name of a city. It requires that **Option Strict** be **Off**.

```
Function MatchUp (CityName As String) As String
   Return Microsoft.VisualBasic.Switch(CityName = "London", "English", _
      CityName = "Rome", "Italian", CityName = "Paris", "French")
End Function
```

Since the **System.Diagnostics** namespace contains a class called **Switch**, a call to the **Switch** function must be qualified with the **Microsoft.VisualBasic** namespace.

See Also

Choose Function, IIf Function, Select...Case Statements, Switch Class

SYD Function

Returns a **Double** specifying the sum-of-years digits depreciation of an asset for a specified period.

```
Function SYD( _
   ByVal Cost As Double, _
   ByVal Salvage As Double, _
   ByVal Life As Double, _
   ByVal Period As Double _
) As Double
```

Parameters

Cost
: Required. **Double** specifying initial cost of the asset.

Salvage
: Required. **Double** specifying value of the asset at the end of its useful life.

Life
: Required. **Double** specifying length of the useful life of the asset.

Period
: Required. **Double** specifying period for which asset depreciation is calculated.

Exceptions/Errors

Exception type	Error number	Condition
ArgumentException	5	*Salvage* < 0, *Period* > *Life*, or *Period* <=0.

Remarks

The *Life* and *Period* arguments must be expressed in the same units. For example, if *Life* is given in months, *Period* must also be given in months. All arguments must be positive numbers.

Example

This example uses the **SYD** function to return the depreciation of an asset for a specified period given the asset's initial cost (`InitCost`), the salvage value at the end of the asset's useful life (`SalvageVal`), and the total life of the asset in years (`LifeTime`). The period in years for which the depreciation is calculated is `PDepr`.

```
Sub TestSYD()
   Dim InitCost, SalvageVal, MonthLife, DepYear, LifeTime, Pdepr As Double
   Dim Fmt As String = "###,##0.00"    ' Define money format.
   Const YEARMONTHS As Integer = 12  ' Number of months in a year.
   InitCost = CDbl(InputBox("What's the initial cost of the asset?"))
   SalvageVal = CDbl(InputBox("What's the asset's value at the end of its life?"))
   MonthLife = CDbl(InputBox("What's the asset's useful life in months?"))
```

(continued)

(continued)

```
    Do While MonthLife < YEARMONTHS   ' Ensure period is >= 1 year.
       MsgBox("Asset life must be a year or more.")
       MonthLife = CDbl(InputBox("What's the asset's useful life in months?"))
    Loop
    LifeTime = MonthLife / YEARMONTHS   ' Convert months to years.
    If LifeTime <> Int(MonthLife / YEARMONTHS) Then
       LifeTime = Int(LifeTime + 1)   ' Round up to nearest year.
    End If
    DepYear = CInt(InputBox("For which year do you want depreciation?"))
    Do While DepYear < 1 Or DepYear > LifeTime
       MsgBox("You must enter at least 1 but not more than " & LifeTime)
       DepYear = CInt(InputBox("For what year do you want depreciation?"))
    Loop
    Pdepr = SYD(InitCost, SalvageVal, LifeTime, DepYear)
    MsgBox("The depreciation for year " & DepYear & " is " & Format(Pdepr, Fmt) & ".")
End Sub
```

See Also

DDB Function, FV Function, IPmt Function, IRR Function, MIRR Function, NPer Function, NPV Function, Pmt Function, PPmt Function, PV Function, Rate Function, SLN Function

SyncLock Statement

Allows statements to be synchronized on a single expression.

```
SyncLock expression
...[ block ]
End SyncLock
```

Parts

expression
    Required. A unique collection of operators and values that yield a single result.

block
    Optional. The statements that will execute in sequence.

End SyncLock
    Terminates a **SyncLock** procedure.

Remarks

The **SyncLock** statement ensures that multiple threads do not execute the same statements at the same time. When the thread reaches the **SyncLock** block, it evaluates the expression and maintains this exclusivity until it has a lock on the object that is returned by the expression. This prevents an expression from changing values during the running of several threads, which can give unexpected results from your code.

Note The type of the expression in a **SyncLock** statement must be a reference type, such as a class, a module, an interface, array or delegate.

Example

```
Class Cache
   Private Shared Sub Add(ByVal x As Object)
      SyncLock GetType(Cache)
      End SyncLock
   End Sub

   Private Shared Sub Remove(ByVal x As Object)
      SyncLock GetType(Cache)
      End SyncLock
   End Sub
End Class
```

SystemTypeName Function

Returns a **String** value containing the system data type name of a variable.

```
Public Function SystemTypeName(ByVal VbName As String) As String
```

Parameter

VbName

Required. A **String** variable containing a Visual Basic .NET type name.

Remarks

SystemTypeName returns the fully qualified common language runtime type name corresponding to the Visual Basic type name. For example, if *VbName* contains "Date", **SystemTypeName** returns "System.DateTime". If **SystemTypeName** does not recognize the value of *VbName*, it returns **Nothing** (not the string "Nothing").

Example

This example uses the **SystemTypeName** function to return data type names for several variables.

```
Dim VbLongName As String = "Long"
Dim VbDateName As String = "Date"
Dim VbBadName As String = "Number"
Dim MySysName As String
MySysName = SystemTypeName(VbLongName)   ' Returns "System.Int64".
MySysName = SystemTypeName(VbDateName)   ' Returns "System.DateTime".
MySysName = SystemTypeName(VbBadName)   ' Returns Nothing.
```

See Also

Data Type Summary, String Data Type, VbTypeName Function

TAB Function

Used with the **Print** or **PrintLine** functions to position output.

```
Public Overloads Function TAB() As TABInfo
```

-or-

```
Public Overloads Function TAB(ByVal Column As Short) As TABInfo
```

Parameters

Column

Optional. The column number moved to before displaying or printing the next expression in a list. If omitted, **TAB** moves the insertion point to the beginning of the next print zone.

Remarks

If the current print position on the current line is greater than *Column*, **TAB** skips to the column value equal to *Column* on the next output line. If *Column* is less than 1, **TAB** moves the print position to column 1. If *Column* is greater than the output line width, **TAB** calculates the next print position using the formula:

```
Column Mod width
```

For example, if *width* is 80 and you specify **TAB**(90), the next print will start at column 10 (the remainder of 90/80). If *Column* is less than the current print position, printing begins on the next line at the calculated print position. If the calculated print position is greater than the current print position, printing begins at the calculated print position on the same line.

The leftmost print position on an output line is always 1. When you use the **Print** or **PrintLine** functions to print to files, the rightmost print position is the current width of the output file, which you can set using the **FileWidth** function.

Note Make sure your tabular columns are wide enough to accommodate wide letters.

Example

This example uses the **TAB** function to position output in a file and in the **Output** window.

```
FileOpen(1, "TESTFILE", OpenMode.Output) ' Open file for output.
' The second word prints at column 20.
Print(1, "Hello", TAB(20), "World.")
' If the argument is omitted, cursor is moved to the next print zone.
Print(1, "Hello", TAB(), "World")
FileClose(1)
```

The **TAB** function can also be used with the **WriteLine** method. The following statement prints text starting at column 10.

```
Debug.WriteLine(TAB(10), "10 columns from start.")
```

See Also

Mod Operator; Print, PrintLine Functions; Space Function; SPC Function; FileWidth Function

Then

The **Then** keyword introduces a statement block to be compiled or executed if a tested condition is true.

The **Then** keyword is used in these contexts:

#If...Then...#Else Directives

If...Then...Else Statements

See Also

Visual Basic Language Keywords

Throw Statement

Creates an exception within a procedure.

```
Throw expression
```

Part

expression
Required. Provides information about the exception to be thrown.

Remarks

The **Throw** statement creates an exception that you can handle with structured exception-handling code (**Try**...**Catch**...**Finally**) or unstructured exception-handling code (**On Error GoTo**). You can use the **Throw** statement to trap errors within your code, because Visual Basic moves up the call stack until it finds the appropriate exception-handling code.

Example

The following code uses the **Throw** statement to create an exception:

```
' Throws a new exception.
Throw New System.Exception("An exception has occurred.")
```

See Also

Try...Catch...Finally Statements, On Error Statement

TimeOfDay Property

Returns or sets a **Date** value containing the current time of day according to your system.

```
Public Property TimeOfDay() As DateTime
```

Remarks

The **Date** data type includes date components. When returning the system time, **TimeOfDay** sets these all to 1, so the returned value represents the first day of the year 1. When setting the system time, **TimeOfDay** ignores the date components.

To access the current system time as a **String**, use the **TimeString** property.

To get or set the current system date, use the **Today** property.

Example

This example uses the **TimeOfDay** property to return the current system time.

```
Dim MyTime As Date
MyTime = TimeOfDay   ' Return current system time.
```

See Also

Timer Property, TimeString Property, Today Property

Timer Property

Returns a **Double** value representing the number of seconds elapsed since midnight.

```
ReadOnly Public Property Timer() As Double
```

Remarks

The **Timer** property returns both the seconds and the milliseconds since midnight. The seconds are in the integral part of the return value, and the milliseconds are in the fractional part.

Example

This example uses the **Timer** function to pause the application. It can perform other processing during the pause.

```
Dim Start, Finish, TotalTime As Double
If (MsgBox("Press Yes to pause for 5 seconds", MsgBoxStyle.YesNo)) = _
   MsgBoxResult.Yes Then
   Start = Timer   ' Set start time (seconds).
   Finish = Start + 5.0   ' Set end time for 5-second duration.
```

```
   Do While Timer < Finish
      ' Do other processing while waiting for 5 seconds to elapse.
   Loop
   TotalTime = Timer - Start   ' Calculate total time.
   MsgBox "Paused for " & TotalTime & " seconds"
Else
   End
End If
```

See Also

Randomize Statement, TimeOfDay Property, Today Property

TimeSerial Function

Returns a **Date** value representing a specified hour, minute, and second, with the date information set relative to January 1 of the year 1.

```
Public Function TimeSerial( _
   ByVal Hour As Integer, _
   ByVal Minute As Integer, _
   ByVal Second As Integer _
) As DateTime
```

Parameters

Hour

Required. **Integer** expression from 0 through 23. However, values outside this range are also accepted.

Minute

Required. **Integer** expression from 0 through 59. However, values outside this range are also accepted. The value of *Minute* is added to the calculated hour, so a negative value specifies minutes before that hour.

Second

Required. **Integer** expression from 0 through 59. However, values outside this range are also accepted. The value of *Second* is added to the calculated minute, so a negative value specifies seconds before that minute.

Exceptions/Errors

Exception type	Error number	Condition
ArgumentException	5	Argument is outside the range –2,147,483,648 through 2,147,483,647
ArgumentOutOfRangeException	9	Calculated time is less than negative 24 hours.

Remarks

The following example demonstrates negative, zero, and positive argument values. Here, the **TimeSerial** function returns a time representing 15 minutes before three hours before noon, or 8:45:00 A.M.:

```
Dim AlarmTime As Date = TimeSerial(12 - 3, -15, 0)
```

If either *Minute* or *Second* exceeds its normal range, it is applied to the next larger unit as appropriate. For example, if you specify 75 minutes, it is evaluated as one hour and 15 minutes. If any argument is outside the range –2,147,483,648 through 2,147,483,647, an **ArgumentException** error occurs.

TimeSerial reduces the total seconds modulo 86,400, which is the number of seconds in a day. Therefore, the returned time is always between 00:00:00 and 23:59:59.

The **Date** data type includes date components. **TimeSerial** sets all of these to 1, so the returned value represents the first day of the year 1. However, if the values of the arguments cause the calculated time to exceed 24 hours, the day is incremented as necessary. In the following example, the values of *Hour* and *Minute* result in a combined time of more than 24 hours.

```
MsgBox(TimeSerial(23, 75, 0))  ' Displays "1/2/0001 12:15:00 AM"
```

If the values of the arguments result in a negative calculated time, the date information is set to 1/1/0001 and the time information is adjusted to be between 00:00:00 and 23:59:59. However, if the calculated time is less than negative 24 hours, an **ArgumentOutOfRangeException** error occurs.

Since every **Date** value is supported by a **DateTime** structure, its methods give you additional options in assembling a **Date** value. For example, you can employ one of the overloaded **DateTime** constructors to populate a **Date** variable using the desired combination of components. The following example sets `NewDateTime` to May 6, 1978 at one tenth of a second before 8:30 in the morning:

```
Dim NewDateTime As Date = New Date(1978, 5, 6, 8, 29, 59, 900)
```

Example

This example uses the **TimeSerial** function to return a time for the specified hour, minute, and second.

```
Dim MyTime As Date
MyTime = TimeSerial(16, 35, 17)   ' Return the time in a Date data type.
```

See Also

DateSerial Function, DateValue Function, Hour Function, Minute Function, Now Property, Second Function, TimeValue Function

TimeString Property

Returns or sets a **String** value representing the current time of day according to your system.

```
Public Property TimeString As String
```

Exceptions/Errors

Exception type	Error number	Condition
InvalidCastException	5	Invalid cast.

Remarks

TimeString always returns the system time as "HH:mm:ss", which is a 24-hour format.

If you attempt to set **TimeString** with an invalid value, an **InvalidCastException** occurs.

To get or set the current system date as a **String**, use the **DateString** property.

To access the current system time as a **Date**, use the **TimeOfDay** property.

Example

This example uses the **TimeString** property to display the current system time.

```
MsgBox("The current time is " & TimeString)
```

See Also

Now Property, DateString Property, TimeOfDay Property

TimeValue Function

Returns a **Date** value containing the time information represented by a string, with the date information set to January 1 of the year 1.

```
Public Function TimeValue(ByVal StringTime As String) As DateTime
```

Parameter

StringTime
Required. **String** expression representing a date/time value from 00:00:00 on January 1 of the year 1 through 23:59:59 on December 31, 9999.

Exceptions/Errors

Exception type	Error number	Condition
InvalidCastException	13	*StringTime* includes invalid time information.

Remarks

You can enter valid times using a 12-hour or 24-hour clock. For example, `"2:24 P.M."` and `"14:24"` are both valid *StringTime* arguments.

If the *StringTime* argument includes date information, **TimeValue** does not include it in the returned value. However, if *StringTime* includes invalid time information such as "January 32," an **InvalidCastException** error occurs.

Example

This example uses the **TimeValue** function to convert a string to a time. You can also use date literals to directly assign a time to a **Date** variable.

```
Dim MyTime As Date
MyTime = TimeValue("4:35:17 PM")    ' Return the time in a Date data type.
MyTime = TimeValue(#4:35:17 PM#)    ' Return the time in a Date data type.
```

See Also

DateSerial Function, DateValue Function, Hour Function, Minute Function, Now Property, Second Function, TimeSerial Function

To

The **To** keyword separates the beginning and ending values of a loop counter or of a value match range.

The **To** keyword is used in these contexts:

For...Next Statements

Select...Case Statements

See Also

Visual Basic Language Keywords

Today Property

Returns or sets a **Date** value containing the current date according to your system.

```
Public Property Today() As DateTime
```

Remarks

The **Date** data type includes time components. When returning the system date, **Today** sets all of these to 0, so the returned value represents midnight (00:00:00). When setting the system date, **Today** ignores the time components.

To access the current system date as a **String**, use the **DateString** property.

To get or set the current system time, use the **TimeOfDay** property.

Example

This example uses the **Today** property to return the current system date.

```
Dim MyDate As Date
MyDate = Today    ' Return current system date.
```

See Also

Format Function, Now Property, DateString Property, TimeOfDay Property

Tristate Enumeration

When you call number-formatting functions, you can use the following enumeration members in your code in place of the actual values.

Constant	Value	Description
True	–1	True
False	0	False
UseDefault	–2	Default setting

See Also

FormatNumber Function, FormatCurrency Function, FormatPercent Function

True

The **True** keyword represents a Boolean value that passes a conditional test.

See Also

Boolean Data Type, False

Try...Catch...Finally Statements

Provides a way to handle some or all possible errors that may occur in a given block of code, while still running code.

```
Try
   [ tryStatements ]
[ Catch [ exception [ As type ] ] [ When expression ]
   [ catchStatements ] ]
[ Exit Try ]
...
[ Finally
   [ finallyStatements ] ]
End Try
```

Parts

tryStatements
Optional. Statement(s) where an error can occur. Can be a compound statement.

Catch
Optional. Multiple **Catch** blocks permitted. If an exception occurs while processing the **Try** block, each **Catch** statement is examined in textual order to determine if it handles the exception. *Exception* represents the exception that has been thrown.

exception
Optional. Any variable name. The initial value of *exception* is the value of the thrown error. Used with **Catch** to specify the error caught.

type
Optional. Specifies the type of class filter. If the value of *exception* is of the type specified by *type* or of a derived type, the identifier becomes bound to the exception object.

When
Optional. A **Catch** statement with a **When** clause will only catch exceptions when *expression* evaluates to **True**. A **When** clause is only applied after checking the type of the exception, and *expression* may refer to the identifier representing the exception.

expression
Optional. Must be implicitly convertible to **Boolean**. Any expression that describes a generic filter. Typically used to filter by error number. Used with **When** keyword to specify circumstances under which the error is caught.

catchStatements
Optional. Statement(s) to handle errors occurring in the associated **Try** block. Can be a compound statement.

Exit Try
Optional. Keyword that breaks out of the **Try...Catch...Finally** structure. Execution resumes with the code immediately following the **End Try** statement. Not allowed in **Finally** blocks.

Finally
Optional. A **Finally** block is always executed when execution leaves any part of the **Try** statement.

finallyStatements
Optional. Statement(s) that are executed after all other error processing has occurred.

End Try
Terminates the **Try...Catch...Finally** structure.

Remarks

If errors occur that the programmer has not handled, Visual Studio for Applications simply provides its normal error message to a user, as if there was no error handling.

The **Try** block contains code where an error can occur, while the **Catch** block contains code to handle any error that does occur. If an error occurs in the **Try** block, program control is passed to the appropriate **Catch** statement for disposition. The *exception* argument is an instance of the **Exception** class or an instance of a class that derives from the **Exception** class corresponding to the error that occurred in the **Try** block. The **Exception** class instance contains information about the error including, among other things, its number and message.

> **Note** If a **Try** statement does not contain at least one **Catch** block it must contain a **Finally** block.

Example

The following simplified example illustrates the structure of the **Try...Catch...Finally** statement:

```
Public Sub TryExample()
   Dim x As Integer = 5   ' Declare variables.
   Dim y As Integer = 0
   Try   ' Set up structured error handling.
      x /= y   ' Cause a "Divide by Zero" error.
   Catch ex As Exception When y = 0   ' Catch the error.
      MsgBox(ex.toString)   ' Show friendly error message.
   Finally
      Beep()   ' Beep after error processing.
   End Try
End Sub
```

See Also

End Statement, Err Object, Exit Statement, On Error Statement

Type Conversion Functions

These functions are compiled inline, meaning the conversion code is part of the code that evaluates the expression. Execution is faster because there is no call to a procedure to accomplish the conversion. Each function coerces an expression to a specific data type.

```
CBool(expression)
CByte(expression)
CChar(expression)
CDate(expression)
CDbl(expression)
CDec(expression)
CInt(expression)
CLng(expression)
CObj(expression)
CShort(expression)
CSng(expression)
CStr(expression)
```

Part

expression

Required. Any **String** expression or numeric expression.

Return Types

The function name determines the return type, as shown in the following table:

Function name	Return type	Range for *expression* argument
CBool	**Boolean**	Any valid **String** or numeric expression.
CByte	**Byte**	0 through 255; fractions are rounded.
CChar	**Char**	Any valid **String** expression; value can be 0 through 65535.
CDate	**Date**	Any valid representation of a date and time.
CDbl	**Double**	–1.79769313486231E+308 through –4.94065645841247E–324 for negative values; 4.94065645841247E–324 through 1.79769313486231E+308 for positive values.
CDec	**Decimal**	+/–79,228,162,514,264,337,593,543,950,335 for zero-scaled numbers, that is, numbers with no decimal places. For numbers with 28 decimal places, the range is +/–7.9228162514264337593543950335. The smallest possible non-zero number is 0.0000000000000000000000000001.

Function name	Return type	Range for *expression* argument
CInt	**Integer**	–2,147,483,648 through 2,147,483,647; fractions are rounded.
CLng	**Long**	–9,223,372,036,854,775,808 through 9,223,372,036,854,775,807; fractions are rounded.
CObj	**Object**	Any valid expression.
CShort	**Short**	–32,768 through 32,767; fractions are rounded.
CSng	**Single**	–3.402823E+38 through –1.401298E–45 for negative values; 1.401298E–45 through 3.402823E+38 for positive values.
CStr	**String**	Returns for **CStr** depend on the *expression* argument. See "Returns for CStr."

Remarks

If thc *expression* passed to the function is outside the range of the data type to which it is being converted, an error occurs.

In general, you can use the data type conversion functions to force the result of some operation to a particular data type rather than the default data type. For example, use **CDec** to force decimal arithmetic in cases where single-precision, double-precision, or integer arithmetic normally would occur.

When the fractional part is exactly 0.5, **CInt** and **CLng** always round it to the nearest even number. For example, 0.5 rounds to 0 and 1.5 rounds to 2. **CInt** and **CLng** differ from the **Fix** and **Int** functions, which truncate, rather than round, the fractional part of a number. Also, **Fix** and **Int** always return a value of the same type as is passed in.

Use the **IsDate** function to determine if a value can be converted to a date and time. **CDate** recognizes date literals and time literals as well as numbers that fall within the range of acceptable dates.

CDate recognizes date formats according to the locale setting of your system. You must provide the day, month, and year in the correct order for your locale, or the date may not be interpreted correctly. A long date format is not recognized if it contains a day-of-the-week string, such as "Wednesday".

The **Date** data type always contains both date and time information. For purposes of type conversion, Visual Basic .NET considers 1/1/1 (January 1 of the year 1) to be a neutral value for the date, and 00:00:00 (midnight) to be a neutral value for the time. If you convert a **Date** value to a string, **CStr** does not include neutral values in the resulting string. For example, if you convert `#January 1, 0001 9:30:00#` to a string, the result is "9:30:00 AM"; the date information is suppressed. However, the date information is still present in the original **Date** value and can be recovered with functions such as **DatePart**.

The **CType** function takes a second argument, *typename*, and coerces *expression* to *typename*, where *typename* can be any data type, structure, class, or interface. For more information, see "CType Function."

CBool Example

This example uses the **CBool** function to convert expressions to **Boolean** values. If an expression evaluates to a nonzero value, **CBool** returns **True**; otherwise, it returns **False**.

```
Dim A, B, C As Integer
Dim Check As Boolean
A = 5
B = 5
Check = CBool(A = B)    ' Check is set to True.
' ...
C = 0
Check = CBool(C)    ' Check is set to False.
```

CByte Example

This example uses the **CByte** function to convert an expression to a **Byte**.

```
Dim MyDouble As Double
Dim MyByte As Byte
MyDouble = 125.5678
MyByte = CByte(MyDouble)    ' MyByte is set to 126.
```

CChar Example

This example uses the **CChar** function to convert a the first character of a **String** expression to a **Char** type.

```
Dim MyString As String
Dim MyChar As Char
MyString = "BCD"    ' CChar converts only first character of string.
MyChar = CChar(MyString)    ' MyChar is set to "B".
```

The input argument to **CChar** must be of data type **String**. You cannot use **CChar** to convert a number to a character, because **CChar** cannot accept a numeric data type. This example obtains a number representing a code point (character code) and converts it to the corresponding character. It uses **InputBox** to obtain the string of digits, **CInt** to convert the string to type **Integer**, and **ChrW** to convert the number to type **Char**.

```
Dim MyDigits As String    ' Input string of digits to be converted.
Dim CodePoint As Integer    ' Number to be represented as a character.
Dim MyChar As Char
MyDigits = InputBox("Enter code point of character:")
CodePoint = CInt(MyDigits)    ' Convert entire string to Integer.
MyChar = ChrW(CodePoint)    ' MyChar is set to Char value of code point.
```

CDate Example

This example uses the **CDate** function to convert strings to **Date** values. In general, hard-coding dates and times as strings (as shown in this example) is not recommended. Use date literals and time literals, such as #Feb 12, 1969# and #4:45:23 PM#, instead.

```
Dim MyDateString, MyTimeString As String
Dim MyDate, MyTime As Date
MyDateString = "February 12, 1969"
MyTimeString = "4:35:47 PM"
' ...
MyDate = CDate(MyDateString)   ' Convert to Date data type.
MyTime = CDate(MyTimeString)   ' Convert to Date data type.
```

CDbl Example

This example uses the **CDbl** function to convert an expression to **Double**.

```
Dim MyDec As Decimal
Dim MyDouble As Double
MyDec = 234.456784D    ' Literal type character D makes MyDec a Decimal.
MyDouble = CDbl(MyDec * 8.2D * 0.01D)   ' Convert result to a Double.
```

CDec Example

This example uses the **CDec** function to convert a numeric value to **Decimal**.

```
Dim MyDouble As Double
Dim MyDecimal As Decimal
MyDouble = 10000000.0587
MyDecimal = CDec(MyDouble)   ' Convert to Decimal.
```

CInt Example

This example uses the **CInt** function to convert a value to **Integer**.

```
Dim MyDouble As Double
Dim MyInt As Integer
MyDouble = 2345.5678
MyInt = CInt(MyDouble)   ' MyInt is set to 2346.
```

CLng Example

This example uses the **CLng** function to convert values to **Long**.

```
Dim MyDbl1, MyDbl2 As Double
Dim MyLong1, MyLong2 As Long
MyDbl1 = 25427.45
MyDbl2 = 25427.55
MyLong1 = CLng(MyDbl1)   ' MyLong1 contains 25427.
MyLong2 = CLng(MyDbl2)   ' MyLong2 contains 25428.
```

CObj Example

This example uses the **CObj** function to convert a numeric value to **Object**. The **Object** variable itself contains only a four-byte pointer, which points to the **Double** value assigned to it.

```
Dim MyDouble As Double
Dim MyObject As Object
MyDouble = 2.7182818284
MyObject = CObj(MyDouble)   ' Double value is pointed to by MyObject.
```

CShort Example

This example uses the **CShort** function to convert a numeric value to **Short**.

```
Dim MyByte as Byte
Dim MyShort as Short
MyByte = 100
MyShort = CShort(MyByte)   ' Convert to Short.
```

CSng Example

This example uses the **CSng** function to convert values to **Single**.

```
Dim MyDouble1, MyDouble2 As Double
Dim MySingle1, MySingle2 As Single
MyDouble1 = 75.3421105
MyDouble2 = 75.3421567
MySingle1 = CSng(MyDouble1)   ' MySingle1 is set to 75.34211.
MySingle2 = CSng(MyDouble2)   ' MySingle2 is set to 75.34216.
```

CStr Example

This example uses the **CStr** function to convert a numeric value to **String**.

```
Dim MyDouble As Double
Dim MyString As String
MyDouble = 437.324
MyString = CStr(MyDouble)   ' MyString is set to "437.324".
```

This example uses the **CStr** function to convert **Date** values to **String** values.

```
Dim MyDate As Date
Dim MyString As String
' ...
MyDate = #February 12, 1969 00:00:00#   ' INVALID format.
' Date literals must be in the format #m/d/yyyy# or they are invalid.
' ...
MyDate = #2/12/69 00:00:00#   ' Time is midnight.
' The neutral time value of 00:00:00 is suppressed in the conversion.
MyString = CStr(MyDate)   ' MyString is set to "2/12/1969".
' ...
MyDate = #2/12/69 00:00:01#   ' Time is one second past midnight.
' The time component becomes part of the converted value.
MyString = CStr(MyDate)   ' MyString is set to "2/12/1969 12:00:01 AM".
```

CStr always renders a **Date** value in the standard short format for the current locale, for example, '2/15/2003".

See Also

Conversion Functions; CType Function; Asc, AscW Functions; Chr, ChrW Functions; Format Function; Hex Function; Oct Function; Str Function; Val Function; DatePart Function; Returns for Cstr; Type Conversions

TypeName Function

Returns a **String** value containing data type information about a variable.

```
Public Function TypeName(ByVal VarName As Object) As String
```

Parameter

VarName
Required. **Object** variable. If **Option Strict** is **Off**, you can pass a variable of any data type except a structure.

Remarks

The following table shows the **String** values returned by **TypeName** for different contents of *VarName*.

***VarName* contents**	**String returned**
16-bit **True** or **False** value type	"Boolean"
8-bit binary value type	"Byte"
16-bit character value type	"Char"
64-bit date and time value type	"Date"
Reference type indicating missing or nonexistent data	"DBNull"
128-bit fixed point numeric value type	"Decimal"
64-bit floating point numeric value type	"Double"
32-bit integer value type	"Integer"
Reference type pointing to an unspecialized object	"Object"
Reference type pointing to a specialized object created from class *<objectclass>*	"*<objectclass>*"
64-bit integer value type	"Long"
Reference type with no object currently assigned to it	"Nothing"

(continued)

(continued)

VarName **contents**	**String returned**
16-bit integer value type	"Short"
32-bit floating point numeric value type	"Single"
Reference type pointing to a string of 16-bit characters	"String"

If *VarName* is an array, the returned string can be any one of the strings in the preceding table with empty parentheses appended. For example, if *VarName* points to an array of integers, **TypeName** returns "Integer()".

When **TypeName** returns the name of a reference type such as a class, it only returns the simple name, not the qualified name. For example, if *VarName* points to an object of class **System.Drawing.Printing.PaperSource**, **TypeName** returns "PaperSource".

Example

This example uses the **TypeName** function to return data type information about several variables.

```
Dim MyType As String
Dim StrVar As String = "MyString"
Dim DecVar As Decimal
Dim IntVar, ArrayVar(5) As Integer
MyType = TypeName(StrVar)   ' Returns "String".
MyType = TypeName(IntVar)   ' Returns "Integer".
MyType = TypeName(ArrayVar)   ' Returns "Integer()".
```

See Also

Data Type Summary, IsArray Function, IsDate Function, IsDBNull Function, IsError Function, IsNothing Function, IsNumeric Function, IsReference Function, Object Data Type

TypeOf

The **TypeOf** keyword introduces a comparison clause that tests whether an object is derived from or implements a particular type, such as an interface.

The **TypeOf** keyword is used in this context:

If...Then...Else Statements

UBound Function

Returns the highest available subscript for the indicated dimension of an array.

```
Public Function UBound( _
   ByVal Array As System.Array, _
   Optional ByVal Rank As Integer = 1 _
) As Integer
```

Parameters

Array

Required. Array of any data type. The array in which you want to find the highest possible subscript of a dimension.

Rank

Optional. **Integer**. The dimension for which the highest possible subscript is to be returned. Use 1 for the first dimension, 2 for the second, and so on. If *Rank* is omitted, 1 is assumed.

Exceptions/Errors

Exception type	Error number	Condition
ArgumentNullException	9	*Array* is **Nothing**
RankException	9	*Rank* is less than 1 or *Rank* is greater than the rank of array.

Remarks

Since array subscripts start at 0, the length of a dimension is greater by one than the highest available subscript for that dimension.

For an array with the following dimensions, **UBound** returns the values in the following table:

```
Dim A(100, 5, 4) As Byte
```

Call to UBound	Return value
`UBound(A, 1)`	100
`UBound(A, 2)`	5
`UBound(A, 3)`	4

You can use **UBound** to determine the total number of elements in an array, but you must adjust the value it returns to account for the fact that the subscripts start at 0. The following example calculates the total size of the array `A` in the preceding example:

```
Dim Total As Integer
Total = (UBound(A, 1) + 1) * (UBound(A, 2) + 1) * (UBound(A, 3) + 1)
```

The value calculated for `Total` is 3030, which is 101 * 6 * 5.

Example

This example uses the **UBound** function to determine the highest available subscript for the indicated dimension of an array.

```
Dim Highest, MyArray(10, 15, 20), AnyArray(6) as Integer
Highest = UBound(MyArray, 1)    ' Returns 10.
Highest = UBound(MyArray, 3)    ' Returns 20.
Highest = UBound(AnyArray)   ' Returns 6.
```

See Also

LBound Function, Dim Statement, ReDim Statement

UCase Function

Returns a string or character containing the specified string converted to uppercase.

```
Public Shared Function UCase(ByVal Value As Char) As Char
```

-or-

```
Public Shared Function UCase(ByVal Value As String) As String
```

Parameter

Value

Required. Any valid **String** or **Char** expression.

Remarks

Only lowercase letters are converted to uppercase; all uppercase letters and nonletter characters remain unchanged.

Example

This example uses the **UCase** function to return an uppercase version of a string.

```
Dim LowerCase, UpperCase As String
LowerCase = "Hello World 1234"    ' String to convert.
UpperCase = UCase(LowerCase)   ' Returns "HELLO WORLD 1234".
```

See Also

LCase Function

Unicode

The **Unicode** keyword indicates that strings are converted to Unicode values regardless of the name of the method being declared.

The **Unicode** keyword is used in this context:

Declare Statement

See Also

Visual Basic Language Keywords

Until

The **Until** keyword specifies a condition that terminates the execution of a **Do** loop.

The **Until** keyword is used in this context:

Do...Loop Statements

See Also

Visual Basic Language Keywords

User-Defined Data Type

The user-defined type (UDT) supported by previous versions of Visual Basic is generalized to a *structure* in Visual Basic .NET. A structure is a concatenation of one or more *members* of various data types. The structure is treated as a single unit, although its members can also be accessed individually.

A structure declaration starts with the **Structure** statement and ends with the **End Structure** statement. The **Structure** statement supplies the name of the structure, which is also the identifier of the data type being defined by the structure. Other parts of the code can use this identifier to declare the data type of variables, arguments, and function return values.

The following paradigm shows the declaration of a structure.

```
[Public|Private|Protected] Structure structname
   {Dim|Public|Private|Friend} member1 As datatype1
   ...
   {Dim|Public|Private|Friend} memberN As datatypeN
End Structure
```

The declarations between the **Structure** and **End Structure** statements define the members of the structure. Every member must be declared using a **Dim** statement or a statement that specifies access, such as **Public**, **Private**, or **Friend**. If a **Dim** statement is used, the access defaults to public.

Note As with all composite data types, you cannot safely calculate the total memory consumption of a structure by adding together the nominal storage allocations of its members. Furthermore, you cannot safely assume that the order of storage in memory is the same as your order of declaration.

All structures inherit from the .NET class **System.ValueType**.

See Also

Data Type

User-Defined Date/Time Formats (Format Function)

The following table identifies characters you can use to create user-defined date/time formats:

Character	Description
(:)	Time separator. In some locales, other characters may be used to represent the time separator. The time separator separates hours, minutes, and seconds when time values are formatted. The actual character used as the time separator in formatted output is determined by your system's **LocaleID** value.
(/)	Date separator. In some locales, other characters may be used to represent the date separator. The date separator separates the day, month, and year when date values are formatted. The actual character used as the date separator in formatted output is determined by your locale.
(%)	Used to indicate that the following character should be read as a single-letter format without regard to any trailing letters. Also used to indicate that a single-letter format is read as a user-defined format. See below for further details
d	Displays the day as a number without a leading zero (for example, `1`). Use **%d** if this is the only character in your user-defined numeric format.
dd	Displays the day as a number with a leading zero (for example, `01`).
ddd	Displays the day as an abbreviation (for example, `Sun`).
dddd	Displays the day as a full name (for example, `Sunday`).
M	Displays the month as a number without a leading zero (for example, January is represented as `1`). Use **%M** if this is the only character in your user-defined numeric format.
MM	Displays the month as a number with a leading zero (for example, `01/12/01`).
MMM	Displays the month as an abbreviation (for example, `Jan`).
MMMM	Displays the month as a full month name (for example, `January`).

Character	Description
gg	Displays the period/era string (for example, `A.D.`)
h	Displays the hour as a number without leading zeros using the 12-hour clock (for example, `1:15:15 PM`). Use **%h** if this is the only character in your user-defined numeric format.
hh	Displays the hour as a number with leading zeros using the 12-hour clock (for example, `01:15:15 PM`).
H	Displays the hour as a number without leading zeros using the 24-hour clock (for example, `1:15:15`). Use **%H** if this is the only character in your user-defined numeric format.
HH	Displays the hour as a number with leading zeros using the 24-hour clock (for example, `01:15:15`).
m	Displays the minute as a number without leading zeros (for example, `12:1:15`). Use **%m** if this is the only character in your user-defined numeric format.
mm	Displays the minute as a number with leading zeros (for example, `12:01:15`).
s	Displays the second as a number without leading zeros (for example, `12:15:5`). Use **%s** if this is the only character in your user-defined numeric format.
ss	Displays the second as a number with leading zeros (for example, `12:15:05`).
f	Displays fractions of seconds. For example **ff** will display hundreths of seconds, whereas **ffff** will display ten-thousandths of seconds. You may use up to seven **f** symbols in your user-defined format. Use **%f** if this is the only character in your user-defined numeric format.
t	Uses the 12-hour clock and displays an uppercase `A` for any hour before noon; displays an uppercase `P` for any hour between noon and 11:59 P.M. Use **%t** if this is the only character in your user-defined numeric format.
tt	Uses the 12-hour clock and displays an uppercase `AM` with any hour before noon; displays an uppercase `PM` with any hour between noon and 11:59 P.M.
y	Displays the year number (0–9) without leading zeros. Use **%y** if this is the only character in your user-defined numeric format.
yy	Displays the year in two-digit numeric format with a leading zero, if applicable.
yyy	Displays the year in four digit numeric format.
yyyy	Displays the year in four digit numeric format.
z	Displays the timezone offset without a leading zero (for example, `-8`). Use **%z** if this is the only character in your user-defined numeric format.
zz	Displays the timezone offset with a leading zero (for example, `-08`)
zzz	Displays the full timezone offset (for example, `-08:00`)

Example

The following are examples of user-defined date and time formats for `December 7, 1958, 8:50 PM, 35 seconds`:

Format	Displays
M/d/yy	12/7/58
d-MMM	7-Dec
d-MMMM-yy	7-December-58
d MMMM	7 December
MMMM yy	December 58
hh:mm tt	08:50 PM
h:mm:ss t	8:50:35 P
H:mm	20:50
H:mm:ss	20:50:35
M/d/yyyy H:mm	12/7/1958 20:50

See Also

Format Function, Predefined Date/Time Formats (Format Function), User-Defined Numeric Formats (Format Function)

User-Defined Numeric Formats (Format Function)

The following table identifies characters you can use to create user-defined number formats. These may be used to build the style argument for the **Format** function:

Character	Description
None	Displays the number with no formatting.
(**0**)	Digit placeholder. Displays a digit or a zero. If the expression has a digit in the position where the zero appears in the format string, display it; otherwise, displays a zero in that position. If the number has fewer digits than there are zeros (on either side of the decimal) in the format expression, displays leading or trailing zeros. If the number has more digits to the right of the decimal separator than there are zeros to the right of the decimal separator in the format expression, rounds the number to as many decimal places as there are zeros. If the number has more digits to the left of the decimal separator than there are zeros to the left of the decimal separator in the format expression, displays the extra digits without modification.

Character	Description
(#)	Digit placeholder. Displays a digit or nothing. If the expression has a digit in the position where the # character appears in the format string, displays it; otherwise, displays nothing in that position. This symbol works like the **0** digit placeholder, except that leading and trailing zeros aren't displayed if the number has fewer digits than there are # characters on either side of the decimal separator in the format expression.
(.)	Decimal placeholder. The decimal placeholder determines how many digits are displayed to the left and right of the decimal separator. If the format expression contains only # characters to the left of this symbol; numbers smaller than 1 begin with a decimal separator. To display a leading zero displayed with fractional numbers, use zero as the first digit placeholder to the left of the decimal separator. In some locales, a comma is used as the decimal separator. The actual character used as a decimal placeholder in the formatted output depends on the number format recognized by your system. Thus, You should use the period as the decimal placeholder in your formats even if you are in a locale that uses a comma as a decimal placeholder. The formatted string will appear in the format correct for the locale.
(%)	Percent placeholder. Multiplies the expression by 100. The percent character (%) is inserted in the position where it appears in the format string.
(,)	Thousand separator. The thousand separator separates thousands from hundreds within a number that has four or more places to the left of the decimal separator. Standard use of the thousand separator is specified if the format contains a thousand separator surrounded by digit placeholders (**0** or #). A thousand separator immediately to the left of the decimal separator (whether or not a decimal is specified) or as the rightmost character in the string means "scale the number by dividing it by 1,000, rounding as needed." For example, you can use the format string `"##0,,"` to represent 100 million as 100,000. Numbers smaller than 1,000 but greater or equal to 500 are displayed as `1`, and numbers smaller than 500 are displayed as `0`. Two adjacent thousand separators in this position scale by a factor of 1 million, and an additional factor of 1,000 for each additional separator. Multiple separators in any position other than immediately to the left of the decimal separator or the rightmost position in the string are treated simply as specifying the use of a thousand separator. In some locales, a period is used as a thousand separator. The actual character used as the thousand separator in the formatted output depends on the Number Format recognized by your system. Thus, You should use the comma as the thousand separator in your formats even if you are in a locale that uses a period as a thousand separator. The formmatted string will appear in the format correct for the locale.
(:)	Time separator. In some locales, other characters may be used to represent the time separator. The time separator separates hours, minutes, and seconds when time values are formatted. The actual character used as the time separator in formatted output is determined by your system settings.

(continued)

(continued)

Character	Description
(/)	Date separator. In some locales, other characters may be used to represent the date separator. The date separator separates the day, month, and year when date values are formatted. The actual character used as the date separator in formatted output is determined by your system settings.
(**E- E+ e- e+**)	Scientific format. If the format expression contains at least one digit placeholder (**0** or **#**) to the left of **E-**, **E+**, **e-**, or **e+**, the number is displayed in scientific format and `E` or `e` is inserted between the number and its exponent. The number of digit placeholders to the left determines the number of digits in the exponent. Use **E-** or **e-** to place a minus sign next to negative exponents. Use **E+** or **e+** to place a minus sign next to negative exponents and a plus sign next to positive exponents. You must also include digit placeholders to the right of this symbol to get correct formatting.
- + $ ( )	Literal characters. These characters are displayed exactly as typed in the format string. To display a character other than one of those listed, precede it with a backslash (\) or enclose it in double quotation marks (" ").
(\)	Displays the next character in the format string. To display a character that has special meaning as a literal character, precede it with a backslash (\). The backslash itself isn't displayed. Using a backslash is the same as enclosing the next character in double quotation marks. To display a backslash, use two backslashes (\\). Examples of characters that can't be displayed as literal characters are the date-formatting and time-formatting characters (**a**, **c**, **d**, **h**, **m**, **n**, **p**, **q**, **s**, **t**, **w**, **y**, **/**, and **:**), the numeric-formatting characters (**#**, **0**, **%**, **E**, **e**, comma, and period), and the string-formatting characters (**@**, **&**, **<**, **>**, and **!**).
(**"ABC"**)	Displays the string inside the double quotation marks (" "). To include a string in the style argument from within code, you must use **Chr(34)** to enclose the text (**34** is the character code for a quotation mark (")).

Example

The following table contains some sample format expressions for numbers. (These examples all assume that your system's locale setting is English-U.S.) The first column contains the format strings for the *Style* argument of the **Format** function; the other columns contain the resulting output if the formatted data has the value given in the column headings.

Format (*Style*)	"5" formatted as	"-5" formatted as	"0.5" formatted as
`Zero-length string ("")`	5	-5	0.5
`0`	5	-5	1
`0.00`	5.00	-5.00	0.50
`#,##0`	5	-5	1

Format (*Style*)	"5" formatted as	"-5" formatted as	"0.5" formatted as
`$#,##0;($#,##0)`	`$5`	`($5)`	`$1`
`$#,##0.00;($#,##0.00)`	`$5.00`	`($5.00)`	`$0.50`
`0%`	`500%`	`–500%`	`50%`
`0.00%`	`500.00%`	`–500.00%`	`50.00%`
`0.00E+00`	`5.00E+00`	`–5.00E+00`	`5.00E–01`
`0.00E–00`	`5.00E00`	`–5.00E00`	`5.00E–01`

See Also

Different Formats for Different Numeric Values (Format Function), Format Function, Predefined Numeric Formats (Format Function), User-Defined Date/Time Formats (Format Function)

Val Function

Returns the numbers contained in a string as a numeric value of appropriate type.

```
Public Overloads Function Val(ByVal Expression As String) As Double
```

-or-

```
Public Overloads Function Val(ByVal Expression As Object) As Double
```

-or-

```
Public Overloads Function Val(ByVal Expression As Char) As Integer
```

Parameter

Expression
: Required. Any valid **String** expression, **Object** variable, or **Char** value. If *Expression* is of type **Object**, its value must be convertible to **String** or an **ArgumentException** error occurs.

Exceptions/Errors

Exception type	Error number	Condition
OverflowException	6	*InputStr* is too large.
InvalidCastException	13	Number is badly formed.
ArgumentException	438	**Object** type expression not convertible to **String**.

Remarks

The **Val** function stops reading the string at the first character it cannot recognize as part of a number. Symbols and characters that are often considered parts of numeric values, such as dollar signs and commas, are not recognized. However, the function recognizes the radix prefixes `&O` (for octal) and `&H` (for hexadecimal). Blanks, tabs, and linefeed characters are stripped from the argument.

The following returns the value 1615198:

```
Val(" 1615 198th Street N.E.")
```

In the code below, **Val** returns the decimal value –1 for the hexadecimal value shown:

```
Val("&HFFFF")
```

> **Note** The **Val** function recognizes only the period (**.**) as a valid decimal separator. When different decimal separators are used, as in international applications, use **CDbl** or **CInt** instead to convert a string to a number.

Example

This example uses the **Val** function to return the numbers contained in each string. **Val** stops converting at the first character that cannot be interpreted as a numeric digit, numeric modifier, numeric punctuation, or white space.

```
Dim ValResult As Double
ValResult = Val("2457")    ' ValResult is set to 2457.
ValResult = Val(" 2 45 7")    ' ValResult is set to 2457.
ValResult = Val("24 and 57")    ' ValResult is set to 24.
```

See Also

Str Function, Type Conversion Functions, OverflowException

VariantType Enumeration

When you call the **VarType** function, you can use enumeration members in your code in place of the actual values.

The **VariantType** enumeration defines constants used to identify possible **Variant** types. The following table lists the **VariantType** enumeration members.

Member	Constant	Description
VariantType.Array	**vbArray**	Array.
VariantType.Boolean	**vbBoolean**	**Boolean** (**True** or **False**).
VariantType.Byte	**vbByte**	**Byte** (0 through 255).
VariantType.Char		**Char** (0 through 65535).
VariantType.Currency	**vbCurrency**	Currency.

Member	Constant	Description
VariantType.DataObject		DataObject.
VariantType.Date	**vbDate**	**Date** (0:00:00 on January 1, 0001 through 11:59:59 PM on December 31, 9999).
VariantType.Decimal	**vbDecimal**	**Decimal** (0 through +/–79,228,162,514,264,337,593,543,950,335 with no decimal point; 0 through +/–7.9228162514264337593543950335 with 28 places to the right of the decimal; smallest non zero number is +/–0.0000000000000000000000000001).
VariantType.Double	**vbDouble**	**Double** (–1.79769313486231E+308 through –4.94065645841247E–324 for negative values; 4.94065645841247E–324 through 1.79769313486231E+308 for positive values).
VariantType.Empty	**vbEmpty**	Null reference.
VariantType.Error		
VariantType.Integer	**vbInteger**	**Integer** (–2,147,483,648 through 2,147,483,647).
VariantType.Long	**vbLong**	**Long** (–9,223,372,036,854,775,808 through 9,223,372,036,854,775,807)
VariantType.Null	**vbNull**	Null object.
VariantType.Object	**vbObject**	Any type can be stored in a variable of type **Object**.
VariantType.Short		**Short** (–32,768 through 32,767).
VariantType.Single	**vbSingle**	**Single** (–3.402823E+38 through –1.401298E–45 for negative values; 1.401298E–45 through 3.402823E+38 for positive values).
VariantType.String	**vbString**	**String** (0 to approximately 2 billion Unicode characters).
VariantType.UserDefinedType	**vbUserDefinedType**	User-defined type. Each member of the structure has a range determined by its data type and independent of the ranges of the other members.
VariantType.Variant	**vbVariant**	**Variant**.

See Also

VarType Function

VarType Function

Returns an **Integer** value containing the data type classification of a variable.

```
Public Function VarType(ByVal VarName As Object) As VariantType
```

Parameter

VarName
Required. **Object** variable. If **Option Strict** is **Off**, you can pass a variable of any data type except a structure.

Remarks

The integer value returned by **VarType** is a member of the **VariantType** enumeration.

The following table shows the values returned by **VarType** for special cases of *VarName*.

Data type represented by *VarName*	Value returned by *VarType*
Nothing	**VariantType.Object**
DBNull	**VariantType.Null**
Enumeration	Underlying data type (**Byte**, **Short**, **Integer**, or **Long**)
Array	Bitwise OR of array element type and **VariantType.Array**
Array of arrays	Bitwise OR of **VariantType.Object** and **VariantType.Array**
Structure (**System.ValueType**)	**VariantType.UserDefinedType**
System.Exception	**VariantType.Error**
Unknown	**VariantType.Object**

Example

This example uses the **VarType** function to return data type classification information about several variables.

```
Dim MyString As String = "MyString"
Dim MyObject As Object
Dim MyNumber, MyArray(5) As Integer
Dim MyVarType As VariantType   ' Integer enumeration.
MyVarType = VarType(MyVarType)   ' Returns VariantType.Integer.
MyVarType = VarType(MyString)   ' Returns VariantType.String.
MyVarType = VarType(MyObject)   ' Returns VariantType.Object.
MyVarType = VarType(MyArray)   ' Returns the bitwise OR of _
                                 VariantType.Array and VariantType.Integer.
```

See Also

Data Type Summary, Object Data Type, VariantType Enumeration

VBFixedArrayAttribute Class

Used to declare fixed-sized arrays.

```
<System.AttributeUsage(System.AttributeTargets.Field, _
   Inherited := False, AllowMultiple := False)> _
Public NotInheritable Class VBFixedArrayAttribute
   Inherits System.Attribute
```

Remarks

Visual Basic .NET arrays are of variable length by default. This attribute is useful when using Visual Basic .NET file input and output functions, such as **FileGet** and **FilePut** that require fixed length arrays.

Example

```
Structure Book
   <VBFixedArray(6)> Public Chapter() As Integer
End Structure

Sub WriteData()
   Dim FileNum As Integer = FreeFile()
   Dim MyBook As Book
   '  Add code here to populate the array.
   FileOpen(FileNum, "C:\testfile", OpenMode.Binary, _
            OpenAccess.Write, OpenShare.Default)
   FilePut(FileNum, MyBook) ' Write data.
   FileClose(1)
End Sub
```

See Also

VBFixedArrayAttribute Class Members, VBFixedStringAttribute Class, FileGet Function, FilePut Function, FileOpen Function

VBFixedArrayAttribute Constructor

Initializes the bounds of a fixed sized array.

```
Public Sub New( _
   ByVal size1 As Integer, _
   Optional ByVal size2 As Integer = -1 _
)
```

Parameters

size1
: Initializes the value of **FirstBound** field, which represents the size of the first dimension of the array.

size2
: Initializes the value of the **SecondBound** field, which represents the size of the second dimension of the array.

Remarks

The constructor runs when the **VBFixedArrayAttribute** attribute is applied to a class.

See Also

ComClassAttribute Class

VBFixedArrayAttribute.FirstBound Field

Gets or sets the size of the first dimension of an array.

```
Public Dim FirstBound As Integer
```

Field Value

Contains an integer that represents the size of the first dimension of an array.

Remarks

The constructor sets this field when the **VBFixedArrayAttribute** is applied to an array.

See Also

VBFixedStringAttribute Class, ComClassAttribute Class

VBFixedArrayAttribute.SecondBound Field

Gets or sets the size of the second dimension of a two dimensional array.

```
Public Dim SecondBound As Integer
```

Field Value

Contains an integer that represents the size of the second dimension of a two dimensional array.

Remarks

The constructor sets this field when the **VBFixedArrayAttribute** is applied to an array.

See Also

VBFixedStringAttribute Class, ComClassAttribute Class

VBFixedStringAttribute Class

Used to declare fixed-sized strings.

```
<System.AttributeUsage(System.AttributeTargets.Field, _
   Inherited := False, AllowMultiple := False)> _
Public NotInheritable Class VBFixedStringAttribute
   Inherits System.Attribute
```

Remarks

Visual Basic .NET strings are of variable length by default. This attribute is useful when using Visual Basic .NET file input and output functions, such as **FileGet** and **FilePut** that require fixed length strings.

Example

```
Structure Person
   Public ID As Integer
   Public MonthlySalary As Decimal
   Public LastReviewDate As Long
   <VBFixedString(15)> Public FirstName As String
   <VBFixedString(15)> Public LastName As String
   <VBFixedString(15)> Public Title As String
   <VBFixedString(150)> Public ReviewComments As String
End Structure
```

See Also

VBFixedArrayAttribute Class, ComClassAttribute Class, FileGet Function, FilePut Function, FileOpen Function

VBFixedStringAttribute Constructor

Initializes the value of the **SizeConst** field.

```
Public Sub New( _
   ByVal size As Integer _
)
```

Parameters

size

The size of the fixed string.

Remarks

The constructor runs when the **VBFixedStringAttribute** attribute is applied to a class.

See Also

VBFixedStringAttribute Class

VBFixedStringAttribute.SizeConst Field

Gets or sets the length of the string.

```
Public Dim SizeConst As Integer
```

Field Value

Represents the length of the string.

Remarks

Use this field to specify the length of a fixed-length string.

See Also

VBFixedStringAttribute Class

VbStrConv Enumeration

When you call the **StrConv** function, you can use the following enumeration members in your code in place of the actual values.

VbStrConv Enumeration Members

The *Conversion* argument takes the following **VbStrConv** enumeration members:

Member	Constant	Description
UpperCase	**vbUpperCase**	Converts the string to uppercase characters.
LowerCase	**vbLowerCase**	Converts the string to lowercase characters.
ProperCase	**vbProperCase**	Converts the first letter of every word in the string to uppercase.
Wide	**vbWide**	Converts narrow (single-byte) characters in the string to wide (double-byte) characters. Applies to Asian locales.
Narrow	**vbNarrow**	Converts wide (double-byte) characters in the string to narrow (single-byte) characters. Applies to Asian locales.
Katakana	**vbKatakana**	Converts Hiragana characters in the string to Katakana characters. Applies to Japanese locale only.
Hiragana	**vbHiragana**	Converts Katakana characters in the string to Hiragana characters. Applies to Japanese locale only.
SimplifiedChinese	**vbSimplifiedChinese**	Converts the string to Simplified Chinese characters.
TraditionalChinese	**vbTraditionalChinese**	Converts the string to Traditional Chinese characters.
LinguisticCasing	**vbLinguisticCasing**	Converts the string from file system rules for casing to linguistic rules.

See Also

StrConv Function

VbTypeName Function

Returns a **String** value containing the Visual Basic data type name of a variable.

```
Public Function VbTypeName(ByVal UrtName As String) As String
```

Parameter

UrtName

Required. **String** variable containing a type name used by the common language runtime.

Remarks

VbTypeName returns the Visual Basic .NET type name corresponding to the common language runtime type name. For example, if *UrtName* contains "Int32" or "System.Int32", **VbTypeName** returns "Integer". If **VbTypeName** does not recognize the value of *UrtName*, it returns **Nothing** (not the string "Nothing").

The type name in *UrtName* can be obtained from various sources, for example from the **Name** property of the **System.Type** class.

Example

This example uses the **VbTypeName** function to return data type names for several variables.

```
Dim SysDateName As String = "System.DateTime"
Dim SysShortName As String = "Int16"
Dim SysBadName As String = "Nonsense"
Dim MyVbName As String
MyVbName = VbTypeName(SysDateName)    ' Returns "Date".
MyVbName = VbTypeName(SysShortName)    ' Returns "Short".
MyVbName = VbTypeName(SysBadName)    ' Returns Nothing.
```

See Also

Data Type Summary, String Data Type, SystemTypeName Function

Weekday Function

Returns an **Integer** value containing a number representing the day of the week.

```
Public Function Weekday( _
   ByVal DateValue As DateTime, _
   Optional ByVal DayOfWeek As FirstDayOfWeek = FirstDayOfWeek.Sunday _
) As Integer
```

Parameters

DateValue

Required. **Date** value for which you want to determine the day of the week.

DayOfWeek

Optional. A value chosen from the **FirstDayOfWeek** enumeration that specifies the first day of the week. If not specified, **FirstDayOfWeek.Sunday** is used.

Settings

The *DayOfWeek* argument can have one of the following settings.

Enumeration value	Value	Description
FirstDayOfWeek.System	0	First day of week specified in system settings
FirstDayOfWeek.Sunday	1	Sunday (default)
FirstDayOfWeek.Monday	2	Monday (complies with ISO standard 8601, section 3.17)
FirstDayOfWeek.Tuesday	3	Tuesday
FirstDayOfWeek.Wednesday	4	Wednesday
FirstDayOfWeek.Thursday	5	Thursday
FirstDayOfWeek.Friday	6	Friday
FirstDayOfWeek.Saturday	7	Saturday

Exceptions/Errors

Exception type	Error number	Condition
ArgumentException	5	*DayOfWeek* is less than 0 or more than 7.

Remarks

The value returned by the **Weekday** function corresponds to the values of the **FirstDayOfWeek** enumeration; that is, 1 indicates Sunday and 7 indicates Saturday.

If *DayOfWeek* is less than 0 or more than 7, an **ArgumentException** error occurs.

Note **Weekday** uses the current calendar setting from the **CurrentCulture** property of the **CultureInfo** class in the **System.Globalization** namespace. The default **CurrentCulture** values are determined by **Control Panel** settings.

Example

This example uses the **Weekday** function to obtain the day of the week from a specified date.

```
Dim MyDate As Date
Dim MyWeekDay As Integer
MyDate = #2/12/1969#    ' Assign a date.
MyWeekDay = Weekday(MyDate)    ' MyWeekDay contains 4 because
   ' MyDate represents a Wednesday.
```

See Also

Day Function, Month Function, Now Property, WeekdayName Function, Year Function, DatePart Function

WeekdayName Function

Returns a **String** value containing the name of the specified weekday.

```
Public Function WeekdayName( _
   ByVal WeekDay As Integer, _
   Optional ByVal Abbreviate As Boolean = False, _
   Optional ByVal FirstDayOfWeekValue As FirstDayOfWeek = FirstDayOfWeek.System _
) As String
```

Parameters

WeekDay
: Required. **Integer**. The numeric designation for the weekday, from 1 through 7; 1 indicates the first day of the week and 7 indicates the last day of the week. The identities of the first and last days depend on the setting of *FirstDayOfWeekValue*.

Abbreviate
: Optional. **Boolean** value that indicates if the weekday name is to be abbreviated. If omitted, the default is **False**, which means the weekday name is not abbreviated.

FirstDayOfWeekValue
: Optional. A value chosen from the **FirstDayOfWeek** enumeration that specifies the first day of the week. If not specified, **FirstDayOfWeek.System** is used.

Settings

The *FirstDayOfWeekValue* argument can have one of the following settings.

Enumeration value	Value	Description
FirstDayOfWeek.System	0	First day of week specified in system settings (default)
FirstDayOfWeek.Sunday	1	Sunday
FirstDayOfWeek.Monday	2	Monday (complies with ISO standard 8601, section 3.17)
FirstDayOfWeek.Tuesday	3	Tuesday
FirstDayOfWeek.Wednesday	4	Wednesday
FirstDayOfWeek.Thursday	5	Thursday
FirstDayOfWeek.Friday	6	Friday
FirstDayOfWeek.Saturday	7	Saturday

Exceptions/Errors

Exception type	Error number	Condition
ArgumentException	5	*WeekDay* is less than 1 or greater than 7, or *FirstDayOfWeekValue* is less than 0 or greater than 7.

Remarks

The string returned by **WeekdayName** depends not only on the input arguments, but also on the Regional Options settings specified in the Windows Control Panel.

If *WeekDay* is less than 1 or more than 7, or if *FirstDayOfWeekValue* is less than 0 or more than 7, an **ArgumentException** error occurs.

> **Note** **WeekdayName** uses the current calendar setting from the **CurrentCulture** property of the **CultureInfo** class in the **System.Globalization** namespace. The default **CurrentCulture** values are determined by **Control Panel** settings.

See Also

MonthName Function

When

The **When** keyword adds a conditional test to a **Catch** statement.

The **When** keyword is used in this context:

Try...Catch...Finally Statements

See Also

Visual Basic Language Keywords

While

The **While** keyword specifies a condition that allows the execution of a **Do** loop to continue. The **While** keyword is not the same as the opening statement of the **While...End While** block.

The **While** keyword is used in this context:

Do...Loop Statements

See Also

While...End While Statements

While...End While Statements

Executes a series of statements as long as a given condition is **True**.

```
While condition
   [ statements ]
End While
```

Parts

condition
Required. Expression. Must evaluate to **True** or **False**. If *condition* is **Nothing**, *condition* is treated as **False**.

statements
Optional. One or more statements following **While** that are executed while *condition* is **True**.

End While
Terminates execution of the **While** block.

Remarks

If *condition* is **True**, all of the *statements* are executed until the **End While** statement is encountered. Control then returns to the **While** statement and *condition* is again checked. If *condition* is still **True**, the process is repeated. If it is **False**, execution resumes with the statement following the **End While** statement.

You can nest **While** loops by placing one loop within another.

Example

This example uses the **While...End While** statement to increment a counter variable. The statements in the loop are executed as long as the condition evaluates to **True**.

```
Dim Counter As Integer = 0
While Counter < 20   ' Test value of Counter.
   Counter += 1   ' Increment Counter.
End While   ' End While loop when Counter > 19.
Debug.WriteLine (Counter)   ' Prints 20 in the Output window.
```

See Also

Do...Loop Statements, With...End With Statements

With...End With Statements

Executes a series of statements making repeated reference to a single object or structure.

```
With object
   [ statements ]
End With
```

Parts

object
   Required. Expression. Can evaluate to any data type, including elementary types.

statements
   Optional. One or more statements following **With** that are executed on *object*.

End With
   Terminates execution of the **With** block.

Remarks

With...End With allows you to perform a series of statements on a specified object without requalifying the name of the object. For example, to change a number of different properties on a single object, place the property assignment statements within the **With...End With**, referring to the object once instead of referring to it with each property assignment. The following example illustrates use of **With...End With** to assign values to several properties of the same object:

```
With MyLabel
   .Height = 2000
   .Width = 2000
   .Text = "This is MyLabel"
End With
```

> **Note** Once you have entered a **With...End With**, you cannot reassign *object* until you have passed the **End With**. Therefore, you can access the methods and properties of only the specified object without qualifying them. You can use methods and properties of other objects, but you must qualify them with their object names.

You can nest **With...End With** statements by placing one within another. However, because members of outer statements are masked inside the inner statements, you must provide a fully qualified object reference in an inner **With...End With** to any member of an object in an outer statement.

You cannot use **GoTo** to branch from outside a **With...End With** to a label inside it. If you with to exit before all the statements have been executed, put a label on the **End With** statement and branch to that.

Example

This example uses the **With** statement to execute a series of statements on a single object. The object `MyObject` and its properties are generic names used for illustration purposes only.

```
With MyObject
   .Height = 100    ' Same As MyObject.Height = 100.
   .Text = "Hello World"   ' Same As MyObject.Caption = "Hello World".
   With .Font
      .Color = Red    ' Same As MyObject.Font.Color = Red.
      .Bold = True    ' Same As MyObject.Font.Bold = True.
   End With
End With
```

WithEvents

The **WithEvents** keyword indicates that a declared object variable refers to a class instance that can raise events.

The **WithEvents** keyword is used in this context:

Dim Statement

See Also

Visual Basic Language Keywords

Write, WriteLine Functions

Writes data to a sequential file. Data written with **Write** is usually read from a file with **Input**.

```
Public Sub Write( _
   ByVal FileNumber As Integer, _
   ByVal ParamArray Output As Object _
)
```

-or-

```
Public Sub WriteLine( _
   ByVal FileNumber As Integer, _
   ByVal ParamArray Output() As Object _
)
```

Parameters

FileNumber
Required. An **Integer** expression containing any valid file number.

Output
Optional. One or more comma-delimited expressions to write to a file.

Exceptions/Errors

Exception type	Error number	Condition
IOException	52	*FileNumber* does not exist.
IOException	54	File mode is invalid.

Remarks

If you omit *Output*, a blank line is printed to the file. Multiple expressions can be separated with a comma.

Unlike the **Print** function, the **Write** function inserts commas between items and quotation marks around strings as they are written to the file. You don't have to put explicit delimiters in the list. When **Write** is used to write data to a file, only the following data formats are supported and several universal assumptions are followed so the data can always be read and correctly interpreted using **Input**, regardless of locale:

- Numeric data is always written using the period as the decimal separator.
- For **Boolean** data, either `#TRUE#` or `#FALSE#` is printed. The **True** and **False** keywords are not translated, regardless of locale.
- Date data is written to the file using the universal date format. When either the date or the time component is missing or zero, only the part provided gets written to the file.
- Nothing is written to the file if *Output* data is empty. However, for null data, `#NULL#` is written.
- For **Error** data, the output appears as `#ERROR errorcode#`. The **Error** keyword is not translated, regardless of locale.

WriteLine inserts a newline character (that is, a carriage return-linefeed, or `Chr(13) + Chr(10)`), after it has written the final character in *Output* to the file.

Note You should not write strings that contain embedded quotation marks for use with the **Input** function (for example, `"1,2""X"`): the **Input** function parses this string as two complete and separate strings.

Example

This example uses the **Write** function to write raw data to a sequential file.

```
FileOpen(1, "TESTFILE", OpenMode.Output) ' Open file for output.
Write(1, "This is a test.")  ' Print text to file.
WriteLine(1)  ' Print blank line to file.
WriteLine(1, "Zone 1", TAB(), "Zone 2")   ' Print in two print zones.
WriteLine(1, "Hello", " ", "World")     ' Separate strings with space.
WriteLine(1, SPC(5), "5 leading spaces ")    ' Print five leading spaces.
WriteLine(1, TAB(10), "Hello")   ' Print word at column 10.

' Assign Boolean, Date, and Error values.
Dim aBool As Boolean
Dim aDate As DateTime
aBool = False
aDate = DateTime.Parse("February 12, 1969")

' Dates and Booleans are translated using locale settings of
' your system.
WriteLine(1, aBool, " is a Boolean value")
WriteLine(1, aDate, " is a date")
FileClose(1)   ' Close file.
```

See Also

Input Function; FileOpen Function; Print, PrintLine Functions

WriteOnly

The **WriteOnly** keyword indicates that a property can be written but not read.

The **WriteOnly** keyword is used in this context:

Property Statement

See Also

Visual Basic Language Keywords

Xor Operator

Performs a logical exclusion operation on two **Boolean** expressions, or a bitwise exclusion on two numeric expressions..

```
result = expression1 Xor expression2
```

Parts

result
Required. Any **Boolean** or numeric variable. The result for **Boolean** comparison is the logical exclusion of two expressions. For bitwise operations the result is a numeric value resulting from the bitwise exclusion of two numeric expressions

expression1
Required. Any **Boolean** or numeric expression.

expression2
Required. Any **Boolean** or numeric expression of the same type as *expression1*.

Remarks

For **Boolean** comparisons, if one and only one of the expressions evaluates to **True**, *result* is **True**. Otherwise, *result* is **False**. If either expression is stated as Nothing, that expression is evaluated as **False**.

If *expression1* is	And *expression2* is	Then *result* is
True	**True**	**False**
True	**False**	**True**
False	**True**	**True**
False	**False**	**False**

For numeric expressions, the **Xor** operator performs as a bitwise operator. A bitwise comparison of two expressions using exclusive-or logic to form the result, as shown in the following table:

If bit in *expression1* is	And bit in *expression2* is	Then *result* is
0	0	0
0	1	1
1	0	1
1	1	0

Note Since the logical/bitwise operators have a lower precedence than other arithmetic and relational operators, any bitwise operations should be enclosed in parentheses to insure accurate execution.

If the operands consist of one **Boolean** expression and one numeric expression, the result **Boolean** expression will be converted to a numeric value (–1 for True, and 0 for False) and the bitwise operation will result.

Example

This example uses the **Xor** operator to perform logical exclusion on two expressions. The result is a **Boolean** value representing whether *only* one of the expressions is true.

```
Dim A As Integer = 10
Dim B As Integer = 8
Dim C As Integer = 6
Dim myCheck As Boolean
myCheck = A > B Xor B > C   ' Returns False.
myCheck = B > A Xor B > C   ' Returns True.
myCheck = B > A Xor C > B   ' Returns False.
```

This example uses the **Xor** operator to perform logical exclusion of the individual bits of two numeric expressions. The bit in the result pattern is set if only one of the corresponding bits in the operands are set.

```
Dim A As Integer = 10
Dim B As Integer = 8
Dim C As Integer = 6
Dim myCheck As Integer
myCheck = (A Xor B)   ' Returns 2.
myCheck = (A Xor C)   ' Returns 12.
myCheck = (B Xor C)   ' Returns 14.
```

See Also

Logical/Bitwise Operators, Operator Precedence in Visual Basic, Operators Listed by Functionality, Logical Operators

Year Function

Returns an **Integer** value from 1 through 9999 representing the year.

```
Public Function Year(ByVal DateValue As DateTime) As Integer
```

Parameter

DateValue
Required. **Date** value from which you want to extract the year.

You can also obtain the year by calling **DatePart** and specifying **DateInterval.Year** for the *Interval* argument.

Example

This example uses the **Year** function to obtain the year from a specified date. In the development environment, the date literal is displayed in short date format using the locale settings of your code.

```
Dim MyDate As Date
Dim MyYear As Integer
MyDate = #2/12/1969#   ' Assign a date.
MyYear = Year(MyDate)   ' MyYear contains 1969.
```

See Also

Day Function, Month Function, Now Property, Weekday Function, DatePart Function

APPENDIX A

Operators

Operators Listed by Functionality

Operators	Description
Arithmetic Operators	These operators perform mathematical calculations.
Assignment Operators	These operators perform assignment operations.
Comparison Operators	These operators perform comparisons.
Concatenation Operators	These operators combine strings.
Logical/Bitwise Operators	These operators perform logical operations.
Miscellaneous Operators	These operators perform miscellaneous operations.

See Also

Operators,Operator Precedence in Visual Basic

Operator Precedence in Visual Basic

When several operations occur in an expression, each part is evaluated and resolved in a predetermined order called *operator precedence*.

When expressions contain operators from more than one category, they are evaluated according to the following rules. The arithmetic and concatenation operators have an order of precedence that is described below, and all have higher precedence than the comparison and logical operators. Comparison operators have higher precedence than the logical operators, but lower precedence than the arithmetic and concatenation operators. All comparison operators have equal precedence; that is, they are evaluated in the order, left to right, in which they appear. Arithmetic, concatenation and logical/bitwise Operators are evaluated in the following order of precedence:

Arithmetic/Concatenation Operators

Exponentiation (^)

Negation (-)

Multiplication and division (*, /)

Integer division (\)

Modulus arithmetic (**Mod**)

Addition and subtraction (+, -), String concatenation (+)

String concatenation (**&**)

Comparison Operators

Equality (=)

Inequality (<>)

Less than, greater than (<,>)

Greater than or equal to (>=)

Less than or equal to (<=)

Like

Is

TypeOf...Is

Logical/Bitwise Operators

Negation (**Not**)

Conjunction (**And, AndAlso**)

Disjunction (**Or, OrElse, Xor**)

When multiplication and division occur together in an expression, each operation is evaluated as it occurs from left to right. When addition and subtraction occur together in an expression, each operation is evaluated in order of appearance from left to right. Parentheses can be used to override the order of precedence and force some parts of an expression to be evaluated before others. Operations within parentheses are always performed before those outside. Within parentheses, however, operator precedence is maintained.

The string concatenation operator (**&**) is not an arithmetic operator, but in precedence, it does follow all arithmetic operators and precede all comparison operators.

The **Is** operator is an object reference comparison operator. It does not compare objects or their values; it checks only to determine if two object references refer to the same object.

See Also

= Operator, Is Operator, Like Operator, Operators Listed by Functionality, Operators

Arithmetic Operators

The following are the arithmetic operators defined in Visual Basic .NET.

^ Operator

* Operator

/ Operator

\ Operator

Mod Operator

+ Operator

- Operator

See Also

Operator Precedence in Visual Basic, Arithmetic Operators

Assignment Operators

= Operator

^= Operator

*= Operator

/= Operator

\= Operator

+= Operator

-= Operator

&= Operator

Comparison Operators

Compares expressions.

```
result = expression1 comparisonoperator expression2
result = object1 Is object2
result = string Like pattern
```

Parts

result
Required. Any numeric variable. The result is a **Boolean** value representing the result of the comparison.

expression
Required. Any expression.

comparisonoperator
Required. Any comparison operator.

object
Required. Any reference object name.

string
Required. Any **String** expression.

pattern
Required. Any **String** expression or range of characters.

Remarks

The following table contains a list of the comparison operators and the conditions that determine whether *result* is **True** or **False**.

Operator	True if	False if
< (Less than)	*expression1 < expression2*	*expression1 >= expression2*
<= (Less than or equal to)	*expression1 <= expression2*	*expression1 > expression2*
> (Greater than)	*expression1 > expression2*	*expression1 <= expression2*
>= (Greater than or equal to)	*expression1 >= expression2*	*expression1 < expression2*
= (Equal to)	*expression1 = expression2*	*expression1 <> expression2*
<> (Not equal to)	*expression1 <> expression2*	*expression1 = expression2*

Note The **Is** and **Like** operators have specific comparison functionality that differs from the operators in the table.

When an expression of type **Single** is compared to one of type **Double**, the **Single** expression is converted to **Double**. This behavior is opposite to the behavior found in Visual Basic 6.

Similarly, when an expression of type **Decimal** is compared with an expression of type **Single** or **Double**, the **Decimal** expression will be converted to **Single** or **Double**. For **Decimal** expressions, any fractional value less than 1E–28 may be lost. Such fractional value loss may cause two values to compare as equal when they are not. For this reason, care should be taken when using equality (=) to compare two floating point variables. It is better to test that the absolute value of the difference between the two numbers is less than a small acceptable tolerance.

Comparing Strings

When Strings are compared, the string expressions are evaluated based on their alphabetical sort order. The sort order for strings is evaluated based upon the **Option Compare** setting.

Option Compare Binary results in string comparisons based on a sort order derived from the internal binary representations of the characters. Sort order is determined by the code page. In the following example, a typical binary sort order is shown:

```
A < B < E < Z < a < b < e < z < À < Ê < Ø < à < ê < ø
```

Option Compare Text results in string comparisons based on a case-insensitive, textual sort order determined by your system's locale. When you sort the same characters using **Option Compare Text**, the following text sort order is produced:

```
(A=a) < (À=à) < (B=b) < (E=e) < (Ê=ê) < (Ø=ø) < (Z=z)
```

Typeless programming with comparison operators

The use of comparison operators with **Object** expressions is not allowed under **Option Strict On**. When **Option Strict** is **Off**, and *expression1* or *expression2* are **Object** expressions, their runtime type determines how they are compared. The following table shows how the expressions are compared and the result from the comparison, depending on the runtime type of the operands:

If operands are:	Comparison will be:
Both strings	Sort comparison based on string sorting characteristics.
Both numeric values	Objects will be converted to **Double**, and numeric comparison performed.
One numeric value, and one **String**	The **String** is converted to a **Double** and numeric comparison is performed. If the **String** cannot be converted to **Double**, an **InvalidCastException** will be thrown.
Either or both are reference types other than **String**	An **InvalidCastException** will be thrown.

For numeric comparisons, **Nothing** is treated as 0. For string comparisons, **Nothing** is treated as " ".

Example

This example shows various uses of comparison operators, which you use to compare expressions. Comparison operators return a **Boolean** result that represents whether or not the stated expression is true. When the > and < operators are applied to strings, the comparison is made between the normal alphabetical sorting order of the strings. This may be dependent on locale. Whether the sort is case-sensitive or not depends on the Option Compare setting.

```
Dim myResult As Boolean
myResult = 45 < 35    ' Returns False.
myResult = 45 = 45    ' Returns True.
myResult = 4 <> 3    ' Returns True.
myResult = "5" > "4444"    ' Returns True.
```

See Also

= Operator, Is Operator, Like Operator, Option Compare Statement, Operator Precedence in Visual Basic, Operators Listed by Functionality, Comparison Operators

Concatenation Operators

& Operator

+ Operator

See Also

Operator Precedence in Visual Basic, Concatenation Operators

Logical/Bitwise Operators

And Operator

Not Operator

Or Operator

Xor Operator

AndAlso Operator

OrElse Operator

See Also

Operator Precedence in Visual Basic, Logical Operators

Miscellaneous Operators

AddressOf Operator

GetType Operator

See Also

Operators Listed by Functionality

APPENDIX B

Summary Lists

#Compiler Directive Summary

Visual Basic language keywords and run-time library members are organized by purpose and use.

Action	Language element
Define a compiler constant.	#Const
Compile selected blocks of code.	#If...Then...#Else
Collapse and hide sections of code.	#Region
Indicate a mapping between source lines and text external to the source.	#ExternalSource

See Also

Keywords and Members by Task, Visual Basic Language Keywords, Visual Basic Run-Time Library Members

Arrays Summary

Visual Basic language keywords and run-time library members are organized by purpose and use.

Action	Language element
Verify an array.	IsArray
Declare and initialize an array.	Dim, Private, Public, ReDim
Find the limits of an array.	LBound, UBound
Reinitialize an array	Erase, ReDim

See Also

Keywords and Members by Task, Visual Basic Language Keywords, Visual Basic Run-Time Library Members

Collection Object Summary

Visual Basic language keywords and run-time library members are organized by purpose and use.

Action	Language element
Create a **Collection** object.	Collection
Add an item to a collection.	Add
Remove an object from a collection.	Remove
Reference an item in a collection.	Item
Return a reference to an **IEnumerator** interface.	GetEnumerator

See Also

Keywords and Members by Task, Visual Basic Language Keywords, Visual Basic Run-Time Library Members

Control Flow Summary

Visual Basic language keywords and run-time library members are organized by purpose and use.

Action	Language element
Branch.	GoTo, On Error
Exit or pause the program.	End, Exit, Stop
Loop.	Do...Loop, For...Next, For Each...Next, While...End While, With
Make decisions.	Choose, If...Then...Else, Select Case, Switch
Use procedures.	Call, Function, Property, Sub

See Also

Keywords and Members by Task, Visual Basic Language Keywords, Visual Basic Run-Time Library Members

Conversion Summary

Visual Basic language keywords and run-time library members are organized by purpose and use.

Action	Language element
ANSI value to string.	Chr, ChrW
String to lowercase or uppercase.	Format, LCase, UCase
Date to serial number.	DateSerial, DateValue
Decimal number to other bases.	Hex, Oct
Number to string.	Format, Str
One data type to another.	CBool, CByte, CDate, CDbl, CDec, CInt, CLng, CSng, CShort, CStr, CType, Fix, Int
Date to day, month, weekday, or year.	Day, Month, Weekday, Year
Time to hour, minute, or second.	Hour, Minute, Second
String to ASCII value.	Asc, AscW
String to number.	Val
Time to serial number.	TimeSerial, TimeValue

See Also

Keywords and Members by Task, Visual Basic Language Keywords, Visual Basic Run-Time Library Members

Data Type Summary

The following table shows the Visual Basic .NET data types, their supporting common language runtime types, their nominal storage allocation, and their value ranges.

Visual Basic type	Common language runtime type structure	Nominal storage allocation	Value range
Boolean	**System.Boolean**	2 bytes	**True** or **False.**
Byte	**System.Byte**	1 byte	0 through 255 (unsigned).
Char	**System.Char**	2 bytes	0 through 65535 (unsigned).
Date	**System.DateTime**	8 bytes	0:00:00 on January 1, 0001 through 11:59:59 PM on December 31, 9999.

(continued)

(continued)

Visual Basic type	Common language runtime type structure	Nominal storage allocation	Value range
Decimal	**System.Decimal**	16 bytes	0 through +/–79,228,162,514,264,337,593,543,950,335 with no decimal point; 0 through +/–7.9228162514264337593543950335 with 28 places to the right of the decimal; smallest nonzero number is +/–0.0000000000000000000000000001 (+/–1E–28).
Double (double-precision floating-point)	**System.Double**	8 bytes	–1.79769313486231570E+308 through –4.94065645841246544E–324 for negative values; 4.94065645841246544E–324 through 1.79769313486231570E+308 for positive values.
Integer	**System.Int32**	4 bytes	–2,147,483,648 through 2,147,483,647.
Long (long integer)	**System.Int64**	8 bytes	–9,223,372,036,854,775,808 through 9,223,372,036,854,775,807.
Object	**System.Object** (class)	4 bytes	Any type can be stored in a variable of type **Object**.
Short	**System.Int16**	2 bytes	–32,768 through 32,767.
Single (single-precision floating-point)	**System.Single**	4 bytes	–3.4028235E+38 through –1.401298E–45 for negative values; 1.401298E–45 through 3.4028235E+38 for positive values.
String (variable-length)	**System.String** (class)	Depends on implementing platform	0 to approximately 2 billion Unicode characters.
User-Defined Type (structure)	(inherits from **System.ValueType**)	Depends on implementing platform	Each member of the structure has a range determined by its data type and independent of the ranges of the other members.

Note For strings containing text, use the **StrConv** function to convert from one text format to another.

Memory Consumption

When you declare an elementary data type, it is not safe to assume that its memory consumption is the same as its nominal storage allocation. The common language runtime assigns storage based on the characteristics of the platform on which your application is executing. In some circumstances it packs your declared elements as closely together as possible; in other cases it aligns their memory addresses to natural hardware boundaries. Also, storage assignment is different on a 64-bit platform than it is on a 32-bit platform.

The same considerations apply to each member of a composite data type such as a structure or an array. Furthermore, some composite types have additional memory requirements. For example, an array uses extra memory for the array itself and also for each dimension. On a 32-bit platform, this overhead is currently 12 bytes plus 8 bytes for each dimension. On a 64-bit platform the requirement is doubled. You cannot rely on simply adding together the nominal storage allocations of the components.

An **Object** referring to any elementary or composite data type uses 4 bytes in addition to the data contained in the data type.

See Also

Boolean Data Type; Byte Data Type; Char Data Type; Date Data Type; Decimal Data Type; Double Data Type; Integer Data Type; Long Data Type; Object Data Type; Short Data Type; Single Data Type; String Data Type; User-Defined Data Type; Type Conversion Functions; Int, Fix Functions; StrConv Function

Data Types Summary

Visual Basic language keywords and run-time library members are organized by purpose and use.

Action	Language element
Convert between data types.	CBool, CByte, CChar, CDate, CDbl, CDec, CInt, CLng, CObj, CShort, CSng, CStr, Fix, Int
Set intrinsic data types.	Boolean, Byte, Char, Date, Decimal, Double, Integer, Long, Object(default), Short, Single, String
Verify data types.	IsArray, IsDate, IsDbNull, IsError, IsNothing, IsNumeric, IsReference

See Also

Keywords and Members by Task, Visual Basic Language Keywords, Visual Basic Run-Time Library Members

Dates and Times Summary

Visual Basic language keywords and run-time library members are organized by purpose and use.

Action	Language element
Get the current date or time.	Now, Today, TimeOfDay
Perform date calculations.	DateAdd, DateDiff, DatePart
Return a date.	DateSerial, DateValue, MonthName, WeekDayName
Return a time.	TimeSerial, TimeValue
Set the date or time.	DateString, TimeOfDay, TimeString, Today
Time a process.	Timer

See Also

Keywords and Members by Task, Visual Basic Language Keywords, Visual Basic Run-Time Library Members

Declarations and Constants Summary

Visual Basic language keywords and run-time library members are organized by purpose and use.

Action	Language element
Assign a value.	Get, Property
Declare variables or constants.	Const, Dim, Private, Protected, Public, Shadows, Shared, Static
Declare a class, delegate, enumeration, module, namespace, or structure.	Class, Delegate, Enum, Module, Namespace, Structure
Create objects.	CreateObject, GetObject, New
Get information about an object.	GetType, IsArray, IsDate, IsDbNull, IsError, IsNothing, IsNumeric, IsReference, SystemTypeName, TypeName, VarType, VbTypeName
Refer to the current object.	Me
Require explicit variable declarations.	Option Explicit, Option Strict
Handle events.	AddHandler, Event, RaiseEvent, RemoveHandler
Implement inheritance.	Inherits, MustInherit, MustOverride, MyBase, MyClass, New, NotInheritable, NotOverridable, Overloads, Overridable, Overrides

See Also

Keywords and Members by Task, Visual Basic Language Keywords, Visual Basic Run-Time Library Members

Directories and Files Summary

Visual Basic language keywords and run-time library members are organized by purpose and use.

Action	Language element
Change a directory or folder.	ChDir
Change the drive.	ChDrive
Copy a file.	FileCopy
Make a directory or folder.	MkDir
Remove a directory or folder.	RmDir
Rename a file, directory, or folder.	Rename
Return the current path.	CurDir
Return a file's date/time stamp.	FileDateTime
Return file, directory, or label attributes.	GetAttr
Return a file's length.	FileLen
Return a file's name or volume label.	Dir
Set attribute information for a file.	SetAttr

See Also

Keywords and Members by Task, Visual Basic Language Keywords, Visual Basic Run-Time Library Members

Errors Summary

Visual Basic language keywords and run-time library members are organized by purpose and use.

Action	Language element
Generate run-time errors.	Clear, Error, Raise
Get exceptions.	GetException
Provide error information.	Err
Trap errors during run time.	On Error, Resume, Try...Catch...Finally
Provide line number of error.	Erl
Provide system error code.	LastDLLError

See Also

Keywords and Members by Task, Visual Basic Language Keywords, Visual Basic Run-Time Library Members

Financial Summary

Visual Basic language keywords and run-time library members are organized by purpose and use.

Action	Language element
Calculate depreciation.	DDB, SLN, SYD
Calculate future value.	FV
Calculate interest rate.	Rate
Calculate internal rate of return.	IRR, MIRR
Calculate number of periods.	NPer
Calculate payments.	IPmt, Pmt, PPmt
Calculate present value.	NPV, PV

See Also

Keywords and Members by Task, Visual Basic Language Keywords, Visual Basic Run-Time Library Members

Information and Interaction Summary

Visual Basic language keywords and run-time library members are organized by purpose and use.

Action	Language element
Run other programs.	AppActivate, Shell
Call a method or property.	CallByName
Sound a beep from computer.	Beep
Provide a command-line string.	Command
Manipulate COM objects.	CreateObject, GetObject
Retrieve color information.	QBColor, RGB
Control dialog boxes.	InputBox, MsgBox

See Also

Keywords and Members by Task, Visual Basic Language Keywords, Visual Basic Run-Time Library Members

Input and Output Summary

Visual Basic language keywords and run-time library members are organized by purpose and use.

Action	Language element
Access or create a file.	FileOpen
Close files.	FileClose, Reset
Control output appearance.	Format, Print, Spc, Tab, FileWidth
Copy a file.	FileCopy
Get information about a file.	EOF, FileAttr, FileDateTime, FileLen, FreeFile, GetAttr, Loc, LOF, Seek
Manage files.	Dir, Kill, Lock, Unlock
Read from a file.	FileGet, FileGetObject, Input, InputString, LineInput
Return length of a file.	FileLen
Set or get file attributes.	FileAttr, GetAttr, SetAttr
Set read-write position in a file.	Seek
Write to a file.	FilePut, FilePutObject, Print, Write

See Also

Keywords and Members by Task, Visual Basic Language Keywords, Visual Basic Run-Time Library Members

Math Summary

Visual Basic language keywords and run-time library members are organized by purpose and use.

Action	Language element
Derive trigonometric functions.	Atn, Cos, Sin, Tan
General calculations.	Exp, Log, Sqr
Generate random numbers.	Randomize, Rnd
Get absolute value.	Abs
Get the sign of an expression.	Sgn
Perform numeric conversions.	Fix, Int

See Also

Keywords and Members by Task, Visual Basic Language Keywords, Visual Basic Run-Time Library Members

Registry Summary

Visual Basic language keywords and run-time library members are organized by purpose and use.

Action	Language element
Delete program settings.	DeleteSetting
Read program settings.	GetSetting, GetAllSettings
Save program settings.	SaveSetting

See Also

Keywords and Members by Task, Visual Basic Language Keywords, Visual Basic Run-Time Library Members

String Manipulation Summary

Visual Basic language keywords and run-time library members are organized by purpose and use.

Action	Language element
Compare two strings.	StrComp
Convert strings.	StrConv
Reverse a string.	InStrRev, StrReverse
Convert to lowercase or uppercase.	Format, LCase, UCase
Create a string of repeating characters.	Space, StrDup
Find the length of a string.	Len
Format a string.	Format, FormatCurrency, FormatDateTime, FormatNumber, FormatPercent
Manipulate strings.	InStr, Left, LTrim, Mid, Right, RTrim, Trim
Set string comparison rules.	Option Compare
Work with ASCII and ANSI values.	Asc, AscW, Chr, ChrW
Replace a specified substring.	Replace
Return a filter-based string array.	Filter
Return a specified number of substrings.	Split, Join

See Also

Keywords and Members by Task, Visual Basic Language Keywords, Visual Basic Run-Time Library Members

APPENDIX C

Member Lists

Visual Basic Run-Time Library Members

The Visual Basic .NET run-time library members include functions, methods, and properties you can use in your code. The library is divided into modules representing categories of functionality.

Microsoft.VisualBasic.Collection

Add	Item
Count	Remove
GetEnumerator	

Microsoft.VisualBasic.Conversion

ErrorToString	Oct
Fix	Str
Hex	Val
Int	

Microsoft.VisualBasic.DateAndTime

DateAdd	Day	Second	Today
DateDiff	Hour	TimeOfDay	WeekDay
DatePart	Minute	Timer	WeekDayName
DateSerial	Month	TimeSerial	Year
DateString	MonthName	TimeString	
DateValue	Now	TimeValue	

Microsoft.VisualBasic.ErrObject

Clear
Description
Erl
GetException
HelpContext
HelpFile
LastDLLError
Number
Raise
Source

Microsoft.VisualBasic.FileSystem

ChDir
ChDrive
CurDir
Dir
EOF
FileAttr
FileClose
FileCopy
FileDateTime
FileGet
FileLen
FileOpen
FilePut
FileWidth
FreeFile
GetAttr
Input
InputString
Kill
LineInput
Loc
Lock
LOF
MkDir
Print
PrintLine
Rename
Reset
RmDir
Seek
SetAttr
SPC
TAB
Unlock
Write
WriteLine

Microsoft.VisualBasic.Financial

DDB
FV
IPmt
IRR
MIRR
NPer
NPV
Pmt
PPmt
PV
Rate
SLN
SYD

Microsoft.VisualBasic.Globals

ScriptEngine
ScriptEngineBuildVersion
ScriptEngineMajorVersion
ScriptEngineMinorVersion

Microsoft.VisualBasic.Information

Err	IsError	LBound	TypeName
IsArray	IsNothing	QBColor	UBound
IsDate	IsNumeric	RGB	VarType
IsDBNull	IsReference	SystemTypeName	VbTypeName

Microsoft.VisualBasic.Interaction

AppActivate	CreateObject	GetSetting	SaveSetting
Beep	DeleteSetting	IIf	Shell
CallByName	Environ	InputBox	Switch
Choose	GetAllSettings	MsgBox	
Command	GetObject	Partition	

Microsoft.VisualBasic.Strings

Asc	FormatNumber	Len	Space
AscW	FormatPercent	LSet	Split
Chr	GetChar	LTrim	StrComp
ChrW	InStr	Mid	StrConv
Filter	InStrRev	Replace	StrDup
Format	Join	Right	StrReverse
FormatCurrency	LCase	RSet	Trim
FormatDateTime	Left	RTrim	UCase

Microsoft.VisualBasic.VbMath

Randomize

Rnd

See Also

Visual Basic Language Keywords, Keywords and Members By Task

Err Object Members

Properties

Description Property	Read/write. Returns or sets a descriptive string associated with an error.
Erl Property	Read-only. Returns an integer indicating the line number of the last executed statement.
HelpContext Property	Read/write. Returns or sets an **Integer** containing the context ID for a topic in a Help file.
HelpFile Property	Read/write. Returns or sets a **String** expression containing the fully qualified path to a Help file.
LastDLLError Property	Read-only. Returns a system error code produced by a call to a dynamic-link library (DLL).
Number Property	Read/write. Returns or sets a numeric value specifying an error.
Source Property	Read/write. Returns or sets a **String** expression specifying the name of the object or application that originally generated the error.

Methods

Clear Method	Clears all property settings of the **Err** object.
Raise Method	Generates a run-time error; can be used instead of the **Error** statement.

See Also

Err Object

Collection Object Members

Properties

Count Property	Read-only. Returns an integer containing the number of objects in a collection.
Item Property	Returns a specific member of a **Collection** object either by position or by key.

Methods

Add Method	Adds a member to a **Collection** object.
Remove Method	Removes a member from a **Collection** object.

See Also

Collection Object

ComClassAttribute Class Members

Properties

ClassID Property	Contains a class ID used to uniquely identify the class.
EventID Property	Contains an event ID used to uniquely identify the event.
InterfaceID Property	Contains an interface ID used to uniquely identify the interface.
InterfaceShadows Property	Indicates that a generated COM interface name shadows another member of the class or base class.

Constructor

ComClassAttribute Constructor	Initializes a new instance of the **ComClassAttribute** class.

See Also

VBFixedArrayAttribute Class, VBFixedStringAttribute Class, ComClassAttribute Class, Shadows

VBFixedArrayAttribute Class Members

Fields

FirstBound Field	Gets or sets the size of the first dimension of an array.
SecondBound Field	Gets or sets the size of the second dimension of a two-dimensional array.

Constructor

VBFixedArrayAttribute Constructor	Initializes the bounds of a fixed-sized array.

See Also

VBFixedStringAttribute Class, ComClassAttribute Class

VBFixedStringAttribute Class Members

Fields

SizeConst Field	Gets or sets the length of the string.

Constructor

VBFixedStringAttribute Constructor	Initializes the value of the **SizeConst** field.

See Also

VBFixedArrayAttribute Class, VBFixedStringAttribute Class, ComClassAttribute Class

Keywords and Members by Task

Visual Basic language keywords and run-time library members are organized by purpose and use.

Category	Description
Arrays	Creating, defining, and using arrays.
Collections	Using collections.
Compiler Directives	Controlling compiler behavior.
Control Flow	Looping and controlling procedure flow.
Conversion	Converting numbers and data types.
Data Types	Data types and object subtypes.
Dates and Times	Converting and using date and time expressions.
Directories and Files	Controlling the file system and processing files.
Errors	Trapping and returning error values.
Financial	Performing financial calculations.
Input and Output	Receiving input and displaying or printing output.
Information and Interaction	Starting other applications and processing events.
Math	Performing trigonometric and other mathematical calculations.
Operators	Comparing expressions and other operations.
Registry	Deleting, reading, and saving program settings.
String Manipulation	Manipulating strings and string type data.
Declarations and Constants	Declaring programming elements and defining constants.

See Also

Visual Basic Language Keywords, Visual Basic Run-Time Library Members

APPENDIX D

Conversion Functions

Asc Function

AscW Function

CBool Function

CByte Function

CChar Function

CDate Function

CDbl Function

CDec Function

Chr Function

ChrW Function

CInt Function

CLng Function

CObj Function

CShort Function

CSng Function

CStr Function

CType Function

Format Function

Hex Function

Oct Function

Str Function

Val Function

See Also

Type Conversion Functions

APPENDIX E

Visual Basic Compiler Options

The Visual Basic .NET command-line compiler is provided as an alternative to compiling programs from within the Visual Studio .NET integrated development environment (IDE). This section contains descriptions for the Visual Basic compiler options.

Visual Basic Compiler Options Listed Alphabetically

The Visual Basic .NET command-line compiler is provided as an alternative to compiling programs from within the Visual Studio .NET integrated development environment (IDE). The following is a list of the Visual Basic command-line compiler options sorted alphabetically.

Option	Purpose
@ (Specify Response File)	Specifies a response file.
/?	Displays compiler options. This command is the same as specifying the **/help** option. No compilation occurs.
/addmodule	Causes the compiler to make all type information from the specified file(s) available to the project you are currently compiling.
/baseaddress	Specifies the base address of a DLL.
/bugreport	Creates a file that contains information that makes it easy to report a bug.
/debug	Produces debugging information.
/define	Defines symbols for conditional compilation.
/delaysign	Specifies whether the assembly will be fully or partially signed.
/help	Displays compiler options. This command is the same as specifying the **/?** option. No compilation occurs.
/imports	Imports a namespace from a specified assembly.
/keycontainer	Specifies a key container name for a key pair to give an assembly a strong name.

(continued)

(continued)

Option	Purpose
/keyfile	Specifies a file containing a key or key pair to give an assembly a strong name.
/libpath	Specifies the location of assemblies referenced via the /reference option.
/linkresource	Creates a link to a managed resource.
/main	Specifies the class that contains the **Sub Main** procedure to use at startup.
/nologo	Suppresses compiler banner information.
/nowarn	Suppresses the compiler's ability to generate warnings.
/optimize	Enables/disables code optimization.
/optioncompare	Determines whether string comparisons should be binary or use locale-specific text semantics.
/optionexplicit	Requires explicit declaration of variables.
/optionstrict	Enforces strict language semantics.
/out	Specifies an output file.
/quiet	Prevents the compiler from displaying code for syntax-related errors and warnings.
/recurse	Searches subdirectories for source files to compile.
/reference	Imports metadata from an assembly.
/removeintchecks	Disables integer overflow checking.
/resource	Embeds a managed resource in an assembly.
/rootnamespace	Specifies a namespace for all type declarations.
/target	Specifies the format of the output file using one of four options: /target:exe, /target:library, /target:module, or /target:winexe.
/utf8output	Displays compiler output using UTF-8 encoding.
/verbose	Outputs extra information during compilation.
/warnaserror	Promotes warnings to errors.
/win32icon	Inserts a .ico file into the output file.
/win32resource	Inserts a Win32 resource into the output file.

See Also

Visual Basic Compiler Options Listed by Category

Visual Basic Compiler Options Listed by Category

The Visual Basic .NET command-line compiler is provided as an alternative to compiling programs from within the Visual Studio .NET integrated development environment (IDE). The following is a list of the Visual Basic command-line compiler options sorted by functional category.

Compiler Output

Option	Purpose
/nologo	Suppresses compiler banner information.
/utf8output	Displays compiler output using UTF-8 encoding.
/verbose	Outputs extra information during compilation.

Optimization

Option	Purpose
/optimize	Enables/disables optimizations.

Output Files

Option	Purpose
/out	Specifies an output file.
/target	Specifies the format of the output file using one of four options: /target:exe, /target:library, /target:module, or /target:winexe.

.NET Assemblies

Option	Purpose
/addmodule	Causes the compiler to make all type information from the specified file(s) available to the project you are currently compiling.
/delaysign	Specifies whether the assembly will be fully or partially signed.
/imports	Imports a namespace from a specified assembly.
/keycontainer	Specifies a key container name for a key pair to give an assembly a strong name.
/keyfile	Specifies a file containing a key or key pair to give an assembly a strong name.

(continued)

(continued)

Option	Purpose
/libpath	Specifies the location of assemblies referenced via the /reference option.
/reference	Imports metadata from an assembly.

Debugging/Error Checking

Option	Purpose
/bugreport	Creates a file that contains information that makes it easy to report a bug.
/debug	Produces debugging information.
/nowarn	Suppresses the compiler's ability to generate warnings.
/quiet	Prevents the compiler from displaying code for syntax-related errors and warnings.
/removeintchecks	Disables integer overflow checking.
/warnaserror	Promotes warnings to errors.

Help

Option	Purpose
/?	Displays the compiler options. This command is the same as specifying the **/help** option. No compilation occurs.
/help	Displays the compiler options. This command is the same as specifying the **/?** option. No compilation occurs.

Language

Option	Purpose
/optionexplicit	Requires explicit declaration of variables.
/optionstrict	Enforces strict type semantics.
/optioncompare	Determines whether string comparisons should be binary or use locale-specific text semantics.

Preprocessor

Option	Purpose
/define	Defines symbols for conditional compilation.

Resources

Option	Purpose
/linkresource	Creates a link to a managed resource.
/resource	Embeds a managed resource in an assembly.
/win32icon	Inserts an .ico file into the output file.
/win32resource	Inserts a Win32 resource into the output file.

Miscellaneous

Option	Purpose
@ (Specify Response File)	Specifies a response file.
/baseaddress	Specifies the base address of a DLL.
/main	Specifies the class that contains the **Sub Main** procedure to use at startup.
/recurse	Searches subdirectories for source files to compile.
/rootnamespace	Specifies a namespace for all type declarations.

See Also

Visual Basic Compiler Options Listed Alphabetically

@ (Specify Response File)

Specifies a file that contains compiler options and source code files to compile.

```
@response_file
```

Arguments

response_file

Required. A file that lists compiler options or source code files to compile.

Remarks

The compiler processes the compiler options and source code files specified in a response file as if they had been specified on the command line.

To specify more than one response file in a compilation, specify multiple response file options. For example:

```
@file1.rsp @file2.rsp
```

In a response file, multiple compiler options and source code files can appear on one line. A single compiler option specification must appear on one line (cannot span multiple lines). Response files can have comments that begin with the # symbol.

You can combine options specified on the command line with options specified in one or more response files. The compiler processes the command options as it encounters them. Therefore, command-line arguments can override previously listed options in response files. Conversely, options in a response file override options listed previously on the command line or in other response files.

> **Note** The /@ option is not available from within the Visual Studio development environment; it is available only when compiling from the command line. It cannot be changed programmatically.

Example

The following are a few lines from a sample response file:

```
# build the first output file
/target:exe
/out:MyExe.exe
source1.vb
source2.vb
```

/addmodule

Causes the compiler to make all type information from the specified file(s) available to the project you are currently compiling.

```
/addmodule:module[,module2]
```

Arguments

module, module2
: Required. A file that contains metadata but not an assembly manifest. To import more than one file, separate file names with a comma.

Remarks

module is a file created with /target:module, or another compiler's equivalent to **/target:module**.

All modules added with **/addmodule** must be in the same directory as the output file at run time. That is, you can specify a module in any directory at compile time, but the module must be in the application directory at run time. If it is not, you get a **System.TypeLoadException** error.

If you specify (implicitly or explicitly) any /target option other than **/target:module** with **/addmodule**, the files you pass to **/addmodule** become part of the project's assembly. An assembly is required to run an output file that has one or more files added with **/addmodule**.

'se /reference to import metadata from a file that contains an assembly.

Note The **/addmodule** option is not available from within the Visual Studio development environment; it is available only when compiling from the command line. It cannot be changed programmatically.

xample

'he following code creates a module:

```
 t1.vb
 Compile with vbc /target:module t1.vb.
 Outputs t1.netmodule.
/
ublic class TestClass
  Dim i As Integer
nd class
```

'he following code imports the module's types:

```
 t2.vb
 Compile with vbc /addmodule:t1.netmodule t2.vb.
ption Strict Off
odule Module1
  Sub Main()
     Dim x As TestClass
     x = New TestClass
     x.i = 802
     System.Console.WriteLine(x.i)
  End Sub
nd Module
```

Vhen you run `t1`, it outputs `802`.

ee Also

.arget

/baseaddress

'pecifies a default base address when creating a DLL.

```
/baseaddress:address
```

rguments

ddress

Required. The base address for the DLL. This address must be specified as a hexadecimal number.

Remarks

The default base address for a DLL is set by the .NET Framework.

Be aware that the lower-order word in this address is rounded. For example, if you specify 0x11110001, it is rounded to 0x11110000.

To complete the signing process for a DLL, use the **-R** option of the Strong Naming tool (Sn.exe).

This option is ignored if the target is not a DLL.

To set /baseaddress in the Visual Studio integrated development environment

1. Open the project's Property Pages dialog box.
2. Click the Configuration Properties folder.
3. Click the Optimizations property page.
4. Modify the DLL base address property.

See Also

/target

/bugreport

Creates a file you can use when filing a bug report.

```
/bugreport:file
```

Arguments

file
: Required. The name of the file that will contain your bug report.

Remarks

The following information is placed in *file*:

- A copy of all source code files in the compilation.
- A list of the compiler options used in the compilation.
- Version information about your compiler, common language runtime, and operating system.
- Compiler output, if any.
- A description of the problem, for which you are prompted.
- A description of how you think the problem should be fixed, for which you are prompted.

Because a copy of all source code files is placed in *file*, you may want to reproduce the (suspected) code defect in the shortest possible program.

Note The **/bugreport** option is not available from within the Visual Studio development environment; it is available only when compiling from the command line. It cannot be changed programmatically.

xample

'he following example compiles `t2.vb` and puts all bug reporting information in the .le `problem.txt`:

```
bc /bugreport:problem.txt t2.vb
```

ee Also

lebug

/debug

'auses the compiler to generate debugging information and place it in the output file(s).

```
/debug[+ | -]
```

or-

```
/debug:[full | pdbonly]
```

rguments

| -

Optional. Specifying +, or just **/debug**, causes the compiler to generate debugging information and place it in a .pdb file. Specifying -, which is in effect if you do not specify **/debug**, causes no debug information to be created.

ull | pdbonly

Optional. Specifies the type of debugging information generated by the compiler. *full*, which is in effect if you do not specify **/debug:pdbonly**, enables attaching a debugger to the running program. *pdbonly* allows source code debugging when the program is started in the debugger, but displays assembly-language code only when the running program is attached to the debugger.

emarks

Jse this option to create debug builds. If you do not specify **/debug**, **/debug+**, or **/debug:full**, you vill be unable to debug the output file of your program.

By default, debugging information is not emitted (**/debug**-). To emit debugging information, pecify **/debug** or **/debug+**.

To set /debug in the Visual Studio integrated development environment

1. Open the project's Property Pages dialog box.
2. Click the Configuration Properties folder.
3. Click the Build property page.
4. Select the Generate debugging information check box.

Example

The following example puts debugging information in output file `app.exe`:

```
vbc /debug /out:app.exe test.vb
```

See Also

/bugreport

/define

Defines conditional compiler constants.

```
/define:symbol=value[,symbol=value]
```

-or-

```
/d:symbol=value[,symbol=value]
```

Arguments

symbol
   Required. The symbol to define.

value
   Required. The value to assign *symbol*.

Remarks

The **/define** option has the same effect as using a **#Const** preprocessor directive in your source file.

You can use symbols created by this option with the **#If...Then...#Else** directive to compile source files conditionally.

/d is the short form of **/define**.

You can define multiple symbols with **/define** by using a comma to separate symbol definitions.

set /define in the Visual Studio integrated development environment

Open the project's Property Pages dialog box.

Click the Configuration Properties folder.

Click the Build property page.

Modify the Conditional compilation constants property.

xample

he following code defines and then uses two conditional compiler constants:

```
bc /define:DEBUGMODE=True,TRAPERRORS=False test.vb
ub mysub()
  #If debugmode Then
     ' Place debug statements here.
      MsgBox("debug mode")
  #Else
     ' Place default statements here.
     '
  #End If
nd Sub
```

ee Also

If...Then...#Else Directives, #Const Directive

/delaysign

pecifies whether the assembly will be fully or partially signed.

```
/delaysign[+ | -]
```

rguments

| -

Use **/delaysign-** if you want a fully signed assembly. Use **/delaysign+** if you only want to place the public key in the assembly. The default is **/delaysign-**.

emarks

he **/delaysign** option has no effect unless used with /keyfile or /keycontainer.

Vhen you request a fully signed assembly, the compiler hashes the file that contains the manifest assembly metadata) and signs that hash with the private key. The resulting digital signature is tored in the file that contains the manifest. When an assembly is delay signed, the Assembly inker (Al.exe) does not compute and store the signature, but reserves space in the file so the ignature can be added later.

For example, using **/delaysign+** allows a tester to put the assembly in the global cache. After testing, you can fully sign the assembly by placing the private key in the assembly.

This option is not available within the development environment.

See Also

/keyfile, /keycontainer

/help, /?

Displays the compiler options.

```
/help
```

-or-

```
/?
```

Remarks

If you include this option in a compilation, no output file is created and no compilation takes place.

> **Note** The **/help** option is not available from within the Visual Studio development environment; it is available only when compiling from the command line. It cannot be changed programmatically.

Example

The following code displays help from the command line:

```
vbc /help
```

/imports

Imports a namespace from a specified assembly.

```
/imports:namespace[, namespace]
```

Arguments

namespace
  Required. The namespace to be imported.

Remarks

The **/imports** option imports any namespace defined within the current set of source files or from any referenced assembly.

he members in a namespace specified with **/imports** are available to all source code files in the ompilation. Use the Imports Statement to use a namespace in a single source code file.

set /imports in the Visual Studio integrated development environment

Open the project's Property Pages dialog box.

Click the Common Properties folder.

Click the Imports property page.

Modify the Namespace property.

set /import programmatically

See "Add Method."

xample

he following code compiles when **/imports:system** is specified:

```
odule MyModule
  Sub Main
     Console.WriteLine("test")
     ' Otherwise, would need
     ' System.Console.WriteLine("test")
  End Sub
nd Module
```

/keycontainer

pecifies a key container name for a key pair to give an assembly a strong name.

```
/keycontainer:container
```

or-

```
/keycontainer:"container"
```

rguments

ontainer

Required. Container that contains the key. Place the string in double quotation marks (" ") if it contains a space.

emarks

he compiler creates the sharable component by inserting a public key into the assembly manifest nd signing the final assembly with the private key. To generate a key file, type **sn -k** *file* at the ommand line.

You can also pass your encryption information to the compiler with /keyfile. Use /delaysign if you want a partially signed assembly.

This option is not available within the development environment.

Example

The following code compiles source file `input.vb` and specifies a key container:

```
vbc /keycontainer:key1 input.vb
```

See Also

/keyfile

/keyfile

Specifies a file containing a key or key pair to give an assembly a strong name.

```
/keyfile:file
```

-or-

```
/keyfile:"file"
```

Arguments

file

Required. File that contains the key. Place the string in double quotation marks (" ") if it contains a space.

Remarks

The compiler inserts the public key into the assembly manifest and then signs the final assembly with the private key. To generate a key file, type **sn -k** *file* at the command line.

If you compile with **/target:module**, information about the key file is held in the module and incorporated into the assembly that is created when you compile an application with **/reference**.

You can also pass your encryption information to the compiler with /keycontainer. Use /delaysign if you want a partially signed assembly.

This option is not available within the development environment.

Example

The following code compiles source file `input.vb` and specifies a key file:

```
vbc /keyfile:myfile.sn input.vb
```

See Also

/target:module, /reference

/libpath

```
/libpath:dir1[.dir2]
```

rguments

ir1

A directory for the compiler to look in if a referenced assembly is not found in either the current working directory (the directory from which you are invoking the compiler) or the common language runtime's system directory.

ir2

Additional directories to search for assembly references. Separate additional directory names with a comma.

emarks

he **/libpath** option specifies the location of assemblies referenced via the /reference option.

he compiler searches for assembly references that are not fully qualified in the following order:

- Current working directory. This is the directory from which the compiler is invoked.
- The common language runtime system directory.
- Directories specified by **/libpath**.
- Directories specified by the LIB environment variable.

ibpath is additive; specifying it more than once appends to any prior values.

Jse **/reference** to specify an assembly reference.

o set /libpath in the Visual Studio integrated development environment

- Open the project's Property Pages dialog box.
- Click the Common Properties folder.
- Click the Reference Path property page.
- Modify the Folder property.

xample

he following code compiles `t2.vb` to create a .exe file. The compiler looks in the working irectory and in the root directory of the C drive for assembly references:

```
bc /libpath:c:\ /reference:t2.dll t2.vb
```

/linkresource

Creates a link to a managed resource.

```
/linkresource:filename[,identifier[,public|private]]
```

-or-

```
/linkres:filename[,identifier[,public|private]]
```

Arguments

filename
    Required. The resource file to link to the assembly.

identifier[,public|private]
    Optional. The logical name for the resource; the name used to load the resource. The default is the name of the file. Optionally, you can specify whether the file is public or private in the assembly manifest; for example, `/linkres:filename.res,myname.res,public`. By default, *filename* is public in the assembly.

Remarks

The **/linkresource** option does not embed the resource file in the output file; use the **/resource** option to do this.

/linkresource requires one of the **/target** options other than **/target:module**.

If *filename* is a .NET Framework resource file created, for example, by the Resource File Generator (Resgen.exe) or in the development environment, it can be accessed with members in the **System.Resources** namespace. To access all other resources at run time, use the methods that begin with **GetManifestResource** in the Assembly Class class.

The short form of **/linkresource** is **/linkres**.

Note The **/linkresource** option is not available from within the Visual Studio development environment; it is available only when compiling from the command line. It cannot be changed programmatically.

Example

The following code compiles `in.vb` and links to resource file `rf.resource`:

```
vbc /linkresource:rf.resource in.vb
```

See Also

/target, /target:module, /resource

/main

Specifies the class or module that contains the **Sub Main** procedure.

```
/main:location
```

Arguments

location

Required. A full qualification to the **Sub Main** procedure to be called when the program starts. This may be in the form **/main:module** or **/main:namespace.module**. *location* also can be a class that inherits from **System.Windows.Forms.Form**.

Remarks

Use this option when creating an executable file or Windows executable program. If the **/main** option is omitted, the compiler searches for a valid shared **Sub Main** in all public classes and modules.

When *location* is a class that inherits from **System.Windows.Forms.Form**, vbc.exe lets you compile code at the command line that was created in the development environment:

```
' Compile with /r:System.dll,SYSTEM.WINDOWS.FORMS.DLL /main:MyC.
Public Class MyC
   Inherits System.Windows.Forms.Form
End Class
```

To set /main in the Visual Studio integrated development environment

1. Open the project's Property Pages dialog box.
2. Click the Common Properties folder.
3. Click the General property page.
4. Modify the Startup object property.

Example

The following code compiles `t2.vb` and `t3.vb`, specifying that the **Sub Main** procedure will be found in the `Test2` class:

```
vbc t2.vb t3.vb /main:Test2
```

See Also

/target:winexe, /target:exe

/nologo

Suppresses display of the copyright banner and informational messages during compilation.

```
/nologo
```

Remarks

If you specify **/nologo**, the compiler does not display a copyright banner. By default, **/nologo** is not in effect.

> **Note** The **/nologo** option is not available from within the Visual Studio development environment; it is available only when compiling from the command line. It cannot be changed programmatically.

Example

The following code compiles `t2.vb` and does not display a copyright banner:

```
vbc /nologo t2.vb
```

/nowarn

Suppresses the compiler's ability to generate warnings.

```
/nowarn
```

To set /nowarn in the Visual Studio integrated development environment

1. Open the project's Property Pages dialog box.
2. Click the Configuration Properties folder.
3. Click the Build property page.
4. Modify the Enable build warnings property.

Example

The following code compiles `t2.vb` and does not display warnings:

```
vbc /nowarn t2.vb
```

/optimize

Enables or disables compiler optimizations.

```
/optimize[ + | - ]
```

Arguments

+ | -

/optimize+, which is the same as **/optimize** and is the default for this option, enables compiler optimizations. **/optimize-** disables optimizations.

Remarks

Compiler optimizations make your output file smaller, faster, and more efficient. However, because optimizations result in code rearrangement in the output file, **/optimize+** can make debugging difficult.

All references (see "/reference") in an assembly must have the same optimization settings.

To prevent an optimized output file, specify **/optimize-**.

You can combine the **/optimize** and **/debug** options.

To set /baseaddress in the Visual Studio integrated development environment

1. Open the project's Property Pages dialog box.
2. Click the Configuration Properties folder.
3. Click the Optimizations property page.
4. Modify the Enable optimizations property.

Example

The following code compiles `t2.vb` and enables compiler optimizations:

```
vbc t2.vb /optimize
```

See Also

/debug

/optioncompare

Specifies how string comparisons are made.

```
/optioncompare:[binary | text]
```

Remarks

You can specify **/optioncompare** in one of two forms: /optioncompare:binary to use binary string comparisons, and /optioncompare:text to use text string comparisons.

/optioncompare:binary is the default.

See Also

/optionexplicit, /optionstrict

/optioncompare:binary

Causes strings to be compared based on their binary representations.

```
/optioncompare:binary
```

Remarks

In Microsoft Windows, the code page being used determines the binary sort order. A typical binary sort order is shown in the following example:

```
A < B < E < Z < a < b < e < z < À < Ê < Ø < à < ê < ø
```

To set /optioncompare:binary in the Visual Studio integrated development environment

1. Open the project's Property Pages dialog box.
2. Click the Common Properties folder.
3. Click the Build property page.
4. Modify the Option Compare property.

Example

The following code compiles `myfile.vb` and uses binary string comparisons:

```
vbc /optioncompare:binary myfile.vb
```

See Also

/optioncompare:text, /optionstrict, /optionexplicit

/optioncompare:text

Causes strings to be compared based on their text representations.

```
/optioncompare:text
```

Remarks

Text-based string comparisons are based on a case-insensitive text sort order determined by your system's locale. A typical text sort order is shown in the following example:

```
(A=a) < ( À=à) < (B=b) < (E=e) < (Ê=ê) < (Z=z) < (Ø=ø)
```

To set /optioncompare:text in the Visual Studio integrated development environment

1. Open the project's Property Pages dialog box.
2. Click the Common Properties folder.
3. Click the Build property page.
4. Modify the Option Compare property.

Example

The following code compiles `myfile.vb` and uses text-based string comparisons:

```
vbc /optioncompare:text myfile.vb
```

See Also

/optioncompare:binary, /optionstrict, /optionexplicit

/optionexplicit

Causes the compiler to report errors if variables are not declared prior to use.

```
/optionexplicit[+ | -]
```

Arguments

+ | -

Specify **/optionexplicit+** to require explicit declaration of variables. **/optionexplicit-** is the default; **/optionexplicit+** is the same as **/optionexplicit**. Both let you declare variables implicitly.

To set /optionexplicit in the Visual Studio integrated development environment

1. Open the project's Property Pages dialog box.
2. Click the Common Properties folder.
3. Click the Build property page.
4. Modify the Option Explicit property.

Example

The following code compiles when **/optionexplicit-** is used:

```
Module Module1
   Sub Main()
      i = 99
      System.Console.WriteLine(i)
   End Sub
End Module
```

See Also

/optionstrict

/optionstrict

Enforces strict type semantics to restrict implicit type conversions.

```
/optionstrict[+ | -]
```

Arguments

+ | -

/optionstrict+ restricts implicit type conversion. The default for this option is **/optionstrict-**; **/optionstrict+** is the same as **/optionstrict**. Both let you use permissive type semantics.

Remarks

When **/optionstrict+** is in effect, only widening type conversions can be done implicitly. Implicit narrowing type conversions, such as assigning a **Decimal** type object to an integer type object, are reported as errors.

To set /optionstrict in the Visual Studio integrated development environment

1. Open the project's Property Pages dialog box.
2. Click the Common Properties folder.
3. Click the Build property page.
4. Modify the Option Strict property.

Example

The following code compiles `test.vb` using strict type semantics:

```
vbc /optionstrict+ test.vb
```

See Also

/optionexplicit

/out

Specifies the name of the output file.

```
/out:filename
```

Arguments

filename
Required. The name of the output file the compiler creates.

Remarks

The compiler expects to find one or more source code files following the **/out** option.

Specify the full name and extension of the file to create. If you do not, the .exe file takes its name from the source code file containing the **Sub Main** procedure, and the .dll file takes its name from the first source code file.

To set /out in the Visual Studio integrated development environment

1. Open the project's Property Pages dialog box.
2. Click the Common Properties folder.
3. Click the General property page.
4. Modify the Assembly name property.

Example

The following code compiles `t2.vb` and creates output file `t2.exe`:

```
vbc t2.vb /out:t3.exe
```

See Also

/target

/quiet

Prevents the compiler from displaying code for syntax-related errors and warnings.

```
/quiet
```

Remarks

By default, **/quiet** is not in effect. When the compiler reports a syntax-related error or warning, it also outputs the line from source code. For applications that parse compiler output, it may be more convenient for the compiler to output only the text of the diagnostic.

In the following example, `Module1` outputs an error that includes source code when compiled without **/quiet**:

```
Module Module1
   Sub Main()
      x
   End Sub
End Module
```

Output:

```
E:\test\t2.vb(3) : error BC30451: The name 'x' is not declared.

        x
        ~
```

Compiled with **/quiet**, the compiler outputs only the following:

```
E:\test\t2.vb(3) : error BC30451: The name 'x' is not declared.
```

> **Note** The **/quiet** option is not available from within the Visual Studio development environment; it is available only when compiling from the command line. It cannot be accessed programmatically.

Example

The following code compiles `t2.vb` and does not display code for syntax-related compiler diagnostics:

```
vbc /quiet t2.vb
```

/recurse

Compiles source code files in all child directories of either the specified directory or the project directory.

```
/recurse:[dir\]file
```

Arguments

dir

Optional. The directory in which you want the search to begin. If not specified, the search begins in the project directory.

file

The file(s) to search for. Wildcard characters are allowed.

Remarks

You can use wildcards in a file name to compile all matching files in the project directory without using **/recurse**. If no output file name is specified, the compiler bases the output file name on the first input file processed. This is generally the first file in the list of files compiled when viewed alphabetically. For this reason, it is best to specify an output file using the **/out** option.

> **Note** The **/recurse** option is not available from within the Visual Studio development environment; it is available only when compiling from the command line. It cannot be changed programmatically.

Example

The following code compiles all Visual Basic files in the current directory:

```
vbc *.vb
```

The following code compiles all Visual Basic files in the Test\ABC directory and any directories below it, and then generates Test.ABC.dll:

```
vbc /target:library /out:Test.ABC.dll /recurse:Test\ABC\*.vb
```

See Also

/out

/reference

Causes the compiler to make type information in the specified assemblies available to the project you are currently compiling.

```
/reference:file[,file2]
```

-or-

```
/r:file[,file2]
```

Arguments

file, *file2*

One or more assemblies. To import more than one file, separate file names with a comma.

Remarks

The file(s) you import must contain assembly metadata. Only public types are visible outside the assembly. /addmodule imports metadata from a module.

At run time, you should anticipate that only one .exe assembly can be loaded per process, even though there may be times when more than one .exe might be loaded in the same process. Therefore, it is not recommended to pass an assembly built with **/target:exe** or **/target:winexe** to **/reference** if you are compiling with **/target:winexe** or **/target:exe**.

If you reference an assembly (Assembly A) which itself references another assembly (Assembly B), you need to reference Assembly B if:

- A type you use from Assembly A inherits from a type or implements an interface from Assembly B.
- You invoke a field, property, event, or method that has a return type or parameter type from Assembly B.

Use /libpath to specify the directory in which one or more of your assembly references is located.

For the compiler to recognize a type in an assembly (not a module), it must be forced to resolve the type, which you can do, for example, by defining an instance of the type. Other ways are available to resolve type names in an assembly for the compiler. For example, if you inherit from a type in an assembly, the type name then becomes known to the compiler.

/r is the short form of **/reference**.

To set /reference programmatically

- See "Add Method."

Example

The following code compiles source file `input.vb` and reference assemblies from `metad1.dll` and `metad2.dll` to produce `out.exe`:

```
vbc /reference:metad1.dll,metad2.dll /out:out.exe input.vb
```

See Also

/target, /target:module, Public

/removeintchecks

Turns overflow error checking for integer operations on or off.

```
/removeintchecks[+ | -]
```

Arguments

+ | -

/removeintchecks- causes the compiler to check all integer calculations for errors such as overflow or division by zero. **/removeintchecks-** is the default for this option.

Specifying **/removeintchecks** or **/removeintchecks+** prevents error checking and can make integer calculations faster. However, without error checking and if data type capacities are overflowed, incorrect results may be stored without raising an error.

To set /removeintchecks in the Visual Studio integrated development environment

1. Open the project's Property Pages dialog box.
2. Click the Configuration Properties folder.
3. Click the Optimizations property page.
4. Modify the Remove integer overflow checks property.

Example

The following code compiles `test.vb` and turns off integer overflow error checking:

```
vbc /removeintchecks+ test.vb
```

/resource

Embeds a managed resource in an assembly.

```
/resource:filename[,identifier[,public|private]]
```

-or-

```
/res:filename[,identifier[,public|private]]
```

Arguments

filename
The resource file to embed in the output file. By default, *filename* is public in the assembly.

identifier[,public|private]
Optional. The logical name for the resource; the name used to load it. The default is the name of the file. Optionally, you can specify whether the resource is public or private in the assembly manifest; for example:

```
/res:filename.res,myname.res,public.
```

Remarks

Use **/resource** to link a resource to an assembly without placing the resource file in the output file.

If *filename* is a .NET Framework resource file created, for example, by the Resource File Generator (Resgen.exe) or in the development environment, it can be accessed with members in the **System.Resources** namespace. For all other resources, use the **GetManifestResource** methods in **System.Reflection.Assembly** class to access the resource at run time.

/res is the short form of **/resource**.

To set /resource in the Visual Studio integrated development environment

1. Add a resource file to your project.
2. Select the file to embed in Solution Explorer.
3. Select Build Action for the file in the Properties Window.
4. Set Build Action to Embedded Resource.

Example

The following code compiles `in.vb` and attaches resource file `rf.resource`:

```
vbc /res:rf.resource in.vb
```

See Also

/win32resource, /linkresource, /target, /target:module

/rootnamespace

Specifies a namespace for all type declarations.

```
/rootnamespace:namespace
```

Arguments

namespace
The name of the namespace in which to enclose all type declarations for the current project.

Remarks

If you use the Visual Studio executable (Devenv) to compile a project created in the Visual Studio integrated development environment, **/rootnamespace** lets you specify the value of the **RootNamespace** property.

Use the common language runtime MSIL Disassembler (ildasm.exe) to view the namespace names in your output file.

To set /rootnamespace in the Visual Studio integrated development environment

1. Open the project's Property Pages dialog box.
2. Click the Common Properties folder.
3. Click the General property page.
4. Modify the Root Namespace property.

Example

The following code compiles `in.vb` and encloses all type declarations in the namespace `mynamespace`:

```
vbc /rootnamespace:mynamespace in.vb
```

/target

Specifies the format of compiler output.

```
/target:[exe | library | module | winexe]
```

Remarks

Use /target:exe to create a .exe console application. This is the default if you do not specify the **/target** option.

Use /target:library to create a dynamic-link library (DLL).

Use /target:module to create a module.

Use /target:winexe to create a Windows program.

Unless you specify **/target:module**, **/target** causes a .NET Framework assembly manifest to be placed in an output file.

Each invocation of vbc.exe produces, at most, one output file. If you specify a compiler option such as **/out** or **/target** more than once, the last one the compiler sees is put into effect. Information about all files in a compilation is placed in the manifest. All output files except those created with **/target:module** contain assembly metadata in the manifest. Use MSIL Disassembler (Ildasm.exe) to view the metadata in an output file.

Example

If you create an assembly, you can indicate that all or part of your code is CLS-compliant with the CLSCompliantAttribute Class attribute, as in the following code:

```
<Assembly: System.CLSCompliant(True)>
<System.CLSCompliant(False)> _
Public Class AClass
End Class

Module Module1
   Sub Main()
   End Sub
End Module
```

/target:exe

Causes the compiler to create an executable console application.

```
/target:exe
```

-or-

```
/t:exe
```

Remarks

The **/target:exe** option is the default when no **/target** option is specified. The executable file is created with a .exe extension.

Use /target:winexe to create a Windows program executable.

Unless otherwise specified with the **/out** option, the output file name takes the name of the input file that contains the **Sub Main** procedure.

Only one **Sub Main** procedure is required in the source code files that are compiled into a .exe file. The **/main** compiler option lets you specify which class contains the **Sub Main** procedure.

/t:exe is the short form of **/target:exe**.

To set /target:exe in the Visual Studio integrated development environment

1. Open the project's Property Pages dialog box.
2. Click the Common Properties folder.
3. Click the General property page.
4. Modify the Output type property.

Example

Both of the following two command lines compile `in.vb`, creating a console application called `in.exe`:

```
vbc /target:exe in.vb
vbc in.vb
```

See Also

/main, /target, /target:library, /target:module, /target:winexe, /out

/target:library

Causes the compiler to create a dynamic-link library (DLL) rather than an executable (EXE) file.

```
/target:library
```

-or-

```
/t:library
```

Remarks

The dynamic-link library file is created with a .dll extension.

Unless otherwise specified with the **/out** option, the output file name takes the name of the first input file.

When building a DLL, a **Sub Main** procedure is not required.

/t:library is the short form of **/target:library**.

To set /target:library in the Visual Studio integrated development environment

1. Open the project's Property Pages dialog box.
2. Click the Common Properties folder.
3. Click the General property page.
4. Modify the Output type property.

Example

The following code compiles `in.vb`, creating `in.dll`:

```
vbc /target:library in.vb
```

See Also

/target, /target:exe, /target:module, /target:winexe, /out

/target:module

Causes the compiler to generate a module that can be added to an assembly.

```
/target:module
```

-or-

```
/t:module
```

Remarks

The output file is created with an extension of .netmodule.

The .NET common language runtime cannot load a file that does not have an assembly. However, you can incorporate such a file into the assembly manifest of an assembly by using **/reference**.

When code in one module references internal types in another module, both modules must be incorporated into an assembly manifest by using **/reference**.

/addmodule imports metadata from a module.

The short form of **/target:module** is **/t:module**.

> **Note** The **/target:module** option is not available from within the Visual Studio development environment; it is available only when compiling from the command line. It cannot be changed programmatically.

Example

The following code compiles `in.vb`, creating `in.netmodule`:

```
vbc /target:module in.vb
```

See Also

/reference, /target, /target:exe, /target:library, /target:winexe

/target:winexe

auses the compiler to create an executable Windows program.

```
/target:winexe
```

or-

```
/t:winexe
```

emarks

he executable file is created with a .exe extension. A Windows program is one that provides a user nterface from either the Services Framework class library or with the Win32 APIs.

se /target:exe to create a console application.

nless otherwise specified with the **/out** option, the output file name takes the name of the input le that contains the **Sub Main** procedure.

nly one **Sub Main** procedure is required in the source code files that are compiled into a .exe file. he **/main** compiler option lets you specify which class contains the **Sub Main** procedure in cases here your code has more than one class with a **Sub Main** procedure.

he short form of **/target:winexe** is **/t:winexe**.

o set /target:winexe in the Visual Studio integrated development environment

1. Open the project's Property Pages dialog box.
2. Click the Common Properties folder.
3. Click the General property page.
4. Modify the Output type property.

xample

he following code compiles `in.vb` into a Windows program:

```
bc /target:winexe in.vb
```

ee Also

nain, /target, /target:exe, /target:library, /target:module, /out

/utf8output

Displays compiler output using UTF-8 encoding.

```
/utf8output[+ | -]
```

Arguments

+|-

The default for this option is **/utf8output-**, which means compiler output does not use UTF-8 encoding. Specifying **/utf8output** is the same as specifying **/utf8output+**.

Remarks

In some international configurations, compiler output cannot be displayed correctly in the console. In such situations, use **/utf8output** and redirect compiler output to a file.

> **Note** The **/utf8output** option is not available from within the Visual Studio development environment; it is available only when compiling from the command line. It cannot be changed programmatically.

Example

The following code compiles `in.vb` and directs the compiler to display output using UTF-8 encoding:

```
vbc /utf8output in.vb
```

/verbose

Causes the compiler to produce verbose status and error messages.

```
/verbose[+ | -]
```

Arguments

+|-

Specifying **/verbose** is the same as specifying **/verbose+**, which causes the compiler to emit verbose messages. The default for this option is **/verbose-**.

Remarks

/verbose displays information about the total number of errors issued by the compiler, reports which assemblies are being loaded by a module, and displays which files are currently being compiled.

Note The **/verbose** option is not available from within the Visual Studio development environment; it is available only when compiling from the command line. It cannot be changed programmatically.

xample

he following code compiles `in.vb` and directs the compiler to display verbose status information:

```
c /verbose in.vb
```

/warnaserror

auses the compiler to treat the first occurrence of a warning as an error.

```
warnaserror[+ | -]
```

rguments

| -

By default, **/warnaserror-** is in effect; warnings do not prevent the compiler from producing an output file. **/warnaserror**, which is the same as **/warnaserror+**, causes warnings to be treated as errors.

emarks

ıbsequent occurrences of the same warning are reported as warnings. The compiler produces no ıtput file.

set /warnaserror in the Visual Studio integrated development environment

Open the project's Property Pages dialog box.

Click the Configuration Properties folder.

Click the Build property page.

Modify the Treat compiler warnings as errors property.

xample

he following code compiles `in.vb` and directs the compiler to display an error for the first ccurrence of every warning it finds:

```
c /warnaserror in.vb
```

/win32icon

Inserts an .ico file in the output file. This .ico file represents the output file in the Windows Explorer.

```
/win32icon:filename
```

Arguments

filename

The .ico file to add to your output file.

Remarks

You can create an .ico file with the Microsoft Windows Resource Compiler (RC). The Resource Compiler is invoked when you compile a Visual C++® program; an .ico file is created from the .rc file. The **/win32icon** and **/win32resource** options are mutually exclusive.

See "/linkresource" to reference a .NET Framework resource file, or "/resource" to attach a .NET Framework resource file. See "/win32resource" to import a .res file.

To set /win32icon in the Visual Studio integrated development environment

1. Open the project's Property Pages dialog box.
2. Click the Common Properties folder.
3. Click the Build property page.
4. Modify the Application icon property.

Example

The following code compiles `in.vb` and attaches an .ico file, `rf.ico`:

```
vbc /win32icon:rf.ico in.vb
```

/win32resource

Inserts a Win32 resource file in the output file.

```
/win32resource:filename
```

Arguments

filename

The resource file to add to your output file.

ːemarks

ʼou can create a Win32 resource file with the Microsoft Windows Resource Compiler (RC).

ʌ Win32 resource can contain version or bitmap (icon) information that helps identify your pplication in the Windows Explorer. If you do not specify **/win32resource**, the compiler generates ersion information based on the assembly version. The **/win32resource** and **/win32icon** options re mutually exclusive.

ee "/linkresource" to reference a .NET Framework resource file, or "/resource" to attach a NET Framework resource file.

Note The **/nologo** option is not available from within the Visual Studio development environment; it is available only when compiling from the command line. It cannot be changed programmatically.

---

xample

ʼhe following code compiles `in.vb` and attaches a Win32 resource file, `rf.res`:

```
bc /win32resource:rf.res in.vb
```

Work Light

A **work light** lets you work on a task in low-light conditions. They literally throw light on the subject at hand so you can keep working if you're in the dark—just like our LANGUAGE REFERENCE series of books, in fact!

At Microsoft Press, we use tools to illustrate our books for software developers and IT professionals. Tools are an elegant symbol of human inventiveness and a powerful metaphor for how people can extend their capabilities, precision, and reach. From basic calipers and pliers to digital micrometers and lasers, our stylized illustrations of tools give each book a visual identity and each book series a personality. With tools and knowledge, there are no limits to creativity and innovation. Our tag line says it all: *The tools you need to put technology to work.*

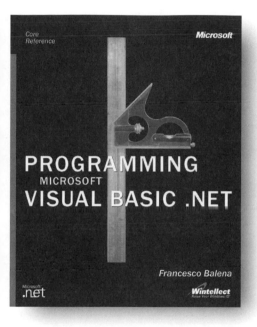